Dharana Darshan

With kind regards, ॐ and prem

Swami Niranjan

Dharana Darshan

A Panoramic View of the Yogic, Tantric and
Upanishadic Practices of Concentration and Visualization

As taught by

Swami Niranjanananda Saraswati

*during the six month Sannyasa Course conducted
at Ganga Darshan from October 1992 to March 1993*

Yoga Publications Trust, Munger, Bihar, India

© Sri Panchdashnam Paramahamsa Alakh Bara 1993
© Bihar School of Yoga 1999

All rights reserved. No part of this publication may be reproduced, transmitted or stored in a retrieval system, in any form or by any means, without permission in writing from Yoga Publications Trust.

The terms Satyananda Yoga® and Bihar Yoga® are registered trademarks owned by International Yoga Fellowship Movement (IYFM). The use of the same in this book is with permission and should not in any way be taken as affecting the validity of the marks.

Published by Sri Panchdashnam Paramahamsa Alakh Bara
    First edition 1993

Published by Bihar School of Yoga
    Second edition 1999 (by Bihar Yoga Bharati with permission of Bihar School of Yoga)

Published by Yoga Publications Trust
    Reprinted 2003, 2006

ISBN: 81-86336-30-3

Publisher and distributor: Yoga Publications Trust, Ganga Darshan, Munger, Bihar, India.

Website: www.yogavision.net

Printed at Thomson Press (India) Limited, New Delhi, 110001

Dedication

*In humility we offer this dedication to
Swami Sivananda Saraswati, who initiated
Swami Satyananda Saraswati into the secrets of yoga.*

Contents

Introduction to Dharana
1. Importance of Concentration — 3
2. Relaxation and Concentration — 11
3. Meditative Process — 17
4. Psychic Symbol — 25
5. Visualization — 32
6. Obstacles in Dharana — 38
7. Yogic, Tantric and Upanishadic Dharanas — 43

Yogic and Tantric Dharana
8. Kaya Sthairyam — 57
9. Chakra Shuddhi — 63
10. Ajapa Dharana — 73
    - One: Frontal Passage Rotation — 81
    - Two: Spinal Passage Rotation — 87
    - Three: Frontal Passage Rotation with Ujjayi and Khechari — 95
    - Four: Spinal Passage Rotation with Ujjayi and Khechari — 101
    - Five: Arohan-Awarohan Rotation — 107
    - Six: Ida-Pingala Elliptical Rotation — 115
    - Seven: Pingala-Ida Elliptical Rotation — 121
    - Eight: Ida-Pingala Spinal Rotation — 127
    - Nine: Pingala-Ida Spinal Rotation — 137
    - Ten: Opening the Granthis — 145
11. Trataka — 156
    - One: Bahya Drishti — 165
    - Two: Bahya-Antar Drishti — 172
    - Three: Antar Drishti — 185
    - Four: Shoonya Drishti — 192

Upanishadic Dharana

12. Bahyakasha Dharana	201
13. Antarakasha Dharana	205
14. Chidakasha Dharana	209
15. Ajna Chakra Dharana	218
16. Hridayakasha Dharana	227
17. Daharakasha Dharana	238
One: Panchatattwa Dharana (A)	243
Two: Panchatattwa Dharana (B)	254
Three: Chakra Dharana (A)	269
Four: Chakra Dharana (B)	277
Five: Chakra Dharana (C)	284
Six: Panchakosha Dharana	290
Seven: Panchaprana Dharana	303
18. Laya Dharana	312
One: Mooladhara and Vishuddhi Drishti	319
Two: Loka Drishti	333
19. Vyoma Panchaka Dharana	340
One: Guna Rahita Akasha	341
Two: Paramakasha	357
Three: Mahakasha	364
Four: Tattwakasha	369
Five: Suryakasha	387
20. Nadanusandhana Dharana	401

Glosssary   430

Introduction to Dharana

1
Importance of Concentration

Concentration is one-pointedness of mind, the ability to hold the awareness of the mind on one point, one place, without wavering. The perfection of concentration leads to meditation. In the state of concentration, the mind is not aware of the external environment or of other peripheral things that surround the object of concentration.

Why is concentration so important? This can be best answered by comparing the mind to a light bulb. The rays of light from the bulb go out in all directions; the energy spreads. If you stand five feet away from the bulb, you can see the light but cannot feel the heat, even though there is great heat at the centre of the bulb, at the filament. In the same way, the mind has great power in a potential form, but it is dissipated in all directions. The mind thinks of different things one after another, without dwelling in depth on any particular subject. Therefore, the average mind does not utilize its power.

In recent times, science has produced the laser and many advances have been made in modern technology through its use. It is a method whereby all the rays of light from a source are lined up with each other so that they go in the same direction and in unison with each other. They vibrate in harmony with each other. The original source of light need not be any greater than the light bulb we have just discussed, yet if you were to stand five feet from a laser beam source, the beam would burn a hole straight through your body. This is the difference between ordinary light and concentrated light.

Similarly, concentrated thought also has great power. It has the power of heightened perception, the ability to see more of the underlying truth behind phenomena. It has the ability to achieve great things and to do unimaginable amounts of work. A concentrated mind is also a relaxed mind. Whenever you become deeply engrossed in anything you automatically come to a state of relaxation. Concentration is vital for everything that you do in life because it prevents the mind from wandering aimlessly in all directions. Without concentration you can achieve nothing. You only need to look around you to see the truth of this statement.

Work done with a concentrated mind becomes more enjoyable. A person with a concentrated mind can do all kinds of work with great efficiency. A person who is unable to concentrate, who thinks of other things while doing the work at hand, makes mistakes and takes an unnecessary length of time to complete the task, if he ever completes it at all. He will continually think about how slowly the time is passing. He will worry about himself, his problems, his family, while he is working. Due to poor concentration there is poor application, so the work is not properly done. Therefore, concentration is essential in daily life as well as in spiritual practice.

Quality of mind

A concentrated mind is a powerful mind and a dissipated mind is a weak mind. In order to develop mental power you must first develop a concentrated mind. A dissipated mind cannot have mental power. If the thoughts are scattered, they can be brought into concentrated focus by specific concentration practices. Then your mind will become so powerful that you can influence the minds of others. You can influence your character, your health, your whole life. If you have a stomach disorder, mental disorder, breathing disorder or any disorder, you can remove it by willpower alone. How can you develop willpower? The secret is to concentrate the mind on one point.

What is meant by a strong mind? A strong mind is one which can carry out its own decisions. In contrast, a weak mind is one which decides one thing but does another. From tomorrow I am going to do this or that but when tomorrow comes you forget everything. You are still the same because your mind is dissipated. All the great men about whom you have read in history, whether artists, writers, musicians, politicians, statesmen, military leaders, scientists or saints, achieved greatness because of the quality of their mind. They did not become great by a freak of nature or a stroke of luck. They became great due to the quality of their mind. They each had a concentrated and hence a gifted mind.

If you want to do something or become something in your life, the quality of your mind has to be improved. If you have a low quality of mind then your performance in all spheres will be poor. If the quality of your mind is high then your performance will be correspondingly very great. To develop a higher quality of mind, you will have to analyze yourself and your aims, and you will have to give some time to the practice of concentration in the morning and evening.

Objects of concentration
Concentration can be practised in many ways. The object of concentration can be seen or located in any of the many centres throughout the body such as chidakasha, hridayakasha, daharakasha, in any of the chakras or in front of the body. Concentration can also be done on the different parts of the body, the physical processes, the stillness of the body, relaxation or tension of the body. The breath is also used as the object of concentration.

Almost any object can be used as the basis for concentration. Once you have selected an object, you should use the same object in your practice day after day. The object should come to your attention spontaneously. For some people the object appears by itself in the form of a vision or a dream. This is the best form of natural selection. Other people, however, will have to find a suitable object for themselves. To assist these people, a very comprehensive list of suitable objects has been compiled. This list should give you some idea of how vast this subject really is and how many objects you can choose from. Actually the number is limitless; the following items are only examples. Go through the list quickly just to get an idea. Perhaps one of the symbols will attract you and perhaps not. Even if you do not find a suitable object in this list, it will spark off something in your own mind or imagination, so that later on the correct symbol will come to you spontaneously. This will probably happen at a time when you are completely relaxed.

Gods, saints, people: Vishnu, Brahma, Shiva, Trimurti, Sita, Rama, Radha, Krishna, Saraswati, Parvati, Ganesha, Hanuman, Lakshmi, Durga, Kali, Varuna, Vayu, Indra, Surya, Soma, Christ, Mary, Buddha, Lao-tzu, Milarepa, Naropa, Saint Francis, Swami Sivananda, Sai Baba, your guru, any other deity or saint, your father, mother, husband, wife, son, daughter, relative, friend, teacher or inspirer.

Sacred objects: shivalingam, trident, shaligram, jyoti, cross, altar, cathedral window, eucharist, chalice, prayer wheel, candelabra, crystal ball, priest, icon or statue of any patron saint, tantric images, archangels, ring of skulls, conch shell, kundalini serpent, Venus de Milo, David and Medici, Perseus and Medusa.

Sacred places: temple, church, chapel, cathedral, chorten, pyramid, mosque, monastery, ashram, pagoda, shrine.

Natural scenes: mountain, hills, valley, desert, oasis, cliffs, sand dunes, white beach, jungle, forest grove, paddy fields, orchard, flower garden, cloudy sky, rain, fog, storm, hail, tornado, earthquake, sea, waves breaking on the shore, Japanese garden, lotus pond, sunshine, sail boat, well, lake, swift stream, spring, pool of water, snow, ice.

Sentient things: elephant, antelope, lion, tiger, monkey, cow, deer, eagle, swallow, swan, flamingo, robin, blue jay, crow, chicken, butterfly, peacock, star fish, octopus, crocodile, cobra, dog, cat, horse, donkey, white lotus, red rose, yellow sunflower, daffodil, blue bells, orchid, cherry blossoms, lawn, coconut palms, moss.

Insentient things: earth, fire, water, air, ether, tamas, rajas, sattwa; Aquarius, Pisces, Virgo, Libra, Gemini, Capricorn, Sagittarius, Scorpio, Leo, Taurus, Cancer and Aries; ruby, onyx, agate, sapphire, diamond, jasper, topaz, crystal, amethyst, opal, jade, garnet, pearl, beryl; pewter, iron, gold, silver, brass, tin, copper; Moon, Mars, Venus, Saturn, Jupiter, Neptune, Mercury, Uranus, Pluto, Sun.

Colour and form: red, blue, green, yellow, indigo, orange, pink, black, white, purple, sunlight, moonlight, firelight, candle flame, lightning, star, hexagon, rectangle, heart, clover leaf, golden egg, square, triangle, crescent, Sanskrit beeja mantra, chakra diagram, yantra, mandala, nadis, prana.

Avoid mental confrontation

You can concentrate on any great saint, any light, any sound, colour, form, thought, or anything you like, but one thing should be clearly understood. When you take up the practice of concentration it is not necessary to select a religious symbol. Sometimes a thought which makes a greater impression on your consciousness can be used instead. There is no use in fighting with the mind. During concentration practice you may be trying to think of a religious symbol, but your mind does not agree because that is how the mind is conditioned. When you try to concentrate on something which is alien to this conditioning, the mind pulls away. However, when you think about very ordinary things there is no distraction.

When you try to concentrate on the wrong symbol, distraction comes and the confrontation begins. It is very necessary to understand that when you are practising concentration, there should be minimal confrontation in the mind. There is no use fighting with your own mind. Who is fighting with whom? There are not two minds. Consciousness is one, but for the sake of diversity there are various *vrittis*, patterns or modifications of the mind. When you confront yourself you are actually creating a quarrel between your own vrittis. When this confrontation between your own vrittis becomes very intense, then you have a schizophrenic attack. Most mental patients are the victims of their own minds.

Therefore, if you are not able to concentrate by using any of the suggested methods, then choose your own. The important thing is that the symbol you choose should become so compelling that your mind is automatically drawn to it and completely integrates with it. When you practise in this way then you will enter into concentration easily. When you practise meditation you can also use distractions as objects of concentration, just like the wise yogi in the story.

There was once a king who was very attached to his riches, but still he wanted to meditate for he was beginning to see the worthlessness of his vast wealth. A yogi gave this king instructions. The king sat down to meditate in earnest, but whenever he tried to fix his mind upon the eternal it went blank. Then, without knowing it, his imagination began to hover around his beautiful gold bracelet which he was particularly fond of. Before his admiring gaze, the bracelet began to sparkle in all the colours of the rainbow. As soon as he found himself in that fantasy, he fought his way back to God. But the harder he tried to fix his mind upon God, the greater was the frustration that he experienced. God invariably changed into the bracelet in his mind.

With much humility, the king now went to the yogi for further instructions. The yogi knew how to turn the weakness into a source of strength. He said to the king, "Since your mind is so attached to the bracelet, start your practice from there. Meditate upon the bracelet. Contemplate on its beauty and sparkling colour. In essence, the bracelet is a configuration of energy vibration solidified into metal. It is the perceptive mind which lends it its beauty and colour. Therefore, try to understand the nature of the mind which created the world as you see it."

Ability to concentrate

Concentration is spoken of in the *Katha Upanishad* (2:3:11) where it is explained by Yama, the Lord of Death, to Nachiketas, a young seeker:

तां योगमिति मन्यन्ते स्थिरामिन्द्रिय धारणाम्।
अप्रमत्तस्तदा भवति योगो हि प्रभवाप्ययों॥

The firm control of the senses and the mind is the yoga of concentration. One must be ever watchful for this yoga is difficult to acquire and easy to lose.

The word 'concentration' means one-pointedness. Just as we need a sharp pencil to write with or a sharp knife to cut with, the mind also must be sharpened through the practices of concentration. We cannot cut with a dull knife or write with an unsharpened pencil, because the pressure applied is spread over too large an area. It is not concentrated. The importance of a concentrated mind in everyday life is widely recognized, but the ordinary mind is not functioning in a concentrated way. It is dissipated, also spread over too large an area and covering too many points. Therefore, we are not able to utilize even a fraction of our potential mental power.

We know many things in life, about our work, our families, our society, our environment, history, science and politics, but we do not know how to wilfully control and direct the mind. The power of concentration has not been developed in most of us as part of our early training. As we grow older the mind becomes more and more dissipated as the tensions and worries mount. This results in increasing loss of mental acuity, wrong decisions, ineffective management, poor memory and finally senility.

We may be masters of technology and of the external word but we are not masters of the mind. Somehow that inner technology which can give us control over the mental functions is eluding us completely. Control over a machine means that we are able to start it, speed it up, slow it down and stop it whenever needed. The same thing is also required of a disciplined mind. The disciplined mind is one which thinks only when you will it and about what you decide. If you want it to think fast or slow or stop thinking altogether, it immediately complies. The thoughts which enter a disciplined mind are immediately cognized and directed. They have no power to sway the mind in one way or another.

If we examine the lives of yogis, sadhus, sannyasins, saints and mystics, we will see that they all have one thing in common. They lead intensely one-pointed and concentrated lives, dedicated totally to the ideal or purpose which they regard as the highest goal. They gain control over themselves and their minds by regular, steady practice. Through their power of concentration they gradually merge the mind into their prayer or meditations until they are able to achieve a state of perfect mind control. Usually on meeting such a person, our first impression is one of deep inner peace, steadiness and self-control.

The ability to concentrate is the root of all higher qualities in man and it requires strenuous effort. To develop a concentrated mind is harder than earning a degree. The average person is not born with the ability to concentrate, so it is necessary to change our nature in order to create something which was not there before. This is different to studying concepts of philosophy from books and lectures. Concentration is something which must be practised and discovered personally to gain full benefit.

The essential thing for developing concentration is regularity in practice. However, before we start practising concentration, we must develop an idea of the broad range which this stage of mental development covers. The practices of concentration and meditation are codified in the yogic and upanishadic texts. This is a subject which should be studied and researched to obtain the best results. Concentration is not a superficial practice. It involves diving deep into the inner dimensions of the mind and consciousness. In order to do this we need three things: (i) correct method, (ii) correct guidance and (iii) correct understanding.

2
Relaxation and Concentration

Concentration is an important means of dealing with mental stress. Most of us never relax properly in our life. In sleep we do not relax. Drinking does not provide relaxation. Pleasant experiences do not provide relaxation. It is the nature of the mind always to be dissipated and distracted, to run in a hundred directions without conscious knowledge. We may think that we are concentrated at this moment, but we are not. There are subtle experiences which are constantly bombarding the mind at the conscious, subconscious and unconscious levels, most of which we have no understanding of. We are never aware that this subterranean activity is happening.

While we are aware of one thing, the input of the other senses is constantly being received, processed and filtered by the brain and mind. So where is concentration? When so many things are happening simultaneously within our personality, how can there be concentration or relaxation? There cannot be. Therefore, yoga has evolved a way to bring about total mental relaxation through a process of mental discipline. In the *Raja Yoga Sutras* of Patanjali this is described as: *atha yoga anushasanam*, which means that yoga is a form of control over the subtle faculties, experiences and expressions of the mind.

Here the word *anu* means 'the most subtle aspect of the personality,' and *shasan* means 'to govern over', 'to control'.

Therefore, this sutra, atha yoga anushasanam, defines the entire yogic process, which is a system of controlling the subtle experiences that are beyond the range of awareness. We may be thinking right now, but we are not aware of those thoughts. At this moment, in the deeper mind many emotions and desires are coming up, but we are not aware of them. How do we relax this state of mind? The formula is very simple. Focus your mind on one point. There has to be intensity of concentration. There has to be a merger of the awareness with an object of concentration. When the awareness is merged with the object, the majority of the mental faculties are pinpointed at one centre. So, there is greater relaxation because all the faculties are working in one direction.

Training the mind
Consciously, subconsciously and unconsciously we are doing a thousand things at any given moment. The sensory faculty which is most active in one situation is making us aware of that experience. For example, if it is very hot in the room and you begin to sweat heavily, then your total attention will be drawn to the feeling of heat, despite your best efforts to concentrate on what you are doing. There will not be much awareness of or attention on anything else.

Take another example: suddenly you remember that you forgot to lock your house. Then, despite your best efforts to be attentive to what you are actually doing, eighty percent of your awareness will be at the door of your house. So, the faculty which is predominant at any given time influences the state of our awareness. In this way the mind blocks off many other areas in which our awareness could be extended. In yoga, by focusing all the faculties at one point, we concentrate and relax the mind. Instead of a hundred things happening simultaneously, perhaps ten things will happen and ninety percent of our faculties will be at one point. This is the concept of dharana, the aspect of mental training in yoga.

The concept of dharana is not just to stop the thoughts, but to bring your attention, your awareness, to a stage where most of the faculties of the body and mind are functioning together. Therefore, in dharana there is greater relaxation, greater mental power, greater concentration. This is the way to train the mind. With this mental training we become objectively aware of our surroundings and our interactions with our surroundings. With greater awareness we are able to control the distressing negative traits of our personality, the negative thoughts and emotions, the feelings of anger, anxiety, frustration, depression and so forth.

Essentially we have the potential to fully develop and express all the faculties at our command together, and this is the aim of dharana. When this state has been achieved then the meditative experience will automatically dawn as the mind becomes relaxed, harmonious and receptive to a broader dimension of consciousness.

Transformation of consciousness

According to yoga, the faculties of body and mind are subject to the influences of prana and chitta. *Prana shakti* is the vital energy, controlling the physical, sensory body. *Chitta shakti* is the mental energy, controlling the consciousness, the mind. In order to understand prana and chitta, and to further clarify our concept of mental training, we must also understand one more point. Pure, transcendental or divine consciousness resides at the level which is beyond elemental consciousness.

Elemental consciousness means awareness or consciousness of earth, water, fire, air, ether and mind. These are the six basic elements of which our being is composed. In kundalini yoga, pure consciousness is represented in our personality as the experience of sahasrara chakra, where there is no duality, no distinction between subject and object. However, when this pure energy, pure awareness, decides to manifest in the world of the senses and objects, it has to go through a process of transformation

This pure awareness is like the high voltage energy coming directly from a power generator, which cannot be carried by the small electrical wires that simply conduct 220 volts for household purposes. This high voltage energy must be conducted through different transformers in order to step it down. These transformers which reduce the voltage of energy in our psychic body are six in number. They are known as the *chakras* or psychic centres.

When we begin to manifest absolute consciousness and energy on the material plane, from pure consciousness, the process of transformation first goes to the mental level, creation of mind. The mental force, located at ajna chakra in the midbrain, is the first *indriya*, or sensory organ, through which we can perceive the world in any colour or form we wish. The second stage of transformation is *akasha tattwa*, the ether element, which is slightly denser than the mind. It is perceived through the sense of sound. Here the energy is stepped down by vishuddhi chakra, located at the throat.

The third stage of transformation is *vayu tattwa*, the air element, which is denser than ether and perceived by touch. Here the energy is stepped down by anahata chakra, located at the heart. The fourth stage is *agni tattwa*, the fire element, which is denser than air. It is perceived by sight. Here the energy is stepped down by manipura chakra, located at the navel.

The fifth stage of transformation is *apas tattwa*, the water element, which is denser than fire. It is perceived by taste. Here the energy is stepped down by swadhisthana chakra, which is located at the pubis. The last dimension of transformation is *prithvi tattwa*, the earth element, which is the densest element. It is perceived by smell. Here the dormant kundalini or spiritual energy force resides in mooladhara chakra at the perineum.

Developing a broader vision

This has been the growth or the evolution of pure energy and transcendental consciousness from the sublime to the ridiculous. We are now functioning almost entirely at the level of matter. The senses express their faculties at this level. Even the mind, which is at the next level down from transcendental consciousness, expresses itself at the level of matter. There is stagnation of the faculties at this level. This stagnation does not have to be defined. We are all living examples of stagnation of consciousness and energy. We cannot see beyond our own limited vision. In order to evolve this vision from the level of matter into the higher realms of perception, we must go through the process of mental training, of concentration and meditation.

The science of meditation transcends the totality of human experience. The aim of meditation is to raise the awareness to such a state or dimension where one no longer experiences the motion of consciousness and energy. It has been described in the Upanishads as a conscious state where 'the sun does not shine, the moon does not give light, the fire does not burn', and once a person reaches that stage, he does not return.

Surya, the sun, represents the pranic energy. Chandra, the moon, represents the mental energy. Surya is the energy which governs the world of matter. Chandra governs the subtle dimension of thought and mind. Agni or fire represents the vitality of prana shakti and chitta shakti, the motion of prana shakti and chitta shakti in the gross and subtle world.

Through the process of dharana we reach a point where there is total cessation of movement, where everything just stops, where there is no activity. In this state of inactivity there is a drowning of human perception. In the state of activity, experiences happen very fast. We sit in the train and as the train moves, we look out the window and see scenery flashing by. Mountains, fields, trees, rivers, villages, towns and cities pass by at great speed. However, when the train stops and we look out the window, then we can see the static world and there is a greater or broader vision.

It is this greater vision of life which is supposed to be the achievement we all aspire for in yoga and meditation. At the ground level our vision is very limited. When we go to the first floor our vision broadens a little bit. When we go to the second floor we see a greater view. If we go to the third floor there is a greater vision. The higher up we go the broader the vision becomes. If we go to the topmost floor of our building, which in our physical body is the seventh floor, then we will have a very broad vision of the world and of ourselves. When we have this vision then we attain *satya*, absolute truth: we become one with reality.

Generally there are two experiences of life. One is related to the appearance and the other to reality. We are more aware of the appearance and less aware of reality. Our vision has to change. We have to become more aware of reality and less aware of the appearance. That is the direction which the practices of dharana take. At the same time there is relaxation, concentration, non-attachment and attainment. When we are able to develop a concentrated mind we will feel, realize and understand that life is like a flower and every unfoldment is beautiful. These are the words of Paramahamsa Satyananda and it is this vision which we must develop.

3

Meditative Process

According to the theory and concept of yoga, meditation is a state of mind and consciousness in which there is alertness, dynamism, dissociation of mind and senses, and total concentration. It is definitely not a process to block out events or experiences which are constantly affecting us. In the *Raja Yoga Sutras* the process of meditation has been divided into eight stages: (i) yama (self-restraint), niyama (fixed rules), (iii) asana (posture), (iv) pranayama (breath control), (v) pratyahara (sensory withdrawal), (vi) dharana (concentration), (vii) dhyana (meditation) and (viii) samadhi (transcendental consciousness).

The first four stages are known as the *bahirangas*, or external yogas, in which an effort is made to harmonize the body, to awaken the pranic energy within the body, and to reach a point of total steadiness and equanimity within the body. The meditative aspect of yoga and yoga itself do not denounce the body as unnecessary. Rather, awareness is first generated for the body because the body affects the stability and peace of mind. If somebody pinches you, where do you feel the pain? In the part of the body that is being pinched or in the mind? The pain is experienced in both places. Therefore, the process of meditation is dealt with in such a way that the mental and physical experiences are totally contained in one field of awareness, so that nothing remains scattered.

So, yoga presents the chakra view of meditation whereby, after having controlled the physical experiences by going through the techniques of bahiranga yoga, one enters the mental dimension and works towards the centre of the mind. This is the basis of the whole philosophy according to yoga. You have to move towards the centre of the mind from the periphery. What are the peripheral experiences of the mind? These are the thoughts, the feelings, the emotions, the desires which we are experiencing constantly and continuously in our lives.

In order to get to the centre of the mind there has to be an awareness of the peripheral activity and control over it. This aspect has been emphasized in the aspect of pratyahara and dharana. The actual practices of meditation are of pratyahara and dharana only. Nowhere in the yogic tradition will you find dhyana mentioned as a practice or technique. But you will find a wide variety of pratyahara and dharana techniques such as tattwa dharana, chidakasha dharana and vyoma panchaka dharana.

These different techniques lead one deeper into the perception of one's own mind, the subtle aspect, the vibratory aspect of the mind. Just as there are many layers of the physical body – on the outside there is the skin, inside are the muscles, nerves, blood vessels, then the bones and inside the bones the marrow – in the same way, there are also many layers or levels in the mental body.

Therefore, meditation is not easy. If you think that closing the eyes and trying to stop the mind is meditation, then you can try it. But you will not be successful unless you have developed very strong willpower. Without the power of anashakti, vairagya or non-attachment, meditation is very difficult to practise. If you are not attached to the experiences of the senses, ego, buddhi (intellect), chitta (memory) and manas (rational mind), then you can experience spontaneous meditation. However, unless and until that happens you will have to work through the practices systematically, stage by stage.

Concept of dharana

The yogic term for concentration is *dharana*, which means 'to hold the mind at one point'. This holding or binding of the mind to one point is the concept of dharana. In Sanskrit, the word dharana is derived from the root *dhri*, which means 'foundation' or 'base'. So, that object or concept upon which the mind is firmly based is the actual definition of dharana. In the yogic tradition, dharana belongs to the internal stages of raja yoga which is the path of mental discipline. Dharana follows the stage of pratyahara in which the mind is withdrawn from the external sensory objects and internalized.

After separating the mind from the senses, the mind can go deep. It can create its own worlds while the senses remain outside. Once we are able to create this differentiation or distinction between the sensory awareness and the mental awareness, then the mind can be directed to go deeper into other states where dharana becomes intense. Dharana, which is termed as mental concentration, is deepening of mental awareness. As the mental awareness deepens, and when there is total absence of sensorial awareness, then dharana takes place.

Intensity of experience

Dharana can take place in any form. We can compare dharana with the experience that two lovers have when they are together for hours and hours, but it seems as if only a few moments have passed. However, if something unpleasant has to be done, then one moment will seem like one whole hour. So the intensity which makes us aware of one moment as being a long time, or of a long time being as one moment, is dharana. In the positive aspect, dharana is deepening of awareness, where the concept of time is lost, where the objective consciousness is lost, and only the awareness of space remains.

When there is sensorial disconnection of mind, then anything which manifests internally in dharana actually becomes more intense and powerful. We have experienced this intensity in the form of an emotional outburst at the time of meditation. There are many people who become highly emotional as they go deep into meditative states. These emotional outbursts are often attributed to some kind of mental, psychological or emotional blockage, however beyond this there is another reason. According to yoga, when an intensity of thought, idea or feeling is experienced unconsciously in the deeper layers of the mind, without the distraction of the senses, at that particular moment the idea or thought form itself becomes a very intensive experience.

Such an emotional outburst is also a state of dharana. The difference is that, in this case, there is no support or basis to which we latch ourselves. Therefore, the intensity is very strong and we feel it coming from deep inside. As that particular emotional outburst takes place, we relate it to some event, situation, circumstance or experience from the past. Childhood memories rise to the surface; images of happy or sad times that we have had in life come rushing up and we go with the force of those feelings. That is the external reaction which takes place in meditation when the mind is without a support. Therefore, it is quite common to see people crying, expressing their emotions and going through different, spontaneous, physical movements in the state of dharana.

Right now, with the externalized mind we are conscious and aware of how our body has to react and behave. In the external state there is also an unconscious control of prana, whereas in meditation that unconscious control is not there. There is no control over the prana. The mind is cut off from the body and the prana begins to move and flow spontaneously. So, the body adopts different postures according to the movement of prana. When this disconnection takes place the prana becomes free. The mental concepts become free from the conditioning of body, environment and even local mentality.

Intensity of concentration
The important thing here is to keep the mind fixed on one point only. Any point of concentration can be used such as a mantra, symbol, thought, idea or any form. Intensity of concentration is generally regarded as dharana. There is a story in the *Mahabharata* which illustrates the intensity of concentration required for this practice. When Acharya Drona was teaching archery to the Pandava and Kuru princes, he asked his pupils to come forward one at a time in order to see a small clay bird that he had placed on a branch at the top of a tree, and to shoot an arrow through the eye of the bird. As each prince came forward, the guru asked them the same question, "What do you see?"

The first prince replied, "I see the forest, the sky, the tree, the leaves, the branch and the bird." The guru said, "Don't shoot. Put your bow down." Then he called the next prince and asked, "What do you see?" The second prince replied, "I see the tree, the leaves, the branch and the bird." The guru told him also to put the bow down. All the pupils who came forward failed to understand the teaching that the guru was trying to impart, because he expected a very specific answer.

Finally Arjuna's turn came and the guru asked him, "What do you see?" Arjuna replied, "I see the bird's eye." The guru asked, "Do you not see the leaves of the tree and the branch on which the bird is sitting?" "No," said Arjuna, "I see only the eye and nothing else." The guru then asked, "Do you not even see even the bird's wings or head?" Arjuna replied, " No, I see nothing but the eye, that is all." So then the guru was satisfied and said to Arjuna, "You have learned well." Arjuna did not have tunnel vision, nor was he blind to the scenery around him. But the intensity of his concentration was so great that all his faculties of perception were fixed on one single point – the bird's eye.

At the time of meditation, if there is oscillation in the mind, then concentration will not be experienced. Dharana is a state in which there is total one-pointedness. It may come only for a second after a lot of practice. If you are trying to practise meditation with an oscillating mind which is moving from one point to the next, while different thoughts and ideas are coming and going, then it is not meditation or dharana, or even pratyahara, because there are too many oscillations and distractions. So just closing the eyes and trying to fix the mind on an image is not enough. Proper training has to be given to the senses, to the mind and also to the mental faculties as and when they manifest, in order to perfect dharana and to come to the meditative state of dhyana.

Approach to meditation

In the *Raja Yoga Sutras* (Samadhipada:14) of Patanjali there is a sutra which describes the process of meditation.

सतु दीर्घकालनैरन्तर्यसत्काराऽऽसेवितो दृढभूमि ॥

That (practice) becomes firmly grounded which is continued for a long time with reverence and without interruption.

This is the main sutra which must be taught to every aspirant. Three qualities are necessary for the achievement or fulfilment of any sadhana, whether it be spiritual or material. The first is faith or conviction. Even if you are working in a factory, there has to be a conviction that through the work you will achieve your goal. Without that conviction there is no motivation to do the work. The same principle applies to the practice of dharana. There has to be faith or conviction that, "Yes, through my practice I am going to attain the goal." Whether it takes a long time or a short time is irrelevant.

Continuity or regularity is the second aspect of sadhana. When you feel that you can fulfil your need with a particular sadhana then you try to become regular in it. During that period of regular practice you try to ignore any distractions which come in the way. Once you set out on a journey, how long it will take you to reach your destination depends on your continuity. You can stop twenty times on the way, or you can just go on continuously. If you stop twenty times on the way, it will take you longer to complete the journey, but if you go on continuously, you will complete the journey sooner. Continuity without a break is necessary in order to obtain the full benefit of the practice.

Many times people say, "I have been practising concentration for many years and nothing has happened." However, most of these people do not practise regularly. Perhaps they practise only once a week or not at all for several weeks and then they may have a spurt of enthusiasm where they practise for long durations. Right from the start it should be understood that practising one day a week is like taking one step forward, and not practising for the remaining six days is like taking six steps back. How can you expect to make any progress in this way? Therefore, in the practice of meditation there has to be continuity and regularity. Just as you find time to do those other things which you consider necessary in your life, in the same way you have to find time to be regular in dharana.

Practice over a long period of time is the third aspect of sadhana which must be fulfilled. The idea of practising one thing for a long period of time is something which puts most people off. If we have to do something for a long time, we tend to get bored and lose interest. In external awareness the mind follows the senses, but when we are internalized, with the senses following the mind, then the time factor is not important. So, we have to be committed to the practice of meditation without any impatience or expectation of achievement within a certain period of time. If there is expectation of achievement within a certain time, then it should be dealt with accordingly.

You also have to consider that your approach to meditation begins just like that of a caterpillar, moving from one small leaf of a huge tree to another. To arrive at the centre of that tree may be the eventual aim, but in the beginning you cannot just go straight to the centre. To do that a different kind of awareness is needed. You have to start crawling from where you are, like a caterpillar which has a leaf as its world. As it passes the leaf, it reaches a tiny twig, which connects to a bigger branch, which connects to another bigger branch, which connects to the trunk of the tree, which goes down into the roots. Our mentality, our expectations, our life, our world, is our leaf and we are nibbling away at it. In fact, we are all caterpillars in our own right, nibbling away at our leaf. From this leaf we have to get to the main trunk and eventually try to bore a hole in the centre. This is the process of meditation.

4
Psychic Symbol

The yogic tradition has described three aspects of meditation: (i) awareness of the practitioner, the person who is practising meditation, (ii) the aim or the goal which the practitioner wishes to attain through the technique or process of meditation, and (iii) the process that the practitioner adopts. When all three become one then the meditative experience dawns and we lose awareness of body and mind. There is nothing but the meditative experience, and that state is called dhyana. When we become one with the meditative experience it becomes a living experience. When the concept of duality no longer exists and there is only one experience, this is known as liberation of the mind.

In the beginning, however, the awareness of each practitioner is different and each aims at a different level of conscious evolution. Although the thoughts and motivations of one practitioner may seem to be similar or the same as those of another, the evolutionary level of the mind is at a different stage. The evolutionary level of the mind has to be observed through a process of self-observation. After observing oneself, one can decide which areas of the personality need to be developed.

Every individual is a composition of head, heart and hands. The head represents buddhi or the intellectual aspect of life. The heart represents the emotional or feeling aspect, the spontaneous, natural, non-rational expressions of life.

The hands represent action, the drive to act, to be a participant in this world club of which we are all life members. We begin like this, by integrating and harmonizing the sensory organs and the organs of action, because the mind itself is a sensory organ.

The spirit is attracted to the dimension of *prakriti*, the world of tangible experiences, which it perceives through the five *jnanendriyas* or sensory organs (eyes, ears, nose, tongue and skin), the five *karmendriyas* or physical organs (hands, feet, anus, sexual organs and speech), and through the total mind or *mahat*, which includes the faculties of *manas* (rational mind), *buddhi* (intellect), *chitta* (memory) and *ahamkara* (ego). Each of these mental faculties is also considered as a separate, subtle sense.

In pratyahara there is a gradual withdrawal of externalized sensory experiences so that dissipation and distraction do not occur. The mind must go through a gradual training process to perfect pratyahara, which may take many years. After mastering sensory withdrawal, dharana begins, where there is total, one-pointed concentration on the symbol, object or process of meditation. Eventually there must be a merging of mind with the experience of mind; a merger of the two identities, 'me' and 'you', subject and object.

As long as we are going through the process of merging, we are in the stages of pratyahara and dharana. When the merger takes place we are in the stages of dhyana and samadhi. However, until we have merged ourselves we cannot say that we practise meditation. We can only say that we are practising methods to improve our awareness and concentration. In order to come to the stage of dhyana and samadhi there must be a pranic awakening as well, because there is a very intimate relationship between prana and mind.

Tools of meditation

In order to consolidate the mind three tools are necessary: (i) psychic sound, (ii) psychic symbol and (iii) psychic breath. These three tools are used in the stages of pratyahara and dharana in order to perfect the meditation process. They provide a basis or a support which the mind can hold on to when the sensory input is cut off. In the process of meditation, as the concentration becomes intensified, the attention is diverted from the sensory perception to the object of concentration. At this time there is a tendency to lose touch with the experience of time, space and object as the awareness moves towards the unconscious dimension.

In this state the mind is overcome by drowsiness as the physical and psychological perceptions are lost. In short it means that we become sleepy. In the state of sleep the mind is diverted to different areas of experience. It begins to dream, imagine and fantasize, and the meditative state is lost. So, there has to be a support on which the mind, that has been divested of its identity with the senses, can rest. That is the purpose of using these three tools of meditation.

There is a story about a caravan in the desert which explains this concept very clearly. A caravan was travelling at night. When it was time to rest, the travellers erected tents and tied up their camels. Unfortunately one man had lost the hook for securing his camel, so the camel remained loose. The man was worried about his camel being untied, so he went to the leader of the caravan and told him his problem. The leader said, "Don't worry about the hook. Just go through the same motion of tying your camel up and the camel will not go anywhere." So the man returned to his camel and went through the motions of tying it up. The camel sat down and did not move from the spot all night.

The next morning everybody was getting ready to resume the journey, but this man's camel would not get up. The man could not understand why his camel would not get up like the other camels had done. So again he went to the leader of the caravan and asked him what he should do. The leader said, "Now go through the motions of unhitching the camel as you would normally do if it had been tied up." So the man went through the motions of untying the rope and the camel immediately stood up.

The meaning of this story is obvious. There is actually no bondage within the mind. However, due to our mental conditioning we feel that we must be bound. The mind feels a need for support, a need to be tied down. So, in our own mind we go through the motions of hitching and unhitching our own mental camel. This is where the tools of meditation are important. We use them as a support for the mind when we are entering the uncharted dimensions of the subconscious and unconscious. This is why there are so many mantras, symbols and meditation practices. They are all intended to act as a support for the mind, as a focal point for concentration, as the awareness penetrates into deeper and deeper levels of consciousness.

The barrier of laya
Every meditation practice utilizes something that the mind can grasp, on which it can take hold. It can be the breath, the mantra, the symbol. In nada yoga it is the gross and subtle sound. In ajapa japa it is the combination of psychic passage, psychic breath and psychic sound. In akasha dharana it is the inner space. In trataka it is various objects viewed externally as well as internally. One's awareness is always fixed on an object or a process. This is because the mind naturally and spontaneously moulds itself around objects of perception. In day-to-day life, the mind does this continually with various external objects and thoughts. Without an object of perception one lapses into a state of unconsciousness.

This also applies to meditation practice. Many people sit for meditation without fixing their attention on a specific object. They merely close their eyes and allow the mind to wander here and there like a wild monkey. They either brood about their problems or fall into a state of sleep. Neither of these states is a meditative experience. We can practise like this for a hundred years and gain absolutely nothing. Therefore, we should try to maintain continuous awareness of an object or whatever process the practice involves. As we progress along the path of meditation we become more and more relaxed. The natural thing to do at this time is to sleep. This is the barrier of laya, unconsciousness, which prevents us from diving deep into our being. This barrier can only be crossed by the adoption of a symbol or method which holds the concentration.

Actually this tendency towards laya or unconsciousness is a safety mechanism. It prevents us from delving into the deeper dimensions of the mind prematurely. The subconscious fears, neuroses and apparitions must be confronted, but the process should take place slowly in a controlled way. The mind has to be gradually purified and harmonized over a period of time. If there is a sudden perception of a great flood of subconscious fears, then we will be overwhelmed by the negative contents of our own mind. So, laya is a protective screen which can only be crossed when the negative karma and samskaras have been exhausted. Then the symbol or the object of concentration must be utilized.

Sakara and nirakara

The word *sakara* means 'with form' and *nirakara* means 'without form'. Whether meditation should be sakara or nirakara has been the main controversy amongst spiritual seekers for millennia. In the *Ishavasya Upanishad* (v.12) it states that: "Those who worship the unmanifest reality enter into blinding darkness; those who worship the manifest enter into even greater darkness." This verse has many meanings, but we will confine our discussion to its implications regarding laya and symbol.

In sakara meditation, where one's awareness is fixed on a definite focal point or object, concentration takes place within the manifest dimension. In nirakara meditation, where one does not fix the awareness at any definite focal point, concentration takes place within the unmanifest dimension. This includes those practices where the awareness is allowed to freely explore the mind and psyche while reflecting on such abstract concepts as infinity, Brahman, God, etc. How is it that both of these types of practice lead to darkness? The reason is that both sakara and nirakara meditation practices are means to an end; they are not the end in itself.

Meditation on form can easily degenerate into mere idol worship. People have worshipped idols and deities without the slightest idea of the purpose behind their worship. The same thing can happen with a mantra, a symbol or any other object of meditation. The symbol becomes an object of intellectual speculation rather than a means of transcendence. Therefore, the Upanishad states that "those who worship the manifest enter into even greater darkness." The purpose of the object is to lead the awareness to that which is beyond intellectual speculation.

Therefore, many people prefer to reflect upon abstract concepts. However, in this regard the Upanishad states that "those who worship the unmanifest reality enter into blinding darkness." This is because most people are not prepared for this type of meditation. In this case meditation on such themes as infinity, Brahman, God, etc. tend to degenerate into intellectual speculations which are not based on deep experience. This leads away from the path of meditation. Nirakara meditation leads to laya, unconsciousness and sleep. Thus the Upanishad warns us to be careful of both sakara and nirakara meditation and to try and understand their purpose and place.

First of all, there must be intense sakara meditation practice in order to purify the mind and make it one-pointed. In the following verse the Upanishad explains, "Meditation on the manifest (sakara) brings a specific experience; meditation on the unmanifest (nirakara) leads to a different experience." Here the Upanishad indicates that sakara meditation leads to a specific level of understanding and experience, while nirakara meditation leads to a different level. Both of them are essential and must be practised at the right time for the evolution of consciousness.

Hence the Upanishad states in the next verse, "He who knows that both the manifest (sakara) and the unmanifest (nirakara) are really one, overcomes death through the manifest and obtains immortality through the unmanifest" This verse indicates the integration of the manifest and the unmanifest, the sakara and the nirakara. One should eventually see the formless in all forms and all forms in the formless. But this understanding can only come after both sakara and nirakara meditation have been perfected. Continuous practice of sakara meditation will eventually lead you across the 'river of death', the barrier of unconsciousness. Then, having obtained this realization, one should reflect upon the formless, unmanifest nirakara. This reflection will arise spontaneously. This is the point where one crosses over from practice into the meditative experience which is beyond intellectual understanding.

5
Visualization

According to yoga, freedom from mental bondage is attained through practice of a mantra or psychic sound. The effect of the mantra is to free the mind from bondage caused by our attraction to the senses. Mantras are sound vibrations which affect the physical, emotional, mental and psychic structure. Every sound vibration creates a particular pattern, image or form. In the initial stage, that sound vibration is known as *nada* or the *pratham spandan*, 'the first remedial vibration'. This remedial vibration is the source from which all life forms emanate.

In the Bible it is said that 'in the beginning was the word'. This is actually the pratham spandan or the nada which is the basis of mantra. In this context mantra becomes a tool for the development of the states of pratyahara and dharana. It provides a base or support on which the mind can rest so that it does not become unconscious. As the mental tensions and distractions diminish, the awareness and concentration improve.

Another aspect of mantra is yantra or psychic symbol. Every mantra is comprised of one or more sound vibrations, and each vibration creates a particular image. Science has also shown that when you play a note on a musical instrument, that note creates a particular form. In the same way the image which a mantra creates in the field of consciousness is known as yantra.

Just as the word mantra (*mananat trayate* or *mansah trayate*) means liberation from the thought processes of the mind, so yantra (*yamyate anena*) means that technique by which the mind is controlled.

When the thought processes are controlled by mantra or yantra, the consciousness presents itself in its purest, true nature. Unless consciousness is experienced in its true nature, the mind remains in a state of relative inertia or inactivity, and cannot understand the reality. The evolution of consciousness in its totality is experienced by the sadhaka only when the clouds of the thought processes are controlled by both mantra and yantra.

Therefore, we have the images of yantras or symbols which can be very simple and also very complicated, depending on the state of our evolution. An individual's mantra can create the image spontaneously. At the time of mantra repetition an image comes to the mind, whether it is a circle, a star, a square, a triangle or any other image. Often one does not understand why it is happening, why this beautiful green, blue, pink light has come into one's meditation. That is the symbol which is being created by the repetition of the mantra in the field of consciousness.

Conceptualization of the mind

What do we do with the symbol that has manifested within the field of consciousness? That is the point of concentration. Generally we sit down for meditation and try to blank out. We try to totally avoid and escape from every kind of sensory and mental identity, idea and experience. Due to the undisciplined nature of the mind, however, we find that there is a struggle with the thoughts. The mind cannot be quiet and we are trying to force it to be quiet. So, instead of meditation we go through a process of mental stress. Instead of experiencing mental peace and tranquility, there is a constant struggle to bring the mind back to the practice, to stop the thoughts from coming, to let go of the worldly worries and anxieties.

Therefore, in order to keep the mind focused at one point we have to use a symbol. At the time of mental dissipation and distraction we have to bring ourselves back to that point again and again. It becomes a visual point to focus our attention upon. It is very difficult to focus the attention on a non-visual point. So mantra and yantra, sound and symbol are necessary tools for meditation. They have the capacity to penetrate far into the depths of the subconscious and unconscious mind in order to manifest or express the hidden potential. They are a scientific process of conceptualizing these unknown areas of the mind. Concentration on these sounds and images influences the brain waves. If we can reorganize, reset, restructure the brain wave patterns, then we can manifest a new quality of consciousness.

Samyama: perfection of concentration
We are surrounded by an ocean of vibrations which are vibrating in different dimensions simultaneously. When we repeat a mantra we begin the process of pratyahara. This requires a gradual withdrawal of the sensory perceptions, and then we are able to focus the mind at one point. After the process of withdrawal is complete, then the mental focusing is total and there is no distraction or dissipation of any type. That state is known as dharana, the capacity of the mind to hold a concept.

For example, we concentrate on a flower and we are able to hold the flower in our mind for a particular period of time. However, we are not able to forget ourselves. We are still aware of time and space. That is called dharana or concentration. Dhyana means total, unfluctuating awareness of the mind in that concept. When you are able to hold the concept of the flower in your mind and you are no longer aware of yourself or of the meditation process, then that is called dhyana or meditation.

When you are able to hold the concept of the flower in your mind, and the flower within you becomes a living experience so that there is no difference between an external flower and the internal flower, when both flowers look alike, that is called samadhi.

All these three stages: dharana, dhyana and samadhi, practised together are known as *samyama*. When you are able to practise these three together, your mind becomes creative, constructive and competent. It is able to hold any idea within itself with greater force and there is no barrier or limitation to its capacities. When you have accomplished samyama you can concentrate on any object. When the mind has achieved perfection in concentration then it attains *siddhis*, psychic abilities.

Living experience

Whatever you can see outside, you can see inside as well. In order to see outside you need the sensory channels; however, to see inside you do not need any sensory medium. That capacity has to be attained. Therefore, do not worry about the quality or the virtue of the practice. Just be sure that the practice is so powerful that you can actually see the object inside clearly, as though it were real. If you find that your practice cannot give you a living experience, then it is necessary for you to review it.

There should be no difference between the external and the internal experience. Both appear to be alike. But when you are able to have the inner experience without depending on your senses, then your mind becomes very powerful. You can influence your destiny and your career. You can change the circumstances of your life. There is nothing that you cannot achieve. That is the ultimate point in mental development which everyone has to reach. That state of mind, that quality of experience is known as supermind, and that supermind is a product of concentration. It is a mind which can create a living experience from anything it thinks about.

Guidelines for visualization

In the preliminary stage of dharana, the symbol can be an external object. However, as your perception becomes more subtle, you should visualize your symbol internally and create an image in chidakasha, the space in front of the closed eyes. This image is more subtle and will take you much deeper.

Many people have trouble maintaining a clear image of the symbol. Either they cannot visualize it or the image tends to fade away. Do not become frustrated if this is the case with you. It is merely an indication of the state of your mind. It is difficult to visualize inner images with a disturbed mind. You will be able to think about the image or imagine it, but you will not be able to see it internally with total clarity, as you would see it externally. As your mind becomes calm and steady, however, you will find it progressively easier to visualize your symbol. When the mind becomes absolutely still and one-pointed, then you will be able to maintain a fixed inner vision of your psychic symbol. It requires regular practice to reach this stage, however, you should not expect to achieve it in one session.

When the mind becomes quiet you should start to use a psychic symbol. You must formulate a pattern of consciousness which acts as a base on which you can fix your awareness. When an astronaut explores space he always relates his position to the earth or the sun. It is the same with the exploration of inner space. You must relate your awareness to a symbol. Your awareness, which normally drifts from one thought to another, must be centred around one form. All the mental forces must be moulded around the symbol. When you can maintain unfluctuating awareness of that one symbol for a few minutes without displacement by other thoughts, then the inner vision will develop.

If you wish to practise visualization, keep the following points in mind:
- Your symbol can be external or internal. However, as your perception becomes more refined, you should utilize a subtle, inner psychic symbol.

- Your symbol should be such that your mind automatically identifies with it, i.e. your symbol should attract and hold your attention without too much effort.
- Do not change your symbol. If you change it then the mind will have to adapt to and mould itself around a new symbol. That takes time and effort.
- Try to develop the ability to clearly visualize a sharp image of the symbol in front of the closed eyes. With practice it should arise spontaneously.
- If you do not have a specific symbol, then practise meditation techniques such as those given in this book. When you are ready the symbol will come to you.

6

Obstacles in Dharana

The practices of dharana are designed specifically to purify the nadis and chakras of the psychic body through techniques of concentration and visualization. When you concentrate, the faculties of mind are made one-pointed. As there are fewer mental distractions, your psychic, astral and pranic bodies come into harmony and alignment with each other. When this alignment takes place you are able to cross over the threshold from outer to inner experiences.

As soon as you become steady in dharana, you cross over this threshold and at this point many obstacles may arise to block your inner progress. These include visions, awakened kundalini, sensuality, illness, disillusionment and oversensitivity. These are the obstacles which arise from within. There are also several obstacles which may arise from without. These include excessive socializing, too many practices, irregularity in lifestyle and practice, and imbalanced diet.

Visions are the first obstacle which one may face on the path of dharana. Here you may see beautiful demigoddesses or apsaras from the other world coming to tempt you away from the practice. Visions may also appear in the form of snakes, lions, tigers, demons and vampires to frighten you. Only if you are able to remain calm and unaffected in such situations will your practice proceed unimpeded. There are many descriptions of different mystics, saints and prophets who experienced such visions at the time of intensive sadhana.

When Christ was living in the desert for forty days, many such visions came to him. Similarly, Lord Buddha had many visions while sitting under the Bodhi tree before his enlightenment.

Kundalini awakening is the next difficulty which arises. In fact, you cannot enter into the stage of dharana without some degree of kundalini awakening. Dharana is usually practised on the different chakras, so this also indicates some degree of awakening which does not happen unless kundalini moves upward into the passage of sushumna. As the kundalini energy begins to penetrate the chakras, dharana begins. If the kundalini experiences become intense during the practice of dharana, you will require the guidance of an experienced guru and a conducive environment in order to continue the sadhana.

Sensuality is another obstacle which one may face on the path of dharana. When dharana occurs, strong sensual feelings develop spontaneously in the lower centres. This can be tolerated once in a while, but during dharana it may happen frequently. As the practice of dharana progresses and the mind becomes controlled, the pranas and chakras are purified. This purification leads to increased production of the sexual fluid. Therefore, sensuality is increased. When sensuality arises during the practice of dharana, you will again need the guidance of an experienced guru in order to clear your path.

Encountering illness is another difficulty which may arise. Often in the lower stages, physical impurities create obstructions. Normally, in the extroverted state of active life, rajo guna is predominant. Through the practice of dharana, however, the process of physical purification takes place very quickly. As a result the unhealthy elements in the body are generated in order to be eliminated as quickly as possible. These may assume the form of an illness that was previously lying dormant.

When illness manifests in the body in this way it is a result of the process of purification. Therefore, you need not worry. The illness will automatically subside through the meditation process itself. Therefore, the dharana practice should not be abandoned at such times, but continued. Under such circumstances, however, medication should be avoided as it interferes with the purification process. You should also abstain from a rich, heavy diet. Take a simple, light diet or take only milk and fruit.

Disillusionment with the practice is yet another obstacle. At this stage it is difficult to assess the degree of your progress correctly. Out of enthusiasm you may tend to overrate your attainment, thinking that dharana can be mastered quickly. However, as you advance you will become disillusioned to find that dharana is not so easy to master. It takes time to steady the mind and develop concentration, inner visualization and control over the image.

When the practice does not go well, you may become uneasy about your progress and begin to doubt whether any benefits have been gained. On the other hand, when some success is attained you may feel overjoyed, thinking that you are on the threshold of samadhi. These kinds of ups and downs will be there at times during the practice. Such illusions about the practice should neither depress nor elate you. It is only by persevering steadily regardless of such ups and downs that actual progress is made.

Oversensitivity develops when you begin to develop concentration. The sound of a pin dropping may feel like a thunderbolt going through your brain. Certain smells, sounds, sights and feelings which you would not have noticed before will repel or irritate you. These are the stages through which you have to pass, but if you have perseverance you will succeed.

Adopting too many practices can create obstacles. There is a danger of wasting your valuable energy and time by trying one practice and then giving it up for another new one. Whatever practice you take up should be continued until you reach the end of it. Before you have completed the practice you should not give it up and take up another. It is better to persevere with one practice until you have mastered it. If you practise a little of this and a little of that, you will never attain the meditation experience. Different and new practices may excite your imagination, but there it will end. It is like the man who dug one hundred wells but never found water. Each time he would give up after digging a few feet and start digging in a new place. Therefore, stick to one practice and go deep, then you will reach the goal.

Excessive socializing is another obstacle to the practice of dharana. If you wish to go deep into the practice, you will have to minimize your social commitments. Companionship with different types of people distracts the mind. Excessive talking also distracts the mind. All types of sensory diversion, excitement and intoxication block the pathway of dharana.

Irregularity in lifestyle and practice is one of the biggest obstacles and for many people the hardest to overcome. In order to attain concentration, the mind and body must be balanced and steady. Irregularity creates imbalance and restlessness. It is important to create regular meal times, sleeping time, work time, recreation time and meditation time. Once you have decided upon your schedule do not deviate from it. A regular lifestyle and practice is the basis for spiritual progress and the development of concentration.

Imbalanced diet is another obstacle to dharana. The digestive system is very delicate. When we enter into the deeper states of consciousness, the digestive power is often diminished. Therefore, in order to progress in dharana you should neither eat too much nor fast too often. A regular sattwic diet is essential. As your system becomes purified through the practice, the least irregularity will throw you out of balance. One portion more or less of food will disturb your entire system until you get perfect control, then you will be able to eat whatever you like.

Tension is also an obstacle. It must always be remembered that concentration is not a state of tension. True concentration of mind can only be achieved in a relaxed personality. A tense person cannot concentrate. Only when you have learned to maintain an easy and steady posture and to relax the body, nerves, brain and mind can you begin to concentrate. In fact, relaxation and concentration are interrelated. You cannot relax any part of your body unless you can focus your mental attention on it. Similarly, you cannot focus the mind unless it is completely relaxed. Trying to focus a tense mind is like tightening a string which is already too tight. Instead of concentration, fragmentation or mental breakdown may be the result. Therefore, concentration must be developed gradually through a systematic meditative process. Do not force yourself to concentrate when you are feeling tired or tense.

Muscular and nervous tension have nothing to do with concentration. Success in the exercise is not to be measured by any bodily sensation or feeling whatever. Some people think that they are concentrating when they feel a tightness between and behind the eyebrows, but they are only producing headaches and other troubles for themselves. Attention without tension is what is required. Concentration must always be practised without the slightest strain. Control of mind is not brought about by fervent effort of any kind, but by constant, quiet, calm practice and avoidance of all agitation and excitement.

These are some of the major points which you will have to observe and be aware of if you wish to take up the practice of dharana in a serious way. Of course, even if you do not wish to develop the practice to such a great extent, it will still give you untold benefits. It will calm your nerves, clear your mind, improve your temperament and health, increase your lifespan and give you a new vision of life.

7
Yogic, Tantric and Upanishadic Dharana

In this book many guided practices of dharana have been presented from the yogic, tantric and upanishadic traditions. These practices represent an advanced level of teaching which up to now has never been elucidated for the general public. They are being given at this time because a need has been expressed by many serious and advanced practitioners for more guidance into the deeper dimensions of meditation. Systematic study and practice of these techniques will help the practitioner to bridge the gap between the preliminary techniques which are being taught today by most schools, and the advanced methods or spontaneous techniques which have traditionally never been taught except through direct transmission from guru to disciple.

YOGIC AND TANTRIC DHARANA

The practices of chakra shuddhi and ajapa dharana which are described here in a very detailed manner, apart from being an integral part of mantra yoga, are also given prominence in the Upanishads. The ten ajapa dharanas are described in the *Hamsa Upanishad*, which is the fifteenth of the one hundred and eight Upanishads and forms a part of the *Atharva Veda*.

There are two levels of ajapa japa practices. At the pratyahara level, the method covers the gross, external aspect, using physical activity, the breathing process, to internalize the awareness. Then mantra is added to stop the self-induced mental fluctuation. At the dharana level, however, the practice is greatly intensified. There is deep concentration on the mantra, chakra and nadis, so that even the causal manifestations, inherent experiences of the senses and world, tend to gradually dissipate.

The ten practices given here represent the advanced level of ajapa japa which belongs to the dharana group. Of course, it should be understood that the ajapa dharana group of practices is not to be attempted until the pratyahara group has been mastered. The practices of ajapa japa are so organized that the concentration on the breath and the mantra in the pathways of sushumna, ida and pingala opens the chakras and brings about the state of dharana spontaneously, without strenuous effort to control and still the mind.

Trataka

After ajapa dharana, trataka, the practice of gazing steadily at one point, is the next technique we come to. These practices of trataka can be taken up progressively, according to one's ability and inclination. Trataka is a fundamental concentration technique in both the yogic and tantric systems as well as in the upanishadic system. Here it is presented at four levels, which cover the entire span of concentration from external and internal to *shoonya drishti*, the culmination of meditation practice.

The trataka practices also fall into two groups: pratyahara and dharana. Pratyahara trataka involves gazing at an external point, whether a candle, symbol, yantra or mandala, or the different forms of trataka that have been described in the yogic texts. Trataka aims to control the dissipation that occurs when we become aware of form. Control over this aspect, the awareness of form, is the aim of trataka. At the dharana level, the form is seen internally. The process is similar, but instead of using an external image on which to focus one's visual perception, we develop and awaken our own internal visual perception. What is stored in the mind in the form of visual impressions is gradually released in this technique, until ultimately the vision of shoonyata occurs.

UPANISHADIC DHARANA

The Yoga Upanishads describe the various methods and levels of akasha dharana. Upanishadic dharana is not just fixation of the mind on some object or point. It is a very complex process where the mind is taken through different states of external, intermediate and internal experiences. These methods all use different visualization techniques which are done through the mediums of akasha or space.

According to the vedic tradition, akasha, space or the sky, is the most effective support for meditation. By dwelling on the image of the sky, an expansion of mind takes place automatically. The opposite of expansion is contraction, which brings discomfort and uneasiness. The ethereal vastness is a source of energy and power. All impetus towards action issues from the immense void.

In the mind there is normally a ceaseless bubbling of thought, feeling and desire, which is like the foam on the surface of the ocean. We can see the foam and the bubbles but not the ocean itself, although it is there. The bubbles and foam represent the mental consciousness. By dwelling upon the limitless space, the mind becomes conscious of the ocean, which is the infinite consciousness.

The Yoga Upanishads describe three different levels of dharana: (i) bahir lakshya (external stage), (ii) madhya lakshya (intermediate stage), and (iii) antar lakshya (internal stage). The various practices of upanishadic dharana have been taught according to these three levels. Some of the practices also contain all three levels within them. Although the range of practices is very broad, it is best to master each of the practices progressively, according to your individual ability and evolution. You should continue with one practice and try to master it gradually, stage by stage, before going on to the next practice.

External level

The first level of dharana is bahir lakshya. The word *bahir* means 'external', *lakshya* means 'aim', and *dharana* means 'concentration'. So, bahir lakshya is an external aim which one focuses upon to achieve concentration. The first technique of bahir lakshya is called bhoochari mudra, which means gazing into space. First, the hand is held horizontally in front of the nose and one focuses on the nail of the little finger, looking at it intensely and fixing the position of the eyes. Gradually, the hand is removed and the same focus of the eyes is maintained for as long as possible.

Bhoochari mudra is a practice of bahir lakshya. It is very difficult to keep the vision fixed on space. The eyes need to focus on something; it is hard to focus on nothing, on space. However, the longer you maintain the focus of the eyes on the point of space, the easier it becomes to control the sensorial inputs and prevent them from distracting the mental attention. The yogic texts state that when this stage is perfected, a blue light is seen upon closing the eyes.

In addition to the first stage of frontal vision, as practised in bhoochari mudra, there is upper vision, as in akashi mudra, which is the second practice. In akashi mudra, one bends the head back and gazes upward into space, keeping the eyes open. This practice can also be performed by combining shambhavi mudra and gazing at the space between the eyebrows at the level of ajna chakra.

Although these techniques are all visual in nature, different nadis are influenced by the position of the eyeballs. In kundalini yoga, for example, it has been stated that in order to awaken mooladhara chakra one has to practise nasikagra drishti, which is nose tip gazing. Focusing the eyes on the tip of the nose creates different sensations in the nadis which are connected with each other in the forehead region, as well as to ida, pingala and sushumna, which in turn create a certain stimulus at mooladhara. These are techniques of bahir lakshya which stimulate the nadis and help to awaken the different psychic centres.

The bahir lakshya techniques aim at awakening the different nadis. Just as the technique of bhoochari mudra (the first of these practices) is known to be perfected when there is a vision of blue light, in the same way, the practice of akashi mudra is known to be perfected when there is a vision of golden light. So, what does this blue and golden light signify here? It signifies the awakening of ida and pingala nadis; the blue represents ida and the gold, pingala. So, in the external aspect of dharana an effort is made to internalize the mind, to fix the mind on one point, to intensify the state of concentration and also to awaken the two nadis, ida and pingala.

Intermediate level: akasha dharana

The next aspect of dharana is madhya lakshya. The word *madhya* means 'intermediate', *lakshya* means 'aim' and *dharana* means 'concentration', so this is the intermediate stage of dharana. In this stage an effort is made to focus the mind on the experience of space. In yoga, three regions of space are generally described within the physical body. These three physical spaces are:
1. *Chidakasha*: the space of chitta or consciousness experienced in the head region between vishuddhi, ajna and sahasrara chakras.
2. *Hridayakasha*: the space of the heart experienced in the chest region, located between manipura, anahata and vishuddhi chakras.
3. *Daharakasha*: the space of the lower regions, encompassing mooladhara, swadhisthana and manipura chakras.

The techniques of dharana meditation, commonly described in the books on meditation, are related to these three spaces which are also experienced physically within the body. These practices are known as: chidakasha dharana, hridayakasha dharana and daharakasha dharana.

Chidakasha dharana is a technique of meditation in which the awareness of space in chidakasha is built up in different ways: seeing the colours, shapes and symbols that manifest, creating and removing mental images, and allowing images to arise spontaneously. As the mind becomes subtle, different shapes, geometric figures, yantras and mandalas will be seen. These represent a state of perception in the mind. Sometimes nothing will be seen. In order to draw water from a well you require a long rope. If the water is eighty feet down and your rope is only forty feet long, you will obviously never get water. So, although you may see nothing in the region of chidakasha it does not mean that nothing exists. There is always some experience at every level; no level is without experience. However, it needs to be understood that the intensity of our effort will determine how far and how deep we can go. This principle applies to every technique and aspect of yoga.

Hridayakasha dharana is concentration on the heart space, and is a vedic meditation process involving the three bodies of prajna, tejas and vaishwanara. In this process the light is experienced in the heart. There are many Upanishads that give descriptions of the hridayakasha dharana techniques. These are techniques which deal with the intensity of emotion and feeling, creation of an emotion, colours of an emotion, changing of an emotion and also the dimension beyond emotion. These are not the conscious emotions that we normally deal with in daily life, but the deep subconscious feelings that are far more intense. These emotions have to be experienced and relived in order to break the conditioning of the mind. The psychotherapeutic aspect of meditation has its roots in hridayakasha dharana.

Daharakasha dharana is concentration on the space of the lower regions, and comprises the techniques found in the kundalini literature. These practices involve concentration on specific images in the region of mooladhara, swadhisthana or manipura chakras. Here one may see a lotus flower, a colour, a symbol, a deity, an animal or an element. This detailed awareness of the chakras is called daharakasha dharana.

Vyoma panchaka dharana – the five subtle spaces

After chidakasha, hridayakasha and daharakasha, the three gross spaces, we come to vyoma panchaka, the five subtle spaces. *Vyoma* means 'space' and *panchaka* means 'five'. The experience of these five subtle spaces is in the realm of the unconscious and beyond. Daharakasha, hridayakasha and chidakasha are experienced in the conscious and subconscious. These five mental spaces, which are collectively known as vyoma panchaka, consist of guna rahita akasha, paramakasha, mahakasha, tattwakasha and suryakasha.

Guna rahita akasha is the attributeless space. *Guna* means 'attribute' or 'quality', *rahita* means 'without', and *akasha* means 'space'. The final experience in this akasha, taken literally from the scriptures, is that "in the morning a complete ring of sunlight or flame of fire is seen." This description gives some idea of what guna rahita akasha is. It is seen that after one has passed through the experiences of the three spaces and beyond the conscious and subconscious planes of life, then in the unconscious level, the prajna purusha or prajna identity is perceived as a luminous body.

A ring of fire or of sunlight, representing the luminous body, is beyond the known attributes of the manifest physical and mental dimensions. It is beyond the realm of the physical and mental gunas. Maintaining this vision or visual experience for an extended period is the experience of guna rahita akasha. The vision of prajna is not involuntary vision, it is voluntary vision. Just as we can imagine the image of a rose or any other object if we wish, in the same way this vision becomes a voluntary visual experience.

Paramakasha is described as 'deep dark space with a twinkling star-like light. There is a state of perception which is known as shoonya or nothingness. Here total absence of light, cognition and knowledge is experienced, with just the awareness remaining in the form of a tiny star or point of light. It is self-contained awareness, not dissipated or expanded awareness but a fixed luminous point of awareness. From this a meditative process has been developed which is known as shoonya meditation. There comes a point after this where there is total absence of external and internal awareness and only undifferentiated awareness is active. That state is the experience of paramakasha. *Param* means 'super', therefore, this is the super space.

Mahakasha is described as 'bright like the middle of the sun which no eyes can see'. You cannot see the brilliance of the sun by going into the middle of it. This shoonya state is evolving. Initially there was total darkness with just a point of light and that represented awareness. The recognition of that point of light is drashta, observing the awareness. But here the merger of drashta with that awareness takes place so that the whole personality is engulfed by total awareness. It is like being in the centre of the sun, surrounded by brilliance and light. That is known as *maha*, the great.

Tattwakasha is the element of space. *Tattwa* means 'element', but here the experience is not of the five gross elements we know as earth, water, fire, air and ether, but of the seed or essence from which the elements are germinated. In this space the tattwas exist in a dormant state; there is no activity, no motion which is expanding outwards. It is perfect stillness or quietness where each faculty is centred on its own being, so there is no action, nor is there any seed which creates action in the form of desire. In this space the concept of duality has vanished, all the experiences relating to name, form and idea have disappeared and there is absolute stillness.

Suryakasha is the luminous space of the sun or the soul, which is pure and untainted. The word *surya* means 'sun', but it is also interchangeable with *atma* or 'sun', which is the internal, self-luminous principle and illumination. This space of surya or atma is considered to be the source of light manifesting in every visible and invisible object of creation. It is both seen and unseen. This space is a permanent reality and it is illumined by the tattwas or elements. It represents the pure form of the tattwas at the time of their creation.

These are the vyoma panchaka or five subtle spaces we become aware of in the intermediate stage of lakshya dharana.

Internal stage of dharana

The next stage of dharana is antar lakshya. The word *antar* means 'internal' and *lakshya* means 'aim'. Here an internal aim has to be aspired for in dharana. This stage can be considered as the preliminary state of dharana, because in this state the awareness and the concentration of mind have passed beyond the experiences which arise out of the conscious and subconscious perceptions. One has acknowledged them and entered into another level of dharana where the psychic awareness becomes active.

Initially it was the mental awareness, knowledge and perception which became active while recognizing the visions arising in chidakasha. Experiencing feelings and merging the mind with feelings arising from hridayakasha, and recognizing the psychic structure of personality in daharakasha, are also activities attributed to mental awareness. Up to this point the mind was in a state of attention. Divide the word 'attention' – *at* plus *tension* equals attention. Initially the effort maintained mental awareness and faculties, at their peak. In this peak experience of mind, going into the deeper aspects of the three akasha experiences, and finally the vyoma panchaka, the awareness was always in a state of alertness.

There is a lot of emphasis in dharana on being observant, and this observation faculty is gradually made subtle. Through observation it is possible to reduce the distractions that arise from the interaction of the senses and the outside environment. So, when the mind is removed from a state of *attention* then psychic awareness, which is more spontaneous and natural, dawns. Being aware of and focusing the mind on our psychic experiences is the last stage of dharana and the first of dhyana. Within this stage there are three demarcations or levels which have been described by the sages and seers. The first is darshan or visualization of sushumna, the second is awareness of nada or inner sound, and the third is vision of the blue light.

Darshan or visualization of sushumna: Antar lakshya dharana begins with awareness or vision of the sushumna nadi. In intermediate dharana we develop awareness of ida and pingala and the experiences of blue and gold light. Beyond that, however, is the realm of sushumna. Although sushumna is generally considered to be one single psychic nadi, it is actually two. Sushumna nadi is like a tube and in the middle of that tube or nadi is another nadi, which is known as brahma nadi. Brahma nadi is the passage through which kundalini travels from mooladhara to sahasrara. Intensifying the awareness of brahma nadi, and observing it in the form of a luminous thread in the middle of sushumna, is the first stage of antar lakshya dharana.

Brahma nadi is visualized in sushumna in the form of a fiery, luminous thread and it is along this thread that kundalini rises. Here the process of seeing is not imagination; it is known as darshan. We imagine with mental awareness. Imagination is the process through which we divert our mind from one type of experience to another. If we try to visualize a flower with our eyes closed, there is no clarity. The image is not seen; there is just a mental idea that "I am seeing a flower". Maybe when there is intensity of thought that flower can be seen in the form of a vague shadowy outline. So, imagination is used in order to pass through the first two stages of dharana. Then, when psychic awareness begins to dawn, the actual process of seeing becomes darshan.

The word *darshan* means 'to see'. It is the actual vision or manifestation of a symbol or an object like a flower appearing in full colour and form. This process is known as visualization. Here there is an actual experience similar to a holographic type experience, where the object of concentration which does not really exist can be seen clearly. This kind of experience is termed as darshan or visualization in yoga. So, at this stage the luminous thread of brahma nadi is not imagined, it is seen in the centre of sushumna, extending from mooladhara to sahasrara. The movement of kundalini is also seen in the form of a point of light moving up and down along this brahma nadi.

The tradition also says that when the light of kundalini, which rises through the brahma nadi, is seen in the head region, the colour of chidakasha changes. Normally when we close our eyes it looks black and dull, but at this time it will be white, as if the whole head is filled with light. Some texts also state that just by seeing this light in the middle of the forehead, the practitioner is liberated from the bondage of the conscious and subconscious dimensions.

Nada – internal sound: Another indication is a hissing sound heard at the time of deep dharana. One hears it but there is no external source, it comes from inside. This happens when the kundalini experience reaches the level of ajna chakra, for it is here that the nadas, the sound vibrations, are heard. One can hear many different kinds of sounds internally such as wind blowing through leaves and branches, crickets, frogs, animals and human sounds.

Yoga recognizes ten types of nada or internal sounds which are acknowledged as the milestones of kundalini awakening at ajna chakra. These are given in order as follows: (i) the sound of a fizzling sparkler, (ii) a distant flute, (iii) a large bell, (iv) a conch, (v) a lute, (vi) cymbals, (vii) a veena (viii) pouring rain, (ix) a double drum, (x) thunder clouds.

While hearing the flute music, many people have seen the darkness in chidakasha change to different bright, flashing colours. There have also been people who could reproduce these vibrant colours in beautiful art works or the flute music into celestial and enchanting compositions.

Blue light: The final indication is seeing the blue light at ajna chakra, the eyebrow centre, and at anahata chakra, the heart centre. This blue light, which appears in the psychic experience or the kundalini experience, represents the fulfilment of the akasha experience. Seeing this blue light signifies that you have gone as far as this technique can take you and that you are ready to move onto the next stage. This is the completion of antar lakshya dharana, which is subtle psychic concentration and holding the mind to an inner experience and having darshan of it, not just imagination.

Yogic and Tantric Dharana

8
Kaya Sthairyam

Kaya sthairyam is the first practice of the dharana series. It is a basic practice of concentration on the steadiness of the body. In Sanskrit the word *kaya* means 'body' and *sthairyam* means 'steadiness'. Because of the interrelation between the body and the mind, when the body becomes steady and still the mind follows suit. Therefore, each of the dharana practices should begin with five to ten minutes of kaya sthairyam. Only when the body is absolutely steady and immobile should the actual dharana practice begin.

It is also important to note that the mind remains one-pointed only while the body is still. As soon as any part of the body moves, the mind also moves. Thus the concentration is broken and once broken it cannot be attained again in the same sitting. During pratyahara practices you can move the body, you can shift your position you can even get up and then come back to the practice. In dharana, however, you cannot move a finger, you cannot bat an eyelid, you cannot even swallow without breaking the concentration.

Before attempting the following practices of dharana, kaya sthairyam must first be mastered. You should be able to sit without moving any part of the body for at least half an hour, then you will be ready to begin the practices of dharana. In the initial stage of kaya sthairyam, the body should be comfortable and relaxed in the meditation posture. Later on, as immobility develops, the physical awareness will gradually subside as awareness of stillness increases. At this time the concentration is shifted from the body to the natural breath, so that the mind still has a focus. Ultimately, the awareness of the breath will also subside so that there is only awareness. At that time you are ready to begin dharana.

With that awareness which is steady and still and unhampered by the body, you must begin to concentrate on the object of meditation. If dharana is attempted with an unsteady body and fluctuating mind, no benefits will result from the practice even if you perform it for a hundred years. The only results will be tension, frustration and a broken mind. Therefore, give your attention to the preparatory practices in the beginning. Master kaya sthairyam, then you will be able to proceed with the practices of dharana without any obstacle.

Technique
Stage 1: Preparation
Sit in a comfortable meditation posture, preferably siddhasana or padmasana. Adjust your position so that you do not have to move any part of the body during the practice. Make sure the spine is erect. Head, neck and shoulders should be slightly back. Place your hands on the knees in chin or jnana mudra. Close your eyes. Become aware of slow deep breathing and count five breaths mentally.

Stage 2: Body posture
Switch your awareness to the body. Concentrate on your meditation posture. Feel your spine rising straight up from the floor, supporting the head. Be aware of the synchronized and balanced position of the arms and legs. Total awareness of the body.

Stage 3: Visualization of body
Visualize your body externally as if you were seeing it in a full length mirror. See your body in the meditation posture from the front, from the back, from the right side, from the left side, from the top. See your body from all sides at one time.

Stage 4: Body tree
Be aware of your whole body. Feel that you are rooted to the floor. Imagine that your body is growing up from the floor like a tree. Your torso is the trunk, your arms and head are the branches, and your legs are the roots. Your body is rooted to the floor and it will not move.

Stage 5: Sensations in the body
Be aware of any physical sensations: cold, heat, wind, itching, pain, uneasiness, tension, stiffness. Direct your awareness to these feelings. Let them be a focus for your mind. If your mind starts to wander, bring it back to the sensations in the body.

Stage 6: Body parts
Direct your awareness to the head. Be aware of the head and nothing else. Feel any sensation in the head. Visualize the head. Shift your awareness to the neck. Feel any sensations in the neck. Continue to be aware. Following the same process, move your awareness to the shoulders, to the right arm, the left arm, the whole of the back, the chest, the abdomen, the right leg, the left leg, and finally the whole body. Be aware of the whole body together. Intensify your awareness of the body. Do another round maintaining full awareness.

Stage 7: Immobility of the body
Make a resolve that, "I will not move my body throughout the whole practice. My body will not move or shake. I will remain steady and motionless like a statue." Even if you feel an impulse to move a finger or toe, to adjust your clothing, or to scratch, try to overcome this urge. When you feel the urge to move you must say to yourself "No, I will not move any part of my body until the end of the practice."

Stage 8: Steadiness and stillness
Be aware of your physical body, of your meditation posture and of nothing else. There should be total uninterrupted awareness of the whole body. The body is perfectly steady and motionless. Develop the feeling of steadiness. Be

aware of your body and steadiness. Be aware of your body and stillness. Your body is absolutely steady and still. Be aware of steadiness. Be aware of your physical body. There is no movement, no discomfort, only steadiness and stillness.

Stage 9: Psychic rigidity

Feel the steadiness and stillness of the body. Gradually your body will become rigid and stiff like a statue, as though all the muscles have frozen. The body should become so stiff that you are unable to move any part, even if you try. Total awareness of the body, of immobility, of psychic rigidity. Feel the locked position of the body. Be aware of the body and of stillness.

Stage 10: Breath awareness

As the body becomes stiff and rigid, you will begin to lose physical awareness. At this time shift your attention to the breath. Become aware of the natural breath, without altering or modifying it in any way. Simply watch the breath as it moves in and out of the body. The breath moves in and out in a rhythmic flow. Follow each movement of the breath with your awareness.

At the same time become aware of the body. Let the awareness alternate from breath to body, then from body to breath. As the body becomes stiffer and stiffer, the awareness will automatically shift more and more to the breath. No effort is required. When the body is absolutely still and motionless the breath will become more and more subtle, until it seems that you are hardly breathing at all.

Stage 11: State of concentration

As the breath becomes more and more imperceptible, you will begin to experience the pure awareness which functions through the unfluctuating mind. The breathing is responsible for the movements of the mind and body. When the breath becomes very subtle, the mind becomes one-pointed and still. This is the state in which dharana must be practised.

Stage 12: Ending the practice
Get ready to end the practice. Gradually become aware of the physical body, of the meditation posture. Feel the weight of the body against the floor. Be aware of the hands resting on the knees. Be aware of the whole physical body. Be aware of the breathing. Watch the breath as it flows in and out. Take a deep breath in and chant *Om* three times.

Hari Om Tat Sat

Chakra Shuddhi Dharana

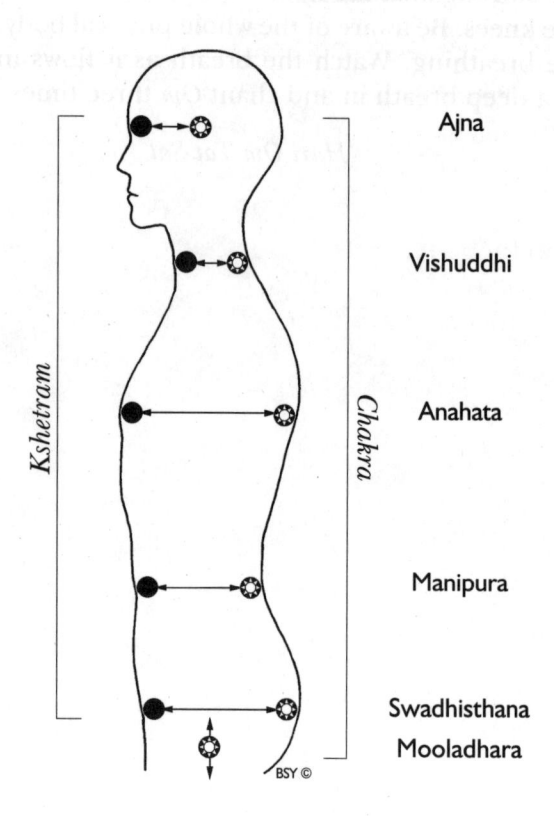

- Ajna
- Vishuddhi
- Anahata
- Manipura
- Swadhisthana
- Mooladhara

Kshetram / *Chakra*

9

Chakra Shuddhi

Chakra shuddhi means 'purification of the psychic centres'. These practices are used in kundalini yoga for the location of the psychic centres. In japa yoga these practices make up a special anusthana which can bring great benefits to the serious practitioner who is able to devote one week or one month uninterruptedly to the practice. In kundalini yoga it is said that before the kundalini awakens the chakras must be purified, opened and awakened. These practices form an important part of this process. Each psychic centre is dealt with individually in separate stages, and in the final stage all the psychic centres are dealt with consecutively.

First each centre is located. Then with the breath, a psychic passage is established between the *chakra kshetram*, or trigger point in the front of the body, and the actual chakra point in the spine. Finally, with the addition of mantra, the chakra is purified and opened. As the sound vibration of the mantra gradually builds up along the psychic passage, the psychic centre is awakened.

While concentrating on the chakra points, the breath and the mantra a high voltage of energy is released and circulated to the brain. This energy helps to remove mental dissipation and steadies the mind, so that even after a few minutes of the practice, the mind becomes one-pointed and still almost effortlessly.

Technique
Stage 1: Mooladhara shuddhi

Mooladhara chakra does not have a kshetram or trigger point, so it must be located directly. To locate this chakra more easily, siddhasana or siddha yoni asana is recommended as a sitting posure, as this will help to centre the awareness at the mooladhara chakra point. Place the hands on the knees in chin or jnana mudra. Close the eyes and relax the whole physical body. Be aware of the meditation posture. Go through each part of the body and make sure that there is no tension or tightness in any part. Let the breath become slow and rhythmical.

Move your awareness to the point of contact where the lower heel is pressing into the perineum or yoni. Become intensely aware of the distinct pressure at that point. Centre your whole awareness at the pressure point. Become aware of a pulse beat in this area as you locate the exact position of mooladhara chakra.

Become aware of the breath. Feel or imagine that you are breathing in and out through this pressure point. Feel the breath moving through the perineal body, or the yoni becoming finer and finer, so that it pierces the point where mooladhara chakra is located. Move your awareness with the steady rhythm of the natural, spontaneous breath. Experience mooladhara chakra being pierced with every inhalation and exhalation. Move the awareness with the breath. Do not allow your attention to become dissipated. Now integrate mental repetition of the mantra *Om* with each breath. As you inhale, repeat *Om*, feeling the vibration moving upward with the breath and piercing mooladhara chakra point. As you exhale again repeat *Om*, feeling the vibration moving downward with the breath, out of the chakra point. Experience the mantra *Om* as it moves in and out through mooladhara chakra. Feel you are purifying and opening mooladhara chakra with the movement of the breath and mantra. Continue with this practice for five minutes.

Stage 2: Swadhisthana shuddhi

Check that you are sitting correctly in siddhasana or siddha yoni asana and that the body is relaxed. Now move your awareness to the point of contact where the upper heel is pressing against the pubic bone. Become intensely aware of the distinct pressure at that point. Centre your awareness at the pubic bone, which is known as swadhisthana kshetram or the trigger point for swadhisthana chakra. Hold your awareness at this point and be aware of the pulse beat there. Now move your awareness in a straight line back to the coccyx bone at the base of the spine. This is the location of swadhisthana chakra. Hold your awareness here for a few moments and become aware of the pulse beat at this point. Intensify your awareness of swadhisthana chakra.

Become aware of the breath. Bring the awareness of the breath down to the pelvic region. Feel or imagine that you are breathing in and out through this area. As you inhale, the breath enters swadhisthana kshetram at the pubic area and moves straight back to the coccyx in the spine, swadhisthana chakra. As you exhale, the breath moves forward from the coccyx or swadhisthana chakra to the pubic bone, the swadhisthana kshetram.

With the movement of your awareness and breath, create a psychic pathway between swadhisthana kshetram at the pubic bone, and the chakra point at the base of the spine. Feel that you are connecting these two points with your breath and awareness. With each inhalation feel the pelvic area expanding and the awareness and breath moving from swadhisthana kshetram straight back to swadhisthana chakra. With each exhalation, feel the pelvic area contracting and the awareness and the breath moving from swadhisthana chakra to swadhisthana kshetram. Feel the breath becoming finer and finer so that it pierces swadhisthana kshetram and the chakra point. Continue with this awareness for five minutes.

Now add mental repetition of the mantra *Om* to the practice. As you inhale, mentally repeat the mantra *Om* and feel the vibration moving from swadhisthana kshetram to swadhisthana chakra. As you exhale, repeat the mantra *Om* and feel the vibration moving from swadhisthana chakra to swadhisthana kshetram. Experience the mantra and the breath moving in this psychic passage. Intensify your awareness of this movement through the psychic pathway. Feel that the mantra and breath are purifying and opening swadhisthana chakra. Continue with this practice for five minutes.

Stage 3: Manipura shuddhi

Leave the awareness of swadhisthana chakra. Bring the awareness back to the meditation posture. If you wish to adjust your position at this time, you may do so. Make sure that the body is comfortable and relaxed.

Bring your awareness to the navel. This is manipura kshetram or trigger point. Intensify your awareness of the navel. Become aware of the pulse beat at this area. Now move your awareness in a straight line back to the spine. This is the location of manipura chakra. Hold your awareness at this point for a few moments. Try to feel the pulse beat at this point, behind the navel in the spine. Be aware of the steady rhythmic pulse beat at manipura chakra.

Become aware of the breath in the abdominal region. Feel the gentle expansion and contraction of the abdomen with the breath. Imagine you are breathing in and out through this area. As you inhale, the breath enters through the navel and travels straight back to the spine, to manipura chakra. As you exhale, the breath travels forward from the chakra point in the spine to the navel.

Continue in this way, moving the awareness with the breath between these two points. With inhalation, feel the abdomen expanding and the breath moving straight back from the navel to manipura chakra. With exhalation, feel the abdomen contracting and the breath moving from the manipura chakra point in the spine to manipura kshetram.

Create a psychic pathway between these two points with the movement of the breath. Feel that you are connecting manipura kshetram to manipura chakra. See the psychic passage clearly. Be aware of the breath becoming finer and finer so that it pierces the manipura kshetram and chakra point. Continue this awareness for five minutes. When this movement becomes spontaneous and effortless, begin to add mental repetition of the mantra *Om*. While inhaling, the mantra moves with the breath from manipura kshetram at the navel straight back to manipura chakra in the spine. While exhaling, the mantra moves forward from manipura chakra to manipura kshetram at the navel. Try to experience the mantra and breath moving in this psychic passage. Intensify your awareness of the vibration of the mantra moving through these two points. Feel that the mantra and breath are purifying and opening manipura chakra. Continue with this practice for five minutes.

Stage 4: Anahata shuddhi

Leave the awareness of manipura chakra. Become aware of the chest, the area contained within the ribcage. Centre your awareness at the sternum in front of the heart. Intensify your awareness at this point. Feel it pulsating in rhythm with your heart beat. Hold your awareness at this point. This is anahata kshetram or the trigger point for anahata chakra. Move your awareness in a straight line back to the spine, to anahata chakra. Centre your attention at the chakra point. Become aware of the anahata chakra pulsation in rhythm with your heart beat. Complete awareness of anahata chakra.

Bring the attention to the natural breath. Feel the expansion and contraction of the chest as you breathe. Now imagine that you are breathing in and out through the chest area. As you inhale, the breath enters the body through anahata kshetram, at the chest, and moves in a straight line back to the spine, to anahata chakra. As you exhale, the breath moves forward from anahata chakra to the sternum, anahata kshetram. With inhalation, the chest expands and the breath moves from the sternum to anahata chakra. With exhalation, the chest contracts and the breath moves from anahata chakra to the sternum, anahata kshetram. Follow the movement of the breath with complete awareness.

Now become aware of the psychic passage between these two points. Feel that you are connecting anahata kshetram to anahata chakra. Intensify your awareness of this psychic passage. Feel the breath becoming finer and finer, so that it pierces anahata kshetram and anahata chakra point. Bring your awareness closer to the breath and become aware of these two psychic points. Continue in this way for some time.

Now add mental repetition of the mantra *Om* to the movement of breath. As you inhale, feel the mantra *Om* moving with the breath from anahata kshetram, at the sternum, to anahata chakra, in the spine. As you exhale, feel the mantra *Om* moving from anahata chakra to anahata kshetram, at the sternum. There should be complete awareness of the vibration of the mantra moving with the breath in the psychic passage between these two points. Feel that the mantra and the breath are purifying and opening up anahata chakra. Continue with this practice for five minutes.

Stage 5: Vishuddhi shuddhi

Leave awareness of anahata chakra. Bring your attention up to the throat area. Become aware of the point at the throat pit. This is the kshetram or trigger point for vishuddhi chakra. Be aware of the pulse beat at the throat. Complete awareness of the pulse beat at vishuddhi kshetram. Now move your awareness straight back to the spine. This is the location of vishuddhi chakra. Hold your attention at this point and feel the pulsation there. Your whole awareness is at vishuddhi chakra.

Become aware of the natural breath. Feel that you are breathing in and out through the throat. Experience the breath entering the body through the throat, vishuddhi kshetram, as you inhale, and moving straight back to the point of vishuddhi chakra, in the spine. Experience the breath moving from vishuddhi chakra to vishuddhi kshetram, at the throat, as you exhale. Keep your awareness moving with the breath between these two points. Feel the gentle expansion and contraction of the throat area with each inhalation and exhalation. While inhaling, the throat area expands and the breath moves from vishuddhi kshetram to vishuddhi chakra. While exhaling, the throat contracts and the breath moves from vishuddhi chakra to vishuddhi kshetram.

Experience the movement of breath in this psychic pathway. Feel that you are connecting vishuddhi kshetram to vishuddhi chakra. Intensify your awareness of the psychic passage and the breath moving between these two points. Be aware of the breath piercing the vishuddhi kshetram and chakra point. Allow your whole awareness to move with the breath through this psychic passage. Continue for some time.

Now add the mantra *Om* to the practice. As you inhale, mentally repeat the mantra *Om*. Feel the mantra moving with the breath from vishuddhi kshetram straight back to vishuddhi chakra. As you exhale, mentally repeat the mantra *Om*. Feel the mantra moving forward with the breath from vishuddhi chakra to vishuddhi kshetram. Experience the vibration of the mantra in the psychic pathway. Feel the mantra and breath moving through vishuddhi kshetram and vishuddhi chakra. Feel the mantra and breath purifying and opening vishuddhi chakra. Continue in this way with steady, unbroken awareness for five minutes.

Stage 6: Ajna shuddhi

Leave your awareness of vishuddhi chakra. Bring the awareness to the eyebrow centre. Hold your attention at this point. Become aware of the eyebrow centre. This point is known as trikuti or bhrumadhya. Centre your whole awareness at this point. Try to feel the rhythmic pulsation at the eyebrow centre. Intensify your awareness of the pulsation at this point. Now move your awareness straight back to the top of the spine, in the middle of the head. This is the location of ajna chakra. Hold your awareness at this point and feel the pulsation there. Intensify your awareness at this point of ajna chakra.

Become aware of the natural breath. Imagine that you are breathing in and out between these two points. Feel the breath entering the body through the eyebrow centre, bhrumadhya, as you inhale, and moving straight back to the top of the spine, ajna chakra. As you exhale, feel the breath moving from ajna chakra forward to the eyebrow centre, ajna kshetram. Move your awareness with the breath between these two points. While inhaling, feel the head expanding as the breath moves from bhrumadhya to ajna chakra. While exhaling, feel the head contracting as the breath moves from ajna chakra forward to bhrumadhya at the eyebrow centre.

Intensify your awareness of this psychic passage. Feel that with every breath you are connecting ajna kshetram to ajna chakra. Feel the breath moving between these two points. Experience the breath piercing the ajna kshetram and chakra point. Centre your whole attention on the movement of the breath in this psychic pathway. Continue for a few moments.

Now begin to integrate the mantra *Om* into the practice. As you inhale, mentally repeat the mantra *Om*. Feel the mantra and breath moving from ajna kshetram straight back to ajna chakra. As you exhale, mentally repeat the mantra *Om*. Feel the mantra and the breath moving forward from ajna chakra to ajna kshetram. Experience the vibration of the mantra as it moves through the psychic pathway between ajna kshetram and ajna chakra. Feel the mantra and breath purifying and opening up ajna chakra. Intensify this awareness. Do not let your awareness slip for a moment. Continue in this way for five minutes.

Stage 7: Chakra shuddhi

Now bring the awareness down to mooladhara chakra at the perineum. Centre your awareness at mooladhara chakra. You must feel the mantra *Om* pulsating slowly and deeply there. The pulsation will feel as if the chakra is being struck from inside. Feel the *Om* mantra pulsating at mooladhara chakra 21 times.

Bring your awareness to swadhisthana chakra at the coccyx. Feel the mantra *Om* pulsating at this point. Experience the *Om* mantra pulsating at swadhisthana chakra 21 times. Come up to manipura chakra behind the navel. Experience the *Om* mantra pulsating at manipura. Count 21 pulsations.

Now move your awareness to anahata chakra behind the heart centre. Feel the *Om* mantra pulsating slowly and deeply at anahata chakra and again count 21 pulsations. Move up the spine to vishuddhi chakra, behind the throat. Be aware of the mantra *Om* pulsating and striking vishuddhi chakra from within. Count 21 pulsations. Come up to ajna chakra at the top of the spine in the centre of the head. Count 21 pulsations of the mantra *Om* at ajna chakra. There should be unbroken awareness of the mantra.

Move your awareness to the top back of the head, to bindu chakra. Experience the mantra *Om* at this point. Feel *Om* pulsating at bindu as you count 21 pulse beats. Move up to sahasrara chakra at the crown of the head. Count 21 pulsations of the mantra at sahasrara chakra. This is one round.

Now bring your awareness back down to mooladhara chakra at the perineum and begin the next round. Continue upwards through each chakra point from mooladhara chakra to sahasrara. Experience the mantra pulsating at each chakra. Count 21 beats at each chakra. There should be continuous, unbroken awareness of the mantra *Om*.

Stage 8: Ending the practice

Now leave your awareness of the mantra and chakras. Become aware of the natural and spontaneous breath. Feel the slow, steady rhythm of the breath.

Become aware of the physical body and the meditation posture you are seated in. Feel the contact between the body and the floor. Become aware of your surroundings. Be aware of the room in which you are sitting, and of any sounds in the external environment. Breathe in deeply and chant *Om* three times.

Hari Om Tat Sat

10
Ajapa Dharana

The word *japa* can be defined as the continuous repetition of a mantra. When the suffix 'a' is added, it implies that the process of mantra repetition becomes spontaneous. So, ajapa is continuous mantra repetition and dharana is one-pointed concentration. Ajapa dharana is, therefore, one-pointed concentration on the spontaneous repetition of mantra. Japa is transformed into ajapa in the stages of dharana where the mantra repeats itself spontaneously, without any effort. As the concentration becomes more and more focused on the japa, one's whole being starts pulsating with the mantra. Japa requires continuous, conscious effort to repeat the mantra verbally or mentally and to turn the beads, but ajapa requires no effort. It is said that japa comes from the mouth whereas ajapa comes from the breath and from the heart. Japa is the preliminary practice of mantra repetition and ajapa is the perfection of this practice.

Vedic sadhana

The sadhana of ajapa is as old as the Upanishads. In some of the Yoga Upanishads, like the *Yogashiksha*, you will find certain passages and stanzas which declare that the breath comes in with the sound of *So* and goes out with the sound of *Ham*. This is the Gayatri ajapa which the jiva repeats continuously. Valmiki was initiated by Narada in 'Ulta Nama' which is this very ajapa. Even now those who follow the

Nirguna Panth (sampradaya) like Radhaswami Panth, Kabir Panth, etc. practise ajapa, just like the ancient sages did.

Gandhi too has written that the name should be repeated from within the heart, not from the mouth. A Muslim saint, while referring to this ajapa said, "I am experiencing the fourth dimension of consciousness." Again he said, "This awareness of *Ham* starts from the nabhi chakra. When it comes up, it is reversed." So, you produce *Ham* from the nabhi chakra. When it has been completed then you reverse it to *So*. Now it becomes *Hamso*.

In the *Bhagavad Gita* there is also a clear reference about ajapa japa. It says, "Some merge prana in apana, others apana in prana, and yet others merge prana in prana." Prana is the ingoing breath, apana is the outgoing breath. *So* represents prana and *Ham* represents apana. So, some aspirants merge prana and apana, i.e. they join *So* with *Ham* which becomes *Soham*. Other aspirants join apana with prana, i.e. they join *Ham* with *So*, which becomes *Hamso*. There are other sadhakas who join prana with prana, which will be dealt with later.

The importance of ajapa dharana

In the *Gita* there is one more reference to ajapa. It says, "Having equalized the prana and apana moving in the nasal region, let the flow of the ingoing and outgoing breath in the nostrils be equal in length and duration." This practice of ajapa has been referred to in the shastras as viloma ajapa. It is a complete practice in itself and through it one can enter the spiritual realms even without the help of a guru. In the successful practice of trataka one attains inner visualization of the object one meditates upon. But after that the way is closed. Thus, you cannot reach the stage of samadhi by yourself without the help of other yogic practices. You need a guru to tell you what the next practice is. In the case of ajapa, however, you do not need a guru.

There are certain practices in yoga which introvert the mind and bring about an automatic suspension of breath.

The difficulty here is that the aspirant becomes extroverted after a short time because the capacity of his lungs is not adequate. This difficulty is experienced by many aspirants. In the practice of ajapa japa, however, this difficulty is eliminated because of the continuous rotation of the breath. Secondly, the ajapa dharana series is complete in itself and through it one can have direct experience of samadhi. In order to attain samadhi, in all other yogic practices one has to control the breath. Whenever the breath is suspended, kumbhaka takes place. However, the breathing remains continuous throughout the practice of ajapa japa, and even in samadhi there is no change.

In the Upanishads it is said that one should practise anahad japa, a japa which never ends. The japa must be coextensive with infinity. We do not know any such mantra, therefore, a method of repeating the mantra so that it does not end is needed. This is achieved through the practice of ajapa japa when the mantra is adjusted with the breathing process and thus its awareness continues throughout.

Swara and sushumna

In the Upanishads there is a parable about two birds, one black and one white, which were tied to a peg with two ropes. They tried to fly many times but each time they had to come back because they were tied up. Ultimately they became tired and slept peacefully near the peg. This illustration refers to ida and pingala. The right nostril flow corresponds to pingala, or *surya nadi*, and the left nostril flow corresponds to ida, or *chandra nadi*. The alternate functioning of ida and pingala keeps one away from one's inner consciousness. So long as they work alternately, samadhi cannot be attained. It is only when the two birds (ida and pingala) are tired and retire to the centre, i.e. the heart or the Self, that sushumna awakens and the process of meditation becomes automatic.

According to swara yoga, when both nostrils flow equally it indicates that sushumna is flowing. At this time one should give up all worldly work and meditate. It is a common experience that sometimes meditation is wonderful because there is harmony in the entire system. When sushumna is not functioning, however, you cannot concentrate, even with effort. So, it is important that the functioning of ida and pingala is harmonized by meditating on them, thus making it possible for sushumna to open.

In order to stop the chain of thoughts you have to observe the breath. You have to see the movement of the breath consciously. During ajapa you must have a complete and unceasing awareness of what you are doing. Let your consciousness be continuous like a stream of oil which does not break in the middle. This is called *swadhyaya*. Here swadhyaya does not mean scriptural studies. It means continuous awareness of what you are doing.

Breath awareness

The first point in ajapa japa is awareness of your own natural breath. You breathe 15 times per minute, 900 times per hour and 21,600 times in 24 hours, but you are never aware of it. You are aware of everything else except this most vital process. Breathing is the key of life and it is also the basis of dharana and meditation.

The second point is awareness of the four different dimensions of the breath which are: (i) natural, (ii) deeper than natural, (iii) relaxed, and (iv) suspended. You can observe these four dimensions yourself when you go to bed. When you lie down your breathing becomes natural. With drowsiness the natural breathing becomes deeper. As you are falling asleep the breathing becomes very relaxed and light snoring can be heard. Sometimes during deep sleep the breathing is suspended, causing you to wake up suddenly.

These same four dimensions of breathing also occur during meditation. If you concentrate on your natural breathing for half an hour or more without making any effort whatsoever, you will find it becoming deeper and deeper. Eventually it will become very relaxed and a faint snoring sound will be heard in the throat. In very deep meditation, suspension of the breath also occurs. During inhalation or exhalation, the breathing stops for half a minute or one minute.

Movement of breath

The third point in ajapa japa is awareness of the movement of breath as it flows through the body. For example, become aware of the natural movement of the breath from the navel to the throat on inhalation and from the throat to the navel on exhalation. After one or two minutes you will find that the dimension of the breath has changed. You will feel it becoming deeper than it is normally as it ascends and descends.

Then you can practise circulating the breath through every part of the body: stomach, chest, top of the head etc. You can also combine the movement of breath with different forms such as a triangle, square, hexagon, circle. Imagine two interlacing triangles at anahata, one inverted and one upright, and try to make them one with the movement of your breath.

Psychic passage

The fourth point in ajapa japa is the psychic passage. Movement of the breath can be practised in as many ways as possible, but the most important is awareness of the breath in the psychic passages. There are an infinite number of psychic passages in the body, but the most important is sushumna nadi in the spinal cord. The other major psychic passages are the frontal passage and the ida and pingala passages.

According to yogic physiology, prana flows through the 72,000 nadis or pranic channels. *Nadi* means 'flow' or 'current'. Out of the 72,000 nadis through which the prana flows, ten are major and three are most important. Of these three, one is the key. That one is known as *sushumna,* which flows through the central canal of the spinal cord. The other two are situated to the left and right of sushumna. They are called *ida*, the mental, and *pingala*, the vital. Sushumna is responsible for spiritual awareness. Ida directs all the mental functions and pingala directs all the vital functions. These three nadis thus control all the functions of the body.

Ida, pingala and sushumna begin at mooladhara chakra in the perineum, which is located midway between the anus and the sexual organ in males and at the cervix in females. From mooladhara these three proceed to the tailbone and go right up the spinal cord to ajna chakra, situated behind the eyebrow centre. Ida and pingala end here but sushumna proceeds on to sahasrara, the highest chakra at the crown of the head, where liberation or moksha takes place. Sushumna is thus the channel through which spiritual awakening takes place. That is why it is the main psychic passage.

Psychic sound

The fifth point in ajapa japa is the psychic sound or mantra which is integrated with the breath. When you inhale the breath spontaneously makes the sound of *So*, and when you exhale the breath makes the sound of *Ham*. The most important thing is that the breath and the mantra should become one. In the beginning you are aware of the breath flowing in and out. Later, however, when you integrate the mantra with the breath, the two become one – *Soham*. While breathing inside the psychic passage, you must become aware of the movement of the breath combined with the movement of the powerful sound, *Soham*.

This process purifies the nadis. When mantra is awakened in the breath, the whole body is recharged. Psychic toxins are eliminated and blocks in the nadis, which are the main source of physical and mental disturbance, are removed. The psychic sound, the mantra *Soham*, should awaken the psychic passages and permeate each and every particle of the body. Sushumna is atma, the highest consciousness. When sushumna begins to vibrate, self-awareness becomes active. When ida starts vibrating the mental force becomes active. When pingala starts vibrating, the prana or life force becomes active and energy flows through one's system, even extending outside the physical body.

Awakening sushumna
When sushumna starts vibrating with the help of concentration on the prana, the breath and the mantra going up and down, there is an awakening in the higher realms of consciousness. Then the inner or psychic sounds, which are called *nada*, are produced. Within the stillness of the inner dimension one begins to hear the sound of the bell, conch, flute, drums, celestial music, roar of the sea, lightning and thunder. Not one but several sounds may be heard. Other inner experiences also take place on new and different dimensions which denote that karmas and samskaras are being eliminated, worked out symbolically.

When the awakening of sushumna takes place with the help of mantra shakti, the elimination of karma takes place symbolically. This results in the arising of inner sounds and fantastic experiences. You hear music and see colours, animals, symbols etc. At times you may feel that the horizon is receding further and further from you or that your body is expanding as if it is being pumped with air to bursting point.

These and many more meaningful, meaningless, relevant, irrelevant, strange and ordinary experiences take place. All of them arise from your deeper consciousness. They all belong to you. You have acquired them in this life or inherited them from your own parents along with your DNA molecules.

Ajapa dharana is the basis for kundalini yoga. With this practice the real dharana or concentration begins. When ajapa dharana is perfected and fully realized, the mind becomes totally one-pointed. In this way, dhyana, or spontaneous meditation, blossoms forth.

Ajapa Dharana One
Frontal Passage: Manipura–Vishuddhi

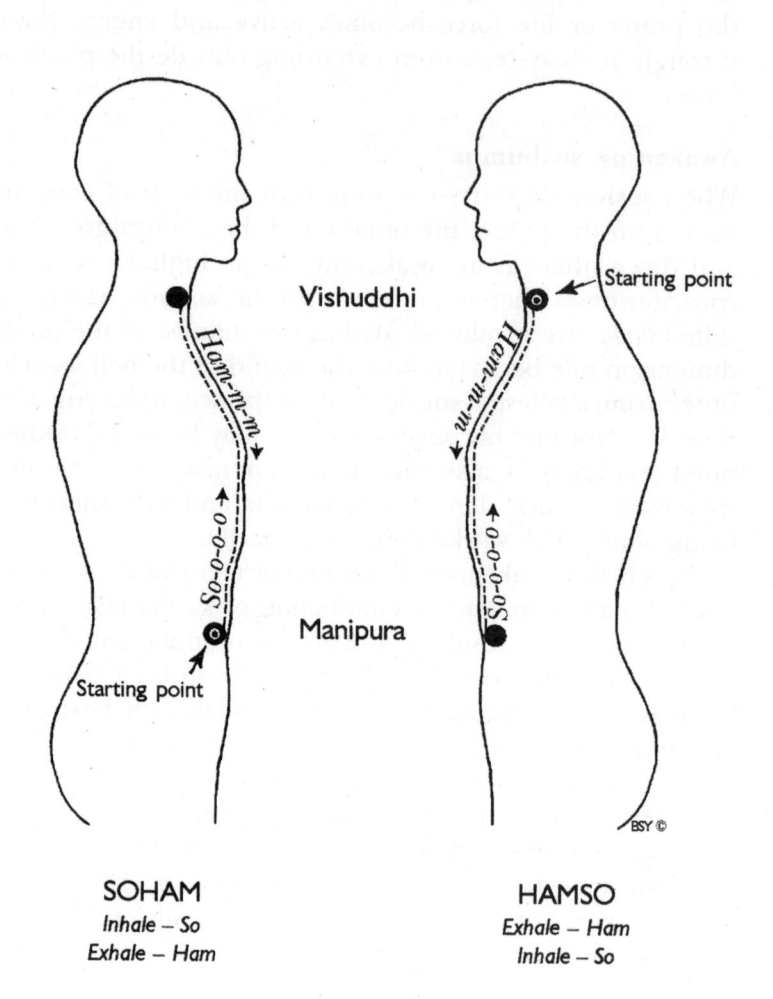

Vishuddhi

Starting point

Ham-m-m

So-o-o-o

Manipura

Starting point

Ham-m-m

So-o-o-o

SOHAM
Inhale – So
Exhale – Ham

HAMSO
Exhale – Ham
Inhale – So

Ajapa Dharana One

FRONTAL PASSAGE ROTATION

In the practices of ajapa dharana, various psychic passages have been utilized in order to channel the awareness, the breath and the mantra. The first one which is given here is the frontal psychic passage which extends from manipura trigger point at the navel to vishuddhi trigger point at the throat. This passage is a powerful psychic channel in its own right as the chakra kshetram or trigger points are located here. These are subtle centres which step down the high voltage of psychic energy transmitted by the chakras in the spine for use by the different organs and parts of the body.

This frontal passage is the first one given because it is the most familiar and therefore the easiest. It takes little effort to visualize the area between the navel and the throat because we are conscious of it most of the time. It is also easy to rotate the breath here as the normal respiratory function is performed in this area. Frontal passage rotation has a very relaxing effect on the heart and lungs, and removes pranic blockages and builds up the prana in this area.

This practice is comprised of several stages which develop the awareness of the psychic passage. First the breath is moved up and down in a straight line from the navel to the throat and from the throat to the navel. Then the frontal psychic passage is visualized as a luminous, transparent tube. Afterwards the breath is rotated inside the psychic passage. When this has been mastered, the rotation of prana is then visualized inside the frontal passage. This is followed by the rotation of the *Soham* and *Hamso* mantra. With each stage an increasing build-up energy inside the frontal passage is experienced and concentration becomes deeper and more one-pointed. This practice follows the principle that an awakening of energy brings about an awakening of consciousness, which makes it easier to concentrate and focus the mind on one point.

Technique
Stage 1: Preparation
Sit in a comfortable meditation asana. Ensure that the spine is straight. The head, neck and shoulders should be slightly back. Place the hands on the knees in chin or jnana mudra. Become aware of your body and meditation posture. Feel the position of the body from the top of the head to the toes. Feel the body posture becoming steady and still. Total awareness of the body and of stillness.
Stage 2: Breath awareness
Switch your awareness from the body to the breath. Practise slow, deep breathing. As you breathe in, count to five. As you breathe out, count to five. Concentrate on the breathing in the throat. As you breathe in and out, feel the breath moving through the throat. As you concentrate on the rhythmic breathing in the throat, you will gradually feel the steadiness of the mind and body as a whole.

Now become aware of the breath moving from the navel to the throat. Bring your awareness to the navel. Inhale slowly in a straight line from the navel up to the throat. Then exhale slowly in a straight line from the throat down to the navel. Count to five each time you breathe in and out. Go on breathing up and down from navel to throat, throat to navel, until the breath moves along this fixed pathway easily without conscious effort. Watch the movement carefully without missing a single breath.

Stage 3: Frontal passage visualization

Leave the awareness of the breath for a few moments and visualize the psychic passage between the navel and the throat, at the front of the body. See the psychic passage as a long, thin, transparent tube, connecting the navel with the throat. This tube is hollow inside and open at both ends, like a flute. You can blow through it from the top or the bottom. Visualize this luminous, transparent tube and move your awareness up and down along the outside surface. Try to see the entire length of the tube very clearly. Take your awareness inside the tube, and move it up and down the centre, visualizing the tube from within.

Stage 4: Breath rotation inside the psychic passage

Resume your awareness of slow, deep breathing. Feel the breath moving inside the frontal passage between the navel and the throat. While inhaling, the breath ascends from the navel to the throat. While exhaling, the breath descends from the throat to the navel. With the ascent and the descent of each breath try to visualize clearly the inside of the psychic passage. Feel as if the awareness is moving together with the breath up and down the centre of the psychic passage. As the breath moves through the passage, the awareness also moves. Develop the feeling of two distinct forces, the breath and the consciousness moving together inside the psychic pathway.

Stage 5: Rotation of prana

Intensify awareness of the breath and the consciousness moving together inside the psychic passage. Feel the flow of breath and consciousness, ascending and descending together through the psychic passage. Gradually become aware of a third force, the pranic force, which is moving together with the breath and the consciousness. It requires a subtle awareness to perceive the flow of prana moving with the breath. The breath moves in the form of wind or air, while prana moves in the form of energy. Become aware of the energy, the prana, moving with the breath. It is actually this flow of prana or energy between the navel and the throat which creates the psychic passage,

in the same way that flowing water creates a stream.
Be aware of the prana moving with the breath inside the psychic passage. Visualize the thin, sparkling stream of energy, of prana, which flows upward from the navel to the throat as you breathe in, and downward from the throat to the navel as you breathe out. Watch carefully and try to experience the movement of prana inside the psychic passage. At first you may need to use your imagination but with practice you will spontaneously feel a powerful current of energy flowing up and down the psychic passage. Be aware of the movement of prana with each breath.

Stage 6: Rotation of Soham
Now leave awareness of the prana and intensify awareness of the breath. Listen carefully to the subtle sound of each breath as it moves up and down the frontal passage. The inherent sound of the breath is the mantra *Soham*. As you breathe in, hear the mantra *So* and as you breathe out, hear the mantra *Ham*. This *Soham* mantra is not separate from the breath. You are not repeating it verbally. It is already going on within the breath each time you breathe. You must become aware of it, that is all.

Listen carefully while inhaling and try to hear the sound *So-o-o-o*. While exhaling hear the sound *Ham-m-m-m*. Concentrate totally on the process of breathing together with the mantra of the breath, which is *Soham*. As the breath moves, the sound moves with it.

Be aware of the movement of the breath and the vibration of the *Soham* mantra inside the frontal passage. Concentrate your entire awareness inside the psychic passage. There should be no other thought, vision or experience.

Try to feel that the entire breathing process is taking place inside the psychic passage only. As the breath becomes more and more subtle, the vibration of the mantra also becomes more subtle. Gradually you will begin to perceive this process as a psychic movement within the frontal passage. The dimension of your consciousness will change as the mind becomes totally absorbed in the psychic movement of the breath and the mantra. Nothing else exists outside of the psychic passage, the breath and the mantra.

Stage 7: Rotation of Hamso

Now we will change the mantra awareness from *Soham* to *Hamso*. The breath awareness in the frontal passage remains the same as in the previous stage, however, the starting point of mantra awareness changes. Instead of beginning the mantra with inhalation from manipura to vishuddhi, you start with exhalation from vishuddhi down to manipura. Bring your awareness to vishuddhi. Exhale from vishuddhi to manipura through the psychic passage and hear the mantra *Ham-m-m-m-m*. Then inhale from manipura to vishuddhi with the mantra *So-o-o-o-o*. The *Ham* mantra still accompanies the exhalation from throat to navel. The *So* mantra still accompanies the inhalation from navel to throat. Only the starting point has changed. Now you begin each round from vishuddhi with exhalation and the mantra *Ham*, which is followed by inhalation from manipura with the mantra *So*.

Continue the *Hamso* awareness for some time, intensifying the perception of the mantra synchronized with the breath inside the psychic passage. With the emphasis on exhalation and the mantra *Ham*, you will feel a further deepening of the awareness. Try not to be disturbed at this time by momentary flashes of light, colours or visions. Whatever arises within the mind, observe it with an attitude of detachment and bring the awareness back to the breathing and the mantra inside the psychic pathway.

Stage 8: Ending the practice

Now get ready to end the practice. Withdraw your awareness from the frontal passage and the mantra. Change over to normal breathing. Again become aware of your physical body which is sitting in the meditation posture. Feel your physical body from head to toe. Be aware of the weight of the body against the floor. Feel the hands resting on the knees. Slowly move your fingers and toes. Breathe in deeply and chant *Om* three times.

Ajapa Dharana Two
Spinal Passage: Mooladhara–Ajna

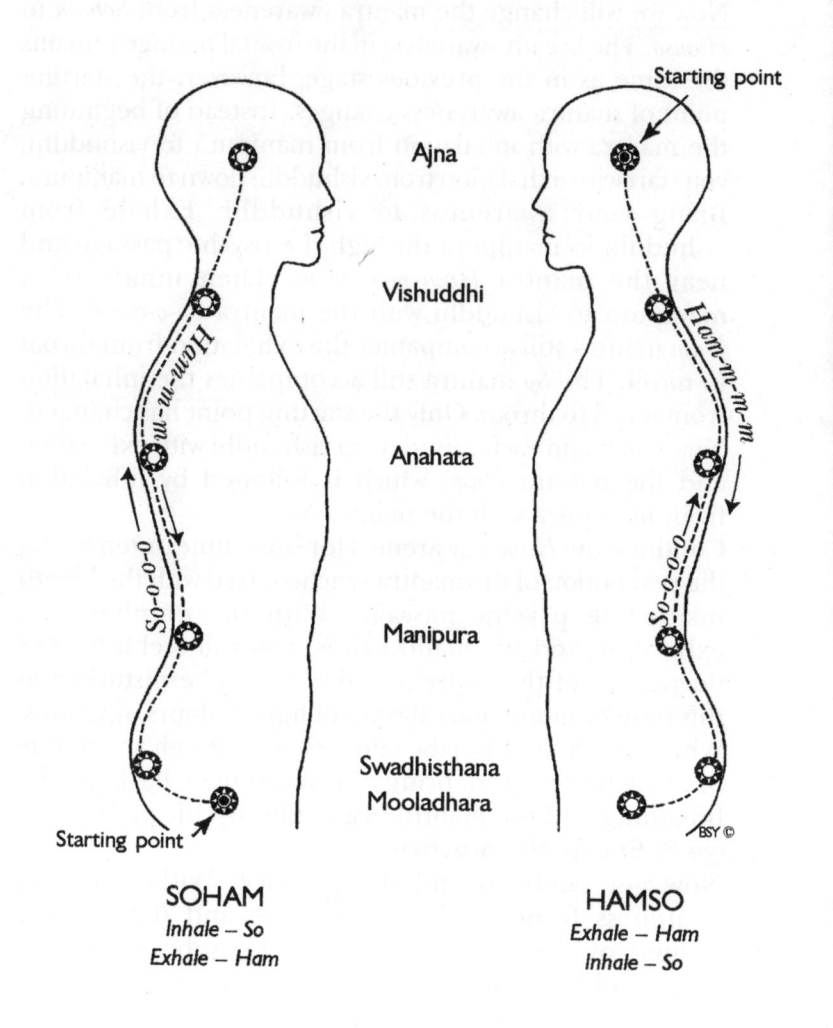

Ajna

Vishuddhi

Anahata

Manipura

Swadhisthana
Mooladhara

Starting point (left figure, bottom) — *So-o-o-o* rising, *Ham-m-m-m* descending

Starting point (right figure, top) — *Ham-m-m-m* descending, *So-o-o-o* rising

SOHAM
Inhale – So
Exhale – Ham

HAMSO
Exhale – Ham
Inhale – So

Ajapa Dharana Two

SPINAL PASSAGE ROTATION

This practice utilizes the most important psychic passage, which is located at the very centre of the spinal cord. This pathway is known as sushumna nadi, which originates from mooladhara chakra at the base of the spine. It is through this pathway that the kundalini shakti, or spiritual energy, must pass enroute to the brain or crown chakra (sahasrara), where it unites with the supreme consciousness for the purpose of illumination. Alongside sushumna nadi are located the fantastic chakras, or psychic switches. These act to illumine the dormant psychic faculties which are currently ensconced in total darkness within the inner recesses of the unawakened brain.

The purpose of this practice is to develop an awareness of this channel which is of great importance to our spiritual evolution and growth. The back is an area which we are not generally conscious of because we cannot see or touch it easily. Furthermore, this passage is located at the centre of the spinal column, which is a bony structure, making it more inaccessible. Because of our general unawareness of this area, it is said that the sushumna passage lies in the state of tamas, or inertia, just outside our conscious perception. In order to awaken our dormant spiritual potential and begin the spiritual journey, this psychic passage must open. As long as sushumna is closed, spiritual awareness cannot develop.

This practice is comprised of various stages which progressively open, purify and awaken the sushumna passage. First the breath is directed up and down the spine in a straight line from mooladhara to ajna and from ajna to mooladhara. Then sushumna is visualized as a luminous channel or thread of light within the framework of the spine. Afterwards the breath is rotated inside sushumna, while maintaining the visualization. Then the rotation of prana is experienced as piercing each chakra or psychic centre in turn. Finally sushumna is purified and awakened by the rotation of *Soham* and *Hamso*.

As this practice is gradually mastered, a tremendous build-up of psychic energy is experienced in the sushumna passage. This build-up of energy helps to awaken the prana, the nadis, the chakras and ultimately brings about an awakening of the inherent spiritual force or kundalini shakti. As this awakening process gains momentum, the concentration and meditative state gradually become steady and one-pointed as the consciousness penetrates the subtle, psychic dimension of our being.

Technique
Stage 1: Preparation
Sit in a comfortable meditation posture. Make sure that your spine is erect. The head, neck and shoulders should be slightly back. Place the hands on the knees in chin or jnana mudra. Check the position of the body and make any adjustments. Feel the relaxed, steady and balanced position of the body. Concentrate on the steadiness and stillness of the body.

Stage 2: Breath awareness
Switch your awareness from the body to the breath. Practise slow, rhythmic breathing. As you breathe in, count slowly to five and as you breathe out, count slowly to five. Total awareness of the breathing and the counting. Feel the breath becoming slow and steady. As you concentrate on the slow, rhythmic breathing, feel the body and mind

coming into attunement. The body and mind are being harmonized by the breathing which is regular and rhythmic. Now bring your awareness to mooladhara chakra below the spine at the perineum. Inhale slowly and move your awareness with the breath up along the spinal cord from mooladhara at the base to ajna chakra at the top. When you reach the top of the spinal card, exhale slowly and descend from ajna back down to mooladhara. Continue breathing in a straight line up and down the spine, from mooladhara to ajna and from ajna to mooladhara. Try to feel the movement of the breath at the centre of the back, along the spine. It is more difficult to develop this awareness because we are not as conscious of this area as we are of the frontal area.

Stage 3: Visualization of sushumna
Now leave the breathing for a few moments. Try to visualize the subtle, psychic pathway which runs up along the very centre of the spinal cord. This pathway is known as sushumna nadi. It is the psychic channel which conducts the kundalini or spiritual force from mooladhara up to sahasrara for the purpose of illumination. Visualize this pathway as a long, thin, luminous tube made out of subtle non-material stuff. See the sushumna pathway between mooladhara and ajna chakras, at the centre of the spinal cord. When you perceive this tube it seems to be transparent, comprised of nothing but light. Particles of white light, fibres of white light, intermingled and interwoven, form this pathway.

Visualize the sushumna passage clearly and move your awareness up and down the outer surface. Experience the luminosity of this subtle channel. The sushumna pathway is also hollow inside and it is open at both ends. Move your awareness up and down through the centre of the sushumna passage. Visualize the entire length of the channel from within clearly. Intensify your awareness, awaken the vision of the sushumna passage at the centre of the spinal cord.

Stage 4: Breathing inside sushumna
Now resume your awareness of slow, deep breathing. Feel the breath moving inside the sushumna passage. While inhaling, ascend through the centre of the spinal passage from mooladhara to ajna. While exhaling descend through the spinal passage from ajna to mooladhara. Concentrate on the movement of the breath inside the passage. Side by side awaken the vision of sushumna, so that you can see the entire length of the passage with clarity as you ascend and descend.

Your entire awareness is riveted inside the psychic passage. As the breath ascends, the awareness also ascends and observes each part of the passage. As your breath descends, the awareness also descends, observing minutely the entire passage. Feel the breath and the awareness as two distinct forces or flows, one of air or wind and the other of consciousness. Be aware of these two forces moving together up and down the spinal passage.

Stage 5: Awareness of prana
Now become aware of a third force moving along with the breath inside the framework of the spinal passage. Try to experience the prana or vital energy which is moving together with the breath up and down the sushumna passage. Prana can be experienced as a stream of light, particles of light or flashes of light moving through the spinal passage. It can also be felt as a stream of heat, cold or electricity. Concentrate your entire awareness on the experience of prana moving together with the breath inside the sushumna pathway. As the breath ascends, the prana also ascends. As the breath descends, the prana also descends. Experience the three forces moving together, the breath, the prana and the consciousness inside the spinal passage.

Stage 6: Piercing the chakras
When the awareness of prana has developed to the point where you are able to experience it moving spontaneously together with the breath, then you must visualize the

different chakra junctions within sushumna. Visualize the chakras as points of light strung together along the psychic passage like the beads of a mala.

Now bring your awareness to the perineum at the base of the spine, where the psychic passage originates. See here the first point of light, which represents mooladhara, the root chakra. Next visualize a point of light at the coccyx or the lower tip of the spine, which represents swadhisthana, the second chakra. Moving upwards see a point of light in the spine directly behind the navel. This is manipura, the third chakra. Next visualize a point of light in the spine, behind the sternum at the heart level. This is anahata, the fourth chakra. Then see a point of light behind the throat pit in the spinal passage. This is vishuddhi, the fifth chakra. Finally see a point of light at the tip of the spinal passage in the midbrain. This is ajna, the sixth chakra.

Now resume your awareness of the breath and the prana ascending and descending through the psychic passage from mooladhara to ajna, ajna to mooladhara. As the breath and the prana ascend and descend the psychic passage, feel that the prana is like a sharp needle piercing each chakra in turn. Experience the piercing and opening of the chakras one after the other, without any break or gap. Do not try to concentrate on the individual chakras or even to name them. The breath and the prana are moving up and down sushumna like an express train which passes through different junctions enroute, without stopping at any of them.

Stage 7: Awareness of Soham

Now leave awareness of the prana and chakras. Become aware of the sound of the breath as it moves up and down the spinal passage. Intensify your awareness. Listen carefully to the subtle sound of each breath as it moves up and down the sushumna passage. Try to experience the inherent nada or sound vibration within the breath itself. As you breathe in, hear the mantra *So-o-o-o-o*. As you breathe out, hear the mantra *Ham-m-m-m*. Concentrate your entire awareness on the process of breathing and the mantra of the breath, which is *Soham*.

As the breath ascends the spinal passage during inhalation, the *So* mantra moves with it. As the breath descends the spinal passage during exhalation, the *Ham* mantra moves with it. The two forces of sound and breath are moving together as if they are one integrated whole. There is no distinction between them. Concentrate on the one movement of breath and sound inside the sushumna passage. Feel the vibrations of the mantra opening and purifying this important pathway and enhancing its luminosity. Your awareness is one with the sound vibration, one with the breath, one with the light. Intensify your awareness of the *Soham* mantra. The sound *So* is ascending on inhalation; the sound *Ham* is descending on exhalation. Practise without missing a single breath.

Stage 8: Awareness of Hamso

Here the awareness of the breath and the psychic passage are the same as in the previous stage. Only the starting point is different. Instead of starting from mooladhara with inhalation and the mantra *So*, the starting point is at ajna with exhalation and the mantra *Ham*.

Bring your awareness to ajna. Exhale from ajna to mooladhara through the spinal passage and hear the mantra *Ham-m-m-m-m*. Then inhale from mooladhara to ajna with the mantra *So-o-o-o-o*. The *Ham* mantra still accompanies the exhalation from ajna to mooladhara, and the *So* mantra still accompanies the inhalation from mooladhara to ajna. The process of breathing is the same; only the starting point has changed. Now you begin each round from ajna with exhalation and the mantra *Ham*, which is followed by inhalation from mooladhara with the mantra *So*. In this way the *Soham* mantra is reversed to *Hamso* in the spinal passage.

Continue the *Hamso* awareness for some time. Intensify the perception of the mantra synchronized with the breath inside the psychic passage. Remember that you do not have to repeat the mantra. It is already going on within the sound of the breath itself. You only have to hear it. Once you are able to hear the mantra within the breath, then you must concentrate on the sound vibration moving through sushumna to the exclusion of all else. You are aware of only the mantra *Ham* with exhalation from ajna to mooladhara, and *So* with inhalation from mooladhara to ajna. Continue the practice without missing a single breath. Complete awareness of the mantra in the breath.

Stage 9: Ending the practice
Now get ready to end the practice. Withdraw the awareness of the mantra and become aware of the natural breath. Be aware of the physical body from head to toe. Become aware of your meditation posture. Feel your hands resting on the knees. Bring your awareness to the environment around you, slowly externalizing the mind. Take a deep breath in and chant *Om* three times.

Hari Om Tat Sat

Ajapa Dharana Three
Frontal Passage: Manipura–Ajna

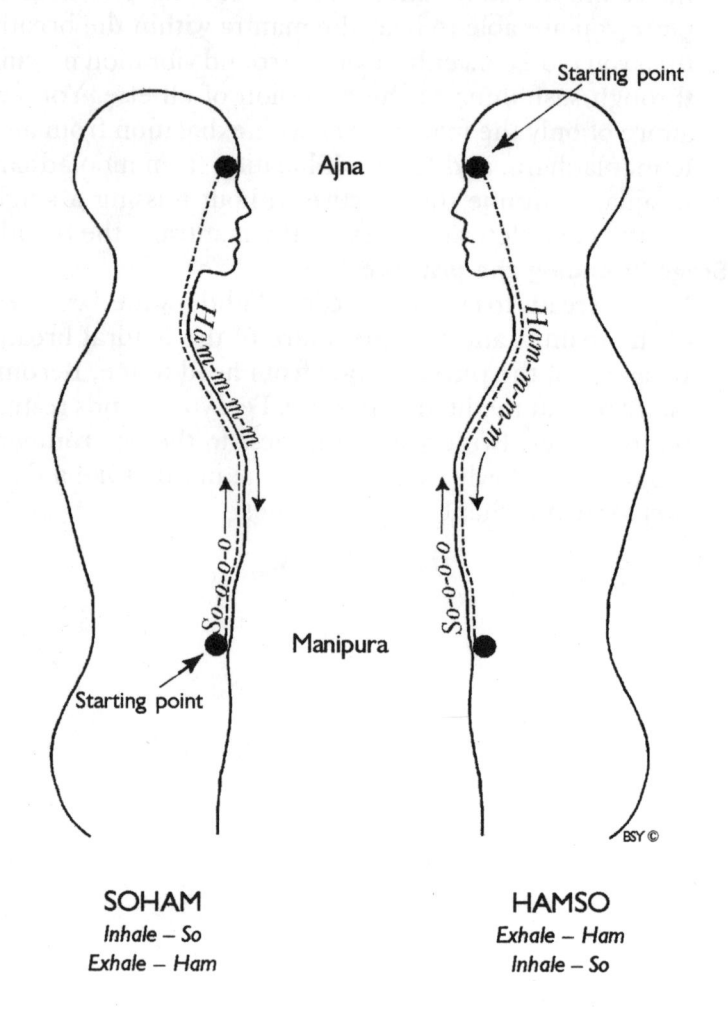

SOHAM
Inhale – So
Exhale – Ham

HAMSO
Exhale – Ham
Inhale – So

Ajapa Dharana Three
FRONTAL PASSAGE ROTATION WITH UJJAYI AND KHECHARI

In this practice all the stages of ajapa dharana one, frontal passage rotation, are performed in the same sequence. Here, however, instead of deep breathing, ujjayi pranayama and khechari mudra are used in order to further develop the awareness of the psychic passage. Ujjayi is known as the psychic breath because of its introverting effect on the mind and senses. The combination of ujjayi with khechari further introverts and deepens the awareness. The frontal passage in this practice is extended from manipura to ajna. This practice should be continued until the ujjayi breathing and the *Soham* mantra flow together through the frontal passage as one force without conscious effort.

Technique
Stage 1: Preparation
Sit in a comfortable meditation asana. Make sure the spine is straight, the shoulders are back and the head is up. Place your hands on the knees in chin or jnana mudra. The eyes and lips should be gently but firmly closed. Become aware of the whole physical body. Move your awareness through each part of the body to ensure there is no tightness or tension in any part. The body should be comfortable and at ease. As your awareness moves through the body, feel the meditation posture becoming steady and still. The body is motionless and

still. Complete awareness of the steadiness and stillness of the whole body.

Stage 2: Breath awareness

Now move your awareness from the stillness of the body to the natural, spontaneous breath. Become aware of each inhalation and exhalation. Follow the breath as it enters and leaves the body, not changing the breath in any way, just allowing the awareness to move with the natural spontaneous breath. Feel the breath becoming steady and rhythmic. As you intensify your awareness of the breath, it will become deeper and slower. Allow the breath to deepen into ujjayi breath and let the tongue slip back into khechari mudra. Keep the awareness flowing with each breath. With each breath the mind and body become more calm and still. There is just awareness of the gentle, subtle flow of the ujjayi breath.

Now bring the awareness to the navel. As you inhale in ujjayi, feel the breath and awareness move from the navel to the eyebrow centre. As you exhale in ujjayi, feel the breath and awareness move from the eyebrow centre to the navel. Your awareness should move with the breath in a straight line from the navel to the eyebrow centre as you inhale. Your awareness should move with the breath in a straight line from the eyebrow centre to the navel as you exhale. Be aware of every inhalation and every exhalation. Feel the movement becoming effortless and spontaneous. Continue with the ujjayi breathing and khechari mudra for the remainder of the practice.

Stage 3: Frontal passage visualization

Begin to visualize the passageway between the navel and the eyebrow centre. This pathway runs in a straight line between the navel and the eyebrow centre. Visualize this psychic passageway as a long, thin, transparent tube which is hollow inside. See this tube clearly.

Let your awareness move along the inside of the hollow tube. Visualize every part of this transparent tube by moving your awareness from the navel to the eyebrow centre and from the eyebrow centre to the navel. Intensify your awareness of the frontal passage which connects the navel to the eyebrow centre. Continue to rotate your awareness along this passageway until you can visualize it clearly.

Stage 4: Breathing inside the psychic passage

Now become aware of the ujjayi breath moving inside this frontal psychic passage. As you inhale feel the breath moving upwards inside the frontal pathway from the navel to the eyebrow centre. As you exhale feel the breath moving downward inside the frontal passage from the eyebrow centre to the navel. Be completely aware of the ascending and the descending breath.

Experience the breath and consciousness moving together within the frontal passage. The consciousness and breath ascend along the psychic passage with inhalation. The consciousness and breath descend along the psychic passage with exhalation. The breath is moving effortlessly along this pathway and you are aware of every movement of the breath. Experience these two forces ascending and descending in the frontal psychic passage.

Stage 5: Awareness of prana

Intensify your awareness of the consciousness and breath moving together within the psychic passage. Be aware of the flowing movement of the breath and consciousness as they ascend and descend with inhalation and exhalation. Experience the steady, rhythmic flow of breath and consciousness.

Now extend your awareness to the prana which is also flowing inside the psychic passage. The prana flows with the breath and consciousness inside the psychic passage. As you inhale, the breath, prana and consciousness flow from the navel to the eyebrow centre. As you exhale, the breath, prana and consciousness flow from the eyebrow centre to the navel. Be aware of the three distinct forces moving inside the frontal psychic passage.

Experience the breath moving in the form of air. Visualize the prana as a stream of white light ascending and descending the psychic passage. Visualize the prana clearly. See the streams of sparkling white light moving with the ujjayi breath within the psychic pathway. While inhaling, see the stream of white light ascending from the navel to the eyebrow centre. While exhaling, see the stream of white light descending from the eyebrow centre to the navel. As your awareness becomes more concentrated and one-pointed, feel the increase of prana within the psychic passage.

Stage 6: Awareness of Soham

Now let go of the awareness of prana and become aware of the breath only. Hear the soft, subtle sound of the ujjayi breath. Concentrate completely on the breath and the subtle sound of the breath. Try to perceive the sound of the *Soham* mantra within the breath as it ascends and descends through the frontal passage. As you inhale, feel the breath and the mantra *So-o-o-o-o* ascending from navel to the eyebrow centre. As you exhale feel the breath and the mantra *Ham-m-m-m-m* descending from the eyebrow centre to the navel.

Your entire awareness is with the ujjayi breath and the mantra of the breath, *Soham*. There is no need to repeat the mantra, just be aware of the sound already going on within the breath. Follow the breath as it ascends the psychic passage with inhalation and hear *So-o-o-o-o*. Follow the breath as it descends the psychic passage and hear *Ham-m-m-m-m*. Bring your awareness closer and closer to the breath and the sound of the breath. There is no other awareness except the breath and the mantra *Soham* within the psychic pathway.

As your awareness becomes more one-pointed and steady, you will begin to perceive the subtler levels of the breath and mantra. Intensify the awareness of the *Soham* mantra. Become aware of the vibration which is created as the mantra ascends with inhalation and descends with exhalation. Do not let your attention be distracted by any thoughts or experiences that may occur. Put these thoughts or feelings aside and concentrate your full attention on the breath and mantra. Steady, continuous awareness of the breath and the mantra.

Stage 7: Awareness of Hamso
For the next stage of the practice the awareness remains the same but the starting point of each round is the eyebrow centre. Bring your awareness to the eyebrow centre. As you exhale, move your awareness with the breath from the eyebrow centre to the navel. Listen to the mantra *Ham-m-m-m-m*. As you inhale, move your awareness with the breath from the navel to the eyebrow centre. Listen to the mantra *So-o-o-o-o*. With this change of starting point, the mantra now becomes *Hamso* instead of *Soham*.

Continue with the practice, intensifying your awareness of the *Hamso* mantra. Feel the ujjayi breath moving within the psychic passage. Hear the mantra *Ham-m-m-m-m* with exhalation and the mantra *So-o-o-o-o* with inhalation. Feel the vibration of *Hamso* as it moves within the frontal psychic passage. Your only focus point right now is the *Hamso* mantra. Follow every breath and perceive the mantra within every breath. Feel your awareness gradually going deeper, moving into more subtle levels of the breath and mantra.

Stage 8: Ending the practice
Continue with the practice for a few more moments. Now prepare to end the practice. Withdraw your awareness of the mantra. Release khechari mudra and stop ujjayi breathing. Become aware of the slow, rhythmic flow of the natural, spontaneous breath. Become aware of the physical body and the posture in which you are sitting. Feel the contact between the body and the floor. Become aware of your surroundings. Listen to the sounds around you. Gradually externalize the mind completely. Now inhale deeply and chant *Om* three times. Slowly move the body and open the eyes.

Hari Om Tat Sat

Ajapa Dharana Four
Spinal Passage: Mooladhara–Ajna

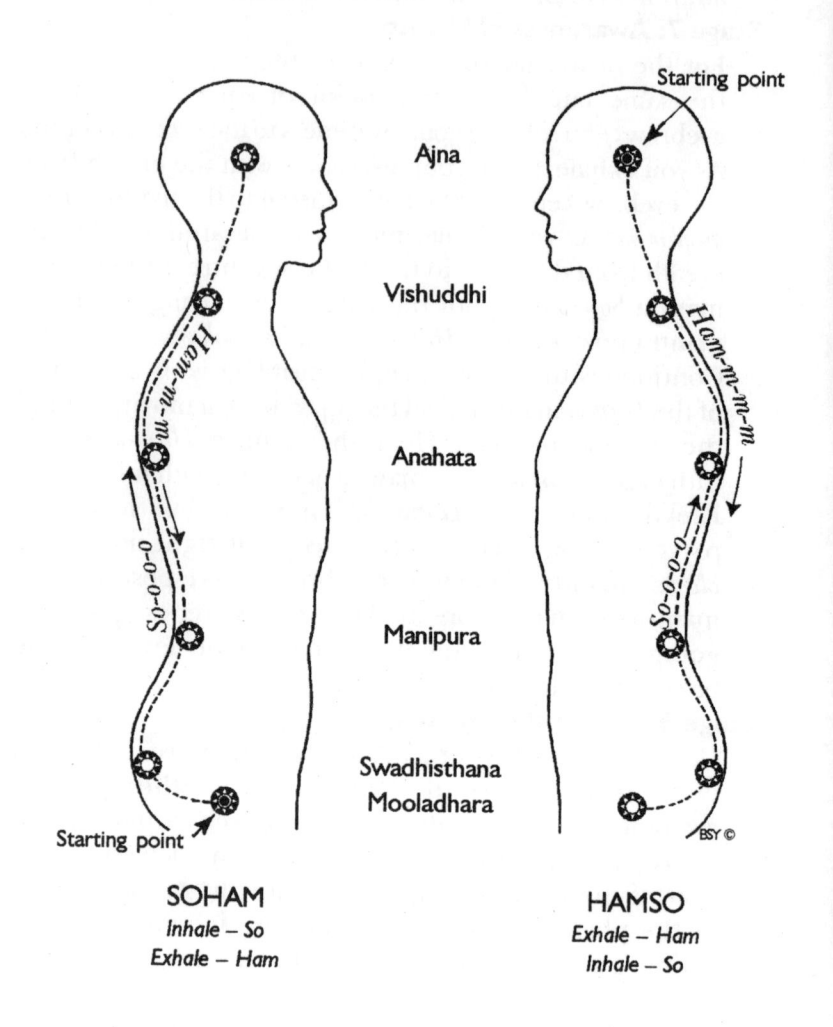

Ajna

Vishuddhi

Anahata

Manipura

Swadhisthana
Mooladhara

SOHAM
Inhale – So
Exhale – Ham

HAMSO
Exhale – Ham
Inhale – So

Ajapa Dharana Four

SPINAL PASSAGE ROTATION WITH UJJAYI AND KHECHARI

In this practice all the stages of ajapa dharana two, rotations in the spinal passage, are performed in the same sequence with the addition of ujjayi pranayama and khechari mudra. Continue this practice until you are able to develop the experience of ujjayi pranayama in the spinal passage with total ease. When the mantra is synchronized with ujjayi breathing you should feel it vibrating through the spinal passage with great force. Alertness and concentration must be maintained throughout the practice.

Technique
Stage 1: Preparation
Sit in any comfortable meditation posture and get ready for the practice of ajapa dharana. Make sure the spine, neck and head are straight. Place the hands on the knees in chin or jnana mudra. Be aware of the whole physical body and check that there in no tightness or tension in any part.
Make any adjustments to your position now so that you can remain steady and still throughout the whole practice. The body should be comfortable and at ease. As you continue to be aware of the body, feel it becoming motionless. Feel stillness spreading through the whole physical body. The body is absolutely motionless, steady and still.

Stage 2: Breath awareness

As the body becomes steady, move your awareness to the breath. Become aware of the natural, spontaneous breath. Feel the slow, rhythmic flow of the breath. Concentrate your whole attention on the natural flow of your breath. As your concentration intensifies, be aware of the breath becoming ujjayi breathing. Hear the soft, subtle sound of ujjayi breathing. Fold the tongue back into khechari mudra. Throughout the practice you will continue with ujjayi breathing and khechari mudra. If the tongue becomes tired, release the tongue lock for a few moments and then again perform khechari mudra.

Continue with your awareness of ujjayi breathing. Experience the steady, even flow of the breath. As you move closer and closer to the breath, feel the mind becoming calm and one-pointed. The gentle, rhythmic flow of ujjayi helps to calm and still the mind. This allows your whole awareness to move with the breath.

Now bring your awareness to the perineum, to mooladhara chakra. As you inhale with ujjayi, move your awareness up along the spinal cord from mooladhara to ajna chakra, at the top of the spine. As you exhale move your awareness back down from ajna to mooladhara. Continue moving your awareness and breath up along the spinal cord with inhalation and down the spinal cord with exhalation. Try to be aware of the whole spinal cord as you inhale and exhale. Use the breath to increase this awareness of the whole spinal cord. Feel the breath passing along each part of the spinal column.

Stage 3: Visualization of sushumna

Deepen your awareness still further and become aware of the psychic passage at the very centre of the spinal cord. Bring your awareness inside the spinal cord, into this psychic passage, the sushumna nadi. Be aware of the sushumna nadi running from mooladhara, just below the spine, to ajna at the very top of the spine. Visualize sushumna nadi as a long, thin, luminous tube. It is not physical like the spinal cord, it is much more subtle.

The sushumna passage should be seen as a transparent, luminous pathway made up of light particles. This pathway is hollow inside. Be aware of the luminosity of sushumna nadi and feel the movement of the light particles. This psychic passage runs from mooladhara up to ajna chakra. Visualize it clearly and become aware of every part of the pathway. Go inside this long, thin, luminous tube. Move along the passage from mooladhara to ajna and from ajna to mooladhara. Intensify your awareness of the psychic passage. Try to perceive this subtle, psychic pathway, which carries the kundalini energy to sahasrara chakra.

Stage 4: Breathing inside sushumna

Maintaining this awareness of the sushumna pathway, again become aware of the ujjayi breathing. Begin to feel the breath moving inside the sushumna passage. As you inhale, the breath ascends from mooladhara up along the psychic passage to ajna chakra. As you exhale, the breath descends from ajna down the psychic passage to mooladhara. Move your awareness along with the breath inside sushumna nadi. Be aware of every breath.

Concentrate completely on the breath ascending and descending inside sushumna. Your awareness, your consciousness, is also moving inside sushumna. As the breath moves, the awareness moves. Be aware of these two forces moving within the long, luminous pathway of sushumna. Focus your whole awareness on the breath moving along the sushumna passage. There is awareness of nothing else. Complete, one-pointed awareness of the movement of breath as it ascends and descends the psychic passage.

Stage 5: Awareness of prana

As you intensify your awareness of the breath moving within sushumna, begin to perceive the prana which is also moving within the psychic pathway. As the breath ascends, the prana descends with it. Become aware of the breath, the prana and the awareness ascending and descending the sushumna passage. Try to perceive prana in the form of light, particles of light, streams of light, moving within the luminous sushumna passage. Intensify your awareness of the prana, the vital energy moving with the breath. Experience the pranic force building up within the psychic pathway with every ascending and descending breath. As you continue with steady one-pointed awareness, the practice will become spontaneous and effortless.

Stage 6: Piercing the chakra

Leave the awareness of prana and the breath for a few moments. Visualize the different chakra points along the sushumna passage. See each chakra in the form of a point of light along the psychic passage.

Bring your awareness down to the perineum, to mooladhara chakra. Become aware of this first chakra and visualize it as a tiny point of light. Now move to the coccyx bone, to swadhisthana chakra. Visualize this second chakra as a point of light. Come up to the part of the spine directly behind the navel, manipura chakra and visualize a point of light. Move up the spine to the heart level behind the sternum. Visualize a point of light at anahata chakra. Next move up the spine until you are directly behind the throat area, vishuddhi chakra. Visualize a point of light at vishuddhi. Now go to the very top of the spine, in the centre of the head, and visualize ajna chakra as a point of light.

Bring your awareness back to the ujjayi breath and the prana ascending and descending the sushumna passage from mooladhara to ajna and from ajna to mooladhara. As you inhale up the psychic passage, feel that the prana is penetrating, piercing each chakra point. As you exhale down the psychic passage, feel that the prana is again penetrating and piercing each chakra point. There is no need to repeat the names of the chakras, just be aware of the prana piercing each chakra point as it ascends and descends sushumna nadi with the breath.

The prana and the breath are moving in a continuous, unbroken flow along the psychic passage. Your awareness should flow in the same way along the pathway. Be aware of each chakra point as the prana passes through each point of light. Keep your awareness flowing with the breath up and down the sushumna passage. Continue the practice and feel your awareness of the movement of prana through the chakra points becoming stronger.

Stage 7: Awareness of Soham

Now let go of this awareness of the chakras and the prana. Bring your awareness back to the ujjayi breath. Listen to the sound of the ujjayi breathing. Hear the subtle sound made by the breath with each inhalation and exhalation. Concentrate your full attention on the breath and the sound of the breath.

Try to perceive the subtle, inherent sound within the breath as the mantra *Soham*. You do not have to make any sound or repeat the mantra, because it is already going on within each and every breath. You must just let your awareness become so one-pointed and clear that you will spontaneously perceive the mantra within the sound of the breath.

With inhalation the breath moves up the sushumna passage with the mantra *So-o-o-o-o*. With exhalation the breath moves down the sushumna passage with the mantra *Ham-m-m-m-m*. Follow the breath as it ascends and descends the luminous sushumna pathway. Make the awareness one with the breath. Inhale and hear the mantra *So-o-o-o-o* as the breath ascends. Exhale and hear the mantra *Ham-m-m-m-m* as the breath descends. Do not let your attention be diverted for a moment. Be aware of every breath and the continuous mantra *Soham*. Feel the vibration of the mantra within the sushumna passage.

Stage 8: Awareness of Hamso

With the next stage of the practice, there is a change in the starting point for the awareness. Everything else remains the same. Continuing with the practice of ujjayi breathing and khechari mudra, bring your awareness to ajna chakra. With exhalation the breathing descends from ajna to mooladhara. Hear the mantra *Ham-m-m-m-m*. With inhalation the breath ascends from mooladhara to ajna. Hear the mantra *So-o-o-o-o*. In this way the mantra changes from *Soham* to *Hamso*.

Continue in this way. Be aware of the *Hamso* mantra. With each exhalation hear the mantra *Ham-m-m-m-m*. With each inhalation hear the mantra *So-o-o-o-o*. Complete concentration on the ujjayi breathing. Try to perceive the mantra of the breath. Continuous awareness of *Hamso*. Feel the vibrations of *Hamso* moving along the entire length of the luminous sushumna pathway. You are not aware of anything except the sound, the vibration of *Hamso* ascending and descending the sushumna passage. Hold this awareness steady and one-pointed.

Stage 9: Ending the practice

Continue with the practice for a few more moments. Now get ready to end the practice. Leave awareness of the mantra and stop the ujjayi breathing. Release khechari mudra. Bring the awareness to the natural breath. Be aware of the steady even rhythm of the breath. Become aware of your physical body and your meditation posture. Awareness of the whole physical body from head to toe. Feel the contact between the body and the floor. Hear any sound in the external environment. Become aware of your surroundings. Externalize your mind fully. Inhale and chant *Om* three times. Now move your body and open your eyes.

Hari Om Tat Sat

Ajapa Dharana Five

AROHAN-AWAROHAN ROTATION

The word *arohan* means 'ascending' and the word *awarohan* means 'descending'. Here ascending refers to the frontal passage and descending refers to the spinal passage. In this practice you are required to move sequentially through these two psychic passages. Hence inhalation takes place while ascending the arohan passage in the front, and exhalation takes place while descending through the awarohan passage in the back.

Previously only part of the frontal passage was used, between manipura and vishuddhi and then between manipura and ajna. Now, however, the entire frontal passage from mooladhara to ajna is used for ascending and this is what is known as arohan. Alongside the arohan or frontal passage are the chakra kshetram or trigger points which correspond to the chakra points in the spine. Mooladhara has no kshetram. The swadhisthana kshetram is located at the pubic bone, manipura kshetram at the navel, anahata kshetram at the sternum, vishuddhi kshetram at the throat pit, and ajna kshetram at the eyebrow centre.

In this practice we will proceed to rotate the awareness, the ujjayi breath, the prana and the mantra, through the arohan and awarohan passages. Concentration upon the arohan-awarohan rotation creates a closed circuit of energy within the two most powerful psychic passages in the body. Both the arohan and awarohan passages are potent energy

Ajapa Dharana Five
Arohan and Awarohan

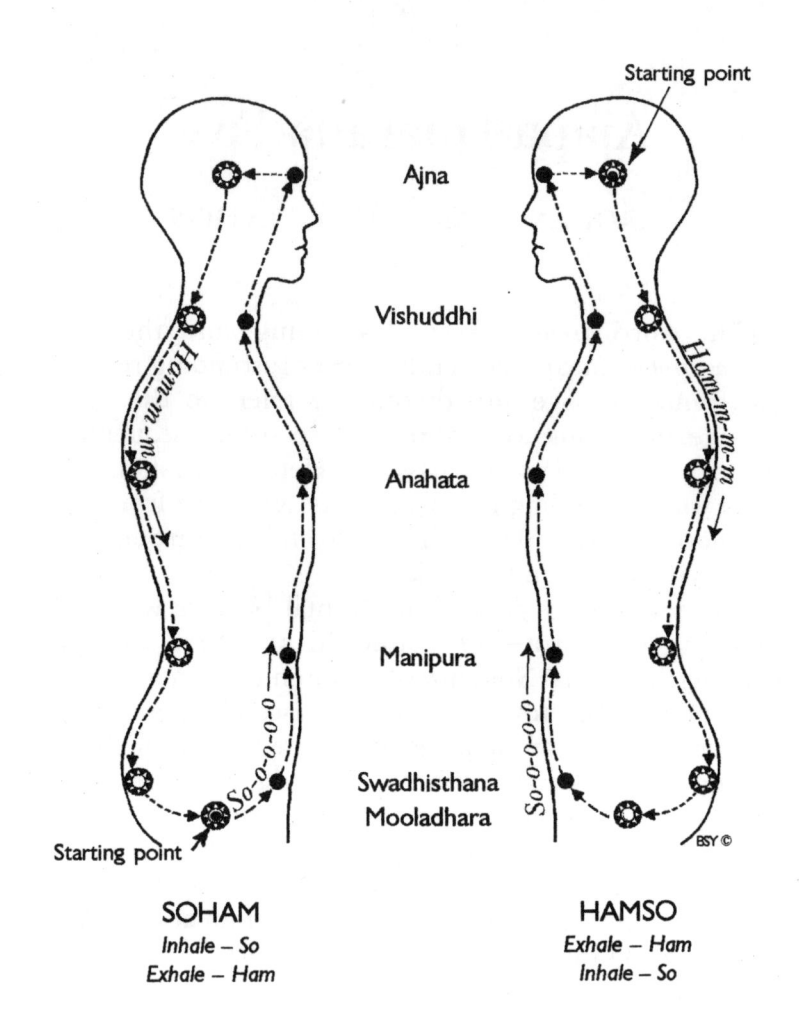

Chakras: Ajna, Vishuddhi, Anahata, Manipura, Swadhisthana, Mooladhara

SOHAM
Inhale – So
Exhale – Ham

HAMSO
Exhale – Ham
Inhale – So

channels. The location of the chakras and their trigger points within these passages make them more powerful than any other channels. By consciously rotating the breath, the prana and the mantra through these passages, we are able to purify them, open the chakras, and awaken that latent psychic potential. Once this is achieved, the spiritual forces arise spontaneously.

Therefore, concentration on these passages is very important and it is considered as a basis for all the higher yogas. Without the awakening of these passages, the meditation process proceeds very slowly and one is unable to attain the different stages of dharana, dhyana and samadhi. However, with the awakening of these channels, the various stages of concentration and meditation unfold spontaneously without having to forcefully control or coerce the mind. As the energy awakens, the mind automatically becomes still. With a still mind it bcomes easy to focus on one point or one process for extended durations of time. Ultimately the concentrated mind is experienced as an integral part of one's inner nature.

Technique
Stage 1: Preparation
Sit in a comfortable meditation asana. Make sure that your spine is erect and your head, neck and shoulders are slightly back. Place the hands on the knees in chin or jnana mudra. Close your eyes. Relax your whole body from head to toe. Adjust your position if you feel any discomfort. Bring your awareness inside. Develop the feeling of body stillness and steadiness. Concentrate on the meditation posture and steadiness. Feel your body becoming steady and immobile like a statue.
Stage 2: Rotation of awareness
Breathe normally throughout this stage of the practice. Fix your awareness at mooladhara chakra. This is the starting point for each round. Let your awareness ascend the arohan passage in the front, passing through

swadhisthana kshetram at the pubic bone, manipura kshetram at the navel, anahata kshetram at the sternum and vishuddhi kshetram at the throat pit, until you come to ajna kshetram at the eyebrow centre. As you pass through the arohan passage, visualize the chakra kshetrams as points of light and mentally repeat the name of each one in turn.

After reaching ajna kshetram you should immediately cross over to ajna chakra at the top of the spine. Let your awareness descend through the awarohan passage from ajna to mooladhara. Visualize the chakras as points of light situated alongside the awarohan passage. As your awareness passes through each centre mentally repeat: ajna, vishuddhi, anahata, manipura, swadhisthana, mooladhara.

This completes one round or circuit of awareness. Immediately begin a second round by moving your awareness up through the arohan passage, mentally repeating the name of each centre as you pass through it. Imagine your awareness moving along a thin, luminous, elliptical path within the body. Try to develop the vision of this oval pathway from mooladhara to ajna in the arohan passage and from ajna to mooladhara in the awarohan passage. Visualize the entire luminous loop as you ascend and descend.

Stage 3: Rotation of breath

Fold your tongue back in khechari mudra. Khechari will be practised for the remainder of the practice, although you can release the tongue lock at any time for a short duration if you feel any discomfort. Exhale and direct your awareness to mooladhara chakra. This is the beginning of each round. Contract the mooladhara chakra area slightly in order to experience this point.

Inhale with ujjayi and ascend the passage. As you ascend, visualize each kshetram and mentally repeat its name in turn. There should be a continuous flow of awareness from one kshetram to the next. The inhalation should end when you reach ajna kshetram at the eyebrow centre. Immediately cross over to the ajna chakra point at the top of the spine and begin descending through the awarohan passage. The descent of awareness is synchronized with exhalation in ujjayi. Visualize each chakra point in turn and repeat its name mentally. On reaching mooladhara, the first round is completed. Then begin the next round.

Stage 4: Rotation of prana
Continue the practice until you feel the ujjayi breath moving easily through the elliptical psychic pathway. Experience the breath and consciousness moving together up and down the arohan and awarohan passages. After some time you will begin to experience a third force, the prana or subtle energy which is moving along with the breath and the consciousness. You may experience the movement of prana momentarily as a stream of light, particles of light or flashes of light, ascending and descending through the psychic passages, along with the breath and the consciousness.

Maintain your awareness and concentration. Leave the mental repetition of the chakra names and simply try to visualize the psychic passages and the psychic centres located within them. As you ascend and descend, feel the prana building up in the psychic passages with each breath, and piercing each chakra kshetram and chakra point in turn.

Intensify your awareness of the prana in the psychic passages. Visualize the movement of prana in the form of white light. See the prana piercing each chakra kshetram and chakra point in turn. Experience the build-up of energy and luminosity inside the psychic passages. You may feel heat, cold, lightness, tickling or tingling, as the experience of prana intensifies. But do not allow the sensation to distract your attention. Visualize the rotation of prana in the arohan and awarohan passages with one-pointed concentration.

Stage 5: Rotation with Soham

Now leave your awareness of the prana and listen carefully to the subtle sounds within the breath. The sound of the breath is the mantra *Soham*. Become aware of mooladhara chakra. Inhale with ujjayi pranayama up the arohan passage, in the front from mooladhara to ajna. Hear the sound of *So-o-o-o-o* and feel it piercing each chakra kshetram in turn. The *So* mantra and the inhalation should end when your awareness comes to ajna kshetram. Then cross over to the ajna chakra point and begin exhalation with ujjayi down awarohan passage in the spine. Hear the mantra *Ham-m-m-m-m* and feel it piercing each chakra point in turn. There should be no mental repetition of the chakra names, only awareness. The exhalation and *Ham* mantra should finish when the awareness reaches mooladhara.

Now begin the next round. Maintain your awareness at mooladhara for a few seconds. Then inhale with ujjayi up the arohan passage. Be aware of the *So* mantra piercing each chakra kshetram. Continue the practice until the mind becomes completely one-pointed and still. Feel the powerful vibration of the mantra purifying the psychic passages and opening the psychic centres.

Stage 6: Rotation with Hamso

In this stage the *Soham* mantra is reversed to *Hamso*. The breathing process remains the same, only the starting point is different. Instead of starting with inhalation at mooladhara we will begin with exhalation from ajna.

Bring your awareness to ajna and focus it there for a few moments. Exhale with ujjayi and descend the awarohan passage. Hear the mantra *Ham-m-m-m-m* and feel it piercing each chakra point in turn. When you reach mooladhara, the exhalation and *Ham* mantra should end. Immediately begin inhalation with ujjayi up the arohan passage. Hear the *So-o-o-o-o* mantra and feel it piercing each chakra kshetram in turn. When you reach ajna the inhalation and *So* mantra should end. This is one round.

Then begin the next round. Maintain your awareness at ajna for a few seconds. Exhale with ujjayi down the awarohan passage. Continue the practice until the movement of the breath and the *Hamso* mantra become spontaneous and effortless. Your concentration should become so deep and steady during this stage of the practice that it is literally unshakeable. Nothing can disturb or distract you. Continue to visualize the psychic passage and centres with utmost clarity throughout the practice.

Stage 7: Ending the practice

Now gradually withdraw your awareness from the psychic passage. Release your tongue. Switch back to normal breathing. Again become aware of your physical body. Feel your whole body from head to toe. See your body sitting in meditation posture in the room. Listen to the sounds in the external environment. Feel the weight of your body against the floor. Slowly move your fingers and toes. Breathe in deeply and chant *Om* three times.

Hari Om Tat Sat

Ajapa Dharana Six
Ida-Pingala Curve
(Back view)

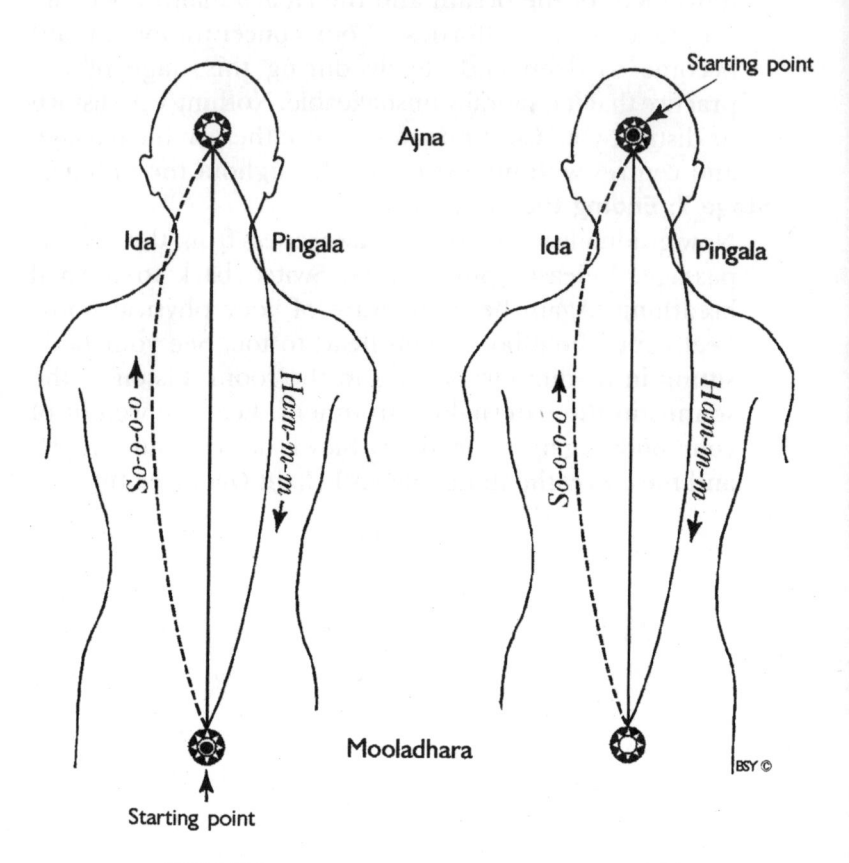

SOHAM
Inhale – So (Ida)
Exhale – Ham (Pingala)

HAMSO
Exhale – Ham (Pingala)
Inhale – So (Ida)

Ajapa Dharana Six

IDA-PINGALA ELLIPTICAL ROTATION

In this practice the two psychic passages of ida and pingala nadis, which represent the mental (ida) and vital (pingala) energies, are used. These passages emanate from mooladhara chakra at the base of the spine and terminate at ajna chakra in the midbrain at the top of the spine. In the earlier practices we practised rotation within sushumna nadi, which moves straight up through the centre of the spine. Ida and pingala are subordinate to sushumna. In this practice, ida is visualized as curving to the left from mooladhara to ajna and pingala as curving to the right. These two channels are represented in the diagram in their simplified version with only one curve in order to develop this awareness more easily.

Just as the sushumna passage represents the spiritual potential, so the two passages of ida and pingala nadis represent the dual forces of prana and consciousness, of body and mind. Ida is said to be the lunar or receptive force while pingala is the solar or dynamic force. In this elliptical rotation the inhalation or activating emphasis is on ida nadi and the exhalation or passive emphasis is on pingala nadi. This means that the mental forces will be activated and the vital forces will be relaxed or subdued, which will become apparent to the practitioner as the different stages of the practice are developed.

Technique
Stage 1: Preparation
Sit in a comfortable meditation posture. Check that your spine is straight and your shoulders and head are slightly back. Place the hands on the knees in chin or jnana mudra. Close your eyes. Relax your whole body. Internalize your awareness. Feel the physical body is sitting straight, steady and still. Concentrate on steadiness and stillness of the body.

Stage 2: Rotation of awareness
Breathe normally. Take your awareness to mooladhara chakra at the base of the spine. Visualize the ida passage which emanates from the left of mooladhara and passes up the left side of the body in one long, sweeping curve, terminating at ajna. Move your awareness up and down the outside of the ida passage, which glows with a soft translucent light. Try to visualize the ida passage clearly on the left side, curving like a bow between mooladhara and ajna.

This passage is hollow inside and it is open at both ends. Move your awareness up through the centre of the ida passage, which curves to the left from mooladhara and terminates at ajna. Then bring your awareness back down through the centre of the same passage, curving to the left from ajna to mooladhara. Intensify your awareness of the ida passage, which curves to the left and glows with a soft translucent light.

Next visualize the pingala passage which emanates from the right of mooladhara and passes up the right side of the body in one long, sweeping curve, terminating at ajna. Move your awareness up and down the outside of the pingala passage. Try to visualize it clearly on the right side, curving like a bow between mooladhara and ajna. Move your awareness up and down the outside of this passage which is dazzling bright, emitting light.

This passage is also hollow inside and it is open at both ends. Move your awareness up through the centre of the pingala passage, which curves to the right from mooladhara and terminates at ajna. Then bring your awareness back down through the centre of the same passage, curving to the right from ajna to mooladhara. Intensify your awareness of the pingala passage, which curves to the right and emits dazzling bright light.

Stage 3: Rotation of breath
Fold the tongue back in khechari mudra. Khechari will be practised for the remainder of the practice, although you may release the tongue lock for short periods whenever you feel discomfort. Take your awareness to mooladhara. Inhale with ujjayi and ascend from mooladhara to ajna through the ida passage which curves to the left. Breathe slowly and visualize the entire length of the passage from inside. When you reach ajna, exhale slowly with ujjayi and descend through the pingala passage which curves to the right from ajna to mooladhara. Breathe slowly and visualize the entire length of the passage from inside.

This is one round. Continue rotating the ujjayi breath up through ida with inhalation and down through pingala with exhalation, until you feel the rotation becoming natural and spontaneous. Try to develop the visualization of the two elliptical passages, one curving to the left and the other to the right. See the soft glow of ida on the left side and the dazzling bright light emitted by pingala on the right. Feel that the entire breathing process is taking place inside these two luminous elliptical passages.

Stage 4: Rotation of prana
As you rotate the awareness and the ujjayi breathing through the ida and pingala passages, gradually become aware of a third force. Experience the rotation of prana, the subtle energy, moving side by side with the breath and the awareness. As you ascend and descend through the ida and pingala passages with ujjayi pranayama, experience a stream of energy moving together with the breath. Visualize a stream of white light rotating in an

elliptical path up the left side and down the right side. Continue rotating the prana with the breath until the experience becomes steady and powerful. This feeling of energy rotating through the elliptical passages must be experienced, accompanied by the vision of light, white light. Intensify the experience and vision of prana rotating through the ida and pingala passages. Synchronize the rotation of prana with the ujjayi breathing.

See the prana curving to the left while ascending from mooladhara to ajna during inhalation, and then curving to the right while descending from ajna to mooladhara during exhalation. Concentrate with one-pointed awareness on the rotation or prana through the ida and pingala psychic passages.

Stage 5: Rotation of Soham

Now leave your awareness of the prana. Listen carefully to the sound of the ujjayi breathing. Try to hear the mantra *Soham*, which is the sound made by the breath itself every time you breathe. While inhaling and ascending through the ida passage, hear the mantra *So-o-o-o-o*. While exhaling and descending through the pingala passage, hear the mantra *Ham-m-m-m-m*.

Experience the *Soham* mantra moving with the breath through the elliptical ida-pingala pathway. Concentrate your entire awareness on the sound vibrations which are moving together with the ujjayi breath up through ida and down through pingala. Feel the *Soham* mantra opening and purifying this psychic pathway. Do not allow anything to distract your awareness. With one-pointed attention, experience the rotation of *Soham* inside the elliptical ida-pingala passage.

Stage 6: Rotation of Hamso

Now we will reverse the *Soham* mantra to *Hamso* by changing the starting point of each round from mooladhara to ajna. Bring your awareness to ajna. Exhale with ujjayi and the mantra *Ham-m-m-m-m* while descending from ajna to mooladhara through the pingala passage which curves to the right. Then inhale with ujjayi and the mantra *So-o-o-o-o* from mooladhara to ajna through the ida passage which curves to the left. Continue rotating the awareness from ajna to mooladhara through pingala and from mooladhara to ajna through ida. Feel the vibrations of the *Hamso* mantra penetrating and permeating the entire elliptical pathway.

Now, with emphasis on the exhalation and the mantra *Ham*, feel your awareness going to a deeper level. Your concentration should be absolutely steady, unwavering and unshakeable. Your awareness is on one thing only – the rotation of *Hamso* through the elliptical psychic passage, and nothing else. If any other thought, vision or experience comes to your mind, immediately remove it and go on with the practice.

Stage 7: Ending the practice

Now get ready to end the practice. Gradually withdraw your awareness and your breath from the ida-pingala passages. Release the tongue lock and return to normal breathing. Become aware of your physical body sitting in the meditation posture. See your body sitting in the room. Feel the weight of your body against the floor. Slowly move your fingers and toes. Breathe in deeply and chant *Om* three times.

Hari Om Tat Sat

Ajapa Dharana Seven
Ida-Pingala Curve
(Back view)

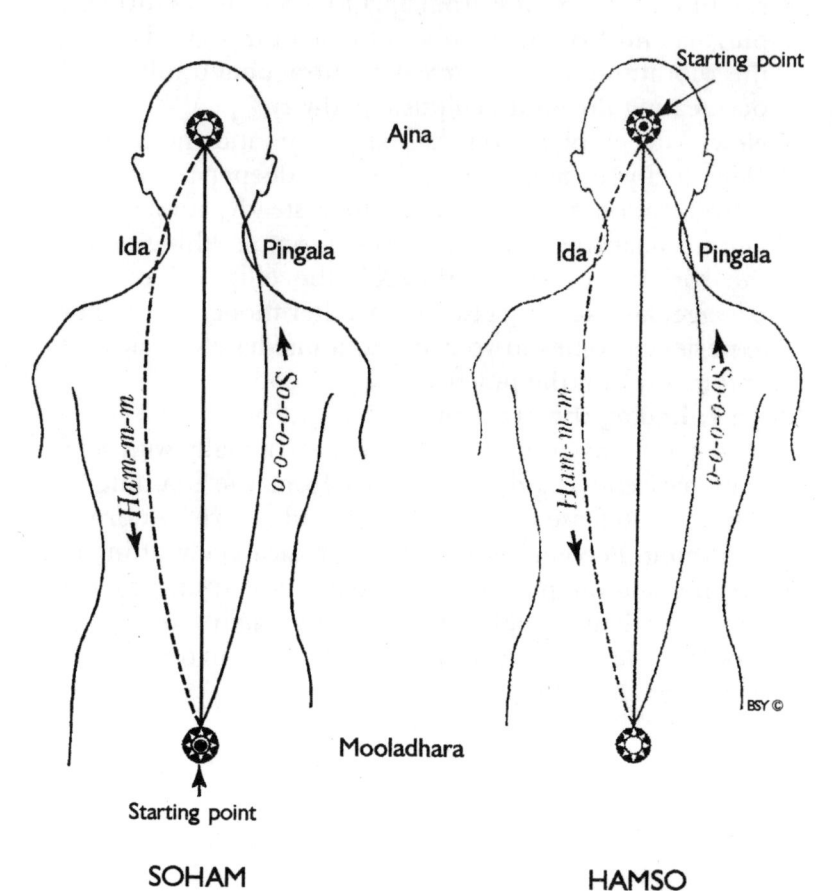

SOHAM
Inhale – So (Pingala)
Exhale – Ham (Ida)

HAMSO
Exhale – Ham (Ida)
Inhale – So (Pingala)

Ajapa Dharana Seven

PINGALA-IDA ELLIPTICAL ROTATION

In this practice the pathway of ascension and descension is alternated so that ascension takes place through pingala and descension through ida. With this rotation the inhalation or activating emphasis is on pingala and the passive or relaxing emphasis is on ida. This means that the vital forces will be activated while the mental forces will be relaxed or subdued, as the practice progresses from stage to stage.

Hence these two rotations involving the ida and pingala nadis can be used with great benefit to balance out or create certain changes in the system and in one's personality and behaviour. At the spiritual level also, it is necessary to balance, regulate and awaken these dual energy forces before the awakening of kundalini can take place. Therefore, these two practices form an important basis for one's physical, mental and spiritual growth.

In yoga it is said that sushumna only opens when ida and pingala are perfectly balanced and awakened. If the quantum of energy in these two nadis can be increased to a high level without creating any imbalance between them, then by their positive and negative polarity they can spark off an awakening of kundalini. When this spark hits mooladhara, the kundalini rises up sushumna and spiritual awakening takes place.

Therefore, the balancing of the nadis is the first prerequisite of yoga. When the nadis are balanced, the body and mind become steady and concentration is achieved. As the nadis become more balanced and regulated, sushumna opens. Spiritual experiences then begin to flow as the awareness penetrates into the deeper dimensions of consciousness. Finally, when the nadis are perfectly balanced and awakened the kundalini rises up sushumna and illumination takes place.

Technique
Stage 1: Preparation
Sit in a comfortable meditation posture. The spine should be erect and the head, neck and shoulders slightly back. Place the hands on the knees in chin or jnana mudra. Close your eyes. Internalize your awareness. Become aware of the straight, comfortable and steady position of your body. Concentrate on body stillness and steadiness. Feel your posture becoming more and more steady and still.

Stage 2: Breath awareness
Switch your awareness to the breath. Practise slow, deep breathing. Count to five while breathing in; count to five while breathing out. As the breathing becomes more and more subtle, gradually feel the tongue slipping back into khechari mudra and the breath changing into ujjayi breathing. Go on practising slow, rhythmic ujjayi with khechari for some time until the mind and body are absolutely calm and still.

Stage 3: Rotation of breath
Take your awareness to mooladhara. Inhale with ujjayi and ascend the pingala passage which curves to the right from mooladhara to ajna. Ascend slowly and observe the entire length of the pingala passage from inside. When you reach ajna, exhale with ujjayi and descend slowly through the ida passage which curves to the left from ajna to mooladhara. Try to observe the interior dimension of the ida passage from top to bottom. Be alert and aware throughout the entire rotation.

This is one round. Continue rotating the ujjayi breath up pingala with inhalation and down ida with exhalation, until you feel the breath rotating by itself in a natural and spontaneous way. Experience the entire breathing process going on within these two psychic passages. Try to develop visualization of the two elliptical passages, one curving to the right and the other curving to the left, forming a closed loop connected by mooladhara at the bottom and ajna at the top. See the dazzling bright light emitted by pingala on the right and the soft translucent glow of ida on the left.

Stage 4: Rotation of prana
Experience the two forces of awareness and breath, moving together up pingala and down ida. Gradually you will begin to experience a third force, the prana or subtle energy, rotating side by side with the breath and the awareness. As you ascend and descend through the elliptical pingala-ida passage or pathway, with ujjayi pranayama, experience a stream of energy moving together with the breath. See a stream of white light, rotating in an elliptical pathway, up the right side and down the left side.

Continue rotating the prana with the breath until the movement becomes steady and effortless. The feeling of energy rotating through the elliptical passages must be experienced, accompanied by the vision of white light. Intensify the vision and the experience of prana, rotating through the pingala and ida passage. Synchronize the rotation of prana with the ujjayi breathing, which by now has become very subtle, almost imperceptible.

See the prana curving to the right from mooladhara to ajna while ascending the pingala passage during inhalation, and curving to the left from ajna to mooladhara while descending the ida passage during exhalation. Concentrate with one-pointed awareness on the rotation of prana through the pingala and ida passages. Nothing should disturb or distract your attention.

Stage 5: Rotation of Soham

Now leave your awareness of the prana. Listen carefully within the sound of the ujjayi breathing. Try to hear the mantra *Soham*, which is being repeated by the breath itself every time you breathe. While inhaling and ascending through the pingala passage, hear the mantra *So-o-o-o-o*. While exhaling and descending through the ida passage, hear the mantra *Ham-m-m-m-m*. Experience the *Soham* mantra moving with the breath through the elliptical pingala-ida pathway.

Concentrate your entire awareness on the sound vibrations which are moving together with the ujjayi breath up through pingala and down through ida. Feel the rotation of the mantra creating a build-up of psychic energy within the elliptical pathway. Intensify your awareness. With one-pointed concentration experience the rotation of the *Soham* mantra inside the pingala-ida passage.

Stage 6: Rotation of Hamso

In the next stage we will reverse the *Soham* mantra to *Hamso*, by changing the starting point of each round from mooladhara to ajna. Bring your awareness to ajna. Exhale with ujjayi and the mantra *Ham-m-m-m-m* while descending from ajna to mooladhara through the ida passage which curves to the left. Then inhale with ujjayi and the mantra *So-o-o-o-o* from mooladhara to ajna through the pingala passage which curves to the right.

Continue rotating the awareness from ajna to mooladhara through ida and from mooladhara to ajna through pingala. Feel the vibrations of the *Hamso* mantra penetrating and permeating the entire elliptical pathway. With emphasis on exhalation and the mantra *Ham*, feel your awareness going deeper. Your concentration should be deep and powerful, like a laser beam, with only one focus, the rotation of *Hamso* through the elliptical pathway, and nothing else. If any other thought or experience comes to your mind, immediately remove it and focus your concentration on the *Hamso* rotation.

Merge your entire awareness in the experience of *Hamso* reverberating down through ida and up through pingala.

Stage 7: Ending the practice

Now get ready to end the practice. Withdraw your awareness and breath from the psychic passages. Release the tongue lock and bring your tongue forward. Switch back to normal breathing. Again become aware of the physical body which is sitting in a meditation posture. Become aware of the external environment. Listen to the external sounds. Feel the weight of your body against the floor. Slowly move your fingers and toes. Breathe in deeply and chant *Om* three times.

Hari Om Tat Sat

Ajapa Dharana Eight
Ida-Pingala Spiral
(Back view)

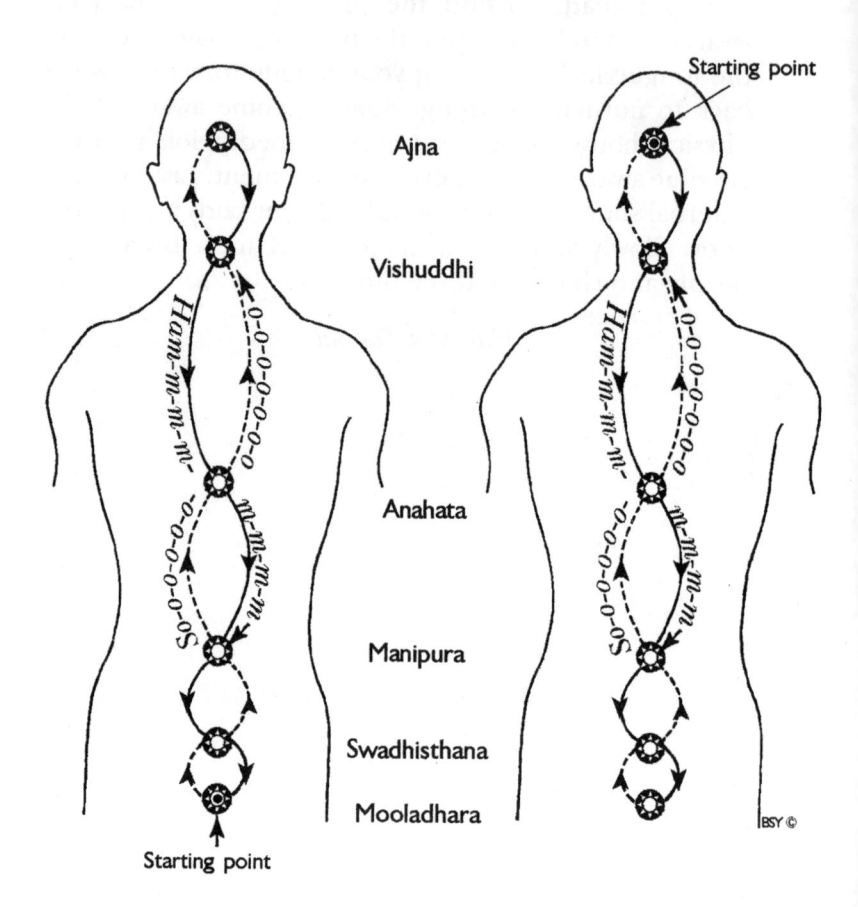

SOHAM
Inhale – So (Ida)
Exhale – Ham (Pingala)

HAMSO
Exhale – Ham (Pingala)
Inhale – So (Ida)

Ajapa Dharana Eight

IDA-PINGALA SPIRAL ROTATION

In this practice ida and pingala are visualized as spiralling passages which cross over at each chakra point. Ida and pingala are channels for the mental and vital forces; they do not actually represent the energy itself. Just as sushumna is a channel for the kundalini and does not represent the actual kundalini energy itself, in the same way, ida and pingala are channels for carrying the dual forces of consciousness and prana through these two spiralling pathways which can be seen in the diagram.

From mooladhara, pingala curves to the right crossing swadhisthana, to the left crossing manipura, to the right crossing anahata, to the left crossing vishuddhi, and to the right where it terminates at ajna. Ida spirals upwards in the opposite direction. From mooladhara, ida curves to the left crossing swadhisthana, to the right crossing manipura, to the left crossing anahata, to the right crossing vishuddhi and finally to the left where it terminates at ajna.

As ida and pingala cross over at each of the chakra centres, an energy exchange is made and the chakra then distributes this energy to the various organs and parts of the body to which it is related. For example, swadhisthana will distribute energy to the reproduction and excretory organs, manipura to the digestive organs, anahata to the heart and lungs, vishuddhi to the ears and throat, and ajna to the eyes, nose and brain.

In this way, ida and pingala are responsible for the transmission of energy which maintains our body and mind. If there is a blockage in the chakra or an imbalance in either of these flows, then different diseases arise. These diseases may be of a mental or physical nature according to the nature of the blockage or imbalance in the energy transmission of these two major channels.

However, when ida and pingala are purified and regulated and there is no blockage in the chakra, then an ongoing state of health is experienced. After regulating the energy flows in these passages, if the quantum of energy can be stepped up, then various stages of concentration can be achieved. Without balancing and raising the pranic level in these two channels, we cannot experience introversion with awareness.

The normal tendency of the introverted mind is to dream or to sleep. The normal tendency of the extroverted mind is to dissipate and become distracted. One-pointed concentration calls for dynamic introversion, awareness which is awake and alert. This condition can only arise when there is a balance between the vital and mental energies.

In this technique we continue with rotation of breath, prana and mantra through the ida and pingala passages. However, we are adding another dimension to the practice. The nadis are seen as spiralling pathways which cross over at each chakra junction. This rotation helps to clear away any obstruction in the transmission of energy through the nadis and chakras. It thereby regulates and expands the entire field of prana, promoting physical health and mental stability.

Here the activating emphasis is on the ida channel or the mental energy, while the passive or subduing emphasis is on the pingala channel or the vital energy. This is very useful for promoting a positive state of mental activity or for developing a state of deep introversion in which the mind remains alert rather then inert. This practice is beneficial for those who are extroverted and dynamic by nature and become restless and distracted easily. This rotation subdues the vital aspect and activates the mental aspect.

Technique
Stage 1: Preparation
Sit in a comfortable meditation posture with the spine erect and your head slightly back. Place your hands on the knees in chin or jnana mudra. Close the eyes. Relax the whole body from head to toe. Develop awareness of the physical body, sitting in the meditation posture. Feel your posture becoming steady and still. Concentrate on steadiness and stillness of the body. Say to yourself mentally, "My body is steady and immovable like a stone statue."
Stage 2: Breath awareness in sushumna
As your body becomes steady and immobile, shift your attention to the breath. Breathe slowly and rhythmically, counting to five each time you inhale and exhale. Continue this practice for one or two minutes.
Bring your awareness to mooladhara chakra at the base of the spine. Inhale slowly up the spinal passage from mooladhara to ajna. When you reach ajna, exhale back down to mooladhara. As you rotate your breath up and down the sushumna pathway, be aware of each chakra junction in turn.
Stage 3: Ida rotation
Now leave the awareness of the breath and of sushumna. Breathe normally and focus your attention at mooladhara chakra. Visualize the ida passage curving to the left from mooladhara and crossing swadhisthana. From swadhisthana it curves to the right and crosses manipura. From manipura it curves to the left and crosses anahata. From anahata it curves to the right and crosses vishuddhi. Then from vishuddhi it curves to the left and terminates at ajna.
Bring your awareness back down along the ida passage. From ajna, ida curves to the left and crosses vishuddhi. From vishuddhi it curves to the right and crosses anahata, and then from anahata it curves to the left and crosses manipura. From manipura it curves to the right and crosses swadhisthana. Then from swadhisthana it curves

to the left and returns to mooladhara, the point of origin. Visualize the entire ida passage spiralling up the spine from left, to right, to left, to right, to left and finally terminating at ajna. Then see the ida passage spiralling downward from left to right, to left, to right, to left and returning to mooladhara. Intensify your awareness of the ida passage.

Be aware of each chakra point as the ida passage curves and crosses over: mooladhara – left, swadhisthana – right, manipura – left, anahata – right, vishuddhi – left, terminating at ajna. Then descend from ajna – left, vishuddhi – right, anahata – left, manipura – right, swadhisthana – left, and come back to mooladhara. Continue this rotation until you can do it effortlessly.

Stage 4: Pingala rotation

Now leave awareness of the ida passage. Continue breathing normally and focus your attention at mooladhara chakra. Visualize the pingala passage curving to the right from mooladhara and crossing swadhisthana. From swadhisthana it curves to the left and crosses manipura. From manipura it curves to the right and crosses anahata. From anahata it curves to the left and crosses vishuddhi. From vishuddhi it curves to the right and terminates at ajna.

Now bring your awareness back down through the pingala passage. From ajna, pingala curves to the right and crosses vishuddhi. Then from vishuddhi it curves to the left crossing anahata. From anahata it curves to the right crossing manipura. From manipura it curves to the left and crosses swadhisthana. Finally from swadhisthana it curves to the right and returns to mooladhara.

Visualize the entire pingala passage spiralling up the spine from right, to left, to right, to left, to right and finally terminating at ajna chakra. Then see the pingala passage spiralling downward from right, to left, to right, to left, to right and returning again to mooladhara chakra. Intensify your awareness of the pingala passage.

Be aware of each chakra point in turn as the pingala passage curves and crosses over: mooladhara – right, swadhisthana – left, manipura – right, anahata – left, vishuddhi – right, terminating at ajna. Then descend from ajna – right, vishuddhi – left, anahata – right, manipura – left, swadhisthana – right and return to mooladhara. Continue this rotation until you can do it effortlessly.

Stage 5: Ida-pingala rotation
Continue breathing normally and focus your awareness at mooladhara. Now begin ascending up through the ida passage: mooladhara – left, swadhisthana – right, manipura – left, anahata – right, vishuddhi – left, and terminate at ajna. Then descend through the pingala passage: ajna – right, vishuddhi – left, anahata – right, manipura – left, swadhisthana – right, and return to mooladhara. This makes one round.

Go on ascending through ida and descending through pingala. Repeat the name of each chakra point mentally as you cross over. Intensify your awareness of the ida-pingala energy circuit. Visualize the two passages clearly as you ascend and descend. Pingala is dazzling bright and ida glows with soft, translucent light.

Stage 6: Ida-pingala breath rotation
Leave the ida-pingala rotation for a few moments and concentrate on slow, deep breathing at the throat. Feel the breathing gradually change over to ujjayi breathing and the tongue slipping back into khechari mudra.

Bring your awareness back down to mooladhara. Visualize the ida and pingala psychic passages, which emanate from the left and right of mooladhara. These passages are hollow inside and you can breathe through them.

Direct your ujjayi breath inside the ida passage. Slowly ascend with inhalation and mental repetition of each chakra point as you curve and cross over: mooladhara – left, swadhisthana – right, manipura – left, anahata – right, vishuddhi – left, and terminate the inhalation at ajna.

Then exhale with ujjayi and descend through the pingala passage. Repeat the name of each chakra point mentally as you curve and cross over: ajna – right, vishuddhi – left, anahata – right, manipura – left, swadhisthana – right, and end the exhalation at mooladhara.

Continue rotating the ujjayi breath along the ida-pingala energy circuit. Feel that the entire breathing process is taking place inside these psychic passages only. Do not allow your awareness to waver or dissipate. Exhale and bring your awareness to mooladhara. Hold the breath outside while concentrating at mooladhara for five seconds. Inhale slowly with ujjayi and ascend the ida passage with mental repetition of each chakra point: mooladhara – left, swadhisthana – right, manipura – left, anahata – right, vishuddhi – left, and terminate the inhalation at ajna.

Retain the breath inside for five seconds while concentrating at ajna. Then exhale slowly with ujjayi and begin descending through the pingala passage with mental repetition of each chakra point: ajna – right, vishuddhi – left, anahata – right, manipura – left, swadhisthana – right, and end the exhalation at mooladhara. This completes one round.

Immediately begin the next round. Hold the breath outside for five seconds while concentrating at mooladhara. Then inhale slowly with ujjayi up the ida passage with mental repetition of the chakras. Continue the breath rotation with mental chakra repetition until you are able to ascend and descend the ida-pingala circuit effortlessly, without any confusion or breathlessness.

Stage 7: Ida-pingala prana rotation

Now intensify your awareness of the ida-pingala breath rotation. Be aware of the dual forces of breath and consciousness rotating together through these psychic passages. As the breath moves, the consciousness also moves along the same pathway. Gradually begin to perceive the movement of a third force, the prana shakti or subtle energy force which is moving side by side with the breath through the ida-pingala circuit.

In this stage there is no mental repetition of the chakras, only awareness. Exhale and take your awareness to mooladhara chakra. Retain the breath outside for five seconds while concentrating at mooladhara. Inhale slowly with ujjayi and ascend the ida passage. Be aware of the location of each chakra junction as you cross over it. Experience the movement of the prana together with the breath. Visualize prana as a stream of white light spiralling up through the ida passage along with the breath.

Inhalation ends when you reach ajna. Retain the breath inside for five seconds and concentrate at ajna. Then exhale slowly with ujjayi and descend through the pingala passage with awareness of each chakra junction as you cross over it. Visualize the spiralling movement of prana down the pingala passage as a stream of white light moving with the breath. Try to feel the pranic force coursing through the nadis, opening and removing any blockages or obstacles in its path.

Continue this rotation until the vision of prana shakti is clear and you are able to concentrate on it to the exclusion of all else. Experience the build-up of pranic force and luminosity in the ida-pingala circuit.

Stage 8: Ida-pingala rotation of Soham

Now leave the vision of prana and listen very carefully to the inherent sound within the breath, which is the mantra *Soham*. Exhale and take your awareness to mooladhara. Retain the breath outside for five seconds while concentrating at mooladhara. Inhale with ujjayi and ascend the ida passage with the mantra *So-o-o-o-o*. Be aware of each chakra junction as you cross over it. When you reach ajna the inhalation ends. Retain the breath inside for five seconds while concentrating at ajna. Then exhale with ujjayi and descend the pingala passage with the mantra *Ham-m-m-m-m*. Be aware of each chakra junction as you pass through it.

When you reach mooladhara immediately begin the next round. Hold the breath outside for five seconds and concentrate at mooladhara. Inhale with ujjayi and ascend the ida passage with the mantra *So-o-o-o-o*. Continue the practice until you experience the *Soham* mantra moving effortlessly with the breath through the ida-pingala circuit. Feel the vibrations of the mantra purifying and awakening these psychic passages. Try to concentrate your entire awareness on the rotation of the mantra. Do not be distracted by any other thoughts or visions. Intensify your awareness of the *Soham* mantra. Your awareness should be focused like a laser on the one point of mantra rotating with the breath through the ida-pingala pathway.

Stage 9: Ida-pingala rotation of Hamso
Next we will reverse the mantra from *Soham* to *Hamso* by changing the starting point of the rotation. In the previous stage the starting point was at mooladhara. Now the starting point is at ajna.

Inhale and bring your awareness to ajna. Retain the breath inside for five seconds while concentrating at ajna. Exhale slowly with ujjayi pranayama and descend the pingala passage with the mantra *Ham-m-m-m-m*. Be aware of each chakra junction as you cross it. When you reach mooladhara, the exhalation is complete. Hold the breath outside for five seconds while concentrating at mooladhara. Then inhale with ujjayi and ascend the ida passage with the mantra *So-o-o-o-o*. Be aware of each chakra junction as you cross over it. When you reach ajna the inhalation is complete. This is one round.

Immediately begin the next round. Retain the breath inside for five seconds while concentrating at ajna. Then exhale with ujjayi and descend through the pingala passage. Continue the *Hamso* rotation until you experience the mantra moving spontaneously through the psychic passage together with the breath. Feel the vibration of the *Hamso* mantra penetrating, purifying and awakening the ida-pingala circuit. As you intensify your concentration on the mantra rotation, feel the build-up of psychic energy within the psychic passages.

Stage 10: Ending the practice
Now leave your awareness of the mantra. Withdraw your attention from the psychic passages. Release the tongue lock. Switch back to normal breathing. Again be aware of your physical body which is sitting in the meditation posture. Feel the body from head to toe. Be aware of the room in which you are sitting. Listen to the sounds coming from the external environment. Feel the weight of your body against the floor. Slowly move your fingers and toes. Breathe in deeply and chant *Om* three times. Open your eyes.

Hari Om Tat Sat

Ajapa Dharana Nine
Pingala-Ida Spiral
(Back view)

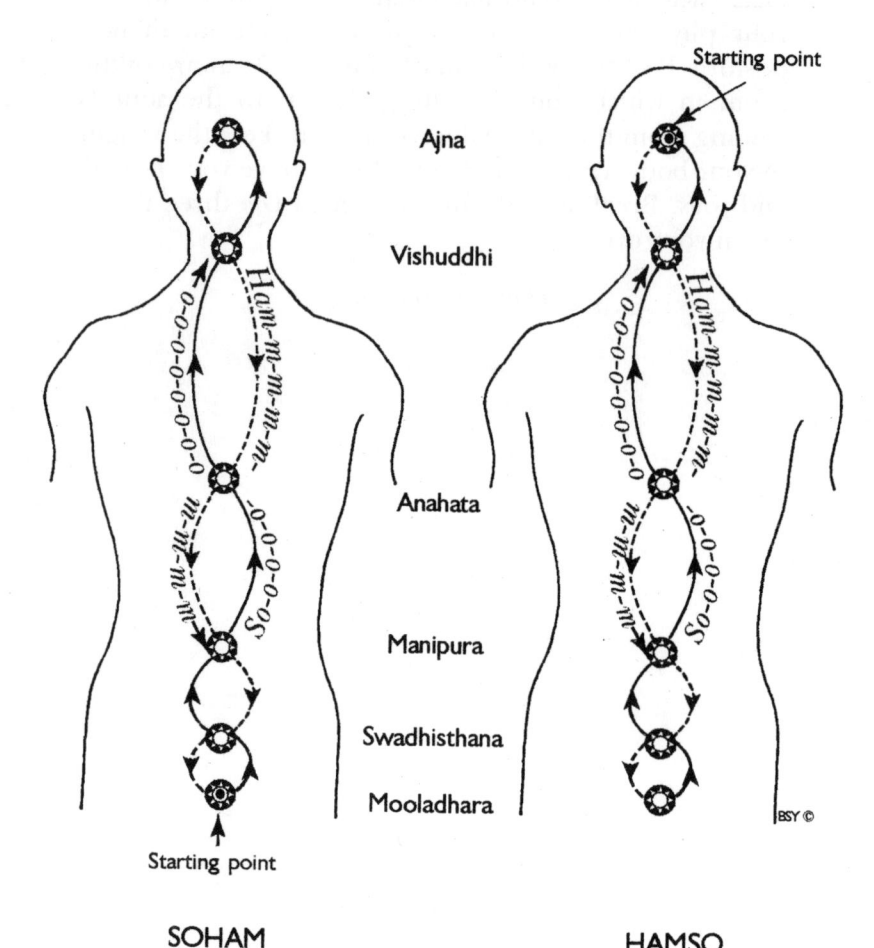

SOHAM
Inhale – So (Pingala)
Exhale – Ham (Ida)

HAMSO
Exhale – Ham (Ida)
Inhale – So (Pingala)

Ajapa Dharana Nine

PINGALA-IDA SPIRAL ROTATION

Here you continue visualizing the nadis as spiralling passages which cross over at each chakra point. However, the rotation is reversed. In this practice ascension is through pingala and descension is through ida. This means that the activating emphasis is now on pingala, the vital or dynamic aspect of our nature, and the passive or subduing emphasis is on ida, the mental aspect.

Hence this rotation is a counterbalance for ajapa dharana eight. It is an important practice for those who wish to strengthen their vitality and personal magnetism. It is very beneficial for those who tend towards dullness, mental depression and introversion, and also for those suffering from chronic, debilitating diseases.

Technique
Stage 1: Preparation
Sit in a comfortable meditation posture, with your spine erect and your head slightly back. Place the hands on the knees in chin or jnana mudra. Close the eyes. Become aware of the whole physical body. Check through the whole body and make sure there is no tension. The body should be completely comfortable and at ease. As you move your awareness through the body, feel your posture becoming steady and still. Be aware of the stillness, the motionlessness of the whole body.

Stage 2: Breath awareness in sushumna

Now bring your awareness to the natural breath. Experience the steady, rhythmic movement of the breath as you inhale and exhale. Keep the awareness moving with the breath.

Bring the awareness to the base of the spine, to mooladhara chakra. Begin to inhale slowly up through the spinal passage from mooladhara to ajna. When you reach ajna, exhale back down through the spinal passage to mooladhara. Continue to move the awareness and the breath up and down the spinal passage. Be aware of each chakra point as the breath moves along the sushumna passage. Keep the breath steady and rhythmic.

Stage 3: Pingala rotation

Leave awareness of the breath in sushumna. For a few moments be aware of the natural breath. Now bring your awareness to mooladhara chakra. Visualize the pingala passage spiralling upwards from mooladhara to ajna. See the pingala passage curving to the right from mooladhara and crossing swadhisthana, curving to the left from swadhisthana and crossing manipura, curving to the right and crossing anahata, curving to the left and crossing vishuddhi, curving to the right and terminating at ajna.

When you reach ajna, bring the awareness back down the through pingala passage. From ajna see the pingala passage curving to the right and crossing vishuddhi, curving to the left and crossing anahata, curving to the right and crossing manipura, curving to the left and crossing swadhisthana, curving to the right and returning to mooladhara.

Visualize the entire pingala pathway. See the spiralling movement of pingala along the spine as it crosses each chakra point. Beginning at mooladhara and moving to the right, it crosses swadhisthana. Moving to the left, it crosses manipura. Moving to the right, it crosses anahata. Moving to the left, it crosses vishuddhi. Moving to the right, it terminates at ajna. Descending from ajna, see pingala moving to the right and crossing vishuddhi. Moving to the left, it crosses anahata. Moving to the right, it crosses manipura. Moving to the left, it crosses swadhisthana. Moving to the right, it returns to mooladhara.

Intensify your awareness of the pingala passage and try to be aware of each chakra point as the pingala passage crosses it.

Your awareness should move steadily up and down the pingala passage. Be aware of the spiralling movement and the chakra points. Feel the rotation becoming spontaneous and effortless.

Stage 4: Ida rotation

Now leave awareness of the pingala passage and again become aware of the steady flow of the natural breath. Bring the awareness to mooladhara and begin to visualize the ida pathway. Visualize the pathway clearly. See the ida passage curving to the left from mooladhara and crossing swadhisthana, curving to the right and crossing manipura, curving to the left and crossing anahata, curving to the right and crossing vishuddhi, curving to the left and terminating at ajna.

When you reach ajna bring the awareness back down through the ida passage. From ajna, see ida curving to the left and crossing vishuddhi, curving to the right and crossing anahata, curving to the left and crossing manipura, curving to the right and crossing swadhisthana, curving to the left and returning to mooladhara.

Visualize the entire ida pathway. Be aware of the spiralling movement of ida as it moves from mooladhara to ajna, crossing each chakra point. Beginning at mooladhara and moving to the left it crosses swadhisthana. Moving to the right it crosses manipura. Moving to the left it crosses anahata. Moving to the right it crosses vishuddhi. Moving to the left, ida terminates at ajna.

Descending from ajna, see ida moving to the left and crossing vishuddhi. Moving to the right and crossing anahata, moving to the left and crossing manipura, moving to the right and crossing swadhisthana, moving to the left and returning to mooladhara.

Intensify your awareness of the ida passage as you continue with the practice. Move your awareness steadily up and down the ida pathway and be aware of each chakra point as the ida passage crosses over. With each round feel the practice becoming natural and spontaneous, without effort.

Stage 5: Pingala-ida rotation

Now leave your awareness of the ida nadi. Bring your awareness back down to mooladhara chakra. Begin ascending along the pingala passage: mooladhara – right, swadhisthana – left, manipura – right, anahata – left, vishuddhi – right and terminate at ajna. Then descend down the ida passage: ajna – left, vishuddhi – right, anahata – left, manipura – right, swadhisthana – left and return to mooladhara. This is one complete round.

Continue with this rotation, ascending through the pingala passage and descending through the ida passage. As you cross each chakra point, mentally repeat the name of that chakra. With each round feel your awareness becoming more intense and steady. Visualize both pathways clearly and vividly, without confusion.

Stage 6: Pingala-ida breath rotation

Now leave awareness of the rotation and bring your awareness to the breath in the throat. Experience the deep, slow steady breathing. Feel the breath becoming ujjayi breathing. Let your tongue slip back into khechari mudra. Be aware of the ujjayi breathing for a few moments. Continue with ujjayi and khechari mudra for the remainder of the practice.

Bring your awareness to mooladhara chakra. From here visualize the ida and pingala pathways. See their spiralling movements from mooladhara to ajna. Become aware of the pingala passage and feel the ujjayi breath moving inside the psychic passage. As you inhale, feel the breath ascending through the pingala passage. Mentally repeat the name of each chakra as the breath crosses over: mooladhara – right, swadhisthana – left, manipura – right, anahata – left, vishuddhi – right, terminating at ajna. The inhalation should end as you reach ajna. As you exhale feel the ujjayi breath descending through the ida passage, mentally repeating the name of each chakra as you cross over: ajna – left, vishuddhi – right, anahata – left, manipura – right, swadhisthana – left, returning to mooladhara. The exhalation should finish as you reach mooladhara. This is one complete round.

Continue with this practice, rotating the ujjayi breath within the pingala-ida pathway. Experience the breath moving inside the psychic passage. Intensify your awareness of the movement of the breath through each curve and chakra point. Do not allow your awareness to be distracted by any thought or sound. Your awareness moves only with the ujjayi breath.

When beginning each round, retain the breath outside for a few seconds and hold your awareness at mooladhara. Then begin inhaling with slow ujjayi breathing. As you ascend the pingala passage, mentally repeat the name of each chakra as the breath crosses over: mooladhara – right, swadhisthana – left, manipura – right, anahata – left, vishuddhi – right, terminating at ajna. Retain the breath inside for a few seconds and hold the awareness at ajna. Then exhaling with the ujjayi breath, descend the ida passage, repeating the name of each chakra: ajna – left, vishuddhi – right, anahata – left, manipura – right, swadhisthana – left, returning to mooladhara.

Begin the next round, again retaining the breath outside for a few seconds with awareness at mooladhara. Then begin ascending pingala passage with inhalation, mentally repeating the names of the chakras.

Continue the practice with complete and unwavering awareness of the pingala-ida pathway. When the awareness is absolutely steady and one-pointed, the practice will become effortless.

Stage 7: Pingala-ida prana rotation

As this awareness of the breath and consciousness moving in the psychic passage continues, gradually become aware of prana. The prana or vital energy is moving within the psychic passages. This prana moves with the breath and the consciousness.

Become aware of these three forces, the prana, the breath and the consciousness, all moving together within the spiralling psychic passage.

This stage of the practice is similar to the previous stage, but there is no chakra repetition as you move through the psychic pathways. Bring the awareness to mooladhara and retain the breath outside for a few seconds. Be aware of mooladhara chakra. Then begin slow ujjayi inhalation and ascend the pingala passage. Be aware of each chakra point as you cross over it. Feel the prana, the breath and the consciousness spiralling upwards through the pingala passage and touching each chakra point. End the inhalation when you reach ajna.

Before exhaling, retain the breath inside for a few seconds with awareness at ajna. Then begin slow, steady exhalation with ujjayi. Feel the prana, the breath and the consciousness descending through the ida passage. Again be aware of each chakra point as you cross over it. Visualize the prana clearly and vividly, feel the breath and the consciousness descending through the curving ida psychic passage.

Try to perceive the prana as streams of white light. See this light flowing freely up the pingala passage and down the ida passage. Centre all your awareness on this movement of prana.

Experience the white light of prana flowing without resistance through the pingala and ida nadis. The prana has swept away all obstacles from the psychic passages. Intensify this awareness of the free flow of prana. With each round experience the prana building up inside the pingala-ida pathway.

Stage 8: Pingala-ida rotation of Soham

Let go of the awareness of prana now. Become aware of the ujjayi breath. Be aware of the slow rhythmic flow of the ujjayi breath. Bring your awareness closer to the breath and try to hear the subtle sound of the breath. Try to perceive the mantra *Soham*, which is inherent within the breath. There is no need to repeat the mantra, the sound is already going on there. You must simply become aware of it.

Exhale and bring your awareness to mooladhara. Retain the breath outside for a few seconds and concentrate on mooladhara. With ujjayi breathing, inhale and ascend the pingala passage. While inhaling listen to the sound of the mantra *So-o-o-o-o*. Be aware of each chakra point as the breath crosses it. End the inhalation as you reach ajna. Retain the breath inside for a few moments. Concentrate on ajna chakra. Then exhale with ujjayi breath, descending slowly through the ida passage. Listen to the mantra *Ham-m-m-m-m* within the exhaling breath. Be aware of each chakra point as the breath crosses it. The exhalation ends when you reach mooladhara. This is one round.

Continue with the practice. Retain the breath outside for a few seconds while concentrating on mooladhara. Then with the ujjayi inhalation again ascend through the pingala passage. Be aware of the mantra *So-o-o-o-o* within the inhalation. Be aware of the mantra *Ham-m-m-m-m* within the exhalation as you descend through the ida passage. Intensify the awareness of the *Soham* mantra ascending and descending the pingala and ida nadis. Experience the mantra touching each chakra point. Experience the breath moving in the psychic passage. Be aware of the *Soham* mantra within the breath.

Stage 9: Pingala-ida rotation of Hamso

In the next stage of this practice, the starting point of the breath and mantra awareness is changed. Instead of beginning at mooladhara, the focus of attention is at ajna. In this way the *Soham* mantra becomes *Hamso*. The rest of the practice remains the same.

Inhale and bring the awareness up to ajna chakra. Retain the breath inside for a few seconds, concentrating at ajna. Then exhale slowly with ujjayi breath and descend through the ida passage with the mantra *Ham-m-m-m-m*. Experience the mantra touching each chakra point as it crosses over. End the exhalation when you reach mooladhara. Retain the breath outside for a few seconds, concentrating on mooladhara chakra. Inhale with ujjayi breath and ascend the pingala passage with the mantra *So-o-o-o-o*. Be aware of the mantra *So* vibrating in each chakra point as it crosses over. This is one complete round.

Now begin the next round by retaining the breath inside for a few moments. Concentrate on ajna. Then exhale and descend through the ida passage with the mantra *So-o-o-o-o*. Continue with the practice in this way. Be aware of the *Hamso* mantra rotating through the pingala-ida pathway. Bring your awareness closer and closer to the breath. There should be awareness only of the mantra of the breath moving within the psychic pathways. Experience the mantra vibration becoming stronger and more intense with each round.

Stage 10: Ending the practice

Continue with the practice for a few moments more. Now get ready to end the practice. Leave awareness of the mantra in the psychic passage. Release khechari mudra and stop ujjayi. Bring the awareness to the natural spontaneous breath. Be aware of the slow, steady rhythm of the breath. Become aware of the physical body. Feel the meditation posture in which you are sitting. Become aware of your surroundings. Listen to any sounds within the external environment. Gradually externalize the mind completely. Inhale deeply and chant *Om* three times. Now slowly move the body and open your eyes.

Hari Om Tat Sat

Ajapa Dharana Ten

OPENING THE GRANTHIS

Granthis are the psychic knots or blocks in our personality where the energy and consciousness interact and manifest in a particular way. According to the yogic tradition, there are three granthis: (i) brahma granthi, (ii) vishnu granthi, and (iii) rudra granthi.

Brahma granthi is the first psychic knot. It is supposed to be the lowest knot covering the area of mooladhara and swadhisthana chakras. It is also known as the perineal knot.

Vishnu granthi is the second knot, which covers the area between manipura, anahata and vishuddhi chakras. It is also known as the navel knot.

Rudra granthi is the third knot, covering the areas of ajna and sahasrara chakras. It is also known as the forehead knot.

These three knots prevent the free flow of prana along sushumna nadi and therefore hamper the awakening of the chakras and prevent the arising of kundalini. It has been the experience of advanced practitioners in the higher techniques that certain spinal contractions can be experienced at these three points with the awakening of prana and sushumna. A tightening of the nadi, where the body adopts different postures such as bending backwards and losing the sense of balance, can occur because the block is being experienced in brahma, vishnu or rudra granthi at the time of pranic awakening.

Ajapa Dharana Ten
Brahma, Vishnu and Rudra Granthis

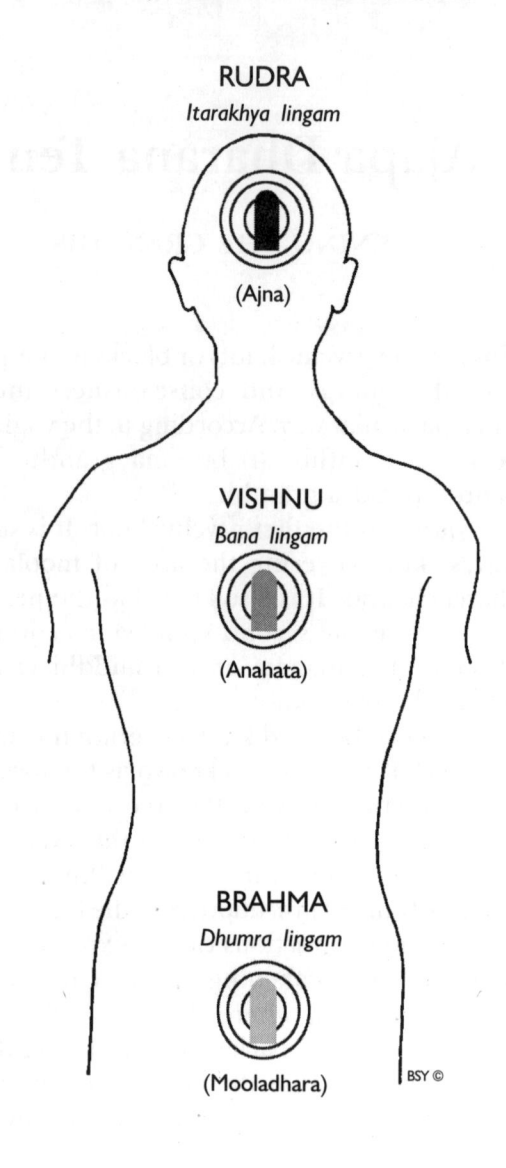

RUDRA
Itarakhya lingam

(Ajna)

VISHNU
Bana lingam

(Anahata)

BRAHMA
Dhumra lingam

(Mooladhara)

Knot of Brahma

Brahma granthi is the knot of Brahma, which is the manifest force of life and creation. In relation to the world in which we live or, according to tantra, the world of yonis or different life forms, brahma granthi controls the energies of mooladhara and swadhisthana. It is linked with the urge to procreate and with deep, instinctive knowledge, awareness and desire. It is known as the blockage of Brahma because it holds our consciousness at that level which is related to the desires of the physical dimension, to sensuality, procreation and the instinctive urge to survive which it cannot transcend.

Once this blockage is removed from the realm of consciousness and energy, instincts of the deep-rooted karmas, samskaras or desires, the other patterns of consciousness and energy are released. The kundalini or primal energy is thus able to rise beyond mooladhara and swadhisthana without being bogged down by the attractions to which our consciousness is hooked.

Knot of Vishnu

Vishnu granthi is the area where the personality and body are sustained. Manipura sustains the physical body in a practical way. The food we consume is converted to energy and distributed throughout the body. The process of converting matter into energy, a form which can be used for maintenance and growth of the body, is a function of manipura.

In the same way, anahata sustains the mental structure in the form of emotions which are intense expressions of subtle energy. The raw, unrefined and unadulterated energy can manifest as anger, hatred, jealousy or in the purified positive aspect as compassion, joy and so on. This energy is the force which sustains the manomaya kosha (mental body) and the pranamaya kosha (pranic body). Vishuddhi, the all-pervading space energy, sustains the vijnanamaya kosha (psychic body) and anandamaya kosha (spiritual body).

So, the sustaining aspect of all our human dimensions is governed by these three chakras which vitalize, feed, nurture and balance the subtle bodies. This is the function of vishnu granthi. Once the vishnu granthi blockage is removed we begin to draw energy to sustain ourselves from the universe and not from a localized centre. The energies of the body become harmonious with the energies of the cosmos. The interaction between the individual personality and the cosmos begins to happen naturally and spontaneously.

Knot of Rudra

Rudra granthi, or the knot of Rudra, governs ajna and sahasrara chakras and represents the transformation of an existing form, idea or concept into the universal aspect. Here there is a breaking away of the old, the ego awareness, the 'I' awareness, the mental awareness, the physical awareness, and an evolving of the sixth sense or the eye of intuition, the third eye.

This sixth sense and beyond is a state where the omniscient nature of consciousness is experienced, where the past, present and future become known. With that omniscient awareness in hand we move on to sahasrara, where the final merger of the individual soul or atma with the universal, cosmic soul, takes place.

Untying the knots

In this practice these three psychic knots which hamper the awakening of prana and kundalini and which limit the boundaries of our consciousness are systematically untied. This is done in the early stages of the practice by developing a conceptual understanding of the three blockages which take the form of attachment, firstly to the senses, secondly to the emotions, and lastly to manifestation.

In the following stages, the practice moves into a symbolic representation of the psychic knots in the form of three lingams: (i) *dhumra lingam* at mooladhara chakra, representing brahma granthi, (ii) *bana lingam* at anahata chakra, representing vishnu granthi, (iii) *itakhya lingam* at ajna chakra, representing rudra granthi.

By performing certain rotations of the breath, the prana and the mantra around these symbols, the three psychic knots which have their archetypal representation at the deeper levels of our consciousness are systematically rooted out and removed. This allows the aspirant to progress in higher sadhana and experience spiritual awakening without the incumbent obstacles and difficulties.

Technique
Stage 1: Preparation

Sit in a meditation posture with the spine erect and the head slightly back. Place the hands on the knees in chin or jnana mudra. Close the eyes. Relax the whole body. Be aware of the physical body and relax it completely while sitting in the meditation posture. You are sitting in a relaxed, comfortable, steady posture. Observe your mental and physical state. Feel the body and mind becoming steady and still. Concentrate on steadiness and stillness.

Stage 2: Awareness of brahma granthi

Focus your awareness at mooladhara. This centre is the highest level of animal evolution and the lowest level of human evolution. The consciousness in mooladhara is still bound firmly by the instincts to concepts of security. There is strong attachment to objects such as money, home, property, possessions, as it is believed that these things give security.

This attachment to the material world is the knot of Brahma, which ties us to the world of the senses. We cannot move beyond the sensory perceptions until this knot of attachment is untied. In order to untie this knot you must begin to consider who you are, what your true nature really is.

Realize "I am not this material body." Be aware of your motionless body and realize that "I am only a temporary inhabitant of this body. This body is not my real nature." Dwelling on this realization, reconsider your attachment to the external world and its material objects.

Stage 3: Awareness of vishnu granthi

Focus your awareness at anahata. Experience the vibration which emanates from the heart centre. Here the focus of awareness has shifted. Material objects no longer offer any security nor hold any special interest. There is still emotional attachment, however, which represents the knot of Vishnu. It is here that family, friends, teachers or guru form your emotional attachment. Your security depends on these relationships, which transcend all forms of material security.

Be aware of the bondage of emotional attachment, the tendency to live life according to your emotions and feelings, rather than in the light of the spiritual quest. Experience your own emotions and feelings. Realize "I am not these feelings." Be aware of your identity with the source of creation. Understand that all beings are manifestations of that same source of creation.

Move deeper into the experience of oneness which underlies the entire manifest world. Feel a oneness with all beings, a part of the universal creation. You are not a separate individual, but an integral part of the undivided whole. Develop the experience of cosmic unity, one without a second.

Stage 4: Awareness of rudra granthi

Focus your awareness at ajna chakra where the knot of rudra is located. The final break from the attachment to the manifest experiences of life takes place here. After untying this knot, one becomes established in the transcendental experience.

The word *rudra* comes from the root *rud* meaning 'to cry'. Whenever our link with the manifest world is broken, we cry. To become established in the unmanifest reality, the transcendental awareness itself, is to untie the knot of rudra granthi.

Be aware of your real nature, your higher self. Realize "I am not the body; I am not the mind. I am the atma, pure consciousness. All else is transitory and illusory."

Stage 5: Brahma/vishnu granthi rotation
a) Fold your tongue back into khechari mudra. Exhale and bring your awareness to mooladhara. Retain the breath outside for a few seconds and concentrate on brahma granthi, which is represented here by the smoky, dhumra lingam. Inhale slowly with ujjayi. Rotate the awareness and the breath three times in a clockwise direction around the smoky dhumra lingam.

As you rotate your awareness and breath around the smoky lingam, be aware of a third force, the prana, which is also rotating side by side with the breath. Experience the force of the breath and the prana, releasing and opening the brahma granthi.

Exhale slowly with ujjayi. Rotate the awareness and the breath three times in a counterclockwise direction around the smoky dhumra lingam. As you rotate, become aware of the pranic force moving with the breath in the form of light. Feel these three forces moving together in one powerful current, loosening and dissolving the knot of brahma. Practise this five times.

b) Inhale slowly with ujjayi and ascend the sushumna passage from mooladhara to anahata. Exhale with ujjayi and retain the breath outside for a few seconds. Concentrate on vishnu granthi, represented here by the red bana lingam which is symbolic of Vishnu. Inhale slowly with ujjayi and rotate the awareness around the red bana lingam three times in a clockwise direction. Be aware of the movement of prana together with the breath.

Exhale slowly with ujjayi Rotate your awareness three times in a counterclockwise direction around the red bana lingam. Side by side with the breath, see the prana moving in a stream of light. Feel the rotation of prana and breath loosening and opening the knot of Vishnu. Practise this five times.

Inhale and retain the breath for a few seconds. Concentrate on the red bana lingam. Then exhale and descend through the sushumna passage to mooladhara. This is one round. When you reach mooladhara immediately begin the next round. Retain the breath outside for a few seconds. Concentrate on brahma granthi which is represented by the smoky, dhumra lingam. Continue the brahma/vishnu granthi rotation until you begin to experience the opening of these psychic knots.

Stage 6: Vishnu/rudra granthi rotation

a) Exhale and bring your awareness to anahata. Retain the breath outside for a few seconds. Concentrate on the vishnu granthi, which is represented here by the red bana lingam.

Inhale with ujjayi and rotate the awareness around the red bana lingam in a clockwise direction three times. Experience the prana rotating with the breath.

Then exhale with ujjayi and rotate the awareness around the red bana lingam in a counterclockwise direction three times. Visualize the pranic force rotating together with the breath and opening the vishnu granthi. Practise this five times.

b) Inhale with ujjayi and raise the awareness through the sushumna passage from anahata to ajna. Exhale and retain the breath outside for a few seconds. Concentrate on the rudra granthi, which is symbolized here by the black itakhya lingam.

Inhale with ujjayi and rotate the awareness around the black itakhya lingam three times in a clockwise direction. Feel the prana moving with the breath, opening the knot. Then exhale with ujjayi and rotate the awareness around the black itakhya lingam three times in a counterclockwise direction. Visualize a stream of prana rotating with the breath and opening rudra granthi. Practise this five times. Now inhale with ujjayi and retain the breath for a few seconds. Concentrate on the black itakhya lingam and the opening of rudra granthi. Exhale with ujjayi and descend the sushumna passage from ajna to anahata. This is one round.

When you reach anahata immediately begin the next round. Retain the breath outside for a few seconds.

Concentrate on vishnu granthi, symbolized here by the red bana lingam. Continue the vishnu/rudra granthi rotation until you begin to experience the opening of these psychic knots.

Stage 7: Granthi rotation with Soham

a) Now leave awareness of the prana rotating with the breath and become aware of the *Soham* mantra. Exhale and bring your awareness to mooladhara. Retain the breath outside for a few seconds. Concentrate on the brahma granthi, symbolized here by the smoky dhumra lingam.

Inhale with ujjayi and rotate your awareness and breath around the smoky dhumra lingam three times in a clockwise direction with the mantra *So-o-o-o-o*, which is heard within the breath. It is one ujjayi breath and one *So* mantra which rotates three times around the lingam.

Exhale with ujjayi and rotate your awareness and breath around the smoky dhumra lingam three times in a clockwise direction with the mantra *Ham-m-m-m-m*. Feel the vibrations of the mantra and the breath purifying and loosening the brahma granthi. Practise this five to ten times.

b) Inhale with ujjayi through the sushumna passage from mooladhara to anahata. Exhale with ujjayi and retain the breath outside for a few seconds. Concentrate on the vishnu granthi, symbolized by the red bana lingam.

Inhale with ujjayi and rotate the awareness and the breath around the red bana lingam three times in a clockwise direction with the mantra *So-o-o-o-o*. Exhale with ujjayi and rotate your awareness and breath around the red bana lingam three times in a counter clockwise direction with the mantra *Ham-m-m-m-m*. Feel the vibration of the mantra and the breath purifying this area and opening the knot of Vishnu. Practise this five to ten times.

c) Inhale with ujjayi and ascend through the sushumna passage from anahata to ajna. Exhale with ujjayi and retain the breath outside for a few seconds. Concentrate on the rudra granthi, symbolized here by the black itakhya lingam.

Inhale with ujjayi and rotate the awareness and the breath around the black itakhya lingam three times in a clockwise direction with the mantra *So-o-o-o-o*. Then exhale with ujjayi and rotate the awareness and the breath around the black itakhya lingam three times in a counterclockwise direction with the mantra *Ham-m-m-m-m*. Feel the vibration of the mantra and the breath purifying and releasing the psychic knot. Practise five to ten times.

Inhale with ujjayi. Retain the breath inside for a few seconds. Concentrate on the black itakhya lingam and on the releasing of rudra granthi. Exhale with ujjayi and descend through the sushumna passage from ajna to mooladhara. This is one round. Immediately begin the next round. Continue this brahma/vishnu/rudra granthi rotation with *Soham* until you feel that the three psychic knots have been purified and opened.

Stage 8: Granthi rotation with Hamso

a) Inhale with ujjayi and take your awareness to mooladhara. Retain the breath inside for a few moments and concentrate on brahma granthi, symbolized by the smoky dhumra lingam.

Exhale with ujjayi. Rotate the awareness and the breath around the smoky dhumra lingam three times in a counterclockwise direction with the mantra *Ham-m-m-m*. Inhale with ujjayi, rotate the awareness and the breath around the smoky dhumra lingam three times in a clockwise direction with the mantra *So-o-o-o-o*. Feel the vibrations of the mantra and the breath releasing the brahma granthi. Do five to ten rounds.

b) Exhale with ujjayi. Retain the breath outside for a few seconds and concentrate on the smoky dhumra lingam. Inhale with ujjayi and ascend the sushumna passage from mooladhara to anahata. Retain the breath inside for a few moments. Concentrate on the vishnu granthi symbolized by the red bana lingam.

Exhale with ujjayi and rotate your awareness and breath around the red bana lingam three times in a counterclockwise direction with the mantra *Ham-m-m-m-m*. Inhale and rotate your awareness around the red bana lingam three times in a clockwise direction with the mantra *So-o-o-o-o*. Feel the vibration of the mantra and the breath opening the knot of Vishnu. Practise this five to ten times.

c) Exhale with ujjayi and retain the breath outside for a few moments. Concentrate on the red bana lingam and the opening of the vishnu granthi. Inhale with ujjayi and raise your awareness through the sushumna passage from anahata to ajna. Retain the breath inside and concentrate on rudra granthi, represented by the black itakhya lingam. Exhale with ujjayi and rotate the awareness and the breath around the black itakhya lingam three times in a counterclockwise direction with the mantra *Ham-m-m-m*. Inhale with ujjayi and rotate the awareness and the breath around the black itakhya lingam three times in a clockwise direction with the mantra *So-o-o-o-o*. Feel the vibrations of the mantra and the breath purifying and releasing the knot of Rudra. Practise this five to ten times. Exhale with ujjayi and descend through the sushumna passage from ajna to mooladhara. This is one round. Immediately begin the next round. Inhale with ujjayi and retain the breath at mooladhara for a few seconds. Concentrate on the brahma granthi, symbolized by the smoky dhumra lingam. Continue the brahma/vishnu/rudra granthi rotation with *Hamso* until you feel the three psychic knots have been purified and released by the breath and the mantra.

Stage 9: Ending the practice

Now prepare to end the practice. Withdraw your awareness from the granthis. Release the tongue lock and return to normal breathing. Become aware of the physical body and the meditation posture. Feel your body from head to toe. Be aware of the room in which you are sitting. Listen to the external sounds. Breathe in deeply and chant *Om* three times.

Hari Om Tat Sat

11

Trataka

Trataka is one of the most direct, simple and effective techniques for attaining concentration of mind. It can be practised by everyone and the benefits are enormous. The word *trataka* means 'steady gazing'. The practice of trataka involves gazing at a point or object without winking or blinking the eyes. It is a method of focusing the eyes, and in turn the mind, on one point to the exclusion of all else. The object can be either external, in which case the practice is called *bahir* trataka (outer gazing) or internal, in which case the practice is called *antar* trataka (inner gazing). Through this method all the attention and power of the mind is channelled into one continuous stream, allowing the latent potential to arise spontaneously.

The practice of trataka is used in one form or another by almost every religious and spiritual system. In Hinduism it is an integral part of the religious practice to sit in front of a picture or statue of the deity and concentrate upon it. Although this is regarded as a form of worship, it is actually a form of trataka, for the aim is to concentrate the mind on the external deity. From this practice the devotee obtains mental peace and a meditative state. Furthermore, the ability to create internal visualizations at will is developed.

In Christianity the same thing is done, although in a less obvious manner. In every church there are idols of Christ, candles and the symbolic cross. These objects act as focal points for trataka. In Tibetan Buddhism, trataka is often done on various deities, yantras and mandalas. Even Zen Buddhism utilizes trataka in the form of staring at a blank wall. So, the practice of trataka is universal and has been used throughout the ages as a method of transcending normal experience. It is very simple yet very powerful, and this is why it has been utilized by so many different systems as a means of spiritual upliftment.

Minimizing visual distraction
In the classical hatha yoga texts, trataka is described as one of the six shatkarma, or cleansing techniques. Here it acts as a stepping stone between the physically oriented and mentally oriented techniques which lead to higher awareness. In this sense trataka forms a bridge between hatha yoga and raja yoga. When you practise until the tears roll down then it is part of hatha yoga, but when you practise with inner visualization then it is part of raja yoga.

The eye is the most powerful indriya or sensory organ in this manifest world. The range of vision extends beyond all kinds of physical dimensions. One can see for miles and miles. One can perceive what is happening many miles away without actually being there. It is the vision that is focused in the practice of trataka. The visual distractions which affect our concentration and awareness must be minimized, and this can be achieved through the practice of trataka, steady gazing.

Through the practice of trataka one can develop the ability to focus the mind at any time. This is necessary in the higher practices of yoga. There is a very deep meaning behind the practice of trataka also. Patanjali's *Yoga Sutras* declare that even in the highest state of samadhi or meditation, there are certain impressions, ideas or experiences which remain in our consciousness. Those ideas or impressions can also be experienced in the state of samadhi, and thus they disturb the concentration of mind. These deep impressions or ideas are known as *pratyaya*.

When the mind has not been taught to concentrate, and meditation has been practised only superficially, then in deep meditation states the pull or attraction of these pratyaya is very powerful, because there is no means of balance. Therefore, the ability that is gained through trataka becomes useful at that moment. When the visual distraction is stopped, we are able to experience a frame of mind that is quiet like a still pond or lake. The different forms of trataka also help to channel or focus the pranic energies.

Physiological and mental functions
Physiologically trataka relieves eye ailments such as eyestrain and headache, myopia, astigmatism and even early stages of cataract. The eyes become clear and bright, able to see the reality beyond appearances. Trataka benefits not only the eyes, but a whole range of physiological and mental functions. It is therapeutic in depression, insomnia, allergy, anxiety and postural problems. Its most important effect is on ajna chakra and the brain. Trataka unlocks the inherent energy of the mind and channelizes it in the dormant areas of consciousness. Further results of one-pointedness of mind are strong willpower, improved memory and concentration.

Trataka is a process of concentrating the mind and curbing its oscillating tendencies. The purpose is to make the mind completely one-pointed and to arouse inner vision. One-pointed concentration of mind is called *ekagrata*. There are numerous distractions which obstruct ekagrata. In fact, distraction only occurs when the senses are tuned to the external world, which means an energy leakage is occurring. Association and identification through the eyes are major contributing factors to this leakage.

Furthermore, the eyes constantly move either in large movements – saccades, or tremors – nystagmus. Even when the eyes are focused on an external object, the view perceived is always fluctuating because of these spontaneous movements. When the same object is constantly seen, the brain becomes accustomed or habituated and soon stops registering that object. Habituation coincides with an increase of alpha waves indicating diminished visual attention to the external world. When alpha waves are produced, particular areas of the brain cease functioning.

Vision depends not only on the eyes, but upon the entire optic tracts. The lens of the eye is only the medium of external visual perception. Via the lens, an image is projected onto the retina. This is a stimulus which excites the retina to fire impulses back to the visual cortex of the brain where an inner image is mapped out.

If you close your eyes and gently push and release them, you will also see flashes of light, not because light is entering the eyes, but because the optic nerve has been stimulated. When the image of an external object is stablilized on the retina, after a period of time, perception of the image will completely disappear and a suspension of the mental processes will occur.

In fact, if there is absolutely no visual stimulus, for example, if you sit in a pitch dark room or cover the eyes with opaque cups, then after some time the mind will turn off just as in sleep. Therefore, during the practice of trataka it is essential to maintain inner awareness so that when the mind is suspended all that remains is the awareness. This is not only in relation to trataka but in any practice of concentration. When the awareness is restricted to one unchanging sensory stimulus, like touch or sound, the mind is turned off. Complete absorption in a single perception induces withdrawal of contact with the external world.

In trataka, the result is a blanking out of visual perception and in the wake of this suspension, the central nervous system begins to function in isolation. This experience is known by yogis as sushumna awakening. When the brain is isolated from the sense modalities and the associated mental processes, ideas, memories, etc. triggered by these thought impressions, the spiritual consciousness emerges. The higher mind, liberated from time and space, is experienced. Sushumna is awakened.

Modes of practice

Trataka consists of five different modes of practice:
1. *Bahya drishti* (outer trataka)
2. *Bahya-antar drishti* (outer and inner trataka combined)
3. *Antar drishti* (inner trataka)
4. *Shoonya drishti* (gazing into the void)
5. *Nirantra drishti* (continuous gazing)

In outer trataka, or external gazing, the eyes remain open and focused on any steady object. Techniques of outer trataka include *agochari mudra* (nose tip gazing) and *shambhavi mudra* (eyebrow centre gazing). This form of trataka can also be practised by focusing the gaze on objects such as the flame of a candle, a dot, the rising sun and so on. By steadying the eyes in this manner you are automatically concentrating the mind.

When outer and inner trataka are combined, first you gaze at an external point or object for some time, then you close your eyes and gaze at the after image or inner reflection of the same object. Any object can be used for concentration. A luminous object such as a candle flame is often used by beginners because the brightness attracts the eyes and holds the gaze. It also imprints a clear image on the retina of the eyes which can be seen clearly when the eyes are closed. This inner image becomes the object of concentration during antar trataka. If it is bright and clear enough, it will hold your inner gaze so that you are aware of nothing else. This leads to concentration of the mental forces.

The method of outer and inner trataka combined is useful for people who are not able to develop an inner image at will, without an external counterpart. Those who can create a steady, distinct inner image without the assistance of an outer object can practise inner trataka alone. In inner trataka the awareness is focused only on an internal image. Therefore, this practice is more difficult than outer trataka alone or outer and inner trataka combined.

Inner trataka is most conducive to concentration because there is no external sensory contact, as there is with the other two forms. You should practise inner trataka when you are able to create a clear inner image and when your mind is reasonably tranquil and steady. If you have a vague inner image or no image and you attempt the practice of inner trataka, then you will either fall asleep or lose your awareness in the usual patterns of thought play.

Gazing into the void should be practised after internal trataka has been mastered. This practice is also known as shoonya drishti. *Shoonya* means the 'void' or 'formless state'. It is not chidakasha. In shoonya drishti there is no object of awareness. This form of trataka is to be done with the eyes open, gazing at nothingness. It takes a long time to get into this state. Your eyes are open, but you are unable to see anything because the mind has become introverted. After some time the eyes become dim. They are half open and you can see nothing. Continuous gazing is looking at any point without blinking the eyes for hours together. It is what Ramana Maharishi used to practise, sitting for ten, eleven or twelve hours a day, without blinking his eyes.

Objects of awareness

The object should be something which naturally attracts your attention and holds your gaze. You must decide what is most suitable for yourself. To give you an idea, we have given a list of commonly used objects: candle flame, shivalingam, cross, nose tip, Om symbol, eyebrow centre, sky, another person's eyes, water, yin yang symbol, ishta devata, yantra or mandala, flower, one's own shadow, black dot, darkness, rising sun, reflection in a mirror, moon, crystal, star, shoonya, reflection of sun or moon in clear water.

You can choose anything as your object, but once you decide, try not to change because this will decrease the effectiveness of your practice. If you develop the awareness of one particular object and then suddenly change, you must start from the beginning again to assimilate the new object. The mind has to mould itself around a particular object so that it is automatically drawn towards it. This takes time, so choose your object carefully and then stick to it.

Multi-purpose practice

Trataka develops the power of concentration as the conscious energy is directed towards one point of attention. The practice automatically leads to meditation. Even beginners will have experiences after a short period of practice. There are also many methods of trataka by which different purposes can be achieved. If you want to practise trataka for the purpose of telepathic communication, there is one method. If you want to practise in order to influence the minds of others, there is another method. If you wish to practise in order to improve your eyesight, then the method will differ again. In order to obtain different results, different methods are followed.

There is a particular practice called chhaya upasana (shadow gazing), concerned with reading the aura and obtaining knowledge of the exact time of death. Any imminent danger can be foretold. Trataka is the main component of this practice. Trataka also awakens the faculties of clairvoyance, telepathy and telekinesis. A person can be summoned by using the method of trataka on the psychic eye. The psychic language which is spoken by the eyes compels the other person to come. There are certain forms of trataka used to detect the whereabouts of lost or stolen articles, and to find the thief. Healing can also be done through trataka.

Guidelines

Trataka can be done at any time, but it is more effective when practised on an empty stomach. The most suitable time is between four and six in the morning. It should be done in absolute silence, without a fan. If you want to delve deeper into the mind, trataka should be practised late at night before going to bed and before japa or meditation. If there is an uncontrollable flow of thoughts during the practice of trataka, mantra japa can be added at the same time.

Trataka is a heat producing practice. Therefore, it should be done after bathing, when you are feeling fresh. If you practise surya namaskara before trataka, the body becomes heated and at the time of trataka you will feel discomfort.

Try to keep your body cool before the practice of trataka. If you go into meditation after the practice of trataka, the body will again become cool and refreshed.

If you practise trataka on the rising sun, you must never look at the sun directly. This is harmful to the eyes and may cause cataracts. Gaze upon the sun's reflection on clear water. When the reflection is disturbed by heavy wind or storm, then you should not practise this form of trataka.

Always practise trataka on a steady object, never on a moving object. Be careful if practising trataka on metal because if the sunrays are reflected by the metal, there may be a reaction on the eyes.

Trataka must be practised in the steadiest possible posture. Although it can be done sitting in a chair or in sukhasana, it is far better to practise it in siddhasana or padmasana. Once the practice begins there should be absolutely no movement of the body.

In both the external and internal forms of trataka, the eyes should not blink or move in any way. Stillness of the eyeballs and eyelids is essential in order to attain clarity of the inner image. If the eyes feel strained, imagine that you are breathing through the mid-eyebrow centre to and from ajna chakra. When you close your eyes and gaze at the counter-image, continue the same awareness of the breath, breathing to and from the image through the eyebrow centre. The mind should be focused on the object or image and nothing else. If the mind wanders or starts to think about other things, you should bring it back to the object of concentration.

If you are using a candle flame, there should be no other light. If you are using a black dot or any other object, there should be good light. Crystal gazing is done in dim light. Trataka on a candle flame must be practised in a room without a fan, where there is no breeze. The candle flame should not flicker. The candle should be placed on a firm stand at eye level, about an arm's length away. Trataka on any object should be practised without eyeglasses or contact lenses. If you have defective vision, position the object so that you do not see double and the object is not blurred.

Trataka
Sri Yantra

Trataka One

BAYHA DRISHTI

Technique 1: Agochari mudra or Nasikagra drishti
Sit in a comfortable meditation pose. Relax the whole body and close the eyes. Feel the body becoming still and steady. Now open the eyes and focus on the nose tip. Do not strain the eyes, but try to hold both eyes on the tip of the nose. If the attention is truly directed inwards to the tip of the nose then you should see a double outline of the nose. These two outlines become one and solid where they merge with each other. The two outlines cross each other at the nose tip to form a V-shaped point.
If you do not see this V-shape then it means that your eyes are not both fixed on the nose tip. In this case it is best to hold one finger in front of your eyes at a distance of about 45 cms. Focus both eyes on the finger. Slowly move the finger nearer and nearer to the nose, all the time keeping the eyes fixed on the finger. Continue to bring the finger closer to the nose until it touches the nose tip. The eyes should still be focused on the finger. Then merely transfer the attention of the eyes to the nose tip and lower the hand. Your eyes will now be focused on the correct point.
At first you will find that you can hold your attention on the nose tip for only a few seconds, but with practise you will be able to extend this time. When you feel the eyes becoming uncomfortable or if they begin to feel strain,

then release the position of the eyes for a few seconds. When the eyes are rested then again open them and repeat the practice. In this manner you will gradually increase the period of time of actual nose tip gazing as the eyes become more accustomed to the practice. Under no circumstances should you strain the eyes. Proficiency in the practice should be developed over a period of weeks.

When you can gaze at the nose tip for a minute or so without the slightest difficulty, then become aware of your breath as well as your nose tip. Feel the breath moving in and out through the nose. At the same time you will hear a slight sound as the breath moves through the nostrils. Become aware of this sound also.

Try to be completely absorbed in the practice to the exclusion of all other thoughts. Maintain awareness of the nose tip, movement of the breath and the accompanying sound. Continue in this manner for some time.

Technique 2: Shambhavi mudra

Sit in a comfortable meditation posture. Place the hands on the knees and close the eyes. Relax the whole body. The body should be steady and still. Now open your eyes and try to focus both eyes at the eyebrow centre. It is difficult to actually fix the eyes on the eyebrow centre as it is out of the normal field of vision. However, you must direct your eyes inwards and upwards so that they point as much as possible in the direction of the eyebrow centre. If this is done correctly, you will see two curved images of the eyebrows, which merge with each other. They will meet at a point at the top of the nose and form a solid V-shaped point.

You have to be aware of the V-shaped point. This is the approximate location of the eyebrow centre. If you do not see this V formation, then this is an indication that your eyes are not converging as they should. In this case place one finger at the nose tip. Focus both eyes on the fingertip. Then slowly move the finger upwards, keeping the eyes focused on the fingertip. If this is done correctly, the eyes will be drawn upward to focus on the eyebrow centre.

Be sure not to strain the eyes. If you experience any discomfort, relax the eyes for a few seconds. When the eyes are rested open them again and focus on the eyebrow centre. Continue with the practice in this way. In this manner you will slowly increase the duration of eyebrow centre gazing. Continue with the practice for some time.

Technique 3: Trataka on a candle flame

Place the candle in the correct position in front of you and light it. Sit in a comfortable meditation posture. Close your eyes. Concentrate on steadiness of the body. Feel your entire body becoming steady and motionless like a statue. Be aware of absolute steadiness and stillness. Make a resolve not to move your body during the practice. If you move even slightly, your concentration will be broken.

Open your eyes and gaze at the candle flame. Focus your gaze at the tip of the wick, without straining. Your eyes should be completely relaxed. If you try too hard to focus on the flame, there will be more tension and movement of the eyes. Consciously relax the eye muscles. Try not to blink or move the eyes in any way. Keep your focus steady as you gaze at the wick of the candle flame.

Let your whole awareness be on the candle flame and wick. If thoughts come, let them. Be aware of them and then gently bring your whole awareness back to the candle flame. See the candle flame clearly. Though your vision is focused on one point you can see the whole candle. Be aware of the shape and colours of the candle flame. Allow your attention to be completely absorbed in the flame. There is only the flame.

If you need to close your eyes, then do so and rest them for a few moments. During this practice tears should not fall, so close your eyes before you feel this will happen. When they are rested, then again open them and focus at the tip of the wick. Continue with the practice in this way.

Technique 4: Trataka with breath awareness

While gazing at the candle flame become aware of your breath. Begin to practise ujjayi pranayama. Let the tongue slip back into khechari mudra. Now imagine that you are drawing your breath from the candle flame to the eyebrow centre and back to ajna chakra at the centre of the head. When you exhale, imagine that the breath flows from ajna chakra, pierces the eyebrow centre and returns to the candle flame. You must split your awareness so that you are simultaneously aware of the candle flame and the movement of the breath. The eyes should remain steady and relaxed throughout.

Continue in this way, breathing in and out while you feel or imagine the breath moving backwards and forwards from the candle flame through the eyebrow centre to ajna chakra and back again to the flame. Be aware of the candle flame, the breath and the subtle sound of the ujjayi breath. Intensify your awareness of this pathway between the candle flame and ajna chakra. Feel you are connecting these points, the flame, bhrumadhya and ajna chakra. Be aware of every breath. Continue in this way for some time.

Technique 5: Trataka on the sun and moon

When practising trataka on the sun or moon you should never gaze directly at them. The sun's rays can damage the retina and cause cataracts in the eyes. Practising trataka directly on the moon can create mental imbalance and a person can become moonstruck. So, anyone suffering from any kind of mental disturbances or depression should not do this practice. Trataka on the sun and moon are very powerful practices as they have a direct effect on the ida and pingala energies in the body and mind, so care should be taken if this practice is undertaken. The sun increases the flow of energy in the pingala nadi, increasing dynamism, while the moon affects ida nadi, increasing the mental force. Those wishing to increase their dynamic, vital powers should do trataka on the rising or setting sun. Those wishing to delve into and uncover their mental potential should practise trataka on the rising or setting moon.

When doing trataka on the sun or moon a pea-sized circular hole should be cut in the centre of a large square of dark coloured cloth. This cloth should be attached to a window facing the sun or moon or to a separate frame that can be used outside. Trataka should then be done by gazing at the sun or moon through this hole.

The practice is done in the same way as the previous practices, gazing both at the external image and the internal image. Try to be aware of the finer and more subtle effects the sun or moon have upon the prana, the body and mind. Be aware of any changes in the flow of energy/prana and any mood changes. Allow the awareness to become deeper and more subtle.

Technique 6: Trataka on a moving scene (while travelling)

This practice can be done while travelling by train or car. Sit beside the open window and relax the whole body. Be aware of the whole body and if there is tension or tightness in any part, try to consciously let go of it. Bring the awareness to the natural breath for a few moments. Feel the steady, rhythmic flow of the breath. Let the sounds of the passengers and the noise of the train fade into the background.

Now, with the eyes open, gaze at the distant scene. This may be difficult at first as the eyes will automatically follow the moving scenery. Take a few moments to allow the eyes to settle on one point. Then hold the eyes steady, without straining. The eyelids should not flicker and the eyeballs should not move even though the scene is constantly changing. Keep the eyes focused on the middle of the scene in front of you.

There should be no thoughts or emotions as you gaze at the distant scene. The mind should be completely steady and devoid of all emotions. You are aware of the continuously changing scenes but you are not judging them or becoming involved in them. Your eyes are focused steadily on one point.

Concentrate completely on the centre of the distant scene. If the eyes become tired then close them for a few moments and relax them completely. While the eyes are closed, bring the awareness to the eyebrow centre. Do not allow yourself to become distracted by the sounds and movements around you. Bring the awareness continually back to the practice. When the eyes feel rested, again open them and gaze at the distant scene.

Continue with the practice in this way. When you finish the practice, close your eyes and relax them completely.

Practice note: This practice should not be done while driving.

Technique 7: Trataka on a needle

When doing trataka on a needle, the needle should be hung on a plain coloured wall at eye level. There should be nothing else hanging on the wall as this will distract the attention during the practice.

Sit down comfortably in any meditation posture. Place the hands on the knees or on the lap. Close your eyes. Become aware of the whole body and make sure that there is no tension in any part.

Bring the awareness to the breath in the nostrils. Be aware of each inhalation and each exhalation. Do not change the breath in any way, just be aware of the natural flow of the breath.

Now open your eyes and focus your gaze at the eye of the needle. See the needle clearly but keep the eyes relaxed. You do not have to make a great effort to gaze at the needle; this will only create tension which will distort your vision. Just gaze in a natural, relaxed way at the needle hanging on the wall.

See the needle clearly. Be aware of the size of its eye, the brightness of the needle as it reflects back the light, the length of the needle. Concentrate fully on the needle. If thoughts come, do not become involved in them. Put them aside and bring your attention back to the needle. Continue in this way with the practice. Make sure that your visual perception of the needle is clear at all times. If the image of the needle becomes blurred, the thoughts begin to wander and concentration will become dissipated. So check that the needle is clearly focused throughout the practice. Your awareness is focused at the eye of the needle but you can see the whole needle. Continue with the practice for as long as is comfortable. Then close the eyes and relax them completely.

Technique 8: Trataka on a current of water
To practise trataka on moving water sit on a river bank or raised ground near the river. You should be able to see the flow of water for a long distance. Sit in a steady comfortable posture so that the body will not move in any way during the practice. Always remain fully alert when you practise trataka on water. Fix your gaze on one point and practise trataka. Your gaze should remain steady. Be aware of the continuous flowing movement of the water, but your gaze should not move along the ripples. If this happens just gently bring the gaze back to the central point of concentration. There should be complete one-pointed awareness. Continue to gaze at the current of water for as long as you can without straining the eyes. Then close the eyes and relax them completely. Bring the awareness to the eyebrow centre. Become aware of the effects of the practice on different levels, from the physical to the more subtle.

Hari Om Tat Sat

Trataka Two

BAHYA-ANTAR DRISHTI

Technique 1: Trataka on a candle flame
Sit in any comfortable meditation posture. Place the hands on the knees and close the eyes. Relax the body completely. Move your awareness through the body and make sure there is no tension or tightness in any part. Feel the whole body becoming steady and still.
Now become aware of the position of the legs. Feel that the legs are comfortable and the hands are relaxed. Become aware of the hands and arms. Feel that the arms are relaxed and still. Become aware of the whole back. The back is straight but without tension. Bring your awareness to the front of the body. Check that there is no tension in the abdomen or chest. Become aware of the head. There should be no tension between the eyebrows or around the jaw.
Next become aware of the whole body together. Be aware of every part of the body. Feel the stillness of the body. There is no movement in any part of the body. The whole body is comfortable and still. Intensify this awareness of stillness throughout the whole body. Experience stillness and quietness.
Now open the eyes and gaze intently at the candle flame. Try not to wink or blink. Continue gazing steadily for three minutes. Then close your eyes and try to visualize the after image of the candle flame at the eyebrow centre.

Gaze at the inner image in the same way that you gazed at the external candle flame. Here is a combination of trataka on the external object and the internal after-image.

See somewhere in chidakasha a tiny, luminous, coloured dot. Gaze steadily at the dot. It is similar to a small grain of wheat, rice or barley in shape, but the colour changes from moment to moment. The colour depends on how long you have been gazing at the candle flame. After one minute the colour will be black, white or dull brown. After about five minutes, the colour of the dot will be bright red.

If the image is not clear at first, just be aware of whatever you can see. Keep the eye muscles relaxed throughout the practice; this helps you to get a clear inner image. If the image is moving, follow it and gently bring it back to the eyebrow centre. Take a few moments to steady the image. If the image fades or disappears, do not worry; just try to recreate it again. The image will become clear and vivid as the eyes become relaxed and steady.

From moment to moment the dot becomes dimmer and suddenly disappears. All this happens within a few seconds, but you should be careful not to open the eyes. Even if the psychic point disappears keep your eyes closed. Again try to assemble the psychic awareness and recollect the psychic point. In a few seconds the internal object will reappear, and when it reappears it will have a different colour altogether.

Continue gazing at the internal point with the help of your inner perception, your inner vision, your inner eye. It will grow fainter and fainter and still fainter, and then it will disappear. Do not open your eyes. Assemble your awareness again. Recollect the internal point and see it come once more before your vision.

Thus this psychic point appears, disappears, reappears, disappears, again reappears, becomes dim, disappears, reappears, again grows dimmer and dimmer. Ultimately it becomes absolutely black and merges with the psychic background.

In the beginning one round will only take about five minutes, but after some practice one single round will take half an hour: three minutes gazing at the external candle flame and twenty-seven minutes visualizing the psychic point which is appearing and disappearing.

Eleven rounds of trataka make one dharana, which means that the mental image becomes absolutely clear. When you think of an object and see the object clearly in your mind, it is called dharana. When you are only thinking about it and not seeing it, then it is called *kalpana*, which is really a lower state of imagination. Dharana is a higher state of kalpana, imagination with a clearcut concept.

After practising eleven rounds of trataka on the candle flame in front of you, you will see every detail of the candle mentally: the colour, the wick and the light. You can see that the wax is melting and dripping down. That should be the intensity of your psychic connection. When this state has arrived then dharana begins.

Technique 2: Trataka on a black dot

Trataka on a dot can be done in two ways. The black dot can be drawn on a white background and hung on a plain wall at eye level. The second way to prepare the dot is to take a betel leaf, prepare collyrium with the help of castor oil and make a black dot on the betel leaf. Then fix this to cardboard. When practising trataka on a dot there should be good light so that you can see the dot clearly without straining the eyes, and the light should be behind you.

The size of the dot used for this practice differs for each individual. If you are unable to see the dot, then you should have a bigger dot. But if you cannot focus the eyes on a bigger dot, then you should have a smaller dot. You must decide on the size of the dot, according to your eyesight. The important thing is not to strain the eyes. If you see two dots, it means you should use either a smaller or a larger dot. The same principle applies to concentration on the picture of your guru, Shiva, Krishna, a yantra, mandala, Om or anything that is printed. This is to avoid adversely affecting the retina during the three minutes of external gazing.

So, a dot of the proper size should be placed at the proper distance according to the eyesight capacity. After gazing upon it for three minutes, close your eyes and look within. You will find a shadow with the same outline. If it is a cross then you will see a cross-like shadow. If it is an Om symbol then an Om-like shadow will appear. If it is a crescent moon then a crescent shadow will appear. If it is a human figure then you will see a human shadow.

Concentrate on this shadow in the same manner as in trataka on the candle flame. The effect on the retina is different, however, because you are not seeing a luminous object. When you gaze at the shadow of the black dot it may be black, blue, grey, or any colour. It will disappear, reappear, disappear, etc. When you can no longer see it then you will have to start again. Eleven such rounds make one dharana.

Technique 3: Trataka on a flower

Any flower may be used for this practice. It is best if the colour is deep and strong. If it is a red rose, then trataka is performed in a bright place. If the flower is white, yellow or pink, then take a black or dark green cloth about two feet wide and three feet long. Pin the flower to the centre of this cloth. Trataka should then be practised in a dimly lit place.

Sit in a meditation posture with the spine upright and straight. Check that the head is straight. Place the hands on the knees or on the lap. Close your eyes. Be aware of the entire body. Let go of all internal tensions, whether muscular, mental or emotional. Be aware of the whole body, from the top of the head to the soles of the feet. Feel the body becoming still and steady like a statue. Be aware of complete stillness.

Now open the eyes and gaze at the flower. Focus your

gaze at the very centre of the flower. Let your eyes become steady and your focus clear. See the flower clearly. Then become aware of each and every petal of the flower. Be aware of the soft, velvety texture of the petals. Become aware of the vibrant, glowing colour of the flower. Hold your focus steady and be completely aware of the flower. Let your awareness merge with the flower as you take in each and every detail. Gaze at the flower until you cannot keep the eyes open any longer. Then close them.

Bring the awareness to the eyebrow centre and become aware of the after image of the flower. At first it will just appear as a circle of colour and will be the opposite colour of the real flower. Concentrate on this counter image in a relaxed manner. There should be no tension or great effort made to make the image clearer. This will happen as the eyes become steady and relaxed.

As in the previous practices the counter-image will disappear and reappear several times. Each time the image disappears keep the attention steady at the eyebrow centre and in a few moments the image will reappear. Continue to gaze at the image. With practice the counter-image will become more vivid and will appear more and more like the external flower.

When the image finally disappears, again open the eyes and begin to gaze at the external flower with complete concentration. Continue in this way with the practice. When you finish the practice, rub the palms of the hands together and practise palming.

Technique 4: Trataka on a chosen deity

For this practice have a small picture of your chosen deity. Then take a sheet of black paper, approximately one foot square and from the centre of this sheet cut a circle two inches in diameter. Fix the picture of the deity to the back of this paper in such a way that only the face is seen. The picture should be placed at eye level, approximately one arm's length from the eyes.

Before beginning, practise kaya sthairyam for some time, until the body becomes completely still and steady. Then open the eyes and gaze at the picture of the deity. The eyes should not blink or flicker in any way. While you are gazing at the picture of the deity, try to hold your vision within the circle. Do not let your attention wander from the image of the deity. Gaze intently at the image as if you were looking for something. Your gaze should be steady but without strain. At the same time you should gaze with a purpose.

Keep the eyes open for as long as possible. Then close your eyes and look at the counter-image at the eyebrow centre. As in the previous practice allow the image to disappear and reappear as you continue to hold your awareness at the eyebrow centre. When the image finally disappears, open the eyes and gaze at the outer image.

Try to be aware of nothing but the image of the deity. As you gaze at the image let your awareness become deeper and deeper. Try to perceive the deeper meaning portrayed by the deity. Keep your awareness steady and one-pointed as you gaze at both the external and internal image. Become completely absorbed in the image. Continue with the practice.

Technique 5: Trataka on a yantra

Select a suitable yantra, for example, Sri Yantra. Place the yantra on a stand so that it is upright and at eye level. You should be able to see the entire diagram clearly without any strain to the eyes. The yantra should be drawn in black and white or on a copper plate in the beginning. Later on you may use yantras in colour.

Close your eyes for a few minutes and concentrate on total steadiness and stillness of the body. When you have achieved this state open your eyes and gaze at the very centre point of the yantra. In Sri Yantra the centre point is inside the innermost tiny triangle.

If you look at the diagram closely, you can see the

innermost inverted triangle. Inside that triangle is a tiny dot. Concentrate on that point for three to five minutes, then close the eyes and try to see the dot internally. Do not try to reconstruct the whole yantra. When the vision fades resume external gazing.

After a week or so, when you are able to see the dot clearly, then practise gazing at the innermost upright triangle around the dot. Gaze steadily at the triangle for five minutes and then close your eyes. Try to see the innermost triangle mentally.

When you have perfected the vision of the innermost triangle, see the next triangle surrounding it. Surrounding the innermost triangle, there are five upward and four downward, symmetrical triangles. Now you should see only the innermost triangle and the inverted triangle surrounding it. Concentrate on the two triangles for five minutes. Then close your eyes and try to see them clearly from within.

When you have mastered this practice, concentrate on the first three inverted triangles, and week by week, add one more triangle until you are able to see all the inverted triangles clearly at one time, externally and internally.

Then proceed to the upright triangles. Develop the vision of these triangles, one by one, until you can see them all clearly at one time, externally as well as internally.

Then begin combining one upright and one inverted triangle, two upright and two inverted triangles. Week by week add one or two triangles until you are able to see the entire inner diagram at a glance, externally and internally. Gradually add the circle, lotus petals and bhupura in the same way, until finally you are able to see the entire diagram at one time. When you close your eyes you should also be able to mentally reconstruct the entire yantra effortlessly.

At this point you can begin to practise with yantras and mandalas in colour.

Technique 6: Trataka on a three-dimensional form

Whenever you practise trataka on objects with a three-dimensional form, you must be particularly aware of the dimensions. Here it is not only awareness of the object, but awareness of the dimensions which is important. In the previous practice also, when you close your eyes and the psychic counterpoint appears in your consciousness, you should become aware of the dimensions which this object has. If it has no dimensions, you should create them.

There are two types of dharana: (i) dharana on an object without dimension, and (ii) dharana on an object with dimension.

With this second type of dharana, dhyana begins. Eleven rounds of trataka on an object with dimensions makes one dhyana. When dharana becomes steady in the case of trataka on a candle flame, it can lead to dhyana. Then the candle flame will appear with dimensions.

There are people who do not dream in three dimensions, but there are also people who see dreams and visions in three dimensions as clearly as they would see the external reality. That is because their psyche is specially developed. With this second type of dharana on an object with dimensions, dhyana begins, because there is no difference between what is seen internally in dhyana and what is seen in external life. If you see an object in dhyana, it is as real to you as it would be in actual life because of the three-dimensional awareness. In this practice that vivid awareness has to be developed.

When doing this practice choose a pleasant object and concentrate on that object. You may have chosen a dog, for example. Do not keep your mind totally absorbed in the dog, but try to relate it to relevant objects and ideas which are connected with the dog. Always, however, keep the dog as your central theme. Do not let your mind wander off onto a completely irrelevant line of thought. Think of the shape of the dog. Think of the different types of dogs. Bring your mind back to your central object, the dog. Think of the food the dog eats. Think of the close relationship that exists between dog and man. Return to the central object. Continue in this way, bringing in as many related topics as possible. Do not let your mind think of anything that is unrelated.

Different objects can be chosen when you have exhausted the exploration of one object. This is an excellent way of developing the power to control ideas and thoughts at will. It is an invaluable method of training the mind to follow a fixed path of association, instead of jumping from one subject to a totally unrelated topic. It is useful for training the mind for meditation, as well as everyday activity.

Technique 7: Trataka on an external scene

This practice is useful for developing a deeper awareness of your surroundings. It helps to improve your perception, observation, inner visualization and memory. It can be practised in any surroundings and in almost any situation. In this practice try to observe every detail within your full field of vision, while holding the gaze steadily on one central point. Then close your eyes and try to recreate the same scene within. The internal image must become as clear and as detailed as the external scene. When beginning the practice it is easier to choose a place where there are not too many objects to be observed. When you can visualize the simpler scenes clearly and vividly then choose a place with a greater variety.

Make sure the body is completely at ease during the practice. Your gaze should be steady and your awareness should move through each object in the scene in front of you. Try to observe as much detail as possible; see the colour, shape and texture of every object. When you feel you have taken in the whole scene then close your eyes. Try to recreate the scene within. Keep your awareness at the eyebrow centre and let the image build up for you as it did when you looked at it externally. You must try to visualize the whole scene in its three-dimensional form.

When the image fades then again open the eyes. Gaze steadily at the image again and try to observe even finer and more subtle details of the scene. Continue in this way for some time.

A variation of this practice is looking at a scene which has a central figure. Centre your gaze on the central form and study the whole scene for some time. Then close the eyes and visualize the same scene internally. Try to see a clear inner picture. Then progressively erase the background from the scene. For example, remove the sky, then remove the trees in the background, then progressively remove what surrounds the central theme of the scene. Eventually you should only picture the central object or theme, perhaps a cow or a man. Keep your awareness on this object for a short time. Then start progressively to build up the picture in the reverse order to which you broke it down previously. Eventually you should see the whole scene again.

Technique 8: Trataka on one's shadow

This practice is known as *chhaya upasana*, 'concentration on one's shadow'. Stand with the sun at your back. Open your eyes and gaze at your shadow cast in front of you on the ground. Focus your gaze at the point of vishuddhi chakra on the shadow. There is no special indication there: you have to create this point mentally. Continue gazing steadily at vishuddhi on the shadow for five minutes or for as long as you can do so.

When it is not possible for you to gaze at the shadow for even one second longer, stop and look directly up into the sky. While gazing upward, you will perceive a great shadow cast over the background of the sky. It is silver in colour and somewhat hazy. Go on gazing at the shadow until it disappears, then try to reassemble it as in the previous practice. It is difficult to gather it again in the beginning, but you may be able to do it once or twice.

Now close the eyes and relax them completely. When

they are rested then again resume gazing on your shadow at the point of vishuddhi. After a few minutes look up quickly without any delay and gaze steadily into the sky. Continue in this way until the shadow in the sky takes on the form of your own shadow.

Technique 9: Trataka on one's own reflection

You can practise trataka on your own reflection in a mirror or in a still body of water, such as a pond or lake. The best time to practise this is when the sun is high in the sky, not at night or on a cloudy or rainy day. If it is dark outside, there should be sufficient light in the room so that the eyes are not strained.

When you practise trataka on your own reflection you must always remember that whatever you see is a projection or manifestation of your own self. Nothing comes from outside. While practising this form of trataka, if you experience the emergence of any psychic apparitions, then it is better to leave the practice.

Sit down on the bank of a pond or lake at midday. If you are going to use a mirror then spread a black cloth on the floor and practise standing or sitting in front of a full length mirror.

Adjust your position and centre your awareness. Concentrate on steadiness and stillness of the body. Open your eyes and gaze at your reflection in the mirror or in the water. Focus your gaze at the point of bhrumadhya (eyebrow centre). Continue gazing steadily for five minutes or so, at this point, until the eyes become tired and you are unable to hold the gaze for even one second longer.

At this time close your eyes and visualize your own reflection within. At first you will see only a vague, hazy outline. Gradually, with practice, the outline will become clearer and clearer, until you are able to see the entire reflection distinctly. Then you should concentrate on the internal reflection at the point of bhrumadhya.

As in the previous practices, the internal image will become dim, disappear and reappear. You should try to reassemble it for as long as you can do so. Then open your eyes and resume gazing externally on your reflection in the water or in the mirror.

Technique 10: Trataka on crystal

When crystal is used as an object for concentration you must practise in dim light, in a room which is neither too bright or dark. First spread a black cloth on a table. Then place a stand on the table and the crystal on the stand.

Sit down and centre your awareness. Concentrate on steadiness and stillness of the body. Open your eyes and gaze into the crystal. You must look into the crystal, not at the outside of it. The consciousness and the vision must penetrate the centre of the crystal.

When you gaze into the centre of the crystal you will see nothing. Here trataka on an external object and on shoonya are combined. When you gaze into the crystal for a long time, the mind goes blank and then visions begin to come, even while your eyes are open.

Usually the period fixed for gazing upon an external object is from three to five minutes. However, there is an exception to the rule in this practice. In crystal gazing you can concentrate for ten minutes, but tears should not fall and the eyes should not be strained.

You have to continue gazing into the crystal for as long as possible without blinking the eyes. The eye muscles should remain absolutely relaxed. The eyelids should not flicker. The moment you feel strain you should close the eyes and rest them. You do not have to think of the crystal when the eyes are closed.

Concentration comes very quickly while concentrating on crystal. This practice develops telepathy, for crystal has the property of attracting sound waves. Radios also contain crystals which attract sound waves, but these are synthetic crystals. The properties of real crystals are more subtle and powerful.

Technique 11: Trataka on a jyotirlingam

The best form of trataka is gazing on the jyotirlingam. This is a luminous, oval shaped crystal found in India by the Narmada river. If you place the jyotirlingam under a flow of water at any time of day, it produces different shades of colours, visions and outlines, where snakes, elephants, jungles, rivers, landscapes and worlds being born and destroyed may be seen.

There are twelve places in India where jyotirlingams have been established: Somnatheshwar, Mallikarjuna, Mahakaleshwar, Omkareshwar, Kedareshwar, Bheemashankar, Vishweswar, Tryambakeshawar Vaidyantheshwar, Nageshwar, Grishneshwar and Rameshwar. These are the jyotirlingams on which trataka is practised.

Everything which exists in the physical universe is drawn from the basis of an inner reality. The great seers saw the lingam inside and that vision gave rise to an outer symbol. In the Upanishads it is said that trataka on an external shivalingam is synonymous to concentration on the internal astral body. The oval shape, which is seen outside, is the same shape seen within yourself as your astral body.

By practising trataka on the jyotirlingam, the aspirant comes face to face with himself and learns the secret of birth and death. He is able to fulfil his spiritual ambitions. Finally, he sees the eternal life inside himself. This jyotirlingam is *swayambhu*, 'self-created', 'self-born'. Nobody created it. It existed before you were born because the subtle body existed before the physical body.

This jyotirlingam manifests differently on different planes. In the physical world it is seen in temples. On the higher planes of consciousness it is seen in the form of light. In order to worship this jyotirlingam you need not use prayer, mantra or flower offerings. You simply have to sit down before the lingam, place a bilwa leaf in front of it, pour water over it and gaze into it, trying to assimilate its physical form within. Nothing else is necessary. It does not matter if you are a believer not. It is a universal symbol.

Trataka Three

ANTAR DRISHTI

Technique 1: Antar trataka on a candle flame

Sit in a comfortable, steady position. Close your eyes and keep them closed for the duration of the practice. Practise kaya sthairyam. Be aware of the steadiness of the whole body. Feel that the body is immovable. It is fixed to the floor, in fact, it is part of the floor. Continue to practise kaya sthairyam for a few minutes until you feel the body becoming stiff and rigid like a statue.

Now bring your awareness to bhrumadhya, at the eyebrow centre. Without creating any strain focus your total attention on the sensation between the eyebrows. Try to think of nothing else apart from the eyebrow centre. Continue in this manner until you can feel a definite sensation at this point.

Now visualize the flame of a candle at the eyebrow centre. Try to hold the image steadily. If you cannot see it, then imagine it. If the image fades or disappears, you must recreate it. Maintain the inner vision of the candle flame. Go on watching it. It may vanish and reappear. Continue to recreate the image at the eyebrow centre. With practice the image should be as clear and vivid as if you were looking at it with open eyes. Hold the image of the candle flame steadily at bhrumadhya. Do not let it waver.

There should be continuous, unbroken awareness of the candle flame. Gradually let everything dissolve and just be aware of the candle flame. Try to identify, to merge your mind totally with the image. Continue in this way for as long as possible.

Then slowly let go of the image. Bring the awareness to the natural, spontaneous breath. Be aware of the slow, steady flow of the breath. Become aware of the body and your meditation posture. Listen to any sounds inside and outside the room. Breathe in deeply and chant *Om* three times. Then slowly move the body and open the eyes.

Technique 2: Looking into the image

For this practice you should choose a symbol or object that holds meaning for you. You should feel some attraction to or interest in that object or symbol. Then it will be easier for you to visualize it and hold your whole attention on the symbol or object for the duration of the practice and to delve deeply into the meaning within it.

Sit in a comfortable meditation posture. Become aware of the whole body. Let go of any tensions whether physical, mental or emotional. Practise kaya sthairyam for some time. Feel the body and mind becoming still and steady. Bring the awareness to the eyebrow centre, bhrumadhya. Become aware of the sensations at this point. There should be no effort or strain, just relaxed awareness of the sensation at bhrumadhya. Let awareness of everything else slip away until there is only awareness of the point of bhrumadhya. Now slowly begin to create your chosen symbol or object. Create every detail of the object. See every curve and line. See the colour and dimensions of the object. Visualize the object as clearly and vividly as it would appear if you were looking at it with open eyes. If you have chosen the symbol *Om*, see the bright silvery *Om* at bhrumadhya. Trace each curving line. See the bindu. Visualize the *Om* symbol bright and vibrant. Intensify your awareness of the symbol. There is no other awareness, only awareness of *Om*. The symbol should remain clear and vivid at the eyebrow centre throughout the practice.

As your awareness becomes deeper, feel that you are looking into the symbol and peeling away layer after layer. Feel you are going deeper into the symbol and beginning to see and understand the nature and essence behind it. Intensify your awareness. Look more deeply into the symbol. There is no effort, just total awareness. Allow yourself to open up to the subtle meaning within the symbol. Continue the practice with complete awareness.

Now slowly let the image fade. Bring your awareness to the natural breath. Follow the slow, steady flow of the breath for a few moments. Become aware of the body. Feel the meditation posture in which you are sitting. Become aware of the contact between the body and the floor. Listen to any sounds in the external environment. Externalize yourself completely. Open your eyes and move your body.

Technique 3: Antar trataka on a star

Sit in any comfortable meditation posture, with the spine erect, the head up and the eyes closed. Place the hands on the knees in chin or jnana mudra. Become aware of the whole body. Move through each part of the body systematically and try to consciously relax each part. Feel the body becoming still and steady. Feel the contact between the body and the floor. Intensify this awareness of the contact between the body and the floor. Feel as if your body is part of the floor, like a tree growing out of the floor. Feel the body rooted to the ground. Awareness of the whole body still and motionless.

Become aware of the slow, rhythmical movement of the breath. Watch each inhalation and exhalation. Now bring your awareness to bhrumadhya at the eyebrow centre. Intensify your awareness of the eyebrow centre. Try to be aware of the sensation at this point. Be completely aware of bhrumadhya and nothing else. Hold your awareness at this point for some time and feel the sensation growing stronger.

Now, at this point of bhrumadhya visualize a tiny, shining star. Try to create the image of the star clearly and vividly at bhrumadhya. Keep on watching the star. See this one single tiny star in an endless sky. Sometimes you can see the star twinkles.

If you find the image fading or moving then again centre your awareness at bhrumadhya. See the tiny, twinkling star in the centre of the vast sky. Visualize it clearly, but without effort or strain. This relaxed gazing at the image will help to make it clearer and keep the image from moving from the eyebrow centre. If you can visualize the star clearly this is an indication that you are awakening the third eye, the symbol of cosmic consciousness. Continue to gaze steadily at the tiny star.

Now let the image fade into the space of chidakasha. Become aware of any images, thoughts, emotions that are manifesting within the inner space. Do not judge or suppress or become involved with any of them. Just be a witness of what is manifesting in this space. See each image or thought, let it pass and move to the next one. There may be no images or thoughts, then just be aware of this. Continue in this way for a few moments with complete awareness. Then again bring your awareness back to the physical body. Feel the contact between the body and the floor. Become aware of your surroundings. When you feel ready, move the body and open your eyes.

Technique 4: Antar trataka on a shivalingam

Antar trataka on a shivalingam is done in the same way as the previous practice. For the practices of antar trataka a steady body and mind are essential. Therefore, before beginning any of the practices always practise kaya sthairyam for some time. In this way you develop physical steadiness. Develop homogeneous awareness of the whole physical body. Kaya sthairyam is a powerful means of pacifying the mind as well as the body.

When the body and mind are quiet and still then bring

your awareness to bhrumadhya, the eyebrow centre. Visualize a black shivalingam. See the inky black oval shape of the shivalingam. Visualize water being poured over the shivalingam. Intensify your awareness of this shivalingam at bhrumadhya. As with the previous practice, if the image fades or moves, you must recreate it clearly and vividly and centre the image at bhrumadhya. Your awareness should be completely steady and one-pointed. Do not allow your attention to become involved with any images or thoughts that may arise. Concentrate fully on the black shivalingam. Deepen your awareness of the image so that it becomes clearer and more alive to you. The shivalingam is the symbol of your astral consciousness. Continue your awareness of the image for as long as possible. Then let it fade into the background. Watch the space of chidakasha. Witness whatever is manifesting there. After a few moments bring the awareness back to the body and your surroundings. When you are ready, move your body and open your eyes.

Technique 5: Antar trataka on the psychic eye
Sit comfortably in a meditation posture and practise kaya sthairyam for some time. Feel the body and mind becoming quiet and motionless. The body should remain completely motionless throughout the practice. Become aware of the psychic breath, witness each subtle breath passing in and out of the throat area. The breath is slow and deep.
Bring your awareness to the eyebrow centre, bhrumadhya. Concentrate on the eyebrow centre and locate the pressure point there. Develop the vision of the human eye. Visualize a closed human eye. See all the details clearly. See the eyelashes and eyebrow, see the curve and shape of the eye. The image may appear for a few seconds and then vanish. This does not matter. Just reconstruct the image again. Keep on watching this closed human eye at bhrumadhya.

Now make an effort to open this eye. This is not a physical but a psychic effort. You must make a psychic effort to open this eye, which represents the third eye, the eye of intuition. Concentrate your whole awareness on this eye. The body and mind should not become tense or tight, but should remain relaxed throughout. The effort you are making is from within. Continue with this effort to open the third eye. As you continue to gaze intently at the eye, see it slowly begin to open. Continue the practice in this way. As the third eye becomes active, then a new kind of vision is developed and intuitive powers are awakened.

Now let go of the image of the psychic eye. Bring your awareness back to the physical body and the external surroundings. When you are ready, move the body and open your eyes.

Technique 6: Awareness of the drashta (seer)

Allow the body to become comfortable in any meditation posture. The spine should be erect and the eyes closed, the hands on the knees or on the lap. Become aware of the whole body and practise kaya sthairyam for some time. Develop complete motionlessness. The body and mind should be calm and still.

Bring the awareness to the inner space. Become aware of your whole being, not only the body and the thoughts but the whole of your being. Be aware of the 'I' which is the whole self. Concentrate on the 'I' which does not change, which will not change regardless of changes in the body, in the emotions or in the environment. Concentrate on 'I' the seer of this body, 'I' the seer of the thoughts, 'I' the witness of everything inside and outside. The homogeneous awareness of 'I'. Do this in whatever way is right for you.

When you develop homogeneous awareness of 'I', everything becomes one with it. Nothing is different from it. Everything is included in it. Develop self-awareness: 'I am' in everything. Include every awareness in this 'I' awareness. Become aware of your whole self. Become aware of being aware.

Now ask yourself the question "Who am I?" 'I' is the awareness by which everything is known, including myself. I not only exist but I know that I exist. I experience my body. I am thinking. I am the seer of all my thoughts. I am the seer of myself. Now concentrate on this seer, this awareness of everything. It is awareness of both the seer and the seen. Develop this dual awareness of both the seer and the seen. The seer is abstract and the seen is on the material, physical plane. See the body. Be aware of the process of seeing, a faculty which is aware of the body. Go deeper and become aware of who is seeing, who is witnessing the body. Move deeper into yourself. Be aware of the seer and the seer of that seer. Ask yourself "Who am I?"

Now get ready to end the practice. Bring your awareness back to the physical body sitting in a meditation posture. Become aware of the weight of the body on the floor. Listen to the sounds around you. Externalize yourself completely. When you feel ready then move the body and open the eyes.

Hari Om Tat Sat

Trataka Four

SHOONYA DRISHTI

This stage of trataka, known as shoonya drishti, differs from the previous stages in that there is no object on which to focus your attention. In the following practices the gaze is fixed on nothingness or space, and the awareness must be steady and one-pointed throughout the practice. This is difficult to do because the mind will wander or sleep will come. Therefore, the practice of antar trataka should be perfected before shoonya drishti is attempted so that the practitioner can gain the full benefits from the practice.

Technique 1: Bhoochari mudra

Bhoochari mudra is an allied technique to agochari and shambhavi mudra and all three are excellent forms of trataka. Agochari and shambhavi mudras are often integrated with other yogic techniques or done specifically during one's yogic practice program. Bhoochari mudra, on the other hand, though it can be done in your daily program, can easily be practised in everyday life without other people realizing that you are practising a yogic technique. It is an excellent, simple yet effective practice that brings tranquility and concentration of mind if done for a reasonable period of time with awareness.

The word *bhoo* means 'earth', and *chari* means 'that which moves', but the practice is usually called 'nothingness gazing'. This mudra can be practised in any position and in almost any place. You can do it while standing, sitting, lying, as you wish. You can do it in the privacy of your own house, at work or at play, whatever is convenient. However, if you practise at home in a sitting pose, it is best to face a blank wall. This ensures that there are no obstructions in your vision which can distract your attention from the practice. This is not essential, only preferable.

When beginning this practice, initially it is best to use the following technique until the eyes become used to focusing on nothingness. When the practitioner is proficient in this then the technique can be discontinued and bhoochari mudra practised without preliminaries.

Allow the body to become comfortable and steady. Keep the eyes open throughout the practice. Raise your right hand in front of your face. Hold the palm so that it is flat and facing downwards, with the fingers together. Place the side of the thumb so that it is in contact with the top of the upper lip. The elbow should point to the side of the body. Focus your eyes on the tip of the little finger, which will be the furthest point of your hand from the eyes.

Gaze intently at the tip of the little finger for some time, if possible without blinking or flickering the eyes. If other thoughts arise, let them come but try to maintain continuous awareness of the fingertip. Then after a minute or so, remove your hand, but continue to gaze at the space where the little finger was situated.

Gaze intently at the nothingness in front of the face where the little finger was positioned. Become fully engrossed in the nothingness, the empty space. Be aware of other thoughts if they arise, but anchor your awareness to the nothingness at the same time. Even if other things are occurring in front of the eyes, they should only be blurred. In fact, if you are totally aware of the nothingness, then you should not even notice them. Even if your eyes see outer events, there should be no registration of the fact in the field of conscious perception. All you can see and are aware of is the nothingness. This is the aim.

From this practice will come calmness, introspection and concentration of mind. Continue for as long as you have time or as circumstances will permit.

Bhoochari mudra can be practised almost anytime or anywhere. At first this practice is fairly difficult for there are so many outer distractions that continually lure one's attention in other directions. As with every other yoga technique, it is a matter of 'practise makes perfect'.

Technique 2: Unmani mudra

The word *unmani* literally means 'no mind, no thinking'. Therefore, this mudra can also be called the attitude of thoughtlessness or the attitude of meditation. The state of unmani arises during meditation. Though one may be acting in the world, there is a state of thoughtlessness. This is called *unmani avastha*, the state of no thought. The mind functions but without the hindrance of conflicting thoughts and analysis. One is conscious and the mind functions, but it seems to be nowhere. In this state the eyes perceive but one does not see. This is unmani.

The state of unmani is widely mentioned in the traditional yogic-tantric texts. The *Hatha Yoga Pradipika* states: "Without support for the mind one should become thoughtless; then one will remain like the space which is both inside and outside a jar." It also states, "Whatever there is in the world, animate and inanimate, is only the scenery of the mind. When the mind achieves a state of unmani, then ignorance and duality cease." Unmani implies that state which is beyond thought – meditation. Unmani mudra is a simple technique that helps to induce the meditation experience.

When practising unmani mudra, sit in a steady, comfortable meditation posture. Become aware of the whole body. Go to each part of the body and mentally relax all tensions from each part. The body should be completely at ease with no tension or tightness. Practise kaya sthairyam for some time, moving your awareness systematically from one part of the body to the next. Feel the body becoming still and steady. Feel the body rooted to the ground, as part of the ground, completely motionless.

Now bring your attention to the eyebrow centre, to the space of chidakasha. Become aware of the mental activity there. Become aware of the different experiences that you may be having right now. See thoughts arising, ideas developing. Become aware of them and gradually try to lessen the mental activity. Just as the physical body is still and quiet, in the same way try to make your mind still and quiet.

Now open the eyes fully, but without strain. Bring your awareness to ajna chakra. Inhale slowly and deeply, keeping the awareness at ajna chakra. Then as you exhale slowly move your awareness down through the spine and at the same time slowly close the eyes. The awareness moving down the spine and the eyelids closing should be synchronized with the exhaling breath. When the exhalation is completed your awareness should be at mooladhara chakra and the eyes are lightly closed. Then again bring your awareness to ajna chakra and open the eyes fully. Inhale slowly and deeply and with awareness at ajna. Exhale moving your awareness down the spine and slowly closing the eyelids.

Although the eyes are open your attention should be on the chakras and the descending awarohan psychic passage. Your eyes are open, but you should be looking inside. Do not use great effort on this practice. Let it become spontaneous and natural. The practice is more mental than physical. Although the eyes are open and then slowly closed, they should not perceive anything on the outside. Your awareness should be with the process happening within. Continue in this way for some time. Feel your awareness becoming deeper and deeper. Your whole awareness is inside, moving deeper into your consciousness. Now get ready to end the practice. Leave awareness of the breath and close the eyes. Just be silent for a few moments and experience whatever you may be feeling internally. Observe the condition and state of the body and mind. Now slowly begin to externalize the mind. Become aware of the external environment, the physical experiences, the sensorial experiences of comfort or discomfort. Become aware of the different sounds in the room and outside. Take a deep breath in and chant *Om* three times. Slowly move the body and open your eyes.

Technique 3: Trataka on the evening sky

When practising trataka on the sky, sit outside in an open place or on a terrace where there is nothing obstructing your view. Sit in any comfortable meditation posture and relax the whole body. Practise kaya sthairyam for some time, until the body becomes still and quiet. Bring the awareness to chidakasha and watch any thoughts or images there. Gradually lessen the mental activity and let the mind become quiet.

Now open the eyes and gaze steadily at the blue sky. The eyes should not blink or flicker in any way. Slowly let the awareness of your surroundings slip away. Be aware only of the vast blue space of the sky. There is nothing else but the sky. As you gaze, feel that the sky is coming closer and closer to you. Feel the sky moving in all directions. Let yourself be enveloped within the vastness of the sky. Feel the sky all around you.

Intensify your awareness of the sky. As your awareness becomes deeper and more intense, experience yourself becoming part of the sky. Feel that there is no difference between you and the sky. You are the sky. Experience the endless space, there is nothing but space. You are aware and experiencing this space, this sky. Steady, continuous awareness of the sky.

Now slowly get ready to end the practice. Close the eyes and let go of the awareness of the sky. Be fully aware of what you are experiencing right now. Become aware of what is happening within the body and mind. Now bring your awareness back to the physical body. Be aware of the posture in which you are sitting. Be aware of comfort or discomfort, heat or coolness. Slowly begin to externalize the mind. Listen to the sounds around you. Then take a deep breath in and chant *Om* three times. Slowly move the body and open the eyes.

Technique 4: Trataka on darkness

This practice is similar to the previous one on the sky. Trataka on darkness should be practised where there is complete darkness, where nothing can be seen, not even your own hand. Then sit with eyes open and gaze into the darkness. Hold the gaze steady and still. Keep looking into that darkness for as long as possible without causing strain to the eyes. If thoughts or emotions come, let them, but keep your attention on the darkness. Try to penetrate the darkness.

After some time the darkness vanishes and visions start floating. According to some psychologists who have made experiments on this particular form of trataka, it is of those practices by which your subconscious mind and behaviour, your suppressed feelings, phobias, fears, all come up in the form of visions and float in that darkness. You must not become caught up and involved in these images and visions. You must be aware of them but not be disturbed by them.

Because this is such a powerful practice it is not recommended for those people who have an impure, restless and abnormal mind to practise it. When the subconscious mind begins to manifest such people will not be able to understand what is happening and their fears will be increased. Therefore, trataka on darkness should only be practised by those who have sufficient mental control and detachment and who have been leading a pure disciplined inner life. In that state they will see the higher astral plane.

Technique 5: Trataka on havan

When performing havan put scented objects into the sacrificial fire. Then sit down comfortably in front of the havan. Relax the whole body. Allow the body to become still and motionless. When the fire is burning steadily for some time then focus your gaze on the centre of the fire. Hold your gaze steadily on the centre point of the fire. Do not move the eyes in any way.

Look deeply into the fire. Let go of your external surroundings. Let any thoughts that come just pass by. Concentrate your full attention on the fire. Feel yourself moving closer to the fire. There is nothing but the fire. Experience the fire as if it were part of yourself. Try to understand the real nature of the fire. Be aware of the divine within the fire.

Continue to intensify your awareness. Do not intellectualize or try too hard in the practice, just allow yourself to be open to the fire. Try to see the fire as it really is. Let your awareness go deeper and deeper into the fire. Continue as long as there is no strain or discomfort.

Then close the eyes. Be silent for a few minutes with the awareness inside. Experience whatever is happening within. Bring the awareness to the physical body and the meditation posture in which you are sitting. Listen to the sounds around you. Externalize the mind fully. Breathe in deeply and chant *Om* three times. Move the body and open the eyes.

Hari Om Tat Sat

Upanishadic Dharana

12

Bahyakasha Dharana

In Sanskrit, the material universe around us is called bahyakasha. The word *bahya* means 'outer' and *akasha* means 'space' or 'ether'. Bahyakasha dharana is the exploration of the external space or ether, not in a rocket ship, but in a meditative way. While the body remains grounded, the consciousness soars into outer space, viewing the planets, the stars and the asteroids. In this practice we experience ourselves as a part of the great space of the external cosmos through which our own individual being and all other beings, both sentient and insentient, have come into existence.

Technique
Stage 1: Preparation
Sit in a comfortable meditation posture. Adjust your position so that you do not need to move any part of the body during the practice. Close your eyes and relax the whole body. Concentrate on your body posture. Feel the body becoming steady and still. Develop the feeling of body steadiness and stillness. Side by side become aware of the natural breath. Continue this process until the body is absolutely steady and immobile.
Stage 2: Visualizing the body
In this practice we are going to externalize the awareness and take a trip into outer space. First of all take your

awareness to the top of the head and look down. Survey your whole body sitting immobile in the meditation posture. See your body from all sides as if you are looking down from the top of the head. See the front side of the body, the back side, the right side, the left side. See the whole body together. See your facial expression. See the clothes you are wearing. See everything in detail.

Stage 3: The room

Raise your awareness up to the ceiling of the room in which your body is sitting. From this point you can easily see everything in the room. See your body sitting in meditation in a particular part of the room. See the floor, the ceiling and the four walls of the room. See the windows and doors. See the furniture. See any other people who are also in the room. View the entire room in one glimpse. See everything in the room at one time.

Stage 4: The building

Imagine that your awareness is connected to the body by a subtle filament of light. Then raise your awareness to the top of the building. Look down and see the inside of the building. See your physical body in the room, in the building. See the different floors of the building. See each floor progressively from the ground floor up. See all the rooms on each floor. See the contents of each room, the people in each room, the colour of each room. Move from floor to floor until you have covered the whole building.

Stage 5: The locality

Raise your awareness fifty metres over the top of your building. Look down and see your body sitting in the same room in the building. See your building and the other buildings that surround it. See the different colours, sizes and shapes of the buildings. See the whole area of your neighbourhood, town or village. See the cars and people moving through the streets. See the children playing. See the trees and grass surrounding the different buildings. See the whole locality in one glimpse, in one view.

Stage 6: The district
Be aware of the filament of light connecting you to your physical body. Raise your awareness another one hundred metres to the level of the low hanging clouds. Look down and see your whole district. See the flat areas of plantation, the hills, the bodies of water. See the towns and villages. See the roads and railroads winding through it from one end to the other. See your town and within your town see your building. See your physical body sitting in the room in the building. See the building, the town and the whole district in one glimpse, in one view.

Stage 7: Country, continent, earth
Raise your awareness straight up several thousand feet, so that you can see the whole state. Continue moving upward and see the whole country. See the whole continent. As you go even higher and leave the earth's atmosphere, look down and see the whole earth as a round globe, hanging in space. Continue on your voyage through outer space. Look down and see the earth growing smaller and smaller until it looks like another star or asteroid.

Stage 8: Outer space
Experience your awareness moving faster than the speed of light through the vast outer space, the bahyakasha. Look into the inky dark space lit up only by stars, asteroids and comets. Experience the space all around you, infinite space, unending. See the solar system and the different planets which comprise it. Go even higher and see the entire Milky Way. See the vast galaxy of stars making up our whole universe. Merge your awareness in the great space, the infinite space. Beyond you, above you, below you, all around you, there is nothing but space, eternal space. Experience this space. Experience the bahyakasha. Experience yourself as a floating entity of awareness within this infinite space. As far as you can see in every direction, there is nothing but space. You are one with the vast space and yet you are also separate.

Stage 9: Returning to earth

Now remember your physical body to which your awareness is still connected by a subtle filament of light. Slowly begin the journey back to earth. Moving downward see the Milky Way, the solar system, the earth. As you re-enter the earth's atmosphere, the globe grows bigger and bigger. See your continent, your state, your district, your town, your building. Enter your building and go to the room in which your body is sitting. See your body sitting in the same posture, in the same place.

Stage 10: Ending the practice

Bring the awareness inside the body. Again experience the physical dimension. Feel the position of the body. Feel the weight of the body against the floor. Feel the hands on the knees. Become aware of the breath, of the external sounds. Be aware of your whole body from head to toe. Slowly release your asana and open your eyes.

Hari Om Tat Sat

13
Antarakasha Dharana

In Sanskrit, the word *antar* means 'inner'. So antarakasha is the inner space which forms the substratum for our own individual creation. According to yogic thought and modern scientific thought as well, the material universe, of which we are all an integral part, has two main aspects – the macrocosmic and the microcosmic. All that exists within the bahyakasha, within the dimension of time, space and object, is part of the macrocosmos. This is the world that we live in. However, whatever exists without, can also be found within, in its own mini form, and that is the microcosmos.

As the macrocosmos exists outside our own individual being, within the space of bahyakasha, so the microcosmos exists inside, within the antarakasha, the inner space. Therefore, in order to experience the microcosmos, the universe within, it is necessary to first develop our perception of the antarakasha, the inner space, through which this inner world takes its subtle form. The inner space is the basic element or the substrata for all the manifestations of consciousness represented by Shiva or Purusha; while the outer space is the substrata for all the manifestations of energy or matter, represented by Shakti or Prakriti. In order to know ourselves, in order to expand our consciousness, the inner space must first be penetrated. It is only then can we begin to experience what is in the deeper dimensions of our being.

Technique
Stage 1: Relaxation of the body
Sit in a comfortable meditation posture. Adjust your position so that you do not need to move any part of the body. Observe the entire body and make sure that from the crown of the head down to the tips of the toes, the whole body is free from all tightness and tension. Move your mind through the different parts of the body. Check each and every part, each and every joint, each and every muscle. Make sure that you are totally at ease physically. Observe and relax your whole body internally. Become aware of the maximum ease that you can experience in the body.

Stage 2: Body steadiness
Maintaining the feeling of total physical relaxation, become aware of your body posture. Concentrate on the position of the body. Feel your body becoming steady and still. Develop the feeling of steadiness and stillness. Side by side become aware of the natural breath. Continue this process until the body is absolutely steady and immobile. Maintain the awareness of the body which is absolutely still and motionless. Concentrate on body stillness, on pindrop silence. There should be no physical movement.

Stage 3: Entering the inner space
Maintain total awareness of the stillness that you can feel within the body. Within the stillness of the body begin to experience the inner space. Leave the concept of the material body made up of bones, flesh, blood and mucus. Develop the concept of the body as space, nothing but space. Experience the body as an empty shell, made of skin with nothing inside.

Within the stillness experience the inner space which pervades the whole body from head to toes, empty space. Feel the internal expansiveness, the lightness, the vacuousness, of the space. It is to this space that you have to direct your consciousness. The body contains the microcosmic experience. Develop the microcosmic awareness within the body. Experience the infinite space within the physical frame.

You do not have to make any effort to experience the inner space. The experience will come to you spontaneously, as you attune your awareness to the subtle dimension of consciousness. This space is not separate from consciousness. It is the medium through which consciousness functions. Where there is consciousness there is space. Attune yourself to the experience of inner space. Beyond the body, beyond the mind, is the dimension of space. Develop this experience.

Stage 4: Inner body space

Maintain total awareness of the space within the body. Observe the vacuousness of the whole body from the head to the toes. Move your awareness from the toes up to the top of the head, observing the space contained within the body. Take your awareness through every part of the body and become aware of the subtle, inner space which pervades it.

Take your awareness to the head. Experience the space within the region of the head. Become aware of the neck and experience the space there. Be aware of the space within the right shoulder, the right arm, the right hand. Experience the space from the right shoulder down to the fingertips. Be aware of the space in the left shoulder, the left arm, the left hand. Experience the space between the left shoulder and the left finger tips.

Experience the space pervading the region of the chest, inside the ribcage. Be aware of the entire chest space from front to back. Experience the space within the abdomen, the upper abdomen, the lower abdomen, from front to back. Experience the space in the buttocks, the right buttock, the left buttock, both buttocks. Experience the entire space between the shoulders and perineum. Be aware of the whole torso and the inner space which pervades it.

Be aware of the space within the right thigh, the right knee, the right calf, the right foot. Experience the inner space between the right hip and the tips of the toes. Be aware of the space pervading the left thigh, the left knee, the left calf, the left foot. Experience the inner space between the left hip and the tips of the toes.

Be aware of the space in both feet together, both legs together. Be aware of the space in both hands together, both arms together. Be aware of the space inside the chest, the abdomen, the whole torso. Be aware of the space inside the neck and head. Develop homogeneous awareness of the space contained within the whole body, the whole body. The whole body space.

Stage 5: Expansion and contraction

Direct your awareness to the natural breath. Watch each ingoing and each outgoing breath. Do not alter the breath flow in any way. Simply observe the natural breathing pattern. Side by side there should be awareness of the inner space. As you breathe in feel that the space is expanding. As you breathe out feel that the space is contracting. Intensify your awareness of the space which is expanding and contracting with each breath.

Stage 6: Ending the practice

Now get ready to end the practice. Withdraw your awareness from the experience of space. Gradually externalize the perception. Feel your physical body sitting in the meditation posture. Feel the weight of your body against the floor. Feel your hands resting on the knees. Be aware of the external sounds. Be aware of the room in which you are sitting. Breathe in deeply and chant *Om* three times.

Hari Om Tat Sat

14
Chidakasha Dharana

The word *chid* or *chitta* means 'consciousness', thus chidakasha is the space of consciousness. This space is located in the region of the head, behind the forehead. Chidakasha is also known as the mind screen or the viewing screen of ajna chakra. If you close your eyes for a few seconds, you will see a space in front. This is the mind screen on which you can view many subtle visions and impressions manifesting from the deeper levels of your consciousness.

Chidakasha can also be likened to a cave. If you look into a cave from outside, all you can see is an impenetrable wall of darkness. It is so dark that you cannot see anything inside. When you enter the cave, however, and your eyes become accustomed to the darkness, then you begin to see things. Although these things were there previously, you were unable to see them. The cave that seemed to be full of blackness before is seen to contain many more things, even things which you did not expect to see.

It is the same with the mind cave. At first when you look into the cave of chidakasha, you will see nothing and you will think that there is nothing there to be seen. But as you become accustomed to it, you will begin to develop awareness of your inner being. This is chidakasha dharana. In this practice chidakasha is visualized as a dark cave or room with four walls, a floor and a ceiling. In the floor is a tunnel leading downward. This is sushumna nadi. On the front wall is the mental screen on which visions appear.

In chidakasha dharana there is a gradual deepening of perception from the physical, sensorial experience to the psychic and pranic experience. The physical sensorial experiences are to be perceived in the region of chidakasha. This is done in three forms: (i) awareness of the existing memory, (ii) awareness of the spontaneous, natural manifestation within chidakasha, and (iii) visualization.

Memory is used in the sense that when we initially become aware of the mind and try to still the jumping mind, the wandering mind, then at that time the mind is usually thinking about, or experiencing something. It is engaged in some other awareness. You may not be conscious of that fact, but the mind is engaged is some thought, in some memory, in some event which was experienced during the day. So, through memory the mind is analyzing and creating some form of understanding of that happening, that process.

It could be a very simple event such as a talk that you might have had with somebody. That talk or that interaction continues inside in the form of a memory. If you become aware of that you will also see the visual image of that connection. As you increase the awareness, then you will also become aware of the other sensory experiences, tactile experiences, such as the wind blowing against the body, the coolness of the wind, the warmth of the clothes, and so forth. Awareness of that memory which has kept the mental awareness engaged is the first process in this technique of chidakasha.

This technique also tends to remove any impression which is in the process of being formed in the mind, and that impression could also be the beginning of some other chain of events which could affect life later on. It is very hard to know what happens in the mind – how insignificant events can alter the mental pattern, mental perception, mental awareness. So, to consciously become aware of the engagement of the mind is the first stage in this process.

The next aspect is the observation of the natural spontaneous manifestations of chidakasha, which is the common practice: images that come up, flashes that are seen, figures that manifest, shadows that cross the screen of chidakasha. So, here we have seen two aspects of chidakasha, one which is mental engagement and the other which is a spontaneous creation of the senses.

In the second aspect you have to identify the colours, shadows and lights. That is the most basic part of the practice. Initially it is difficult to identify different colours. The practice is actually very complex and it takes a long time to master. If you identify the colour blue, then you have to see the blue colour in a point or streak of light, or anything like that which manifests. If you identify the colour red, then you should see red. If yellow, then you should see yellow. In this way, the colour awareness has to develop gradually in chidakasha. This gives control over the visual sensations which are created due to an optical effect in the brain, and which also manifest as a spontaneous, natural production of colours in chidakasha.

The third aspect is where we consciously create the image or impression and visualize it on the mental screen. This is done first by observing any geometrical forms which may arise in chidakasha. Then by visualizing the process of psychic writing in which numbers, letters, and geometrical forms are written psychically on the screen of chidakasha and used as objects of concentration, first individually and then all together.

Visualization is followed by the practice of floating in space which develops the subtle sensation of levitation. This, in brief, is the process of chidakasha dharana.

Technique
Stage 1: Preparation
Sit in a comfortable meditation posture. Adjust your position, so that there will be no need to move your body during the practice. Make sure that the spine is erect and the head straight. Place the hands on the knees or on the lap. Eyelids and lips should be gently but firmly closed, not too tight or loose. For a few moments, observe the position of the body mentally and become aware of how you are sitting. Observe the position of the toes, feet, ankles, knees, legs, fingers, hands, arms, shoulders, back, buttocks, chest, abdomen, trunk, neck and head.

Stage 2: Body mirror
Try to create a mental image of yourself. Mentally imagine that there is a full length mirror in front of you and your body is reflected in that mirror. Try to see the reflection of the body in the mirror. Complete awareness of the body which is being reflected in the mirror. You are watching the reflection of yourself. In that reflection of the body become aware of the position, the posture, in which you are sitting at the moment. Also observe your clothes in the reflection. Observe your hair and your facial expression. It is as if you are sitting in front of a full length mirror, seeing yourself with the eyes open.

Stage 3: Trikon breathing
Shift your awareness to the breathing process. Observe the natural breath as it moves up and down the nostrils. There should be unceasing and unbroken awareness of the breathing. Feel the breath flow in and out of the nostrils. As you breathe in, the two flows of air move upward and meet at the eyebrow centre. As you breathe out, the two flows diverge and move downward. The two breath flows form a triangular pathway with the top of the triangle at the eyebrow centre. Continue to experience the converging and diverging movement of the breath. See the breath moving up and down the sides of the triangle. Feel your awareness merging with the breath.

Stage 4: Entering the head space
Bring your attention to the eyebrow centre. Become aware of the darkness. Observe the black space in front of the closed eyes. Do not tense the eye muscles by concentrating too hard. Just observe the black space, the empty sky. Be aware of the space of chitta, the aspect of the mind which perceives, which experiences the space of consciousness. Experience chidakasha in its totality, the space which extends beyond the realm of the physical senses, the space located in the region above vishuddhi and below sahasrara.

Physically, the entire region of the head is the area of chidakasha. Experience the black sky of chidakasha throughout your head. Become aware of the dark space all around you, inside. Develop total awareness of chidakasha, the inner space, above you, below you, all around you. There is nothing but the sensation of the empty sky.

Stage 5: The cave of chidakasha
Focus your attention on chidakasha, the space inside the head. Imagine the inside of the head is like a cave or a small dark room. The forehead forms the front wall. The back of the head forms the back wall. The sides of the head form the side walls. The base of the brain at the level of the eyes and ears forms the floor, and the crown of the head is the roof. Be aware of chidakasha in the form of a small room or cave. Awareness of the room inside the head, a completely closed, dark room. Observe it.

Visualize yourself standing in the middle of the room. Look all around. Develop the same experience that you would have in a completely dark, closed room, without any lights, doors or windows. Experience the room of chidakasha, the cave of chidakasha. Take your awareness to the front of the room, behind the wall of the forehead. Slowly walk towards the back wall, the back of the head. From the back observe the front. Come to the centre of the head and visualize yourself standing there. Look all around and feel the vastness, the emptiness of chidakasha. Develop the experience of inner silence, inner stillness, mental immobility. Detach yourself, your awareness, from the mind and its perceptions, from the body and its perceptions. Become aware of the inner state of silence, quietness and immobility.

Stage 6: Impressions in the memory

Witness the space of chidakasha, become aware of the sensorial impressions in the memory. Observe the sensory impressions that are active in your mind at this moment. What kind of sensorial experiences are being perceived by you in chidakasha? Be aware of the auditory inputs, the visual inputs, the tactile inputs, the taste inputs, that may be active in the memory, within chidakasha. Just observe them once. Be fully aware of the memory field which is active within the space of chidakasha. Then begin to observe the sensorial manifestations in chidakasha in the forms of colours, shapes, streams of light, or different physiological sensations.

Stage 7: Sensorial manifestations

Keep your attention focused in chidakasha. Be aware of the movement of colour and light. This movement can be seen in the form of streaks of light or colour, in the form of different shades of darkness, in the form of shadowy movements. Be aware of the natural, spontaneous movements of light, shadow and colour in chidakasha. Sometimes they move so fast that it is not possible to identify a colour or a shape. They are created and dissolved every passing moment. Sometimes a cluster of light or colour manifests in chidakasha and remains there for a few moments before it dissolves. When this happens, watch it.

Observe the movement in chidakasha, whether it is of shadow, light or colour. Do not allow your attention to be distracted from the practice. Be aware of nothing but the movement of shadow, colour and light in chidakasha. If there is mental chattering in the form of enquiry, in the form of analysis, or in any other form, stop it. Be fully aware of what you are observing in chidakasha. You do not have to rationalize anything, simply observe.

Gradually develop the awareness of chidakasha, the emptiness, the vast sky. Try to imagine how an astronaut feels when he travels in space. There is complete darkness all around him, and in that darkness he can see the stars twinkling in different colours, sizes, and shapes. You have to evolve a similar experience. Experience that vast space of chidakasha. One part of the consciousness should experience, the other part should only observe the experience, observe the sensations, objectively.

Stage 8: Creating imagery

Think of anything. The first thought that comes to your mind, whatever it may be, try and see a picture of it. Give shape to your thought. If you think of a flower, create an image of the flower in chidakasha. If you think of a tree, create the image of a tree. If you think of fire, create the image of fire. But please remember, only the first thought which comes to your mind should be given form or shape. If you create an image after thinking about it, then it is not valid. The process has to be spontaneous. Create an image with the points of colour and light which float around in chidakasha. Fill up the image that you create with colours, lights and shadows. Make a conscious effort to give colours to the shape that you create in chidakasha.

Stage 9: Yantra visualization

Think of a yantra, a particular geometrical shape or combination of shapes, with intensity of mind. Think of any yantra, even one which you might have heard about from somebody. It does not matter if you have seen a yantra before in your life or not. Just think of one with intensity of mind. Observe it naturally and spontaneously. Observe chidakasha with intensity, whether the geometrical shape of a yantra appears in it or not. The thought, the idea, the perception of the yantra has to come from the subconscious mind. When thoughts appear from the subconscious and there is intensity of thinking and feeling, an image of a yantra is bound to come up. It does not matter whether you see the image of the yantra in one sitting or in ten sittings, now or later. Do not think about it. You are only concerned with the intensity of concentration, with the awareness of chidakasha. Do not allow mental dissipation to distract your awareness of the practice. Do not lose the intensity of your concentration and awareness.

Stage 10: Psychic writing

The next stage of chidakasha dharana is psychic writing. Imagine the whole of chidakasha to be like a big blackboard. You are going to write on the blackboard with different coloured chalks. First of all, with white chalk write your name in capital letters in the top left hand corner of the chidakasha blackboard. After that, with yellow chalk, underneath your name write down the numbers from one to ten with commas in between them. Then with orange chalk draw small circles in the third line. First draw a circle underneath the number one. Draw a second circle underneath the number two. Draw another circle under the number three. Draw another and another. Now with red coloured chalk draw small squares below the circles. Again pick up the white coloured chalk and draw triangles. Underneath each square draw one triangle.

Now look at the whole blackboard. See your name written in the left hand corner. See the numbers on the second line, the circles on the third, the squares on the fourth and the triangles on the fifth.

Stage 11: Floating in space

Now wipe off all the writing. Come back to the awareness of chidakasha. Visualize the whole headspace, the vast sky, in the form of a circle, a ball, a sphere, with a small, round opening. Enter into the sphere through the round opening. You are floating in a sphere. This experience of floating inside the sphere of chidakasha will only take place when there is total, physical balance and steadiness. Once this is achieved there will be a sensation of floating or levitation. You will have to strive to attain this subtle experience of floating in space by first controlling the body, the sensations of the body. Then enter into the sphere of chidakasha and experience yourself floating in it. Try to develop and intensify this feeling which represents coordination and harmony between the physiological experience and the chidakasha experience.

Stage 12: Ending the practice

Become aware of chidakasha, the mental space. Be aware of the same space pervading your whole body. Develop awareness of the physical body, of the meditation posture. Feel the weight of the body against the floor. Total awareness of the physical body. Be aware of the breathing process. Be aware of the room in which you are sitting. Listen to any external sounds. Breathe in deeply and chant *Om* three times.

Practice note: The main aspects of chidakasha dharana have been covered. However, you will have to master each stage, one at a time. We have presented them in stages to give you an idea. But you should try to perfect each stage independently. Only proceed to the next stage after you have achieved full mastery of the previous one. This is necessary in order to gain an experiential understanding of the process rather than a theoretical understanding only.

Hari Om Tat Sat

15
Ajna Chakra Dharana

Ajna chakra visualization is a part of chidakasha dharana, but it is an advanced stage. In the previous practice of chidakasha dharana, we tried to become aware of the various manifestations in the mental screen where different images, colours, figures, forms, shadows, yantras and symbols were seen, created, and eventually blanked out.

Chidakasha dharana deals with the acknowledgement of the mental and subtle activities which are generated spontaneously due to the interaction of body and senses with the four mental components: manas (reasoning), buddhi (intellect), chitta (memory), and ahamkara (ego). Even to perfect that stage of chidakasha dharana takes a long time, though the practices are relatively simple.

In order to go beyond the physical, sensorial experience, to go beyond the mental experience, beyond the manas, buddhi, chitta and ahamkara aspects of the greater mind, the initial practice of chidakasha dharana must be perfected. Then we enter into the various stages of ajna dharana.

Seat of intuition

According to the vedantic theory of yoga and the experience of people who have perfected it, ajna chakra is the place where the greater mind manifests in the form of a desire. That desire which is the first manifestation of the greater mind is known as *ichcha shakti*. The greater mind next manifests in the form of willpower known as *sankalpa shakti*. Then it manifests as a creative process known as *kriya shakti*. That creative process of the supreme intelligence is later on perceived at the level of the different chakras.

So, ajna chakra is a point where the higher intelligence, the unmanifest and the manifest intelligence, are both experienced. Therefore, the yogic traditions have called ajna chakra the seat of intuition, the seat of the guru or the seat of the sixth sense. The five senses belong to the manifest dimension, the manifest experience. The sixth sense or the intuitive experience is the transcendental manifestation of the supreme intelligence. It is here that we have to focus our creativity, willpower and desire to either be a receiver of or a receptacle for the manifest or unmanifest experiences.

Symbolism of the yantra

Ajna works like a radar. What you receive depends on your direction of focus. If you focus downwards you will receive the experiences contained in vishuddhi, anahata, manipura, swadhisthana and mooladhara. The practice of chidakasha dharana is becoming aware of these different levels in ajna, with ajna focusing downwards. When you reverse the focus of ajna then it becomes the practice of ajna dharana. The practice of ajna dharana is a re-focusing of the antenna which receives information and vibrations from above.

There has to be a focus for that antenna. In order to channel the supreme consciousness in the form of a beam and direct it to ajna, so that the information can be received as a transcendental input into the human frame, we have to see the symbolism of the yantra. The yantra we will visualize is a crescent moon with a white circle. That crescent moon is the antenna, the dish which has to be focused in the direction of the white circle. The dish has to be focused in bindu, the white circle represents bindu in ajna.

That bindu in ajna is the shadow reflection of bindu above ajna. It is a mirror image. The bindu above ajna, which we try to see in the form of a blue drop of water, is the hole in the fabric of the supreme intelligence through which the supreme intelligence is actually filtered and pointed at ajna. So, being aware of this link between bindu and ajna is the first stage of ajna dharana.

Elimination of input

In the subsequent practices of ajna dharana there is total elimination, total stoppage, of every kind of input which we receive from the five senses and the four mental aspects. This total stoppage can only happen if the normal awareness can be taken beyond the range of physical and mental perception. Until and unless we reach that point, this practice will be very dry because there is nothing to hang on to. We jump into the void from mooladhara to vishuddhi, where there is nothing to hold onto, and again it is a similar experience in ajna dharana.

In chidakasha dharana we acknowledged the sensory inputs, the mental inputs. Formation of a colour is an input in chidakasha, whether we call it an input of the ocular nerves, of the sensory fields, of the samskaras, or of memory. We are free to associate that input with whatever we wish. It is not without a meaning.

When those inputs are blanked out then a re-focusing of ajna takes place. There are only two channels which the receiver of ajna can pick up, the lower and the upper. So, the moment you turn the dial, one channel goes fuzzy and gradually becomes totally blank. As the other channel comes in, the picture becomes fuzzy, then it gets an outline, a shadow and finally it becomes a clear image. The fuzzy picture, outline, shadow and clear image are the four stages of ajna dharana which come after the basic stage which is given here.

Kundalini yoga approach

This symbolism has also been explained in kundalini yoga in a different way, namely as an actual experience which totally transforms the entire personality. Kundalini yoga states that bindu is the seat or the source of nectar. This is also the tantric belief. From this point, that drop of nectar falls down into the body. When it falls down into the body and is consumed by the fire of manipura, then one is subject to life, birth, death and decay.

However, by means of certain practices this bindu or drop of nectar can be retained at the level of vishuddhi, which is not solar in nature. When the nectar is not allowed to fall down to manipura but is maintained in the chidakasha region, one attains immortality. Hatha yoga goes one step further, using khechari mudra to stimulate that nectar to become active in chidakasha, thus transforming the experience of ajna into an experience of a transcendental nature.

Whatever approach you adopt, whether it be kundalini yoga, tantra or Vedanta, the practices differ only slightly. The method of each practice may differ, but the end results are similar. By the practice of khechari mudra, if you can retain this bindu or drop of nectar at the chidakasha level, then you can actually experience the taste of it physically. This retaining of the bindu in the higher region is a very powerful experience which can be converted into a physical, sensorial kind of experience too.

It is like thinking about something sour. Imagine you are sucking a lemon right now. Those of you who have that intensity can actually feel a tightening up of the salivary glands and the production of saliva. Just by directing the awareness and concentration you can generate that taste so that it becomes a physical experience. If you can do this in a dissipated, distracted frame of mind, imagine what kind of taste you can create with all your mental energies focused on that experience.

It is at this level that both the gross mind and the higher mind combine to create a very deep transformation. We are talking about different levels, not only from the point of view of kundalini yoga, tantra or even from Vedanta. We are trying to combine all three, and that is how we have to understand the higher mental processes.

Changing the focus

Ajna dharana is a process through which intensity of concentration and awareness is developed to such an extent that the whole focus is changed towards bindu. We begin to receive inputs, long distance telephone calls, from heaven. At the level of ajna chakra, if you start receiving telephone calls from God and he says, "Listen, now you have to do this, now you have to do that," then life becomes very difficult.

It is possible to lose our self-awareness at that time. The doubting nature crops up. The gross mind interferes with the transmission of the supreme mind and we begin to think, "Should I or should I not follow it? How can I be sure that this is an intuitive message and not from the one with horns, tail and trident?" This kind of thing happens and often it is recognized by us as a mystical experience. However, once the consciousness reaches the intuitive level, then we no longer get telephone calls from the one with horns, tail and trident. There is only one hot line. But if there is a conflict of mind, a conflict of awareness, then that doubt becomes our own devil.

Therefore, it is necessary to aim for that kind of progression in the practice where you can just take these experiences step by step and perfect them, so that there will be no conflict later on due to having crossed signals. That control over the mental faculty, over the sensorial faculty is a must. It is the control over these faculties, known as tapasya and austerity, which leads to steadiness of the body and mind, and control over the body and mind.

Technique
Stage 1: Preparation
Sit in a comfortable meditation posture. Adjust your position so that the spine is upright and straight. Place the hands on the knees or in the lap and close the eyes. Develop awareness of the whole body from the top of the head to the tips of the toes. Make sure that each and every part of the body is completely at ease and relaxed. Move your mind from one part of the body to the next. Develop complete awareness of the whole body by moving the mind through the different parts internally. Observe the condition, the tension and the relaxation of the different muscles, nerves, inner organs and joints. Relax yourself internally so that there is total ease within your body.

Stage 2: Stillness and silence
Be aware of the posture in which you are sitting. Develop awareness of the physical posture. As you become aware, you will observe the feeling of motionlessness, stillness and silence manifesting within the body and mind. Become aware of physical motionlessness. Become aware of the silence within you and around you. Your body is perfectly still like a statue, totally still and motionless. Be aware of the feeling of silence and stillness pervading the entire physical and mental structure.

Do not identify with any kind of physical experience. No experience of discomfort or comfort, pain or pleasure, can remove your awareness of the sensation of silence and stillness. Dissociate yourself from the physical experiences. Say to yourself mentally, "I am not the body; I am not associated with any mental experience." Dissociate and detach yourself from the body and experiences of the body, from the mind and experiences of the mind.

Stage 3: Pillar of air
Within the body now become aware of the breath as a pillar of air that extends from manipura to ajna. The consciousness ascends from manipura to ajna along this pillar at the time of inhalation, and descends from ajna to

manipura at the time of exhalation. Do not be aware of physical movement. Be aware of the ascent and descent of consciousness along the pillar of air, extending from manipura to ajna. Maintain constant awareness of the feeling of motionlessness and silence. Just be aware of the breath and the ascent and descent of consciousness along the pillar of air.

Stage 4: Akashi mudra

Now bring the entire awareness to ajna chakra in the region of chidakasha and centre it there. Develop total awareness of the experience of space in the region of ajna chakra. By being aware of the space in the region of ajna chakra, gradually dissociate the mind from the rest of the body. Total awareness of the ajna region.

Listen carefully and follow the instructions. First of all, raise your head and let it drop back in a very relaxed way, so that the face points towards the ceiling. Then open the eyes and focus them at the eyebrow centre, as in shambhavi mudra, without blinking the eyelids and without straining the eye muscles. As you continue gazing upward, you will observe that the eyebrows form a triangle with the apex pointing downward.

Concentrate on the apex of the triangle. Then gently close the eyes. Bring the head back to the centre. Become aware of the sensation inside the head. Feel the sensation of lightness, of floating. Isolate the mind from the tension or tiredness of the eye muscles. They will gradually relax. Focus more and more on the sensation that is being experienced inside the head, inside chidakasha.

Once again lift the head up and allow it to drop back. When you are comfortable in that position open the eyes and gaze at the eyebrow centre. Close the eyes and bring the head back to the centre. Be aware of the sensation inside the head. Isolate the mind from the experience of the eyes and the eye muscles.

Again tilt the head backwards. Open the eyes and gaze at the eyebrow centre. Close the eyes and re-centre the head. Be aware of the feeling inside the head and make a conscious effort to relax the neck, the eye muscles, the eye strain. Isolate the perception from those regions and focus it at ajna chakra in the centre of the head.

Stage 5: Yantra visualization

Try to locate the exact point of ajna chakra in the centre of the head. Take the attention from the ajna kshetram, which is located at the eyebrow centre, to the inside of the head, and focus it at the centre, at the midbrain. Visualize an invisible thread extending from one ear to the other and from the eyebrow centre to the back of the head. The point where these two threads meet in the centre of the head is the point of concentration.

At that point create an image of a crescent moon with a white circle over it. Visualize a white crescent moon and a white circle. In the darkness and silence of the infinite space experience, develop the vision of a luminous, white crescent moon with a luminous, white circle on top. This is the vedantic representation of ajna chakra.

While focusing the attention and the awareness on this yantra of ajna, become aware of the vibration which pervades the entire space within the head. That is the vibration of *Om*. The beeja mantra of ajna is *Om*. This yantra of ajna is a white crescent moon with a white circle above it.

Stage 6: No body, no mind

As you focus more and more intensely on the yantra and the beeja mantra vibration of ajna, you will find that gradually the physical awareness, the sensorial awareness diminishes. There will be the feeling of oneness with the deep, dark and silent space which holds the yantra and the mantra of ajna within it.

If you find your awareness being distracted from the image of ajna in the centre of the head towards the front, then make an effort to pull your awareness back to the central point. Try to focus more intensely and merge the awareness into the perception of the image of ajna, the vibration of ajna, in the deep, dark, infinite space of chidakasha.

While maintaining the attention at the region of ajna, observe the diminishing awareness of the four mental aspects of manas, buddhi, chitta and ahamkara. The intensity, the hold and the attachment to these four aspects will gradually diminish as the awareness focuses more intensely on ajna chakra.

While focusing your entire awareness in the region of ajna, develop the 'no body' experience, develop the 'no mind' experience, just the experience of being in ajna. Maintain this awareness all the way through, the 'no body' awareness, the 'no mind' awareness. Just experience the ajna space.

Stage 7: Ajna and bindu

Now move your awareness towards the top back of the head to the region of bindu. Become aware of a point of light, luminous blue in colour, like a droplet of water. Concentrate on this point. At the same time observe ajna at the centre, the white crescent moon with the white circle over it. See bindu, a point of luminous blue light, and ajna, a white crescent moon with a white circle over it. Observe both bindu and ajna simultaneously.

Stage 8: Ending the practice

Now gradually withdraw your mind from these two points of awareness and concentration. Become aware of the space of chidakasha. Gradually externalize the mind. Become aware of the physical body sitting in the meditation posture. Become aware of the natural breathing. Become aware of the room in which you are sitting, of the external environment. Take a deep breath in and chant *Om* three times.

Hari Om Tat Sat

16

Hridayakasha Dharana

In Sanskrit, the word *hridaya* means 'heart'. Therefore, hridayakasha dharana is concentration on the heart space. You may find this practice simple and easy, or you may find it complex and difficult. It all depends on the intensity of feeling you are able to generate, because this particular dharana deals with intensity of feeling. While doing this practice make sure that the intensity of feeling does not alter your mental perception. In this type of meditation it is very easy to feel totally depressed or totally elated. You may feel like crying or you may feel like laughing. But one thing is very important to remember: when you feel the swelling of an emotion, do not try to control it. Do not worry, nothing will happen.

The description of the actual practice of hridayakasha dharana is given towards the end of the practice stages, but first there are different aspects involved which you should know. In brief, the first major points are: creation of an emotion, colours of an emotion, changing of emotions, intensity of emotion, and the dimension beyond emotion. As we go through these practices, you must remember to practise them with total intensity, like dharana, and not just as a passive witness to what is happening. You must make every effort to focus all of your energies, feelings and thoughts during the practice.

Process of hridayakasha
The process of hridayakasha dharana is very lengthy and complex. It is difficult to shorten because a wide range of activities has to be carried on within it at the same time. Most people do not really have enough time to go deeply into each aspect. This is a lifelong process. However, we have tried to present a comprehensive, complete and systematic structure of hridayakasha dharana for the reference and knowledge of serious sadhakas.

To give you a brief idea about its complexity, hridayakasha dharana deals with memories and emotions and the reaction that one feels by recalling all of these. The emotions referred to here are not the normal day-to-day feelings that we know. Day-to-day emotions are not that intense. In these techniques you are told which specific kind of memory or emotion has to be generated in order to remove the blockages that exist on the subtle mental plane.

The psychotherapeutic aspect of meditation is actually a form of hridayakasha dharana because many impressions which are suppressed and blocked are allowed to surface. Of course, one should not take up these practices expecting therapeutic results because it is not the therapy aspect which we are dealing with here. We are concerned with how to transcend the limited mind with its accumulated idiosyncrasies and complexities. Therefore, we are working from a different point of view, with memory, emotion and reaction, which is more important. Even the modern technique of rebirthing has its source in hridayakasha dharana. There are many other techniques known by different names, which are similar to the various aspects of hridayakasha dharana. So, it is a very broad subject. In order to clarify the practice, we have divided it into different stages.

Existing feeling and flame of light
In this process, the first thing that is dealt with is the existing feeling. That existing feeling may be related with the experience of chidakasha. It may be a feeling of anxiety due to a thought process that was witnessed in chidakasha.

It may be feeling of happiness or contentment which is also linked to a sensory input in chidakasha. It may be due to an event which has taken place, which has changed your mood. It may be the feeling of introversion due to concentration or one-pointedness. First there should be awareness of the existing feeling, then identification of that feeling, knowledge of what it is, and finally experiencing that feeling, whether it is contentment, silence, anxiety or joy. The awareness must be merged with that feeling, without losing the knowledge that, "I am merging my consciousness with that feeling".

Behind the existing feeling is the flame of light. This image of the flame represents the seat of the individual soul. According to yogic tradition, the individual soul resides in hridayakasha in the form of the flame or point of light. *Hiranyagarbha*, the golden womb, is a description of this concept. That tiny, unflickering flame, unaffected by the winds of desire, emotion, passion or ambition, is the real you. It represents the spirit, which is beyond the mind, body and experience. It is an acknowledgement that, "Yes, I am That. I am not the body, not the mind. I am the spirit."

Emotion, memory, reaction

It is necessary to become aware of the existing feeling in order to create an emotion and then to try and generate the corresponding colour. If you are not too sure which colour pertains to which kind of emotion, it does not matter. With the intensity of concentration, that colour will come in the course of time. Do not try to condition your mind by reading a book on colour therapy. I know that anger is associated with the colour red so the next time I practise hridayakasha dharana, I will see red. The practice should be spontaneous. You have to allow your feelings to express themselves.

The second aspect of the practice is creating an emotion with intensity. All you have to do is maintain the level of intensity. It is a technique which goes through a wide range of feeling and experiences. It prepares the awareness to deal with reactions that are spontaneous manifestations of memories and emotional combinations. These reactions are not necessarily physical in nature. They may also take the form of another feeling which is generated after the first emotion is seen. So do not consider reaction to be your own individual expression. There is nothing which is your own expression or which stems from you. Reaction is linked to a memory, an emotion, a situation, or to time and space. In the same way, all these experiences are linked with each other. The only thing we have to do is to find the missing link which changes the whole picture.

Memory enaction
In the last stage of the practice, we try to recall the earliest memory which is contained in our consciousness. If you go through this process of enacting that memory within the mind and dissecting the memory, then you will come across certain aspects or ideas, self-generated or existing in the environment, which have helped to shape your present life in one way or another. There is no logical or rational explanation for the power of subconscious impressions. However, the words that were spoken in that memory created a feeling; the actions that were performed then created an impression; the character that you were trying to project then, or the characters that were around you then created an impression. The feeling that you projected then, and the feeling which existed then, created an impression. We are not consciously aware of what happened, but those impressions remain with us today and they are reflected in our behaviour, attitude and character, in our feeling and in our expression.

If we have the ability to go further back, we will observe that many such impressions were accumulated by us as children. Later on these impressions convert themselves into a sweet memory or a sad memory. Whatever their effect may be, we have to come to terms with it. If it is something sweet and pleasant, then we can come to terms with it quite easily. If it is something unpleasant and sad, then we cannot come to terms with it so easily.

The first impressions

If we can go back even further, we can try to recall the exact moment of our birth, with our head sticking out and the feet still inside. That first entry into the external environment from our mother's womb, that first exposure to this world, has also created an impression. Unfortunately this first impression is generally one of insecurity. Coming from a place which is comfortable and warm, protected and secure, to an alien environment which we cannot understand and where we are exposed to the winds, to lack of warmth and comfort – that is the first impression of this world. It is a very correct impression. To be insecure is the first impression, the first teaching that we have received in our lives. From that point our life has come this far. If the seed is bad the plant is going to be weak as well. The seed of insecurity was planted within us when we put our heads into this world.

Even in meditation the sense of insecurity that we encounter is a very big thing. That sense of insecurity has to be dealt with here in a different way, with a different frame of mind. This state of mind is an objective and dispassionate one, not an involved one. If we are involved, then we are caught up in the whirlpool, in the vortex, and we start moving round and round at an incredible speed, but from the periphery of the storm we have to go to the centre. The experience that one has in the womb, of comfort, pleasure, security and contentment, is an experience that one aspires for in higher meditative states. The reason for this kind of meditation is very simple; it is to break the conditioning of the mind which was created when we first arrived.

There is a big difference between the various practices of hridayakasha. In the initial practices an effort is made to live and relive the feeling and to intensify that feeling, to experience that hard, strong, raw and unadulterated feeling and emotion. In the last practice an effort is made in a very simple way to isolate the self-participation from the actual event that is being witnessed.

Technique
Stage 1: Preparation
Sit in a comfortable meditation posture with the spine and head straight. Place the hands on the knees and close the eyes. For a few moments observe the body posture becoming still and motionless. Mentally observe the position of the spine, the legs, arms, head, the entire body. Complete awareness of the entire physical structure. If there is tightness or tension in any part of the body, then you can adjust your position so that you feel comfortable. Try to maintain calmness and quietness of body and mind together.
Say to yourself mentally, "I am going to practise dharana." By saying this, you prepare yourself mentally for the practice. In order to practise dharana, first it is of utmost importance to stop the dissipation, the distraction of mind. Second, you must develop the ability to consciously and wilfully intensify your concentration on the object of meditation or on the sequences of observation in the contemplation process. Say to yourself mentally, "I am going to practise dharana." By saying this to yourself, you are instructing your mind to stop moving towards external objects, and to become centred.
During the practice try to generate an intensity of feeling. Do not analyze or try to think about your experience in words, before, during, or after the practice. Make every effort to intensely feel and experience, by being oblivious to everything around you. You and your God alone exist. There is nothing and nobody else. Develop this feeling of being completely alone within yourself, despite the fact that many people may be around you. Develop the feeling of solitude within.
Now within this inner solitude become aware of the feeling of space, total awareness of the space within the body. In the awareness of space there is the feeling of stillness. Be aware of this feeling which pervades the whole body.

Stage 2: Entering the heart space
Bring your awareness to the region of the chest. Become aware of the space encompassed by the ribcage. This is hridayakasha, the heart space. Observe the space between the sternum in the front and the spine in the back. See the entire space from the diaphragm up to the shoulders. As you breathe in, feel this space expanding. As you breathe out, feel this space contracting.

Develop total awareness of the space contained within the chest, the heart space, hridayakasha. Feel the infinite space which is saturated with silence and stillness. As you observe the silence and stillness that pervades this space, you will notice that the external movement of the thoughts and the senses stops as well. The body and mind experience the same sensation of expansiveness, stillness and silence. This is the result of concentration in the heart space.

In the space of the heart, which is enveloped in darkness, become aware of a tiny flame of light. See that flame of light internally. It is a flame of golden light. Intensify your awareness of the golden light. That flame of light is in the space of the heart, which is known as hridayakasha. This space is filled with the expansion and contraction of the breathing process and the rhythm of the heartbeat.

Visualize this flame of light in the region of the heart. See it brighten and fade to a glow, brighten and fade to a glow. Become aware of the pulsation of light. With each pulsation, the whole space momentarily fills up with light and again the light recedes to a glow. Experience the flame of light which explodes and implodes, filling the entire being with luminosity.

Stage 3: Awareness of feelings
Become aware of the prevailing feeling, the existing feeling in the anahata region. Develop that feeling into a sensation. Develop the feeling of silence, contentment, peace and light within yourself. Whatever feeling may be there, convert it into a feeling of silence, happiness,

peace and light. Work on your existing feeling which you began to observe initially. While you work on it, let the feeling of peace flow through your entire being.

Feel the vibration, feel the energy of peace, supporting, encouraging and strengthening your inner being. Develop the feeling of contentment, light, happiness and peace. Continue to be aware of the space in the heart. Be aware of hridayakasha by concentrating on anahata chakra. Do not allow yourself to be distracted by the external environment. Become aware of the feeling that exists right now within you, whatever it may be, whether it is a feeling of silence and solitude or a feeling of anxiety, worry, tension, of any other feeling.

Stage 4: Colour of your feeling

Try to recognize what the feeling is, and then become aware of its colour. Give a colour to your feeling. See hridayakasha becoming filled with that colour. When the feeling changes, which happens naturally and spontaneously, then you have to change the colour consciously and wilfully. That colour should correspond to the feeling. For example, the emotion, the feeling of anger corresponds to the colour red. If there is such a recognition in the mind, then you should see your heart space filled with red light. If there is a feeling of ill health, if you are not feeling well physically, if there is discomfort and you are very conscious of it, then see the corresponding colour, which in this case would be pale yellow.

If there is a feeling of joy, happiness or contentment, if there is a feeling of ego, pride or self satisfaction, if there is a feeling of sadness, loss or grief, or any other feeling, then recognize it and observe it. Then generate the corresponding colour to that feeling within your hridayakasha. If one feeling persists for a long time, then change it by thinking about another feeling which conveys a different emotion, and see the corresponding colour.

Do not dwell upon one feeling or emotion for a long time. Just give yourself enough time to recognize it.

Then consciously and wilfully generate the corresponding colour awareness in hridayakasha and move on to the next feeling. If the feeling appears spontaneously, observe it. If the feeling does not appear and you have to create a feeling, then do so. Remember that the main objective of the practice is colour observation in hridayakasha and not analysis of the feeling. Dispassionately observe any feeling which may arise and give it colour.

Stage 5: Creation of feeling

Now we will no longer observe the natural feelings as they arise. We must create a feeling. Experience the intensity of that feeling and observe the colour simultaneously. Take the feeling of love, for example. Try to experience the feeling of love with the total intensity at your command. Also observe the colour which manifests naturally along with the feeling of intense love.

Feel love with the total intensity of your heart. If you are wondering for whom or for what, then think about someone whom you love intensely. Think about something which can stir up this kind of feeling within you. Thinking of that, go deep into the intensity of feeling within you. You are not to experience this in your head, in chidakasha. This awareness, process, experience and observation are all taking place in hridayakasha only.

Stage 6: Changing the feeling

Now the process becomes threefold: first, creation of a feeling; second, observation and intensification; and third, changing the feeling. After creating a feeling and observing it with full intensity, you have to change it. Create the feeling of silence, as if you are sitting in the depths of the ocean. Be aware of complete silence all around you. Silence which pervades every part of your being. Make every effort to experience this silence which passes through each and every pore of your being. Next go back in time to the moment you were born. There is no conscious recollection of that moment, but deep within you the experience of that moment still exists. Try to feel it. Feel yourself taking birth again. Try to face what you felt then, with intensity.

Now change to the feeling of anxiety, extreme anxiety. Try to experience each and every feeling. Do not just think about it. Change to the feeling of sleep, the feeling which is experienced just as you are drifting off. Feel yourself floating in the boundary between wakefulness and sleep. That momentary awareness which comes every night at the time of sleep should be developed. That feeling is there; awaken it. That memory of drifting from the conscious to the unconscious state, gradual drifting and drifting, is there; awaken it. Change to the feeling of silence, then to the same feeling of contentment, strength, happiness and peace.

Stage 7: Earliest memories

Next become aware of your earliest childhood memory. Recall that memory, the earliest memory that you can remember. See the event that unfolds before you. While observing the event do not allow yourself to be distracted. Remember your earliest childhood memory and see that memory unfold in the form of a movie or in the form of a picture. Make sure it is the earliest one, the first one that you can remember.

While recalling this memory you may become aware of another preceding one. After completion of the first memory, observe the one that came up in between. Dispassionately observe that event unfolding before the inner eye. There is no personal involvement except that you are recalling that event. Once the whole event unfolds before the inner eye and finishes, then try to find an even earlier memory.

With total intensity of the recall faculty observe the earliest memory. Go as far back as you can in life, to the earliest memory. One part of your being is enacting that event. Dispassionately become aware of the earliest memory.

Now you are going to observe and analyze that earliest memory. What does it mean? Does it convey something?

Does it carry an emotion with it? Dissect the memory, the earliest childhood memory. What has it taught you? What has it conveyed to you? What feeling has it aroused in you? Dispassionately and objectively dissect this memory into little pieces. What were the words that you heard while seeing this recall? Words that may have been spoken about you. Words that may have been spoken to you. What were your actions? What were you doing? With whom do you relate this memory? Of whom do you have this memory? Friends or parents or relatives? Who are the actors? What is their mentality and what is their relationship to you? Who are the actors in this memory apart from yourself? In what space and time did this event take place? What was the emotion? What was the feeling that you felt at that particular moment, not during the re-enaction but at that time? What kind of environment was there?

Be aware. Do not allow any detail to escape your attention. With total awareness be aware of every detail in relation to yourself and in relation to the other actors in that memory. Whenever you feel yourself wandering, whenever you feel your awareness dissipating, focus yourself in the heart space. When you are again centred in your awareness, continue to be aware of that earliest memory of your life.

Stage 8: Ending the practice

After dissecting this memory, centre your awareness in the vision of the golden light at anahata. Become aware of the heart space. Experience the infinite space pervading your whole body. Become aware of your physical body sitting in the meditation posture. Feel the weight of your body. Gradually extrovert your mind. Be aware of the room in which you are sitting. Listen to the external sounds. Be aware of your breathing process. Breathe in deeply and then chant *Om* three times.

Hari Om Tat Sat

17
Daharakasha Dharana

In the akasha dharana practices, chidakasha deals with the practices of concentration in relation to the events, memories and experiences that happen in the dimension of name, form and idea. The external sensorial experiences are witnessed in chidakasha. The subtle, emotional and feeling aspect is witnessed and developed in hridayakasha. The pranic, psychic experiences emanate from and are witnessed in daharakasha. However, in order to recognize the pranic and psychic experiences, the external mind, the mind which is active within us at present, has to be properly guided and trained.

Practices of daharakasha

In the process of training there is a section of dharana practices known as *panchatattwa dharana*, or the dharana of the five elements. This dharana is comprised of two different systems. In the first system the five physical tattwas are seen and an in-depth awareness of them is generated. For example, in the body, which is made up of the solid earth element, matter, the solidity of this element is dissected until its atomic nature is seen. In the same way the other elements are visualized. The second system is related to the panchakosha; observing, understanding and analyzing the experiences of the panchakosha, starting from annamaya and going up to anandamaya kosha.

Panchatattwa dharana is part of daharakasha dharana. In order to train the mind to experience these subtle levels and deeper aspects of the tattwas and the koshas, in order to train the mind to observe and understand this process, we have to follow a system of mental education related to the subtle knowledge and experience of the personality.

In yoga the concept of personality is vast. The psychological concept of personality is limited to one's character, qualities, strengths, weaknesses and so on. According to yogic theory however, the personality is a combination of the five koshas together with their related experiences, belonging to both the manifest lower mind and the unmanifest higher mind.

So the basic principles of these different panchatattwa techniques is what we practise in this meditation. The other techniques are placed on top of this one, like the wooden blocks children use to make houses with. In the same way, we are trying to create a structure within the mind where the faculties of consciousness are free to roam about, to see and to experience different things.

We are all aware of the process of breathing, which is generally seen as something very physical. When we breathe in the lungs expand as they are filled with air. When we breathe out the lungs empty themselves. So the whole breathing process is very physical, but within this physical experience, the subtle experiences have to evolve in order for us to obtain a different vision.

Process of intensification
When we actually begin to feel the subtle process our perception changes. It is like seeing with our eyes the solid world around us and then, with the same eyes and vision, perceiving it differently from underwater. The organ of sight, the eye, does not change. The faculty of sight does not change. It is the perception of the eye that changes from one element to the other. If we look around underwater, for example, there will an absence of clarity. There will be

blurriness and even the perception of colour will be altered. The clear perception of colour that we have now may or may not be there.

As we go deeper into the water the range of vision becomes less and at the same time more intense because it is confined to a limited area. At the same time we become more aware. The broader the range of a sensory experience, the greater the possibility of missing something. When the range of perception is limited, the intensity of awareness increases. So even in dharana, when we are trying to focus the faculties of the mind within a particular range, we are reducing the area of attention and intensifying the awareness more and more.

In this process of intensification the body is the basis. It is the first item that always exists and you can experience the body at any time. So there is an acknowledgement of the physical state, "Yes, this is happening," but there is also awareness of the subtle states. This is a very important point. Generally we make a broad statement, "Become aware of the body," but actually we wish to acknowledge the condition the body is in at that moment. When we say become aware of something else which is not the body, which is slightly more subtle or deeper than the physical experience, we mean we should be more aware within that limited range of vision. That is the training we are trying to achieve in the practices of dharana. Reduce the range of perception so that there is greater intensity of awareness and concentration. That is why the body is the basis from which other experiences evolve.

The first body to evolve after the physical is the mental. In panchatattwa dharana, awareness of the mental body concerns four compartments: buddhi, chitta, manas and ahamkara, and of how these mental activities are vitalized. After all, there is a force which vitalizes the thought process, which gives it dynamism. There is a process which makes our ambitions and desires dynamic. What is that process or that force?

In general terms it is prana. However, in the course of dissecting the concept of prana in relation to the breathing process, the subtle body is energized by the aspect of vitality. This is the first manifestation or aspect of prana in relation to the gross dimension. Generally it is said that prana means vitality. Vitality is one of the descriptions of prana. This vitality is seen as the force which energizes the mental body.

The subtle body here is just a term to describe the deep mental processes. The superficial mental processes are thoughts, ambitions, desires and so forth. The subtle mental processes can be summed up in one word as *samskaras*, the seeds from which plants manifesting in external life take birth. Samskaras are related to character, actions, desires. They are the seeds of which the list is practically endless. This samskara aspect in the subtle body is vitalized by prana, which is visualized in the form of streams of energy particles. The energy body, the psychic body, the realm of actual energy activity, is in the form of vibrating prana, pulsating prana, full of life, full of colour, full of warmth, full of light – multidimensional. This then is the beginning of panchatattwa dharana.

Panchatattwa Dharana

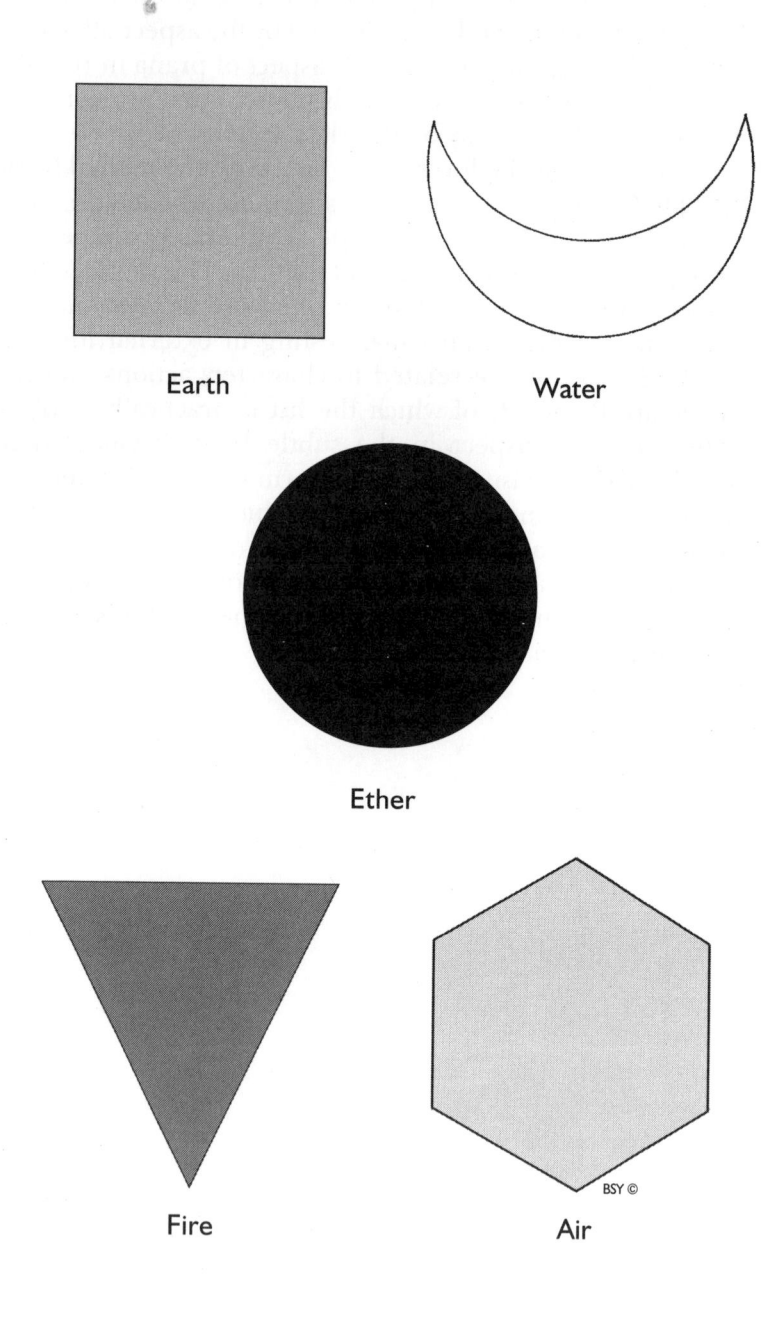

Earth

Water

Ether

Fire

Air

Daharakasha One

PANCHATATTWA DHARANA (A)

According to yogic philosophy, the whole of creation takes place and is sustained by the tattwas. The entire universe is a composition of the tattwas. The Upanishads explain that the five elements or panchatattwa evolved from mind, mind from the cosmic prana and cosmic prana from the superconsciousness. As the human body is made up of the same cosmic elements, the properties of the elements are inherent throughout the body and mind. The influence of these tattwas is so subtle that they affect the entire life pattern and cycle. Everything we do and think is under the influence of the tattwas.

Although these tattwas are known as the five basic elements of earth, water, fire, air and ether, we should not understand them as physical or chemical elements. Rather they should be regarded as the consequences of subtle light and sound emanations which are created by different pranic vibrations. Each tattwa has a particular pranic frequency which affects the body mechanism and the flow of prana. From a particular vibration of prana, sound, light and colour are created. These pranic vibrations, colours and sounds indicate the various tattwas.

The five tattwas form part of an interconnected whole in which each element is derived from the previous one. These five elements are described in the following descending order of evolution.

1. *Akasha* – ether, responsible for void and space
2. *Vayu* – air, responsible for perpetual motion
3. *Agni* – fire, responsible for heat
4. *Apas* – water, responsible for fluidity
5. *Prithvi* – earth, responsible for cohesion and solidity.

The first tattwa to evolve is akasha, which is undifferentiated matter, containing an infinite amount of potential energy. Akasha is the subtle state where both energy and matter exist in the dormant state within the consciousness. As the energy within the particles of akasha begins to vibrate, movement is created and vayu tattwa emerges in the form of air. The particles of vayu have the greatest freedom of movement and, therefore, vayu is seen as all pervading motion.

Due to the excessive movement of energy in vayu, heat is generated, and this acts as the cause for the next tattwa, agni or fire. In agni tattwa the movement of energy is less than that of vayu. This decrease of motion allows agni to dispel part of its radiating heat and thus cool into apas or the water element.

With the birth of apas tattwa, the complete freedom of vayu and the partial freedom of agni are lost and the particles of matter are confined within a definite space, moving only within a small radius. The last tattwa, prithvi or earth, evolves out of a further decrease in energy vibration which causes the water to solidify into earth. Here even the limited freedom of apas movement is lost. Each particle of prithvi has its own place and any vibration within it is confined to the space which it occupies.

Prithvi tattwa

For the purpose of this meditation we will begin with prithvi tattwa dharana or concentration on the earth element, which is the first in the series of the five tattwa dharanas. Here a yellow square is visualized in daharakasha. The square or four-sided figure represents solidity. This figure is at total rest. There is no movement; only perfect stability. It is completely balanced; nothing is imbalanced.

According to kundalini yoga, yellow is the colour attributed to the earth yantra. This yantra is square in shape, which represents the manifestation of cosmic energy from the unmanifest to the manifest and the formation of the physical body. The physical body is the final manifestation of cosmic energy. So the image of the yellow square and of the physical body go hand in hand. Thus there is awareness of these two together in this stage of the practice. The yellow square is the psychic manifestation and the physical body is the gross manifestation of the earth element.

Prithvi tattwa brings stability and permanence in every respect, physically, mentally and in the environment. Physically it is located between the knees and the toes. Mentally it is related to the conscious and subconscious levels. Its psychic location is mooladhara chakra. It is related with *bhuh loka*, the earth plane and *annamaya kosha*, the food or physical body. The subtle sensory perception of prithvi is *gandha* or smell, which is conveyed through the sensory organ of the nose.

Apas tattwa
Apas tattwa or the water element is visualized between the navel and the knees in the form of a silver crescent moon. In the physical body, water is the first tangible tattwa to emerge as matter in the form of fluids. The crescent moon is thus a symbol of fluidity. The silver colour of the moon is very close to the grey colour, representing the merger of light and darkness, black and white, day and night, the manifest and the unmanifest.

Physically apas tattwa is located in the region between the navel and the knees. Mentally it represents mahat tattwa in which all four experiences of manas, buddhi, chitta and ahamkara are contained. It is the source of all subtle mental activities. This element corresponds to *bhuvah loka*, the intermediate astral plane and to *pranamaya kosha*, the energy body. The sensory perception related to apas is taste, which is conveyed through the sensory organ of the tongue.

Agni tattwa

Agni or the fire element is energy in the first stage of manifestation, which is in the form of light and heat. It is by the appearance of light that form is perceived. Thus agni tattwa is responsible for the perception of form which is cognized through the sensory organ of the eye. Without the presence of form there can be no attachment. So agni tattwa is also the first stage where ahamkara or ego begins to assert itself. As light gives form to energy, ahamkara becomes aware of something outside itself. Thus the seed of individual ego is born.

The colour representing the vibrational frequency of agni is red. Thus the yantra of agni is a fiery red inverted triangle. This triangle is made up of particles of red light vibrating and radiating incessantly. In the physical body agni is located between the navel and the heart. It is responsible for the digestive fire as well as the yogic fire which burns away the accumulated dross on the inner levels of our being, making it possible to attain the results of higher sadhana. Mentally it is related to the subconscious mind. Its psychic location is at manipura chakra. It belongs to the dimension of *swah loka*, the divine plane, and to *manomaya kosha*, the mental body.

Vayu tattwa

Vayu or the air element has the nature of movement. This gives rise to the grey-blue colour which is distinctive of this tattwa. Thus the yantra of vayu is visualized as a six-sided grey-blue hexagon. It can also be seen in the form of six grey-blue gaseous dots placed in a hexagonal pattern between the heart and the eyebrow centre. Vayu directly corresponds to prana within the body and hence its physical location is in the chest.

Vayu tattwa is invisible in the material sense. At this subtle stage matter is still in its undifferentiated form. It can be described as energy in motion. In the physical body vayu enables the sensation of touch to be conveyed through the sensory organ *twacha* or skin. Mentally it is related to the subconscious mind. Its psychic centre is anahata, the heart chakra. It corresponds to the dimension of *mahah loka*, the plane of saints and siddhas, and to *vijnanamaya* kosha, the psychic or intuitive body.

Akasha tattwa

Akasha or the ether element is the space in which all matter becomes manifest. It is the subtlest of the panchatattwa, being all pervading, motionless and still. Because the element of ether is limitless and pervades the entire cosmos, it is visualized as the circle of the void. As the void exists in the absence of light, akasha has been described as transparent or black, having no colour. Yet within the blackness all the colours of the spectrum are contained. Thus the circular yantra of akasha is filled with multicoloured dots representing the nature of the void.

The vibration of this tattwa is so subtle that it cannot be perceived by the external senses. Therefore, as long as we function through the senses we cannot perceive this subtle vibration. When the mental frequencies correlate to those of ether, through dhyana one goes beyond time. It is the ether element which is known in yogic terms as 'the space of consciousness.' In the physical body akasha is all pervasive. At the mental level it controls the emotions and passions. It is said that when akasha tattwa is predominant the mind is turned away from sensorial experiences. Therefore, this element is very important for spiritual progress. Physically akasha is located at the top of the head between the eyebrow centre and the crown. Mentally it is related to the unconscious mind. Its psychic location is at vishuddhi chakra. Spiritually it corresponds to *janah loka*, the plane of rishis and munis, and to *anandamaya kosha*, the blissful or causal body.

Technique
Stage 1: Preparation
Sit in a comfortable meditation posture with the spine and head straight. Keep the eyes closed. Internally become aware of the physical posture and areas of discomfort, tightness or tension in the body. In the process of body observation, if you come to an area of physical discomfort, tightness or tension then try to adjust and relax it in order to be at total ease. If you find it necessary to move your body during the practice, do not allow the physical movement to distract your attention or concentration from the practice. Once you have taken your awareness through the different parts of the body, internally develop the feeling of physical stability, comfort and ease.

Stage 2: Sensory awareness
Extend your senses outwards into the environment. Become aware of the existing environment around you. Become aware of every kind of sensory perception being acknowledged by your brain. Become aware of all the auditory, tactile and other sensory inputs. Just acknowledge that these external experiences exist around you in the environment.

Listen to the different sounds, one by one. Allow the awareness to move freely from sound to sound without analyzing, simply listening. Feel the different tactile sensations such as itching, coolness, pressure, tingling. Be aware of different smells. One by one let the awareness register the different sensory perceptions which it receives from the external environment.

Stage 3: Prithvi tattwa dharana
Now internalize the senses and become aware of the inner space that pervades the entire body from head to toe. Total awareness of the space within the body. Take the entire perception, the entire consciousness, to daharakasha, the space that exists in the lower part of the body, in the region of mooladhara, swadhisthana and manipura. Observe the space between the perineum and

the navel. Direct the entire consciousness downward from the head space to daharakasha. Go to the depths of this space. Experience the deep, dark cavernous space of daharakasha.

With your entire awareness and attention centred in daharakasha develop the vision of a large, solid, heavy square. Develop the vision of a square filling up the daharakasha region. Visualize the square, which is yellow in colour. Be alert, be conscious. Be intensely involved in the observation of a square, yellow in colour, in the region of daharakasha. Move your awareness around all four sides of the square. See its yellow colour very clearly. When the vision of a yellow square is clearly seen in daharakasha, then extend that vision of the yellow square so that it covers the entire, physical body, as if the body is placed inside that yellow square. See the physical body inside the large, luminous yellow square. The yellow square is not a dull but a luminous bright colour. Maintain your awareness of the large, luminous, yellow square which covers your whole body and see yourself sitting inside it.

The yellow square is the yantra of the element earth or prithvi tattwa. Prithvi tattwa is represented by the physical body. The square sits firmly on the ground. In the same way the entire physical body is sitting firmly on the floor without loss of balance. There is firmness, stability and solidity in the physical structure. Similarly there is firmness, stability and solidity in the yantra of prithvi tattwa. The luminous yellow square surrounds the entire body and illumines the body with its radiance.

Go deep into the process of observation and feeling. Go deep into the process of visualization. Visualize the physical body inside the yantra of the earth element. Observe the luminosity of the yantra surrounding the entire body. Now deepen your awareness of the yantra and the colour. Try to observe the luminous particles of light which comprise the yantra. See the luminous particles of yellow colour which are contained inside the prithvi tattwa yantra, the earth yantra.

Each particle of this luminous, yellow light is pulsating, vibrating in harmony with the atoms of the body. Feel the harmony of the pulsation. Feel the harmony of the vibration of physical atoms and the particles of light of the prithvi yantra. Be intensely involved in the process of observation and the experience of daharakasha surrounding the entire body. When the vision of prithvi yantra begins to fade, let the yellow square simply dissolve into akasha, into space. Be aware of the clear akasha, the inner space.

Stage 4: Apas tattwa dharana

Now take the awareness back down to daharakasha. Experience the space in the region between mooladhara and manipura, the area between the perineum and the navel. There observe the yantra of the water element. Visualize a silver crescent moon. Develop a clear visualization. Observe the image of a silver crescent moon in daharakasha, representing the water element or apas tattwa.

Once you are able to develop a clear vision of the apas yantra, the silver crescent moon, then expand the yantra to cover the entire mental body. Be aware of the silvery particles of light emanating from the apas yantra and permeating the entire mental body.

The apas yantra represents the entire mental body of the mahat tattwa, the greater mind. In mahat tattwa the four aspects of mind – manas, buddhi, chitta and ahamkara, are contained. It is the source of all the subtle, mental activities. While being aware of this apas yantra, also become aware of the ego identity. Develop the feeling of yourself as an individual. "I am the individual spirit." Ego identity is the awareness of "I am" or "I exist as an independent unit, as an individual".

From the ahamkara experience move into the chitta experience. "I am aware, I observe." Experience the process of individual awareness. Observe the process of self-observation which knows the individual personality and structure. From here move into the buddhi experience. Experience the aspect of analyzing, translating the illogical experiences into logical phrases which are understood by the self. Observe the aspect of analysis, comprehension and conviction.

Then move to the experience of manas. Observe the awareness that jumps from one object to the next, from one name to the next, from one identity to the next, from one form to the next, from one idea to the next. These four aspects comprise the range of mahat, which is being illumined by the apas yantra. Know your mahat to be in harmony with the vibration, with the pulsation of the apas yantra, the silver crescent moon. Now let this vision, this awareness, dissipate into akasha, the space experience.

Stage 5: Agni tattwa dharana

Again become aware of daharakasha. Centre your awareness in the lower space between mooladhara and manipura. Visualize a fiery red inverted triangle within the lower space. See the red triangle filling up the entire space. Move your awareness along the three sides of the triangle. Concentrate on the image of the triangle in daharakasha until it becomes vivid and clear. See the fiery red colour. Total awareness of the red triangle.

When the vision of the triangle becomes clear and steady extend it to cover the whole body. Be aware of red coloured light in the form of a triangle covering your whole body. Visualize yourself sitting inside a large, inverted red triangle. Go deep into the process of observation and feeling. Go deep into the process of visualization. See your own body sitting inside the agni yantra. Observe the luminosity of the yantra surrounding the entire body. See the fiery red colour. Observe the luminous red particles of light which comprise the agni yantra.

Each particle of red light is pulsating and vibrating in harmony with the energy field of your body. Feel the vitality of the colour red. Be intensely involved in the process of observation and the experience of daharakasha surrounding the entire body. If the attention wanders bring it back to the visualization, the experience of agni yantra in daharakasha. When you feel agni yantra beginning to fade, let the red triangle dissolve back into space. Be aware of the clear akasha, the inner space.

Stage 6: Vayu tattwa dharana

Bring the entire awareness back down to daharakasha. Experience the space in the region between mooladhara and manipura. Feel your awareness penetrating into the depths of this lower space, like a deep sea diver going down to the bottom of the ocean. Total awareness of the silent, deep space. Within the depths of daharakasha begin to perceive the blue-grey hexagon of the air element. See the six-sided figure clearly within the lower space. Concentrate on the vayu yantra which fills up the whole of daharakasha with blue-grey light. Move your awareness slowly along each of the six sides of the hexagon. Maintain the vision of the vayu yantra in daharakasha.

When you are able to visualize the blue-grey hexagon clearly, experience the yantra expanding to cover your entire body. Observe the colour which is luminous and bright. Be aware of the blue-grey particles of light emanating from the vayu yantra. Observe these particles of light which are pulsating and vibrating in harmony with your inner being. See yourself surrounded and pervaded totally by the blue-grey light of the vayu yantra. Visualize your body sitting inside the blue-grey hexagon. Maintain the intensity of this vision with total clarity and one-pointed concentration. When the image of vayu yantra begins to fade, let the blue-grey hexagon dissolve into akasha, inner space.

Stage 7: Akasha tattwa dharana

Bring your entire awareness back down to daharakasha. Experience the lower space between the navel and the perineum. Enter into this space fearlessly and go deeper and deeper into the dark, bottomless pit. Within the depths of daharakasha observe the circular yantra of the akasha tattwa. See the circle of the void. As the void exists in the absence of light, this yantra is transparent or black, having no colour. Yet within the blackness or transparency all colours are contained.

Therefore, this circle of the void is filled with multi-coloured dots, tiny multicoloured points of light which are moving at high speed and constantly rearranging themselves. They move at such a high velocity that, at a glance, it seems they are absolutely still. Look into the circle of the void which fills up the entire space of daharakasha. Maintain the vision with total intensity of awareness. Do not allow the attention to slip.

When you are able to visualize the akasha yantra clearly and hold the image, then slowly expand it. Experience the circle of the void surrounding and pervading your entire being. There is nothing but space all through you and all around you. See the tiny points of light moving rapidly in all directions, forming clusters of colour here and there, and then rearranging themselves in completely different patterns. Visualize yourself inside the circle of the void, the akasha yantra.

Merge your entire consciousness, your entire being into the akasha yantra. There is nothing but space, vast, infinite, silent, without beginning or end. Focus your awareness with absolute clarity and intensity on the circle of the void. When this vision begins to fade allow the akasha yantra to dissolve back into the inner space.

Stage 8: Ending the practice

Now get ready to end the practice. Again become aware of the inner space pervading the whole body from head to toe. Develop the feeling of the physical body. Be aware of your meditation posture. Feel the weight of your body. Feel the pressure of the body against the floor. Become aware of the external environment. Listen to the external sounds. Take a deep breath in and chant *Om* three times.

Hari Om Tat Sat

Daharakasha Two

PANCHATATTWA DHARANA (B)

In this practice the different qualities and symbols of the tattwas are explored at three levels: conscious, subconscious and unconscious. In order to understand what these qualities and symbols are and how they relate to human consciousness, let us first look at the theory of evolution which was expounded by the Samkhya school of thought. Samkhya philosophy goes into a detailed explanation of the manifestation of consciousness and energy in the form of Purusha and Prakriti.

There is a universal body of consciousness which is known as Purusha. The word *Purusha* itself means awareness which is contained within a structure and which is in a state of dormancy. That universal consciousness or Purusha is considered to be absolutely pure without any fault or limitation. Alongside Purusha there is another entity, the universal energy. This universal energy is known as *Prakriti* or nature, which governs the whole of creation.

Samkhya has viewed Purusha and Prakriti as the twin forces behind the manifest and unmanifest creation. Originally these two forces were separate. However, something happened in the state of their separateness which brought them together. When these two forces came together and merged as one, an alteration took place in their natural state of being. This alteration is quite natural; we can understand it even now. For example, the combination of hydrogen and oxygen creates a third substance. In the same way the union or merging of Purusha and Prakriti created a third thing; the offspring of their union are known as tattwas.

Tattwa is the final manifestation or the full growth of an expression of Purusha and Prakriti. In the primary stages the tattwas were in the form of bhootas. The word *bhoota* means 'spirit'. It is similar to the concept in the Bible where it says, "...and the spirit moved upon the earth..." These bhootas are the originating point of the tattwas. Metamorphosis from the level of spirit to the physical level then took place. When that metamorphosis took place from something subtle to something concrete, the concrete nature was termed tattwa.

The word *tattwa* means 'a defined body.' The primary tattwas which we already know are: akasha (ether), vayu (air), agni (fire), apas (water) and prithvi (earth). Along with the manifestation of these elements came the nature, quality or perception of these elements. The quality of earth is different to that of water. The quality of water is different to that of fire. Their natures are different and the way of perceiving the different natures is known as *tanmatra*.

The tanmatras are said to be the subtle essence of the tattwas. The five tanmatras are: (i) *shabda* or sound, the subtle essence of akasha tattwa; (ii) *sparsha* or touch, the subtle essence of vayu tattwa; (iii) *roopa* or form, the subtle essence of agni tattwa; (iv) *rasa* or taste, the subtle essence of apas tattwa, and (v) *gandha* or smell, the subtle essence of prithvi tattwa.

These five tanmatra are perceived by the five jnanendriya, organs of knowledge, which are: (i) *srota* or ears, the auditory sense, perception of sound; (ii) *twacha* or skin, the tactile sense, perception of touch or feeling; (iii) *chakshu* or eyes, the optic sense, perception of form; (iv) *jihwa* or tongue, the gustatory sense, perception of taste, and (v) *ghrana* or nose, the olfactory sense, perception of smell.

It is actually from the five tanmatra that the five tattwas have evolved. The tanmatra and the tattwas are also associated with the chakras. Thus in mooladhara we find the yellow square representing the earth element and the tanmatra of smell. Similarly, in swadhisthana there is the white crescent moon of the water element and the tanmatra of taste. In manipura there is the fiery red triangle and the tanmatra of form. In anahata there is the blue hexagon of the air element and the tanmatra of touch. In vishuddhi there is the circle of the void or ether element and the tanmatra of sound.

This practice leads one progressively through the conscious, subconscious and unconscious dimensions of the tattwas. First, the everyday sensory objects are experienced internally by the jnanendriyas. This correlates the tattwas with the conscious level of perception. Second, certain feelings, symbols and scenes are evoked which correspond to the tattwas at the subconscious level. Third, certain devata or aspects of divinity are visualized which correlate the tattwas with the unconscious level.

In this way each of the five tattwas is individually explored and assigned its own particular place in our evolutionary process. By exploring the different dimensions of the tattwas in this way we begin to perceive the interplay of the elements with consciousness and energy or Purusha and Prakriti. By recreating the process of evolution we can experience each aspect as an integral part of the intricate whole.

Technique
Stage 1: Preparation
Sit in a comfortable meditation posture. Adjust your position so that the spine is erect and the head is slightly back. Place the hands on the knees in chin or jnana mudra. The eyes and lips should be gently closed. Become aware of the whole body from the top of the head to the tips of the toes. Move your awareness from one part of the body to the next and make sure there is no tightness or tension in any part. Become aware of the whole body by moving the mind from one part to the next. Be aware of any tension or relaxation in each and every part. Feel the whole body becoming relaxed and comfortable.

Stage 2: Body stillness
Become aware of the posture in which you are sitting. Concentrate on the posture of the body. Feel the body becoming steady and still. As you continue to be aware of the posture feel the stillness and motionlessness. The whole body is completely steady and immobile. Try to experience absolute stillness and silence within the whole physical body.

Stage 3: Prithvi tattwa/smell
Conscious level: Within this silence and stillness become aware of the space within the body. Experience the space which pervades the entire body from the top of the head to the tips of the toes. Experience the *sthoolakasha*, the space throughout the body. Develop total awareness of the space which pervades your whole body. Within this space become aware of prithvi tattwa, the earth element, which is related with the sense of smell. Bring your awareness to the sense of smell. Observe what smells are in the environment right now.

Become aware of the smell of a rose. Recall the scent of a rose and try to smell it right now as if you had just picked the rose. Now change to the smell of jasmine. Be aware of the smell of jasmine. Intensify the awareness of the scent of jasmine.

As the different objects are named try to be intensely aware of each smell, as if the object is right in front of you. Try to hold that awareness for just a few moments and then move on to the next. Be aware of the smell of a guava, of ghee frying, mustard oil, hot rice. Be intensely aware of each separate smell. Smell fresh wood, sandalwood, a tulsi plant. Be aware of the smell of petrol, soap and smoke.

Now recall and be aware of the smell of a hospital, medicines, urine, faeces, perspiration. The smell of tobacco, incense, wet earth after rain, mildew. The smell of the ocean and the smell of camphor.

Subconscious level: Now leave the sense of smell and bring the awareness back to the physical body. Become aware of the whole body. Feel the stillness of your body. Your body is completely motionless and still. Begin to be aware of the heaviness of the body. Feel the body becoming heavy like the earth. Be aware of the stillness of the body and the heaviness of the body. Feel the body becoming heavy and still like the earth.

Create the feeling of your body sitting inside the earth. The earth surrounding the entire body. Above you is earth. Below you is earth. Become one with the earth. You are the earth. Smell the earth.

Within this awareness of earth visualize clearly a deep red lotus flower. See the deep red colour of the lotus flower and the detail of the petals. Let the awareness of the red lotus fade and visualize a yellow square. See a large, bright yellow square. Intensify the awareness of this yellow square. See the four sides of the square enclosing the bright yellow colour.

Do not allow the awareness to be distracted or the mind to wander from the practice. Now let go of the image of the yellow square and visualize a smoky grey shivalingam. Visualize the shivalingam clearly and become aware of the smoky grey colour. See this smoky grey shivalingam encircled by a serpent. See the serpent coiled around the smoky grey shivalingam. This coiled serpent represents the dormant kundalini or spiritual force.

As the image of the shivalingam and the serpent fade, visualize an elephant in the space of the body. This elephant has seven trunks. Visualize this image clearly. See all the details of the elephant with the seven trunks. Feel the heaviness and solidity of this elephant which is symbolic of prithvi tattwa.

Unconscious level: Bring the awareness back to the space pervading the entire body, sthoolakasha. Be completely aware of sthoolakasha. Within sthoolakasha see the image of Bhuh Devi, the earth goddess, black in colour. Visualize the graceful form of Bhuh Devi and see her adorned with many ornaments. Bhuh Devi has four arms. In one hand she is holding sugar cane, in her second hand she holds a bow, in her third hand is new corn, and in her fourth hand is a pitcher, symbols of all we receive from the earth. Visualize clearly the image of Bhuh Devi, who is black in colour.

Now let the image of the earth goddess fade. Create and visualize clearly the image of Ganesh. See Ganesh sitting on a low stool. Visualize his elephant head with the large ears, representing the continuous and intelligent listening ability required by the seeker of truth. See both tusks, one of which is broken, and see the long trunk flowing down between them. He has four arms. In one hand he holds an axe with which he cuts the attachments to the world of plurality, thus ending sorrows. In his second hand is a rope drawing the seeker nearer and nearer to the truth. In his third hand he has a *modaka*, a rice ball, which represents the reward of constant sadhana. His fourth hand is in abhay mudra, by which he gives strength to the seeker and removes all obstacles.

His right foot is resting on his left thigh and his left foot is on the ground, representing the integration of mind and intellect. In front of Ganesh is a bowl of sweets, symbolizing all the glories of existence, which are always at the service of great yogis. Sitting near Ganesh is a little mouse. See the whole image clearly and vividly. Be aware of each and every detail and experience the feeling of contentment and harmony which Ganesh radiates.

Stage 4: Apas tattwa/taste

Conscious level: Let go of these images and of the awareness of the earth element. Become aware again of sthoolakasha. Feel the space pervading the entire body. Now focus your attention on apas tattwa, the water element. Taste is the tanmatra which is related with the water element. Bring your attention to the taste which is in your mouth right now. Be aware of this taste. As different foods are named, try to create and experience each taste with intensity, as if you were eating that food at this moment. Imagine you are eating a rasagula. Recall the taste and experience it right now. Hold it for just a few moments and then let it go. Create the taste of chocolate, ice cream, coca cola. Taste the sweetness of a ripe mango. Taste the sourness of a lemon. Now taste onion, cardamon, cloves, ginger. Experience the taste of milk, butter, curd, cheese. The taste of bitter neem, of salt, sugar, honey and kheer, sweet rice.

Subconscious level: Now let this awareness of taste fade and become aware again of the body pervaded by space. Imagine yourself sitting in a mountain stream underneath a waterfall. Above you is water, below you is water. Water is falling all around you like a curtain. Feel the cool spray of the water. Feel the weight of the water as it falls. Feel the fluidity. Feel yourself becoming fluid and merging with the water. Feel yourself flowing like water, cold water. Experience the feeling of being pulled downstream with the current of the water. You flow without resistance. Taste the cold water.

Still keeping the feeling of fluidity visualize a white lotus. See every detail. The brilliant white colour, the perfect clear petals. The coolness of the white lotus. See the brilliant white lotus filling the entire sthoolakasha. Be intensely aware of the white lotus for a few moments, then let it fade slowly into the space.

As the white lotus merges into the space, visualize a white crescent moon. See the pure white of the crescent moon, the smooth flowing curves of the crescent moon. Let the image fill the entire space. Be aware of the soft, cool radiance of the moon pervading the whole sthoolakasha. Feel your self becoming one with the pure white crescent moon.

Letting this image of the crescent moon fade, begin to visualize a large white crocodile. Allow the white crocodile to fill the space as you see it in greater and greater detail. See the sharp teeth and large mouth. See the long tail of the crocodile, his short feet. The crocodile is white, almost dazzling in its brilliance.

Now let this image of the crocodile fade into the dark ocean. Become aware of the ocean waves, the constant movement of the ocean waves. The night is dark, lit up by a crescent moon and the stars. See this image clearly. The dark sky lit up by a crescent moon and stars. The light of the moon and stars is reflected in the vast dark ocean. Be aware of the depth of the ocean and its constant movement.

Unconscious level: Let go of this image now. In the space visualize Lord Vishnu reclining on Sheshnag, a large black cobra with many hoods. See them floating in the middle of an ocean of milk. Visualize a large pink lotus emerging from Vishnu's navel, upon which Brahma is sitting. See Lakshmi, representing wealth, power and glory, sitting at Vishnu's feet. This image can be seen clearly when the mind is looking inwards, introverted, when it is not running after outside experiences. Try to see the image clearly and with intensity.

Visualize the large black cobra with many hoods. On this cobra Vishnu, blue in colour, representing the infinite, is reclining in yoga nidra. They are floating on a sea of milk which represents human kindness. Brahma is sitting on the pink lotus emerging from Vishnu's navel; the creator is emerging from the infinite. Lakshmi, the consort of Vishnu, is massaging his feet. Visualize this image for a few more moments.

Stage 5: Agni tattwa/form

Conscious level: Again bring the awareness to sthoolakasha. Be aware of the vast space of sthoolakasha. The next stage of the practice is awareness of agni tattwa, the fire element. Form is the tanmatra associated with this tattwa. Here you must become aware of the different forms being created in sthoolakasha. See each form or scene as clearly as you can, bringing as much detail into it as possible.

Visualize snow covered mountains, a rocky mountain, a green fertile mountain. See a wide river with sandy banks on both sides, with green fields on both sides, with jungle on both sides. See a river with fishing boats, sail boats, steam boats. See people bathing in the river. See a mango tree laden with fruit. See a whole mango grove.

Keep moving the awareness from one image to the next. Do not let the attention wander or remain with one particular form. Visualize a small village, a lotus pond, the rising sun. See a clear blue sky, wispy white clouds, dark clouds, heavy rainfall, a rainbow. Visualize a star studded sky with no moon. Visualize the half moon, the full moon. Create the image of a neem tree, a banyan tree, a flowering tree. Visualize birds sitting in the tree, white doves flying, a peacock with tail feathers fanned out, a green parrot, a nilkant, a crow. Visualize a rat, snake, vulture, spider, lizard, dog, goat, lion, monkey, a cow with her calf, a buffalo. See a moving bicycle, moving car, moving truck, bus, tram, train. See a dead body being burned. See a deep, silent forest, a Krishna temple, a Shiva temple.

Subconscious level: Now imagine yourself sitting inside a large blazing fire. See the flames leaping up on all sides of you. Feel the intense heat of the fire. See the golden, red and blue flames on every side. Feel the heat becoming intense, you are becoming hotter and hotter. Do not resist the heat or the flames, allow yourself to merge with the burning heat, feel yourself becoming the fire itself. Feel you are the fire, burning up all that you come into contact with. Be that raging fire.

Slowly begin to let go of this image and allow it to merge with the space around you. Now visualize a bright yellow lotus flower. See the bright glow of the lotus, see each petal separately. Be aware of the vibrancy of the lotus flower. Hold the image for a few moments and then let it dissipate. As the lotus disappears see a red inverted triangle emerge in the space. You can almost feel the heat from the triangle, the red colour is so strong, like a blazing fire.

Now see the sun. Visualize the hot glowing orb of the noonday sun. Feel the intense heat and light from the blazing sun. Be aware of the energy and power of the sun. As this image fades create a picture of a ram, representing manipura chakra, the strength and vitality which is contained in the solar plexus. See the picture of the ram making its way through all obstacles, strong and forward moving.

Unconscious level: Let the awareness come back again to the space pervading the entire body. Now visualize Surya, the god of fire. He is a golden deity. His arms and hands are golden, his hair is golden. He is radiating golden light in all directions. The chariot he rides across the sky is golden and has a golden umbrella to cover him. The chariot is drawn by seven green horses with black manes and red legs.

As he begins his journey across the sky each morning the darkness of the night takes to its heels and the whole world is aroused to activity.

Experience this golden life-giving light which is radiating from Surya. Feel it spreading through your entire being, dispelling the inner darkness which clouds the intellect and causes ignorance. Feel this light filling the whole space around you. Feel yourself one with this light. Surya possesses both heat and light. Light with which he dispels darkness and sustains and energizes the entire world and heat by which he overcomes all obstacles. Experience this light and heat flooding your entire being.

Move now to another aspect of fire. Visualize the god Agni. Agni is visualized as being deep red in colour. He has two faces which represent the two aspects of fire: creative heat and destructive fire. He has three legs and seven arms. When he is mounted he has a ram as his vehicle and his banner bears this animal. From each mouth a forked tongue of flame is issuing. Agni is always youthful, he is never touched by decay. He is immortal.

See Agni burning redly. He is the brightest and most scorching of the deities. He is pure because he burns all impurities. Agni takes us to the highest light. Visualize his ever-expanding fire. Slowly let the awareness of agni tattwa merge with the space.

Stage 6: Vayu tattwa/touch

Conscious level: Now we move on to vayu tattwa, the air element. The tanmatra of touch is the indriya for the air element. Become aware of touch. Feel the touch of your clothes against your skin, your hands resting on your knees. Imagine you are stroking a cat. Feel the soft, smooth, silky fur of the cat as you stroke it. Then change to stroking a dog. Feel the different texture, the rough, wiry hair of the dog.

Experience touching a cow, a bird then a snake. Be aware of the different textures, temperature and sensations created by each animal. Feel the touch of a fish, the cold, scaly skin.

Create the feeling of cold; feel cold air touching the skin, creating goose bumps. Change to the feeling of heat; feel hot air touching the skin. Feel your mother's touch on your cheeks. Experience the feeling of skin touching skin. Feel the touch of a small baby, the touch of a friend, the touch of your husband or wife, be aware of the physical and also the more subtle sensations created by each contact of touch.

Now experience the feeling of tight jeans, silk cloth, velvet, a wire brush, a steel pot, a gunny bag, a woollen blanket. Keep the awareness moving. Be aware of the softness, hardness, coolness or warmth. Be aware of all the different textures of the objects. Imagine you are reaching out and touching each one individually.

Be aware of the tactile sensation of flowers, sand, stone, an apple, an orange, a leaf, the wet earth, an ant biting, the sting of a bee, a mosquito bite, a pinch, a slap. Feel the sharpness and pain these create. The sensation of biting, tickling, dampness, dryness, itching, and the stickiness of glue. Feel the different effect each sensation has on the body, how the body reacts to the contact with each object.

Imagine yourself walking barefoot on wet grass, feel the coolness and softness of the wet grass; walking barefoot on sharp stones, or thorns; walking barefoot on a road which is burning hot from the heat of the sun; walking barefoot on a cold marble floor, in water, on ice, in snow, the cold crunchy feeling of snow under your feet. Be aware of the breeze created by a fan, of cool rain.

Subconscious level: Let these sensations fade and again become aware of the space all around you. See yourself within this space and become aware of a gentle breeze blowing. Feel the wind touching your skin. The wind is growing stronger. Feel the wind blowing all around you, filling up the whole space. Feel the wind on your back, against the front of your body. Feel the wind above you and underneath you. There is nothing but wind all around you, making you lighter and lighter. The wind is emptying your body of weight. You are becoming weightless. Feel yourself being carried by the wind, slowly becoming like the wind until there is no difference between you and the wind. Feel yourself being blown in every direction. There is nothing holding you, you can move freely in every direction, at any speed, with the wind. Experience the touch of the wind.

Slowly let this feeling dissipate and become aware once again of the deep dark space. Visualize a blue lotus. Blue is the colour of vayu tattwa, the unconfined aspect of air. A bright blue lotus. See it clearly. Now let it fade and draw two interlacing triangles, one triangle pointing upward and the other pointing downward. Follow the outline of the triangles as you draw them. Clearly see the two interlacing triangles.

In the darkness of the space become aware of a tiny light. See a tiny jyoti burning in the darkness. See the light radiating and filling the space. The jyoti is steady and unflickering. Watch this tiny, bright, unflickering flame for a few moments. The jyoti represents the still, unchanging self within.

Now visualize a large, still lake. There is no movement on the lake, it is completely still. The surface of the lake is like a mirror reflecting the blue of the sky. As you gaze into the lake become aware of the depth and stillness of the lake. Intensify that feeling of stillness and silence. As you gaze into the deep water of the lake see a black antelope. Visualize a black antelope. See the graceful, flowing movements of this inky black antelope. The antelope is swift and sure in its movements, it is light and free.

Unconscious level: When this image begins to fade let it become part of the space. Within this dark space visualize Vayu, also known as Marut, the god of wind. Vayu is blue in colour, which represents the infinite. He is as fast as thought. His vehicle is the antelope, the symbol of fleetness. In one hand he holds a fan, representing his constant creation of wind. Vayu pervades all things.

He drives a shining car drawn by a pair of ruddy steeds. He possesses the power of healing. Being very powerful, he is often likened to a bull. He holds a sabre, denoting his energy and acuteness. Try to create this image of Vayu. Be aware of his constant, flowing movement. Try to perceive the air element which pervades all things. Hold this awareness for a few moments longer, before letting it fade into the sthoolakasha.

Stage 7: Akasha tattwa/sound

Conscious level: Now we come to akasha tattwa, the ether element. Be aware of the space in which your body is sitting. Feel the space all around your body and pervading your whole body. The space within the body is the same as the space around the body. This is akasha tattwa.

Sound is the tanmatra associated with akasha tattwa. For the next few minutes become aware of the different sounds all around you. Centre your whole awareness on sound. Now create the sound of a bell ringing. Hear the sound of a bell ringing clearly. Hear the sound of a conch. Hear the gentle sound of a flute. Hear the striking of a gong; feel the vibrations of the sound. Hear the sound of cymbals, of a damaru, of a mridanga, of a tabla. Hear the soft sound of anklets jingling, of birds singing, a car horn beeping, a baby crying, mantra chanting, kirtan being sung.

Now hear footsteps, the sound of people talking and laughing, the sound of someone coughing, sneezing, snoring. Hear a telephone ringing, an alarm clock, a train moving, a train whistle, heavy machinery working, the sound of typing.

For the next few moments recall the sounds made by different animals, a cow mooing, a cat meowing, a dog barking, a frog croaking, crickets singing. Hear the crash of thunder and the sound of heavy rainfall. Hear an aeroplane flying overhead.

Subconscious level: Let these sounds fade and bring the awareness back to the space all around you, the space within you. Feel as if you are floating through space. Your body is light, weightless and floating through the vast, inky black space. As you float through the dark space become aware of asteroids passing by. Become aware of the stars scattered through the darkness, bright, twinkling points of light. As you continue to float through space see the moon and the sun. Feel yourself merging into the space in which you are floating, becoming one with the space. Experience akasha tattwa, you are akasha tattwa.

In akasha tattwa, the ether element, see a large, shining symbol of *Om*. See the *Om* symbol vibrating and radiant. Be aware of the soft, continuous unbroken chanting of the mantra *Om*, filling the whole space. Now visualize the full moon. See the cool white light of the full moon. Visualize an elephant, snow white in colour. See the elephant large and clear. There is no speck of colour on the elephant, it is snow white. Now visualize an inky black shivalingam. The shivalingam is dark and dense.

Unconscious level: Now let go of all images and try to imagine Dyaus, the oldest of the vedic gods, representing the sky or the firmament. Visualize the boundless and illuminating firmament, the sky or heaven in the form of a masculine, fatherly deity, god the father. Dyaus represents pure consciousness, which is unchanging and unchangeable, which has no beginning and no end, which is within everything and at the same time beyond everything. This pure consciousness can assume or manifest all forms but in itself it is formless. Try to experience this pure consciousness.

Stage eight: ending the practice

Now get ready to end the practice. Become aware of the space all around you, the space in which you are sitting. Gradually develop the awareness of the physical body. Become aware of the posture in which you are sitting. Feel the contact between the body and the floor. Feel the weight of the physical body. Be aware of any sounds in the external environment as you slowly externalize your mind. Be aware of your surroundings. Now take a deep breath in and chant *Om* three times.

Hari Om Tat Sat

Daharakasha Three

CHAKRA DHARANA (A)

Daharakasha means 'deep space'. There are various books which describe daharakasha or the deep space which lies beyond the boundaries of chidakasha and hridayakasha. Daharakasha is not actually a physical space. There is some literature which describes daharakasha as the space in the lower part of the body, still meaning the deep or the lower space. Each school of yoga follows a different system, but most schools tend to agree that in daharakasha the psychic awareness and psychic faculties are developed. Therefore, in order to experience this space, the main emphasis in on the visualization of chakras.

In this practice of chakra dharana all the chakras are seen in one colour – red. They are surrounded by a golden halo which represents the purity and power of each individual chakra. The visualization is also combined with the beeja mantras. Being aware of the link between each chakra with the help of the mantras is an important aspect of the practice. We have also used two new centres, nasikagra and bindu. Bindu is a minor chakra and nasikagra is the switch for mooladhara. Just as the light above is turned on by the switch on the wall, in the same way, mooladhara is turned on by the switch at the nose tip.

Chakra Dharana

Mooladhara

Swadhisthana

Manipura

Anahata

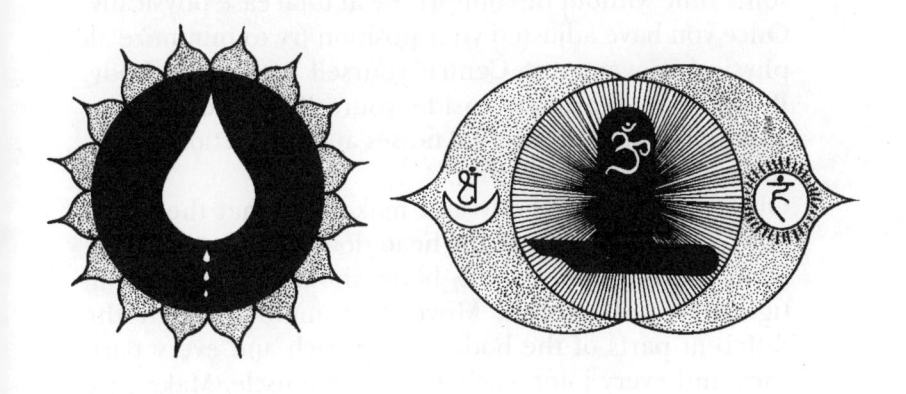

Vishuddhi

Ajna

Bindu

Sahasrara

Technique
Stage 1: Preparation
Sit in a comfortable meditation posture. Make sure the spine is erect and the head is straight. Close the eyes. Adjust your position so that you can remain seated for some time without discomfort. Be at total ease physically. Once you have adjusted your position try to minimize all physical movements. Centre yourself within the body. Bring your awareness inside yourself. Withdraw your attention from the external noises and distractions to the silence and stillness within.

Observe the entire body and make sure that the whole body, from the crown of the head down to the toes, is free from tension. The whole body should be free of all tightness and tension. Move your mind through the different parts of the body. Check each and every part, each and every joint, each and every muscle. Make sure that, physically, you are at total ease.

Observe and internally relax your whole body. Become aware of the maximum ease that you can experience in the body. In the feeling of relaxation, physical relaxation, become aware of internal expansiveness. Bring your mind inside the physical frame. The body contains the microcosmic awareness. The microcosmic experience within the body, within the physical frame, is in itself an infinite experience.

Stage 2: Inner space
Become aware of the whole body and the space within the body. Experience the space which pervades the entire body from the top to the head down to the tips of the fingers, down to the tips of the toes. Visualize the space. Feel as if the body is an empty shell. Visualize the body like a rubber doll which is filled with air and space. When you are aware of space then there is a feeling of expansiveness. When you are aware of air then there is a feeling of motion, movement. These two feelings exist within the body. Observe the pranic movement, the

movement of colours and lights, the movement of the psyche within the body. Be aware of the stillness, the silence and the expansiveness within the body, both representing air and space respectively.

Stage 3: Mooladhara dharana

Now in the inner space that you are seeing, feeling and experiencing, create the image of a four-petalled lotus flower. Please remember that this is the inner space which pervades the entire body and not just chidakasha or hridayakasha. You are not to imagine the mooladhara yantra in any specific place. Within the space that you are perceiving develop the image of a four-petalled lotus flower. Reduce that image and take it down to the mooladhara region. Observe the four petalled lotus flower in the mooladhara region.

Intensify your awareness of the four-petalled lotus flower, red in colour, at mooladhara. See the red lotus surrounded by a halo of golden light. Concentrate in the mooladhara region with total awareness and intensity. Visualize the symbol of mooladhara, a four-petalled lotus flower which is red in colour, representing the element earth. Observe it. Witness it and try to develop a clear image of it in the mooladhara region.

Once the image is perceived, mentally repeat the beeja mantra of mooladhara, *Lam*, during inhalation and exhalation. Do not allow the mind to be distracted by the repetition of the mantra *Lam*. Keep the mind focused on the mooladhara image of a lotus flower with four petals, red in colour, surrounded by a golden halo. With each repetition of the mantra *Lam* during inhalation and exhalation, intensify the awareness of mooladhara. Now stop repeating the beeja mantra of mooladhara.

Stage 4: Swadhisthana dharana

Within the space of your body create the image of a lotus flower with six petals. Create the image of a six-petalled lotus flower, red in colour. Then reduce the image and place it in the region of swadhisthana chakra. The location of swadhisthana is in the sacral region above the genitals. Become aware of it. Now there are two flowers in the space of the body, but you are concentrating on the second one, the six-petalled red lotus flower which is also surrounded by a halo of golden light.

Link both images with the breath and mantra. Inhale and repeat *Lam*, the beeja mantra of mooladhara. Exhale and repeat *Vam*, the beeja mantra of swadhisthana. Try to see both images equally, having similar colour, shape and size. The only difference is that one has four petals and the other has six. Both are red in colour, surrounded by a golden halo. Repeat the beeja mantras *Lam* at the time of inhalation and *Vam* at the time of exhalation.

Stage 5: Manipura dharana

Now stop repeating the beeja mantras and create a third image. Visualize another lotus flower with ten petals which is also red in colour. See this red lotus flower with ten petals in the space of the body. Intensify the awareness of the lotus flower with ten petals. Be sure to observe each petal independently in order to become aware of this red lotus with ten petals. Once you have done that reduce the size of this lotus flower and take it to the region of manipura. In the region of manipura behind the navel, the lotus flower is perceived along with the lotus flowers at swadhisthana and mooladhara.

Visualize all three lotus flowers in a beautiful, bright red colour, surrounded by a golden halo. However, you are aware of manipura more intensely than the others. At the time of inhalation, with the consciousness at mooladhara, repeat *Lam*. As the consciousness continues to move upward with the breath and passes swadhisthana, repeat *Vam*. As the consciousness reaches manipura towards the end of inhalation, repeat *Ram*. Then as the consciousness descends with exhalation from manipura repeat *Ram*, at swadhisthana repeat *Vam*, and at mooladhara repeat *Lam*. So while inhaling and ascending repeat *Lam, Vam, Ram*. Then while exhaling and descending repeat *Ram, Vam,*

Lam. Link the three beeja mantras of the chakras and have the same vision. See the same colours in all three, a bright red lotus, surrounded by a golden halo.

Stage 6: Anahata dharana

Now stop the mantras. Within the space create the image of a red lotus with twelve petals. See the twelve petals internally. Visualize each of the petals individually. Once you are able to develop a clear image of this red lotus with twelve petals, then reduce that image. Place the twelve-petalled lotus flower at the heart centre, the anahata region. Link all four chakras with the breath. The beeja mantra for anahata is *Yam*. Repeat *Lam, Vam, Ram* and *Yam* while ascending with inhalation. Then while descending with exhalation repeat *Yam, Ram, Vam* and *Lam*. Visualize each lotus in turn.

Stage 7: Vishuddhi dharana

Now stop the mantra repetition and develop another image in the space of the body. Visualize a red lotus flower with sixteen petals. Identify and become aware of each of the sixteen petals individually. Reduce the image and place it in the region of vishuddhi. Within the space of the entire body see the red lotus at vishuddhi which is the same colour, size and shape as the lotus flowers in the other chakras. The beeja mantra for vishuddhi is *Ham*. Link all the chakras with mantra and breath. Repeat *Lam, Vam, Ram, Yam, Ham* while inhaling and ascending. Then while exhaling and descending repeat *Ham, Yam, Ram, Vam, Lam*. See all the lotuses in their correct position. All are the same red colour, surrounded by a golden halo. The only difference is in the number of petals. All are linked by the breath and their beeja mantras.

Stage 8: Nasikagra dharana

Now stop the mantra repetition. Create an image of a red circle. Reduce the size of the circle and place it at nasikagra, at the tip of the nose. Concentrate on the red circle there at the tip of the nose. In the space of the body see the red circle at the tip of the nose, with full concentration on the red circle. Concentrate at nasikagra. The beeja mantra for nasikagra is *So*. With inhalation while ascending mentally repeat the mantras *Lam, Vam, Ram, Yam, Ham, So*. During exhalation while descending repeat *So, Ham, Yam, Ram, Vam, Lam*.

Stage 9: Ajna dharana

Now stop the mantra repetition. Within the space create another image of a lotus flower with two petals. Visualize a red lotus flower with two petals that touch each other. Reduce the size of the image and place it in the region of ajna. The beeja mantra of ajna is *Om*. All the chakras are linked by the breath and mantra. They are all of the same red colour, surrounded by a golden halo. While inhaling and ascending repeat *Lam, Vam, Ram, Yam, Ham, So, Om*. While exhaling and descending repeat *Om, So, Ham, Yam, Ram, Vam, Lam*.

Stage 10: Om chanting with chakra visualization

Now stop repeating the mantras. Focus your attention at mooladhara and chant *Om* several times. Then focus the attention at swadhisthana and chant *Om*. Come to manipura and chant *Om*. Bring the awareness to anahata and chant *Om*. Move up to vishuddhi and chant *Om*. Come to nasikagra, nose tip, and chant *Om*. Be aware of ajna and chant *Om*. Come to bindu and chant *Om*. Now dissolve all the lotus flowers into the space. Be aware of the space pervading the entire body.

Stage 11: Ending the practice

Now get ready to end the practice. Become aware of your physical body which is sitting in a meditation posture. Feel the weight of your body against the floor. Be aware of the external environment. Listen to the external sounds. Be aware of your own breathing. Slowly open your eyes and move the body.

Hari Om Tat Sat

Daharakasha Four

CHAKRA DHARANA (B)

When people take up the practice of dharana they always face the same difficulty. They try to concentrate on one point again and again but the mind wanders away. Again they bring it back and again it escapes. They go on like this, alternating between concentration and states of unruliness, but they never achieve dharana because they are constantly struggling with the mind.

Yoga approaches the problem of dharana from a different view point. It says that the state of dharana dawns with the awakening of sushumna nadi. Sushumna is the channel for the spiritual force which flows within the framework of the spine. It originates at mooladhara, the first psychic centre at the perineum and flows straight up through all the other psychic centres to sahasrara at the crown of the head.

Sushumna is the most powerful energy flow in man. It is a non-physical, absolutely transcendental, formless flow. It is a replica of cosmic existence, of the god-like state. Sushumna usually lies in a dormant state and is generally referred to as the sleeping nadi. Once sushumna is awakened you do not have to try to concentrate. It becomes a spontaneous process.

Technique
Stage 1: Preparation

Sit in a comfortable meditation posture with the spine erect and the head straight. Place the hands on the knees in chin or jnana mudra. The eyelids and lips should be gently but firmly closed, not too tight and not too loose. For a few moments observe the position of the body mentally. Become aware of how you are sitting. Observe the position of the feet, toes, knees, legs, fingers, hands, arms, back, trunk, neck, shoulders and head. Try to create a mental image of yourself.

Mentally imagine that there is a full length mirror in front of you and that your body is being reflected in that mirror. Try to see the reflection of your body in this mirror. Complete awareness of the body which is being reflected in the mirror. You are watching the reflection of yourself. In that reflection become aware of the position, the posture, in which you are sitting at this moment. Observe the clothes which you are wearing in the reflection. It is as if you are seeing yourself with the eyes open, sitting in front of a full length mirror.

Stage 2: Awareness in chidakasha

Now bring your attention to chidakasha. Become aware of the darkness, the black sky in chidakasha. Experience chidakasha throughout the head. Become aware of the dark space inside. Total awareness of chidakasha, the inner space, which is above you, below you, behind you, in front of you, and beside you. There is nothing but the empty sky. As you observe chidakasha you will find that there are manifestations of subdued colour, lights, shadows, figures and shapes. You will see different colours, lights and shadows that move and merge with one another constantly.

Intensify the concentration, the awareness. You have to observe the experience in chidakasha, the different manifestations of light, colour, shadow and form. They are the manifestations of the internal activity. Observe them. You do not have to try to rationalize anything, simply observe. Gradually develop the awareness of chidakasha, the feeling of emptiness, the experience of the vast sky, throughout the body. Observe the space of chidakasha throughout the whole body.

Try to imagine how an astronaut feels when he travels in space. There is complete darkness all around him, and in that darkness he can see the stars twinkling in different colours, sizes and shapes. You have to evolve a similar experience. Experience the space throughout the body. One part of the consciousness should experience the space, the other part of the consciousness should only observe the experience. Go on observing the experience, observing the sensation, objectively.

Stage 3: Sushumna darshan

Look down onto your body with the awareness at the top of the head. Look right down to the tips of the toes, to the tips of the fingers. Experience the space pervading the whole body. Take your awareness down to the toes and look up. Experience the space when you look up. Now take your awareness to the tips of the fingers and experience the space around you from that perspective. The same type of feeling, the same type of perception which you experience at night with all the curtains closed, the lights off, and the eyes closed. There is awareness of pitch darkness. With one part of the consciousness experience the complete darkness and with the other part of the consciousness observe the experience. Both should happen simultaneously.

Now bring your awareness to the top of the head and look down into the sushumna passage which is located at the centre of the spinal cord. As you look down into sushumna become aware of the six points of light situated within it. The first point of light, if you observe carefully, is located below the spinal cord, at the perineum, where sushumna originates. The second point of light is situated just above the first, inside sushumna at the point where the coccyx and the sacral bones meet. The third point of light is located in sushumna, behind the navel in the lumbar area of the spine. The fourth point of light is located in sushumna, behind the heart in the thoracic region. The fifth point of light is located in sushumna, behind the throat pit. The sixth point of light is located in sushumna at the top of the spine in the centre of the head, directly behind the eyebrows. The seventh point of light is located at the top of sushumna, at the crown of the head.

Stage 4: Visualization of chakra and colour
Your awareness is above these different points of light and you are looking down. They are like very tiny stars suspended in the sky. You are observing them internally. They are in one straight line. Observe them. Observe sushumna as a luminous, golden cord which connects each point from bottom to top, like pearls on a string. The part of consciousness which is observing can move in any direction. Take that part of the consciousness right down to the first point of light and look at it from the front. As you observe the first point of light, the mooladhara centre, be aware of the other points of light above you. Take your awareness right down and observe the first point of light. Experience the space all around you. Your consciousness, which is observing, is the microscopic self. The point you are observing is the microscopic space.

Go deep into that point of light and generate the experience of colour. As the consciousness enters into that point of light in the mooladhara region, the colour changes. The whole space becomes red. See the whole space filled with red light. With the red colour there is also the feeling of emptiness. See the deep red colour pervading the entire structure.

Now withdraw the awareness from the first point of light and enter the second one. As you come out from the mooladhara light, the red colour dissipates. Again the space becomes dark. Take your awareness up to the second point of light which is at the level of swadhisthana chakra, the coccyx. Observe this point. As your consciousness enters into this light, the colour of the space changes to vermilion. Intensify your awareness and see the orange-red colour pervading the entire space.

Now come out from the second point of light. As you withdraw the awareness, the orange-red colour fades and disappears into the darkness of the inner space. Move your awareness up to the level of the third light, manipura chakra, behind the navel. As you enter the manipura light, the colour changes to golden yellow, the colour of flame, the fire nature. See the entire space pervaded with golden yellow light.

As you withdraw from the manipura light, the golden yellow colour fades and disappears into the darkness of the inner space. Bring your awareness up to the fourth point of light, anahata chakra, behind the heart. As you enter into the anahata light, see the colour change to sky blue. Visualize the space pervaded by sky blue light.

As you withdraw from the anahata light, the light blue colour fades and disappears into the darkness of the inner space. Move your awareness up to the level of vishuddhi, the fifth point of light behind the throat. Observe this point and see the space changing to a violet purple colour. Visualize the entire space pervaded by the violet purple colour.

As you withdraw your awareness from the vishuddhi point of light, see the violet purple colour fade and disappear into the darkness of the inner space. Bring your awareness up to the sixth light at the level of ajna chakra, in the midbrain. As you enter this light see the colour change to silver. Visualize the entire space pervaded by silvery coloured light.

As you come out of ajna see the silver colour fade and disappear into the darkness of chidakasha. Bring your awareness up to the seventh light, at the level of sahasrara, the crown of the head. Here see the colour of the space change to white. Visualize the entire space illumined with brilliant white light. Maintain this awareness for as long as you can.

Stage 5: Spontaneous chakra visualization

As the awareness comes out of sahasrara see all seven points of light, glowing like jewels hanging on a string with a soft, silvery blue light. Now let your mind go spontaneously to any point of light, whether it is mooladhara, anahata or ajna; whether swadhisthana, manipura or vishuddhi. It does not matter where it goes, but observe it carefully.

Allow the mind to follow its own direction and move towards any point of light where it is naturally attracted. Wherever the mind moves spontaneously, observe that point of light. Try to go to the source of that point of light. Go to the nucleus of that point. Within the nucleus of the light see the image of yourself as you are. Acknowledge the chakra, the point of light where your awareness has gone spontaneously. Wherever the mind goes, whether mooladhara, swadhisthana, manipura, anahata, vishuddhi, ajna or sahasrara, just acknowledge it. Observe where the mind goes, without any direction, without any effort, where it is naturally attracted to, just go to that point and acknowledge it.

Stage 6: Om chanting with chakra visualization

Observe all the points of light. Observe all the chakras, all the points of light, simultaneously. Experience the space all around you. Experience voidness, nothingness, shoonyata, all around you, and in that space, awareness of the chakras in the form of points of light. Now chant *Om* and while you chant *Om*, the part of your consciousness which is observing must stand back and watch the vibration of *Om* in all these chakras. As you chant, the different psychic centres, the different points of light, will pulsate with a life of their own. Develop this awareness, develop this feeling of pulsation, of vibration. They will become brighter, they will begin to twinkle. Experience the pulsation, the vibration of the chakras. Visualize that and at the same time be aware of the chanting of the mantra *Om*. Be alert. Breathe in and chant *Om*. Feel the sound of the mantra *Om*, vibrating and pulsating, with the pinpoints of light. *Om, Om, Om,* go on observing. *Om, Om, Om.*

Stage 7: Ending the practice

Now stop the practice and slowly externalize the consciousness. Become aware of the inner space pervading the entire body from head to toe. Become aware of the physical body. Feel your body sitting in the meditation posture. Become aware of the external environment, the external sound, the people around you, different objects around you. When you are fully aware of the outside environment, slowly move your body and open your eyes.

Practice note: It is interesting to note in stage five which chakra your mind is naturally attracted to. This shows the level at which you can most easily express yourself. It denotes your present level of awareness. The natural and spontaneous trait of the personality is known by the gravitational pull of the chakra. However, there should be no application of level here. The chakra which your awareness naturally centres on indicates your natural inclination, what is active and manifesting in you at present. Wherever the attention goes, that is the right chakra. Do not try to judge or choose. There should be no discrimination. It is a natural process because that is where you are now and with that faculty you are experiencing things. It is the faculty that is active within a chakra which makes you see, observe and experience either pain or pleasure. If you are centred in anahata and you feel pain there, that means it is the faculty of anahata which is active and which is taking you through the experience of pain. If mooladhara gives that experience, then it is the mooladhara faculty. So you know that it is necessary to work at developing that chakra.

Hari Om Tat Sat

Daharakasha Five

CHAKRA DHARANA (C)

Technique
Stage 1: Preparation
Sit in a comfortable meditation posture with the spine and head erect. Place the hands on the knees in chin or jnana mudra. Close your eyes. Relax your whole body. Develop complete awareness of your whole body internally and relax each part. Be aware of the posture in which you are sitting. As you become aware of your body you will observe the feeling of motionlessness, stillness and silence emanating from within. Become aware of physical motionlessness. Observe the silence around you and within you.

The entire body is perfectly still, like a statue. The body is totally still and motionless. Be aware of the feeling of silence and stillness pervading the entire physical and mental structure. Do not identify with any kind of physical experience. No experience of comfort or discomfort, of pain or pleasure, can override the feeling of silence and stillness within you. Dissociate yourself completely from the body and the experiences of the body, from the mind and the experiences of the mind.

Stage 2: Pillar of air
Now within the body become aware of the breath as a pillar of air that extends from manipura to ajna. The consciousness ascends and descends up and down this

pillar at the time of inhalation and exhalation. While inhaling, the consciousness ascends from manipura to ajna. While exhaling, the consciousness descends from ajna to manipura. Do not be aware of any physical movement. Observe the ascent and descent of consciousness along the pillar of air, extending from manipura to ajna and from ajna to manipura.

Stage 3: Mooladhara mandala

Become aware of the vast inner space that pervades your entire being. Experience sthoolakasha, the space throughout the body. Develop total awareness of the space that pervades your whole body. Within this space visualize a large yellow square. Try to see the colour and the outline of the square within the body space. The square is large and heavy, representing the earth. Be aware of the vibration of the earth. Feel the element earth, smell the earth as you visualize the yellow square. Here the pranas are at their greatest density, where energy manifests as form.

Inside the yellow square is a red inverted triangle, representing the creative force or shakti. See the red triangle surrounded by the yellow square within the body space. Inside the red triangle is a smoky-grey shivalingam, dumra lingam, which is encircled three and a half times by a sleeping serpent. This sleeping serpent represents the dormant kundalini or spiritual force. See the serpent encircling the smoky-grey shivalingam, inside the red inverted triangle within the yellow square.

There is a sound associated with this mandala, the beeja mantra *Lam*. Visualize the entire mandala clearly, and mentally repeat the beeja mantra *Lam*, *Lam*, *Lam*. See the large yellow square. Inside the square is the red inverted triangle. Inside the triangle is the smoky-grey shivalingam with a serpent coiled around it three times. When you are able to see the entire mandala, reduce it and place it inside daharakasha in the region of mooladhara at the perineum.

Stage 4: Swadhisthana mandala

Again become aware of sthoolakasha. Within the space pervading the entire body visualize a large white crescent moon. Inside the crescent moon see ocean waves on a dark night, lit up by stars. Ocean waves on a dark night represent the unconscious dimension, the region of deep sleep. Here also within the depths of the ocean the *karmashaya*, the repository of karmas, is located. Visualize the swadhisthana mandala clearly within sthoolakasha, the whole body space.

There is a sound associated with this mandala, the beeja mantra *Vam*. See the large white crescent moon hanging in space and repeat the beeja mantra *Vam, Vam, Vam*. Be aware of the water element, of fluidity. Within the moon see ocean waves on a dark night lit up by stars. When you are able to visualize the entire mandala, reduce it and place it inside daharakasha, in the region of swadhisthana at the coccyx.

Stage 5: Manipura mandala

Again bring your awareness back to sthoolakasha. Within the inner space visualize manipura mandala. See a large, fiery red, inverted triangle surrounded on all three sides by black bhupura. See the fiery vibrations of this mandala. Inside the triangle is a ball of blazing fire, representing the solar force, the centre of prana. See the ball of blazing fire inside the red inverted triangle, surrounded by black bhupura. Feel the energy, the heat, the light emanating from this mandala.

There is a sound associated with this mandala, the beeja mantra *Ram*. Visualize manipura mandala and repeat *Ram, Ram, Ram*. When you are able to visualize the entire mandala clearly, reduce it and place it inside daharakasha in the region of manipura, behind the navel.

Stage 6: Daharakasha mandala

Now, concentrating inside daharakasha, try to see the mooladhara mandala clearly and distinctly in its entirety. Repeat the beeja mantra *Lam, Lam, Lam*. Next see swadhisthana mandala and repeat the beeja mantra *Vam Vam Vam*. Then see the manipura mandala and repeat the beeja mantra *Ram Ram Ram*. Inhale – *Lam Vam Ram*. Exhale – *Ram Vam Lam*.

Try to see mooladhara and swadhisthana together. When perfected try to see swadhisthana and manipura together. Finally, visualize all three, mooladhara, swadhisthana and manipura, in their correct locations, in one glimpse.

Stage 7: Anahata mandala

Again become aware of the entire body space. Within sthoolakasha visualize the anahata chakra mandala. See the symbol of a sky blue coloured hexagon formed by two interlacing triangles. Visualize the two interlacing triangles forming the hexagon. They are sky blue in colour. In the centre of that hexagon is a tiny point of bright light. This is the source of eternal, unborn and undying vibration. Try to feel the waves of that vibration travelling to each and every part of the microcosmic universe within you. Try to feel and experience the ripples of the vibration which is subtle, which is deep, travelling from the source of light to the entire microcosmic universe within you.

The ripples of the vibration, the extension of the pulse in the microcosmic universe within the feeling of total stillness and silence, represents the air element. The mandala is the hexagon. See the two interlacing triangles which are sky blue in colour. In the centre of the hexagon is the tiny point of very bright light. See it with total intensity of mind. With one-pointed awareness observe anahata.

It is from this pulse of life, it is from this source, that all the subtle activities manifest in our life. The element air is linked with the mind. The thoughts are experienced in the form of ripples within the mind. The desires are experienced in the form of ripples within the mind. The emotions are experienced in the form of ripples within the mind. Some have more intensity than others. Some have less intensity but everything emanates from this point of light. Be aware of the pulse of life. It is the eternal vibration, the anahada nada. There is also a sound associated with this vibration. The beeja mantra is *Yam*. Visualize anahata mandala and repeat *Yam, Yam, Yam*.

Stage 8: Vishuddhi mandala

Now gradually withdraw the awareness from concentration in anahata and come to the vishuddhi region. In the region of vishuddhi, at the borderline of hridayakasha and chidakasha, is a white circle. See a plain, white circle. That white circle is the mandala of vishuddhi. Vishuddhi means 'the pure'. Develop awareness of a white circle representing the element ether or space. Develop complete awareness of the white circle. Be aware of the purity of space, the expansiveness of space. Be aware of space as the base for the manifestation of all the other elements.

There is a sound vibration associated with vishuddhi or the element of ether, space. That sound is *Ham*. Visualize the white circle and repeat *Ham, Ham, Ham*.

Stage 9: Ajna mandala

Now withdraw your mind and attention from vishuddhi and again bring it to chidakasha. Within the space of chidakasha visualize an ebony black, shining shivalingam with a white *Om* symbol on it. To the right of the lingam is the sun and to the left is the moon. The shining black shivalingam represents the element of mind, the astral mind, the higher mind. The sun and moon here symbolize the union of ida and pingala, and their merging with sushumna. Beyond this point there is no awareness of duality, of ego, of the lower mind.

Concentrate your entire awareness on the ajna mandala within chidakasha. The associated sound is the mantra *Om*. Visualize the shining black shivalingam. See the white *Om* symbol on it clearly and repeat *Om, Om, Om*. Be aware of the element of mind, higher mind, astral mind; subtle awareness of this mandala which has command or control over all the others.

Stage 10: Hridayakasha and chidakasha mandala
Now withdraw the awareness from the ajna mandala. Visualize anahata mandala at the centre of hridayakasha, behind the heart. See the anahata mandala in its entirety and repeat *Yam, Yam, Yam*. Next visualize the vishuddhi mandala between hridayakasha and chidakasha, behind the throat pit, and repeat *Ham, Ham, Ham*. Then visualize the ajna mandala in chidakasha, behind the eyebrow centre, and repeat *Om, Om, Om*. Inhale – *Yam, Ham, Om*. Exhale – *Om, Ham, Yam*.

Visualize anahata and vishuddhi mandalas together. When this is perfected visualize vishuddhi and ajna mandalas together. Finally, visualize the three mandalas – anahata, vishuddhi and ajna, all together, in one glimpse, one vision, clearly.

Stage 11: Chakra mandala darshan
Now visualize each chakra mandala in turn and repeat the beeja mantra. See mooladhara and repeat *Lam*, swadhisthana – *Vam*, manipura – *Ram*, anahata – *Yam*, vishuddhi – *Ham*, ajna – *Om*.

Visualize mooladhara and swadhisthana together. Next see mooladhara, swadhisthana and manipura together. Next see mooladhara, swadhisthana, manipura and anahata together. Now see mooladhara, swadhisthana, manipura, anahata and vishuddhi altogether. Finally see mooladhara, swadhisthana, manipura, anahata and vishuddhi and ajna in one glimpse, in one view, with total clarity. Hold the vision of the chakra mandalas for as long as you can.

Stage 12: Ending the practice
When the vision of the chakras begins to fade, withdraw your awareness to the inner space. Experience the entire sthoolakasha from head to toe. Again experience the physical body which is sitting motionless in the meditation posture. Be aware of the room in which you are sitting. Listen to the external sounds. Breathe in deeply and chant *Om* three times.

Hari Om Tat Sat

Daharakasha Six

PANCHAKOSHA DHARANA

The word *kosha* means 'sheath' or 'body' and *pancha* means 'five'. According to the yogic tradition, the human personality is comprised of five bodies or koshas. These five koshas range from the gross to the transcendental dimensions and they belong to the experience of daharakasha.

Annamaya kosha
The first kosha described in yoga is annamaya kosha or the body of matter, which can be animate or inanimate. A building, a tree and a physical body are all considered to be annamaya kosha. The only difference is that the building is inanimate while the body is animate. So, this annamaya kosha or material body is a vast concept.

There are many kinds of matter. Some forms of matter are totally independent and some are dependent on other matter for their existence. For example, the food that we eat is matter and the body which consumes the food is also composed of matter. So here we find an interaction of matter. One form of matter is consumed to sustain and support the other form. This is known as the dependency of matter on matter. An independent form of matter is a stone. You cannot eat stone and there is no substance received by this form of matter.

Yoga views the whole of creation as the manifestation of matter, which can be compared to the external body, used for the manifestation of creative consciousness and energy. Different objects, whether a stone or a body, have a different composition, but they are all impregnated by energy and consciousness. A stone contains consciousness and energy, but because of its composition these are not manifest. Plant life also contains consciousness and energy, but these are not expressed by them in the form that we perceive.

Consciousness and energy require different agencies in order to manifest creatively. A stone is simply inert matter, annamaya kosha. In plant life we see a combination of annamaya, pranayama and slight manomaya kosha. In human life we see the combination of all five koshas. So the consciousness inherent in a stone or in plant life utilizes a different means of expression.

Unless the koshas are integrated in a unit it is not possible for them to manifest. Annamaya kosha is simply the manifestation of matter regardless of what type of consciousness and energy is contained within it. It is simply a tool, an expression of consciousness and energy in the material or gross world which provides the experience of the dimension being dealt with in the particular kosha.

Pranamaya kosha

After annamaya kosha comes pranamaya kosha. That is the body of energy or prana. What makes the body move? It is the force of energy. If you remove that energy from the body, what will cause the body to move? If you pick a blade of green grass, after some time it will turn brown and die. The force that kept it alive and green was prana.

Yogis have realized that everything in the universe contains energy, and that energy is termed very generally as prana. The prana which pervades and controls the entire universe is known as *mahaprana*. The prana which governs the individual units such as that of a body is subdivided into five categories. According to the various activities of the individual unit, that prana is again divided into five minor categories. So, animate beings have ten different types of prana within them. Inanimate beings have just one type of prana. It is the pranic force which maintains and supports the physical body.

Let us look at prana from the macrocosmic viewpoint. In the macrocosmos, the prana which pervades the entire universe is known as mahaprana, which is the first impulse of life or consciousness. For example, when you sleep at night there is no concept of time and space. There is total unconsciousness. When the alarm goes off there is a slight stirring in the fields of consciousness, which then intensifies as awareness is brought about. Then you become aware of the body, the environment, what time it is, and so on.

In deep sleep, which is a state similar to death, the first movement which takes place in the field of consciousness, which makes one extrovert and creates a link between the body and the mind, is the activity of prana. If the pranic link between the body and mind were not there, the mind would not coordinate with the body. There would be two separate units, body and mind, functioning in one person.

Many times, when we go into deep states of concentration or introversion where we become unconscious of the external world, we find that our mind is alert but there is no control over the body. That pranic link which coordinates the mental and physical activities is temporarily disengaged from the body. So, mahaprana is the first impulse which creates a link between matter and consciousness.

Mahaprana is the pulsation or life force of every atom and planetary body which exists in the universe. Stars and pulsars which emit different kinds of radio waves or gamma rays are also forms of mahaprana. If you started eliminating each wave in the cosmos one by one, eventually there would be just one kind of wave, which could be considered as the originating point of all the others. That point is known as mahaprana.

Mahaprana also manifests differently in the different koshas. In the psychic body prana manifests at the vibratory level. In the physical and mental bodies it manifests in the form of stimulation and impulse. When we get the idea to raise our arm, the impulses which travel from the body to the brain and from the brain to the body are of physical prana.

In pranamaya kosha, prana manifests in the form of currents or energy flows. The current of prana which flows from pranamaya kosha to annamaya kosha, always travels through the energy channels or nadis in the form of currents. These currents can be experienced in the physical body in the form of light, tiny electrical currents, prickly or itchy sensations, within the physical framework.

There are many kinds of energy flows in the physical body. The first is the blood vessels which carry the blood from one part to another. The second is the nerves which carry sensations from the body to the brain. The third is the nadi or pranic flow which connect the prana from pranamaya kosha with the physical body.

Five thousand years ago there was a rishi in India named Kannada. He was the first person to describe the atomic theory. He described how prana interacts within the pranic structure. He said that the nucleus of the atom which is pulsating with energy is prana in its pure form. That prana is the source of movement, the source of life, and that life is visible in our external physical structure.

Manomaya kosha
Third comes manomaya kosha, which comprises the rational mind as well as the emotions. Manomaya kosha also incorporates the various other aspects of the mind. The conscious, subconscious and unconscious expression, behaviour and relationships are all aspects of manomaya kosha. States of mind such as euphoria, happiness, joy, frustration, depression and anxiety are also aspects of manomaya kosha. These various expressions of mind are also related with the samskaras and karmas of vijnanamaya kosha.

Vijnanamaya kosha is considered to be the storehouse of samskara and karma. It is the area where buddhi, chitta and ahamkara manifest in their raw form. When these faculties or impressions have to interact with the external world, they use the agency of mind (manas).

Our interactions with positive and negative things, the problems of dealing with our own mind, nature, desire, strengths and weaknesses, ambitions and needs, are the different aspects of manomaya kosha. It is not just the rational mind which is known as manomaya kosha, but the totality of mind. Manomaya kosha is a very broad term used to define the various expressions of mind and human nature.

Vijnanamaya kosha

Fourth is vijnanamaya kosha, the sheath of wisdom, understanding and realization. These are two aspects or levels of vijnanamaya kosha. The first or lower aspect is that of internal and external knowledge. The second aspect is the understanding of samskara and karma. After one has gone through these two states, the third state or dimension is reached, which is the experience, understanding and realization of ego.

In the course of evolution, when spirit was evolving into matter, the first manifestation was *mahat* or supreme intelligence. From this aspect of mahat there emerged four sub-aspects. These are recognized as: (i) ahamkara, the ego principle, (ii) chitta, process of observation, (iii) buddhi, process of discrimination and understanding, and (iv) manas, mind. These sub-aspects make up the body of vijnanamaya kosha.

Vijnanamaya kosha is generally translated as the body of intellect, but this is not correct. Vijnana is a combination of two words: vi plus jnana. *Jnana* means knowledge and when you add *vi* it becomes subtle knowledge. The body where subtle knowledge is experienced is vijnanamaya kosha.

In manomaya kosha we mentioned buddhi, chitta and ahamkara, but now we will deal with them as parts of vijnanamaya kosha. *Buddhi* means 'intellect', which is also subdivided into two groups. One form of intellect is related to the external world of objects and the other is an internal understanding of the principles which shape our personality.

Apart from the external buddhi or intelligence, there is another aspect which is rooted in the impressions of consciousness not yet manifest.

This consciousness which is not manifest contains the experiences of past lives, experiences which are carried through the agencies of our parents and grandparents, just like DNA. It contains information from the time of creation until now. The subtle buddhi is influenced by this information in the form of samskaras and karmas. So, an aspect of realizing buddhi is gaining knowledge of the samskaras and karmas.

Another area of mahat is *chitta*, which means 'to observe'. Within the personality there is an aspect of the consciousness which is constantly observing everything. Chitta is the little man sitting inside, dispassionately observing everything that is happening. That is known as 'the seer' in the yogic tradition.

After chitta comes the concept of ahamkara or the ego principle. The word *aham* means 'I' and *akara* means 'shape' or 'form'. Spirit which is free from the identity of the self is simply 'aham'. That aham is later known as *atman* or soul. So, in vijnanamaya kosha we are not dealing with aham but with ahamakara, with the soul which is lost in its self-identity. When the soul is lost in its self-identity it does not see beyond.

We know we have a body; we can see and experience the body. We know we have a mind; we can experience it, but we cannot see it. We know we have a soul, but we can neither experience it nor see it. So, there is a decreasing state of awareness. But when we go into vijnanamaya kosha through the process of sadhana, the awareness of the body and mind is lost, and the awareness of the subtle mind takes place along with the awareness of the soul.

Anandamaya kosha

Fifth is anandamaya kosha, the bliss body. This is where the experience of soul or spirit takes place, where the individual fuses with the higher personality. Here the concept of soul becomes a living experience. All the impurities and dross simply drop away and the effulgence of the soul is experienced. The soul is experienced as the governing body of the individual. When anandamaya kosha is experienced one does not remain human any longer. One becomes divine and that is the realization of the Self or God.

Evolving through the koshas

So, the koshas represent an aspect of yogic psychology, because one progresses from annamaya to anandamaya kosha in the course of natural growth. Some people are stuck in annamaya kosha all their lives. Some are stuck in manomaya kosha. Very few people get stuck in pranamaya kosha because they do not know that it exists. However, it is in pranamaya that energy blocks arise in the nadis, chakras and kundalini, which create innumerable problems within the personality.

Sometimes we feel disturbed and we think, "I have no control over myself; I am going crazy". We relate this disturbance to an annamaya or manomaya experience without realizing that it is coming from pranamaya. We have been trained to accept annamaya and manomaya, that is, the body and the mind, and nothing beyond that. If somebody gets stuck in vijnanamaya, they will have intense ego problems or difficulties with karmas and samskaras, which cannot be dealt with because there is no understanding of that level. In the history of humanity there have been very few people who have gone up to anandamaya kosha. They are known as the saints or realized souls.

In this practice the awareness of the five koshas is progressively developed from a conceptual point of view, in order to broaden one's self-understanding. With this experience one gains a better idea about the purpose of sadhana and how we are evolving through the different dimensions of prana and consciousness in this body.

Technique
Stage 1: Preparation

Sit in a comfortable meditation position with your spine erect and head slightly back. Place the hands on the knees in chin or jnana mudra. Close the eyes and relax. For a few moments become aware of the body. Move your awareness through the different parts of the body, from the head to the toes. Develop complete and total awareness of the body.

Stage 2: Entering daharakasha

Once you have become aware of the entire body, then gradually dissociate the awareness from the physical body. Visualize the body in the form of an empty shell with an outer covering of skin filled with the element of space. Develop the awareness of the body in the form of a balloon which is filled with air and space inside, and surrounded by air and space outside. In the same way imagine your body to be filled with space and surrounded by space.

Be totally aware of the space within, totally centred in the experience of space within. Do not allow the physical distractions to disturb the state of your awareness which is centred in the etheric body. As you become more and more aware of the space you will observe a descending feeling of calmness, silence and stillness.

After some time there will be an experience of expansiveness. When you are aware of air you perceive motion within the body space. Two basic experiences exist within daharakasha: stillness and expansiveness. Movement of prana can be seen in the form of colours and lights within the stillness, silence and expansiveness of daharakasha. Be aware of the deep, inner space of the body and the movement within that space, which creates an experience of expansiveness.

Stage 3: Awareness of annamaya kosha

Within the space become aware of the physical body which is composed of matter. The manifestation of various elements combined with the earth element is the annamaya kosha. This is the last manifestation of energy where it solidifies into matter. Feel the physical body which is composed of muscle, bone, blood, mucus and skin. Be aware of the different organs, systems and parts which comprise the physical body.

Within the stillness of the body experience the movement of the breath. Be aware of the body which is breathing in and out. See how the body breathes. Become aware of the heart beat. Feel the rhythmic pulsation of the heart which is responsible for the circulation of blood throughout the body. Experience the muscular and skeletal systems which provide the framework of the body by which we move and act in the world. Develop total awareness of the muscles, bones, organs and systems of the body.

Experience the entire physical body; feel its weight and bulk. Feel its solidity and harmony with the earth upon which it rests, from which it receives nourishment, and to which its elemental nature will one day return. Experience the earth element in your being, in the form of the physical body, annamaya kosha. Annamaya kosha is simply the manifestation of matter, regardless of what type of consciousness and energy is contained within it.

Stage 4: Awareness of the pranic body

Next awaken your awareness of pranamaya kosha, the energy body which interacts with the material body at the gross level, and with the mental and psychic bodies at a more subtle level. Experience pranamaya kosha as an infrastructure of energy channels, currents or flows, which gives life to every part and particle of your being.

Move your awareness into pranamaya kosha and experience prana as a powerful force, full of warmth, light and colour. Just as hot air can be seen rising from a fire in the form of a shimmering, turbulent force, similarly prana can be experienced within the subtler states of the physical body. Intensify this experience of prana. Be aware of the energy field and experience the life force.

In pranamaya kosha, prana manifests in the form of energy currents. These currents can be experienced in the physical body in the form of light. Be aware of tiny electrical currents, prickly or itchy sensations within the physical framework.

Experience the different energy flows in the physical body. Be aware of the blood vessels which carry the blood from one part of the body to another. Be aware of the nerves which carry sensations from the body to the brain. Be aware of the pranic currents flowing from pranamaya kosha into the physical body.

Intensify your awareness of the pranic link between body and mind. Be aware of prana in the form of vital energy and mental energy. Without prana the body would not move and the mind would not think. What we understand as life, living, being, knowing, understanding, feeling, perceiving, all take place through the agency of prana.

Be aware of prana as the cause of life and also the link between the various levels of our being. Intensify your awareness of the pranic field in the form of vital, mental and psychic energy. Even spiritual energy belongs to the dimension of prana. Experience the infrastructure of prana which exists throughout your being at all levels from gross to subtle. Go deep and intensify your perception of the subtle pranic force. Visualize prana in the form of light particles or streams of energy atoms which make up the infrastructure of the pranamaya kosha.

Stage 5: Awareness of manomaya kosha

Now leave your awareness of pranamaya kosha and enter the mental field. Become aware of the mental body which contains every aspect of mental and emotional expression. Observe with awareness whatever you are thinking or feeling inside at this moment. Watch carefully how the mental process functions. Be aware of the different thoughts and feelings as they arise. Watch how they form themselves into complex, interwoven patterns.

Be aware of manas, the thought and counter-thought

process which constantly sifts through all the daily impressions arriving from the external world and relates them with the memories of past impressions in order to process them and decide on the best course of action.

However, manas cannot function alone. The various expressions of mind are related with the samskaras and karma which are stored in vijnanamaya kosha. In order to interact with the outside world, manas (the rational mind) must use the help of buddhi (intellect), chitta (awareness) and ahamkara (self-identity), which belong to the area of vijnanamaya kosha.

Be aware of the constant mental process. Experience manas interacting with buddhi, chitta and ahamkara. See how the various expressions of the mind manifest through this interaction. In order to observe the mind, you require the help of chitta, the observer. With the help of chitta begin to observe dispassionately all the manifestations of manomaya kosha as they arise.

Observe the mental dialogue which goes on internally. Who is talking to whom and for what? Observe how the emotions are sparked off by certain thoughts, especially those with which you most identify. See how the different kinds of thoughts and emotions colour, influence and modify the mental field.

There are five kinds of thinking which modify the mental field in different ways. If you watch the mind carefully, you can identify them. They are: right thinking, wrong thinking, fanciful thinking, thinking influenced by memory, and thinking influenced by sleep. As you watch the mental play, try to see which of these categories your thoughts fall into. Observe when you have right thoughts or wrong thoughts. Observe when you have fanciful thoughts or thoughts arising from memory. Observe when your thoughts are influenced by sleep, as in dream. The continual arising of these five vrittis or mental modifications is responsible for the creation of every feeling, emotion, thought, desire, ambition, action or type of behaviour. In order to observe the mental field you will have to become aware of these five vrittis, and experience how they manifest in the form of all your mental activities. Without these five vrittis there would be no mental functioning. The mind would be still.

Stage 6: Awareness of vijnanamaya kosha

Now leave the awareness of manomaya kosha and become aware of vijnanamaya kosha, the pranic body. Enter the dimension of pure energy which is the pranic realm. The psychic body functions through the agency of the subtle prana which is known as psychic energy. Experience pure energy in the form of vibration inside the psychic body.

Vijnanamaya kosha is not only the body of psychic energy, it also relates to the higher mind. It is experienced as the body of intellect or inner knowledge. In manomaya kosha there was awareness of the manas aspect, interacting with chitta, buddhi and ahamkara. Here we must experience chitta, buddhi and ahamkara in their pure state.

Buddhi means intellect. The lower intellect is related to the external world of objects and senses and the higher intellect is related to the internal understanding of the principles which create and shape our personality. Experience the external buddhi by understanding, observing and analyzing through your rationality. See how your actions and behaviour are shaped according to the external buddhi or intelligence.

Apart from this there is another aspect of buddhi which is rooted in the impressions of consciousness which are not yet manifest. This unmanifest consciousness contains the experience of past lives, experiences which are carried through the agencies of our parents and grandparents, just like DNA and which contain information from the time of creation until now. Be aware of the subtle buddhi. Next we will enter another area known as chitta. Chitta means to observe. Within the mind there is an aspect of consciousness which is constantly observing everything. Become aware of chitta, the little man sitting inside you, dispassionately observing everything that is happening. Experience chitta, the seer, who realizes his own identity. After chitta develop the experience of ahamkara or the ego principle. Try to observe your own self-identity, the feeling of 'I'ness within you which creates duality, which separates I from others, you from me. As you observe your own self-identity realize that the source of this identity is the self or soul, which is pure spirit without any identity.

In vijnanamaya kosha you are not aware of the pure 'I', the pure self, but of the self which is lost in its own identity. Spirit which is lost in self-identity is ahamkara. Spirit which is free from identity is simply aham, 'I am, that I am, that I am'.

Now be aware not of aham, but of ahamkara. Experience the soul which is lost in its own identity. When the soul is lost in its own identity it does not see beyond. As you become aware of vijnanamaya kosha, the awareness of the body and mind is lost. Develop the experience of the subtle mind along with the soul.

Stage 7: Awareness of anandamaya kosha

Finally come to the fifth sheath of bliss and happiness, anandamaya kosha. Here the concept of soul is divine experience. Be aware of all the impurities and dross falling away and experience the effulgence of your soul. Be aware of the soul as the governing body of your individual life. With this realization you become divine. This is the realization of the Self, of God, of *mukti* or liberation.

Stage 8: Ending the practice

Now prepare to end the practice. Withdraw your awareness from the higher koshas and again become aware of annamaya kosha, the physical body. Visualize your physical body sitting in the meditation posture. Feel your whole body from head to toe. Be aware of the room in which you are sitting and slowly externalize your awareness. Be aware of the breath. Breathe in deeply and chant *Om* three times.

Hari Om Tat Sat

Daharakasha Seven

PANCHAPRANA DHARANA

Prana dharana is meditation on the breath and the experience of breathing in the different bodies; the physical body – air breath; the mental body – different vitalities of breath; the causal body – pranic breathing; the psychic body – essence of prana, pulsation of prana. That is the link which we are creating from the physical to the psychic body by following the train of breath. Breathing in and breathing out, inhalation and exhalation, expansion and relaxation, the flaring up and the flaring down of energy, these are the different subtle aspects of breathing which must be experienced in order to develop the perception of prana. This experience is further enhanced by developing the awareness of the blood circulation and then gradually going deeper and experiencing the flow of prana at a more subtle level. When the experience of the flow of prana is awakened then we go on to observe the different dimensions of the pranic body.

The pranic body is a network of flowing energy in the shape of the physical body, which radiates outward just as light emanates from a bulb. Its form is not static but dynamic. It expands and contracts. So, in the first stage of the practice we experience the dynamic nature of the pranic body by breathing in and out through every pore of the skin. With each inhalation the pranic body expands and with each exhalation it contracts.

Panchaprana Dharana

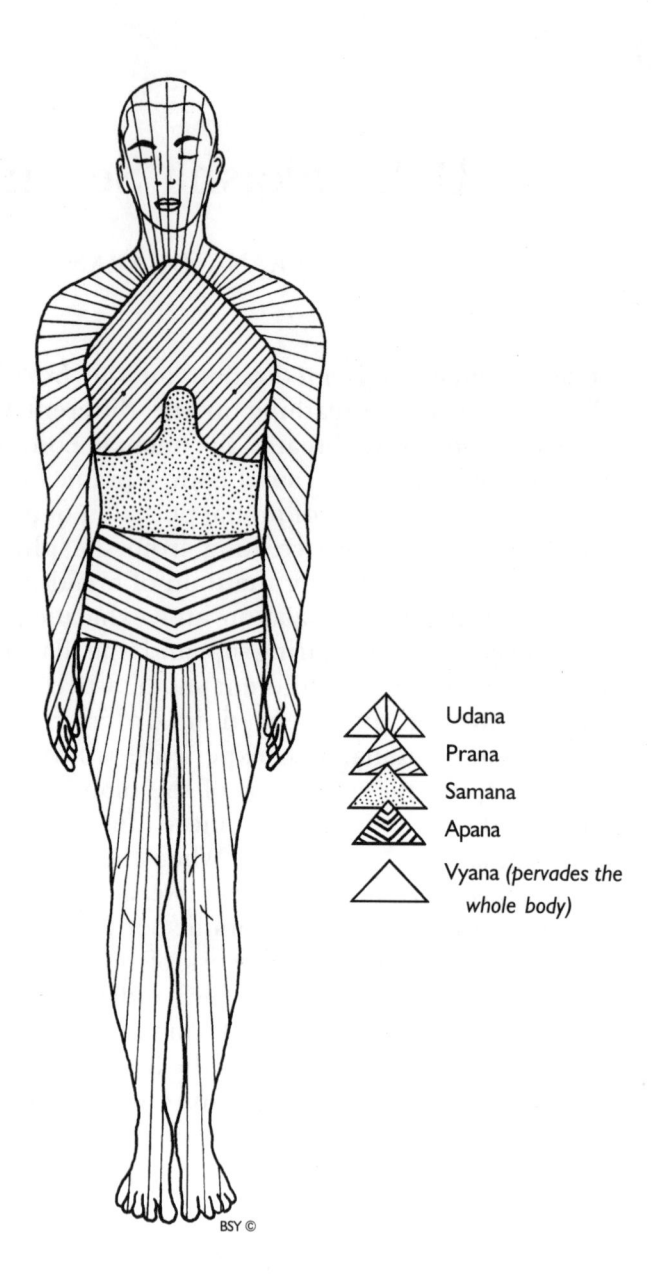

As prana circulates through the body, it is modified and adapted according to the functions of each particular organ and region. According to these different modifications of prana, the prana vayus were classified. There are a total of ten vayus and of these, five are said to have a greater influence over the functioning of the body. They are known as the panchapranas: prana, apana, samana, udana and vyana. The five remaining pranas are called *upa* pranas or subsidiary pranas.

In this practice the awareness of each prana is developed separately. First there is the vision of *vyana vayu*, the all pervading prana, which is seen as tiny points of light moving in all directions all through the pranic body. Then the vision of *udana vayu*, which pervades the extremities of the body, is seen in the form of rings of light moving in a clockwise direction. From udana we come to *prana vayu*, which moves up and down the chest in waves of light. *Apana vayu* is visualized moving in the pelvic region from the navel to the perineum as a downward stream of light. *Samana vayu* is visualized as a stream of light in the abdominal region, moving sideways from right to left and from left to right.

In this way the pranic body is viewed in its separate components, which in reality are all interlinked and which represent the different aspects of pranic expression within the physical body. When we perceive the movements of these five pranas we are actually seeing the movement of the pranic body.

Technique
Stage 1: Preparation

Sit in a comfortable meditation posture with the spine and head erect. Place the hands on the knees in chin or jnana mudra. Close the eyes. Become aware of the whole body. Develop your awareness of the whole body, from the tip of the toes to the top of the head. In one glimpse, in one thought, observe the whole body. Develop complete awareness of the whole body.

Gradually become aware of the etheric body within the physical body. The etheric body is experienced in the form of space. Visualize the body as an empty shell. Dissociate your mind from the physical body, from the awareness of muscles and bones and internal organs. Just be aware of space. Observe the space which pervades the entire body internally and which also exists around the body.

The body is just an empty shell covered with skin. The skin is the shell. Imagine the whole body to be like a balloon which is filled with air, and around the balloon there is also air. In the same way the etheric body is filled with space and space exists all around the etheric body. Intensify the awareness of space. "I am nothing but space, through and through."

With this awareness gradually dissociate your awareness, your perception, your mind from the experience of comfort or discomfort, pleasure or pain. You should know that, "I am not the pain or the pleasure, the discomfort or the comfort, which is being experienced by the physical body. My consciousness is centred in the etheric body. My etheric body is different from my physical body."

Try to forget the physical body and just be aware of the etheric body. Be aware of space and nothing but space. Even if the physical body moves, do not let that movement distract your awareness. Become aware of the feeling of silence and stillness in the etheric body.

Stage 2: Pillar of air

Observe the breath within the etheric body in the form of a pillar of air which extends from manipura to ajna chakra. The consciousness moves up and down this pillar of air. At the time of inhalation the consciousness ascends with the breath along this pillar of air from manipura to ajna. With exhalation the consciousness descends from ajna to manipura. With each ascent and descent of consciousness up and down this pillar of air from manipura to ajna become aware of the stillness and silence which pervades the etheric body. Intensify your awareness of the silence and stillness of the etheric body experienced with the ascent and descent of consciousness up and down the passage of air extending from manipura to ajna.

Stage 3: The subtle aspects of breathing

Now become aware of the breathing process which is happening on different dimensions simultaneously. The physical body breathes in air. The mental body breathes in vitality. The subtle body breathes in prana and the psychic body breathes in pure energy.

The physical body which is composed of the gross elements – bones, muscles etc., breathes in air. For a few moments be aware of the physical breathing process. Once the awareness is established in the physical body go deep and become aware of the three subtle aspects of breathing. Go beyond the physical body consciousness and feel the three other bodies breathing and pulsating with the energy of life.

The mental body, which is composed of the four faculties of manas, buddhi, chitta and ahamkara, breathes in vitality. This is the first subtle body of which you have to be aware with intensity of mind and with concentration. The first subtle aspect, the mental body, breathes in vitality, this vital, active principle which is the cause of the functioning and performance of the mental structure. The mental body is the one that interacts with the world of the senses. Feel it breathe in vitality. The vitality which the mental body breathes is an attribute and aspect of the air that the physical body is breathing. Go deep into the perception, into the awareness, into the feeling of the mental body breathing in vitality.

Now go into the second aspect, the subtle body. The subtle body interacts with the subtle mind and the psychic realm. The subtle body receives its life and stimulation through prana. The subtle body interacts with the mental body and its deeper aspects and also with the superficial aspects of the psychic body.

Prana, which the subtle body breathes in and out, is to be observed in the form of energy particles, in the form of a stream of visualized energy atoms. Go deep, intensify the perception of the subtle body breathing in prana, the manifest prana. The vision of manifest prana is in the form of energy particles, energy atoms, a stream of particles.

Go into the third aspect, the psychic body, the realm of pure energy. The psychic body breathes in the subtle form of prana, where prana is not just a vision but a force full of warmth, heat and colour. Just as hot air rising from a fire can be seen in the form of a shimmering, turbulent force in the open atmosphere, in the same way the subtle prana, the pure form of energy, is to be seen and experienced full of warmth, light, heat and colour.

With intensity of awareness and concentration go on observing, go on witnessing the play of energy within the structure of the psychic body. Intensify the awareness there and be more aware of this energy activity within the different bodies related to the process of breathing.

Stage 4: Heart centre

Now become aware of the heart region within the etheric body. Become aware of the physical heart and observe the heart beat. At the corresponding location in the etheric body visualize a pulsating point of light. This point of light which flares up and diminishes with every heart beat is experienced as expansion and contraction of the point of light in the etheric body. Intensify the awareness of this light in the heart region. The pulsation of light is in rhythm with the heart beat, explosion and implosion of light in the etheric body. The whole of the etheric body fills up with light and becomes dark again with each pulsation.

Stage 5: Blood circulation/pranic flow

Now concentrate on the circulation of blood in the physical body. Become aware of blood flowing through each and every part of the body. Try to hear the sound of blood flowing within the body. Become totally aware of the movement of blood in the body, as it flows continuously through the different veins, arteries and blood vessels. This physical activity is experienced in the etheric body as a flow of prana.

Become aware of the flow of energy which pervades the entire structure. Within the experience of space be aware of the subtle movement of prana. Observe the flow of prana in each and every part of the etheric body. This flow of prana fills the etheric body with the experience of warmth, light and vitality.

Intensify the awareness of prana filling the space of the etheric body with warmth, luminosity and vitality. Try to concentrate totally on this pranic movement. Be aware of this pranic experience.

Be aware of the total etheric body and of the movement of prana within the space. Just as the blood circulation in each and every part of the body provides energy, warmth and comfort to the entire physical structure, in the same way the prana flows into each and every part of the etheric body, filling up the entire space with warmth, light, comfort, vitality and energy.

Try to experience in one glimpse, in one thought, this continuous movement of prana throughout the entire etheric body. Intensify the awareness of prana. Maintain the awareness of space, prana and luminosity in the etheric body and deepen the feeling of inner silence and stillness.

Stage 6: Whole body breathing

Maintain your awareness of the total etheric body and the movement of prana within the space. It is not an awareness of a localized space like chidakasha or hridayakasha. Be aware of the entire space of the body as a whole. Intensify your awareness of sthoolakasha, the space throughout the body. Along with this awareness begin to observe the natural, spontaneous flow of the breath. As you inhale, feel that the whole body breathes in not just through the nostrils but through each and every pore of the skin. As you exhale, experience the breath going out through each and every pore.

With each inspiration there is an experience of expansion. Feel the entire pranic body is expanding. With each expiration there is a feeling of relaxation. Feel the pranic body contracting. As the breath enters the body through the pores of the skin while inhaling, the prana expands within the etheric body, filling it with light. See the etheric space expanding and filling with particles of light, flashes of light, streaks of light. As the breath leaves the body, sthoolakasha relaxes and contracts. Observe this phenomenon. Intensify this awareness.

Stage 7: Awareness of pranamaya kosha

Maintain the awareness of energy, of prana, in each and every part of the body. This is vyana vayu, the prana pervading each and every part of the body. Try to have a visual experience. Try to see the space contained in the body filled with tiny pinpoints of light, streaks of light, streams of light, moving in every direction. Your whole body from head to toe is filled with light particles. Each and every part of the body is filled with light particles, all moving in random patterns.

Now become aware of the udana vayu in the extremities of the body. See udana moving inside the two legs, the two arms and the head, in the form of rings of light and energy moving clockwise. Develop the awareness of udana vayu from the tips of the toes to the hips, from the tips of the fingers to the shoulders, from the neck to the top of the head. Visualize a circular form of energy, moving at great speed in a clockwise direction. Try to develop this experience through instant visualization, instant feeling. You should simply be aware of the process, be aware of the pranic movement which is constantly going on in the extremities of the body.

Next develop the experience of samana vayu in the abdominal region, from the navel to the diaphragm. Samana vayu is moving sideways. Visualize a wave of light moving from left to right and from right to left, across the abdomen. Develop instant visualization, instant feeling. Be aware of the movement of prana in the abdomen with intensity and concentration.

Now become aware of the pranic movement within the chest region. Develop the experience of prana vayu. Visualize the upward flow of prana from the base of the rib cage to the throat pit. See a wave of light, like the wave of the ocean, surging upwards during inhalation from the diaphragm to the neck, and then surging downward during exhalation. Be aware of this pranic movement. Experience the prana vayu moving within the region of the chest with intensity of awareness and concentration.

Finally, observe the movement of apana vayu in the lower abdomen from the navel to the perineum. Visualize a wave of light energy travelling downward at the time of inhalation from the navel to the perineum. At the time of exhalation this light wave travels upward. Intensify the awareness of the movement of apana from the navel to the perineum.

Stage 8: Ending the practice

Allow the vision of the pranic body to fade into sthoolakasha. Experience the space pervading the entire body. Become aware of the physical body and the meditation posture. Become aware of the room. Slowly externalize the mind. Take a deep breath in and chant *Om* three times.

Hari Om Tat Sat

18

Laya Dharana

There are two paths of self-illumination. One path leads to expansion of consciousness and the other path leads to total dissolution, laya or shoonya. The first path includes many spiritual practices and is taught by many teachers. The second path is known as laya and is taught by very few. This was what St John of the Cross was referring to when he said, "By God, I swear I die every night." What is this death and this night? When the mind is withdrawn to the source, when the pranas and the body remain inert, as if dead, that is laya. The only difference between the final stage of laya and the death experience is that after death you do not come back into the same body, whereas after experiencing the laya stage you return to the same body and mind, and resume life as the same individual.

Laya yoga and kundalini yoga
The word *laya* means 'to dissolve'. What does one dissolve? Not the mind because that happens in the normal course of kundalini yoga practice. As you go from mooladhara to swadhisthana and then to manipura, you gradually dissolve the various layers of mind. Dissolution of prana also happens in kundalini yoga. Laya yoga is the Upanishadic version of kundalini yoga and kriya yoga. The Upanishads say that through hatha yoga you are able to overcome the doshas which are accumulated in the body, and after purifying

yourself you become established in the supreme self, which is *chaitanya* or divinity. It is not an experience but an absolute merger. At that level all the winds, all the movements of energy, all the motion of the mind completely stops and dissolution of personality is obtained.

It is not just having a vision or experience, but dissolving oneself completely into the cosmic self. This dissolution is seen in the form of the transformation of the normal patterns of consciousness and the development of the transcendent nature. The manifest nature has to dissolve with the unmanifest nature. So this dissolution of the total life force followed by rebirth is laya yoga.

Kundalini yoga is a tantric process and laya yoga is a vedic process. In the practices of tantra the emphasis has been given to energy, to feeling, to sensitizing the awareness in order to experience the movement of prana shakti. Both kundalini and laya yoga work on the awakening of pranas, chakras and stimulation and purification of the tattwas; however, laya yoga also emphasizes the awareness of consciousness.

Laya yoga aims to sensitize the awareness in order to experience the consciousness so that we become aware of the changes taking place in that dimension. The ability to observe and control the experiences in the field of consciousness enables one to eventually harmonize the pranic awakening, the awakening of chakras and the kundalini. Laya is a system which complements the practices of kundalini and kriya yoga by bringing a balance both in the prana and in the structure of consciousness, thus making our practice more complete.

Entering the unconscious

When first entering the state of laya, the individual consciousness is completely disintegrated. There is no awareness of I; no knowledge of time, space, object or individuality. Even the breath stops in some cases. If one continues practising and experiencing this laya state, the whole body undergoes a condition of rigor mortis. This could continue for half an hour, one hour or a whole night, during which time the body is devoid of prana. In the state of laya, the mind reverts from the state of manifestation to the state of dissolution. During this period the mind returns to the causal state.

Just as a small plant goes back to the seed, so the mind reverts to its original state, which is called *moola prakriti*. In this state there is no creation, activity, movement or vibration. It is a state of status quo where everything stands still. There is no evolution or devolution, no time and no space. At this point the mind enters the unconscious body according to modern psychology, or the anandamaya kosha according to Vedanta. There the consciousness is refreshed and qualified with the unconscious self. The eight siddhis expounded in the *Raja Yoga Sutras* of Patanjali are also cultivated there, so that when consciousness returns to the normal state it is vested with spiritual power.

The black hole and the white hole

According to the theory of laya yoga, within our own consciousness there is a black hole and a white hole. In the process of spiritual awakening it is natural for us to be attracted towards anahata. We have always considered anahata to be associated with the different forms of subtle, mental movements such as emotions and feelings. In sadhana most of us only go as far as anahata.

Beyond anahata a different kind of experience takes place which has nothing to do with the mind or the body or with experiences we have had in our life. Beyond anahata is the white hole from where creation takes place. The yantra of vishuddhi, the white circle, represents that white hole. The black hole of our personality is mooladhara. All our existing and potential behaviour, consciousness, creativity, divine faculties and transcendental awareness are sucked into this area. We have the energy, the ability and the strength, but once that higher awareness is sucked into mooladhara then we become ordinary beings, seeking sensory distractions, sensual pleasures and living our lives as we have done for generations until now.

Since we are so caught up in the bondage of this black hole, the powerful attraction of mooladhara, there is no escape for us. It is here that the wheel of life and the law of karma is experienced. The other side of the spectrum is vishuddhi. This potential has to surface from the white hole of vishuddhi into the realm of human consciousness. This is the theory or concept of laya. So, just as there is the theory of the 'big bang' and the expanding universe externally, in the same way, within us also is a white hole and 'big bang'. The symbolic representation of vishuddhi, the white circle, represents ether, the first of the elements belonging to the physical world. The bang, which is consciously and constantly expanding and creating, stands for these different levels of anahata, manipura, swadhisthana, back to the surface of mooladhara. These are the four waves of manifestation of the 'big bang'

The upside down tree

Vishuddhi is not really associated with any of the experiences that we have known life to be. Rather, vishuddhi is the seed of life, the causal body from where the different bodies take birth. It is the seed from which the tree, the trunk, the branches, the leaves and the fruit emerge. This has been described in a very beautiful and poetic form in the fifteenth chapter of the *Bhagavad Gita*. The example is given of an upside down tree, which has its roots facing up and its branches facing down, representing our growth or evolution in life. The root is akasha tattwa, the first tattwa to come into being. The other tattwas have come forth from akasha tattwa. Anahata represents the trunk. Manipura is represented by the branches, vitality going in all directions, nurturing and supporting the entire being. Swadhisthana is represented by the millions of leaves. These leaves symbolize the *karmashaya*, the karmas which are stored in the deeper levels of our consciousness, and we do not know what each leaf means. Mooladhara is the forbidden fruit that we eat every day, every moment.

Jumping into the void

Although initially we have to work with all the chakras, in order to perfect laya it is necessary that we work with mooladhara and vishuddhi. In the pure vedantic approach these two chakras, mooladhara and vishuddhi, are the most important. Birth and creation are represented by vishuddhi, death and stagnation by mooladhara. In the vedantic approach, the effort here is to reach the last stage, where our consciousness dives into mooladhara and emerges at vishuddhi, where everything is pure, new, with greater creativity, with greater harmony, balance and light.

Mooladhara is a fantastic psychic centre because it is the only chakra which has unlimited potential. It can bind a person with ropes of karma and samskara so strong that they are impossible to break it. Yet this chakra, if handled correctly, can propel you deep within itself to dissolve completely and to again take birth from vishuddhi.

Visualization and vibratory field

Visualization plays a very vital role in the practices of laya dharana. Vision plays an important role in the manifest world and also in the unmanifest dimension. Sixty percent of the stimulation that we receive is visual by nature, so when we block out this input from the brain, the faculty of vision has to develop internally. This development of inner vision gives the ability to eventually alter the patterns of consciousness by focusing the will, attention, and dissipated energies of mind.

Visualization stimulates or awakens the vibratory dimension of our psychic personality. In laya it is necessary that this power of visualization be awakened to its fullest capacity, because it is through visualization that we are able to control the manifestation of energy, by controlling the vibratory field of our psychic personality. It is only through the power of visualization that we can eventually control the altered states of consciousness by again controlling the vibratory field of the body. The vibratory field of the body has the ability to control the energy experience and the consciousness experience. This vibration is known as spandan. Vibration or spandan is the level beyond the tattwas, where the tattwas which represent the interaction of energy and consciousness are in a primordial state.

Laya – the final yoga

In laya yoga there are four levels of practices. The first level is refining and managing the consciousness of the four basic instincts: *maithuna* or the sexual instinct, *bhaya* or fear, *ahara* or craving, and *nidra* or sleep. The second is experiencing the chakras – chakra consciousness. The third aspect is managing the gunas: tamas, rajas and sattwa and the psychic manifestations of the gunas. The fourth level is understanding the transcendental dimensions of consciousness or lokas. Those who have perfected laya yoga have been able to control their life force and, in some cases, even rejuvenate their bodies and their selves, because they gain the ability to direct and channel the life energy. Laya yoga is said to be the last yoga beyond hatha, raja, karma and bhakti yogas. In fact the last stages of all the different yogas aim to bring the aspirant towards the experience of laya.

What is samadhi? Samadhi is the experience of union. It is the experience of dissolution of the outer nature that is the aim of raja yoga. Even in samadhi there are different stages which represent an altered state of consciousness, of human attitude, of human behaviour and interaction, ultimately leading to the state of dissolution of individuality with the cosmic energy. Even in bhakti yoga, nine stages have been defined, and in the final stage there is *sayujya*, which means total identification and oneness with the object of contemplation, fusion with the object of contemplation. So, in this sayujya also there is dissolution of the external nature. In this way we find that towards the end, every yoga takes the aspirant towards the experience of re-emerging with the cosmic, universal consciousness.

Laya yoga is a form of death, death of the known. Therefore, the techniques of laya yoga have been kept secret throughout the ages, until now. Prior to the practice of laya yoga, pratyahara and dharana have to be perfected. The direction of these practices is to enable one to transform the nature of the personality, the body, the brain, the mind, the emotions, the sensitivity, the creativity, so that one will be able to experience the transcendental consciousness. An introduction to the practices of laya yoga is given here in order to develop the ability to move smoothly, naturally and spontaneously into the deeper practices of laya, which include the Vyoma Panchaka series.

Laya Dharana One

MOOLADHARA AND VISHUDDHI DRISHTI

Space has been considered the basis for the growth of every other element. The entire evolution of humanity, whether material or spiritual, happens in the dimension of space. Space contains infinite possibilities of growth and it also supports the nature and the growth of the other elements. Vishuddhi represents the element of space. Anahata chakra represents the next element, air, a denser form of the same energy. Similarly, manipura chakra, representing the fire element, and swadhisthana chakra, representing the water element, are progressively denser forms of the same energy. Mooladhara represents earth, the solid form of that same energy. Matter represents the total potential of cosmic energy. There is concentration of that cosmic energy in one grain of sand, in one atom, so matter is important in every respect.

The concentrated final form of energy is matter, represented by mooladhara, and the expanded form of energy which supports the tattwas and consciousness is space, represented by vishuddhi. Mooladhara also has the immense potential to draw one's energy and to propel one to emerge from vishuddhi by bypassing the other chakras. If you can practise the mooladhara sadhana with total control over yourself, you do not need to pass through the other chakras. You can come to vishuddhi straight away, provided you are able to handle the nature of mooladhara.

Just as energy has manifested in the form of tattwas, elements, from space to earth, so consciousness has manifested in the form of akashas, the different dimensions of space and consciousness in these chakras. In mooladhara chakra the tattwa is earth, which represents energy, and the space is guna rahita akasha, which means the space without attributes. In order to complete this process there has to be a comprehensive understanding of all the chakras, the tattwas and the different states of consciousness that one experiences with chakra awakening. This requires a gradual process of progression and preparation. For most of us it is not possible to totally ignore and bypass the mental vrittis or the manifestations of the pranic forces in our personality. It is only possible for a selected few who have that kind of mentality and determination, who are willing to go through the rigorous process of laya, dissolution of personality within themselves.

Technique 1: Mooladhara and vishuddhi awareness
Stage 1: Preparation

Sit in a comfortable meditation posture. Keep the eyes closed, spine erect and head straight. Place both hands on top of the knees or in front of the body, wherever comfortable. For a few moments, focus your entire attention within your body. Move your mind through the body from part to part. See each part mentally. Acknowledge the existence of the part. Release any kind of tightness or tension which you may experience in that part, by acknowledging the body and being aware of the physical state. Gradually eliminate all physical distractions from the field of your awareness. Become more involved in the observation of your body. As you do so, you will notice that the body begins to attain a state of stillness. You begin to experience quietness and peace.

Stage 2: Awareness of energy

In this state of silence, of motionlessness and peace within the body, become aware of a subtle flow of energy.

The subtle flow is experienced in the form of a rising movement from the base of the spine to the top of the spine, to the crown of the head. Go on tracing this flow and heightening your awareness of it. At the time of natural inhalation, feel the flow ascending from the base of the spine to the top of the spine, moving towards the head. At the time of natural exhalation, the subtle wave descends from the upper regions down towards the base of the spinal cord. Become aware of the subtle movements which are being experienced in the region of the body at the time of inhalation and exhalation.

Stage 3: Awareness of mooladhara

Now focus your attention at the starting point. Bring the awareness to the beginning of the wave that rises from the base of the spine, in the region of mooladhara chakra. Concentrate your entire attention in the region of mooladhara chakra, located in the region of the perineum in males and at the posterior of the cervix in females. While focusing your attention at mooladhara, do not block the perceptions of the upward movement which is experienced spontaneously and naturally at the time of inhalation.

Become aware of the mooladhara centre within the body. Visualize a vortex of energy there, a luminous point of energy. Mooladhara is pulsating and vibrating. Experience these pulsations and vibrations in the form of waves ascending and descending along the full length of the spine. They ascend at the time of inhalation and descend at the time of exhalation.

Stage 4: Om chanting in mooladhara

Now bring your attention to the region of vishuddhi. Inhale deeply and chant *Om* three times. While you are chanting *Om*, centre your entire awareness at mooladhara chakra. When you are inhaling and preparing yourself to chant *Om*, bring the entire awareness to vishuddhi chakra. Again at the time of chanting focus the entire awareness and feel the vibration in mooladhara chakra. As you chant *Om* become aware of mooladhara chakra, and when you are not chanting, as you inhale move the awareness up to vishuddhi chakra.

You may feel an opening up of mooladhara with the chanting of *Om*. Generally, in the state of tension there is contraction of the perineal muscles. At other times there is contraction of the abdominal muscles and of the neck muscles. At the time of chanting *Om* be specifically aware of the release and opening up of mooladhara. Feel that any tightness of the muscles is being released. Make sure that the entire perineal region is completely relaxed and free from any tension or contraction.

As you breathe in, your awareness is at vishuddhi chakra. As you chant the mantra *Om* bring your attention to mooladhara. Then, when you are inhaling, relaxing or listening, bring your attention to vishuddhi. Both of the centres are to be visualized in this practice. As you focus on each chakra point in turn, see it in the form of a burning flame. Continue for several minutes in this way.

Stage 5: Ending the practice

Prepare to end the practice. Stop the chanting of *Om*. Leave the awareness of mooladhara and vishuddhi chakras. Become aware of your body sitting on the floor in a meditation posture. Gradually externalize your mind and senses. Gently move the body and open your eyes.

Technique 2: Mooladhara breathing
Stage 1: Preparation

Prepare your body by coming into a comfortable sitting asana with the head, neck and spine in a straight line, hands resting on the knees, eyes and mouth lightly closed. Spend a few moments becoming aware of your body, and mentally releasing any tension, stiffness or tightness. Feel your body becoming steady, still and comfortable. Now we are going to practise a form of mooladhara breathing. In this process we will have to combine the practice of moola bandha and nasal breathing. At the time of inhalation there is contraction of the perineal muscles. While holding the breath in, maintain the contraction of moola bandha. When breathing out there has to be a gradual relaxation of the block in the abdominal region.

Stage 2: Nadi shodhana and moola bandha in mooladhara
We will begin with a simple practice of nadi shodhana pranayama. In this practice the entire process is to be experienced in mooladhara chakra only. Place the index and the middle fingers of your right hand on your forehead. Use the ring finger to close the left nostril and the thumb to close the right nostril. The practice starts with the right nostril. First breathe in through the right nostril, the pingala side. While breathing in, become aware of mooladhara chakra and gently contract the perineal muscles as much as you can without creating any kind of tension. Hold the inhalation internally for a count of seven, maintaining moola bandha and the vision of a flame at mooladhara. Exhale through ida nadi, the left nostril. At the time of exhalation there will be a gradual release of the contraction. Now hold the breath out for a count of seven. Try to release the contraction from other muscles in the body such as the abdomen and shoulders.

Again repeat this process. Breathe in through the left nostril, hold the breath and maintain moola bandha. Then exhale through the right nostril, pingala swara, and release the contraction. Hold the breath outside for a count of seven. In this way, with intense awareness, you have to move the pranas of mooladhara.

Stage 3: Visualization of a jyoti and square in mooladhara
Bring the entire attention to mooladhara chakra. Visualize mooladhara chakra in the form of a jyoti, a light, a flame. That flame is burning inside a small square, and the entire symbol is in the region of mooladhara. The more clearly you can perceive this image, the better your concentration will be. Inhale through the right nostril

and slowly practise moola bandha. The breath should be slow, deep and long. When you have fully inhaled, close the nostrils, retain the breath and count mentally from one to seven. Open the left nostril and exhale through the left nostril. Exhalation should be slow, deep and long. Hold the breath outside for the count of seven and allow the muscles to relax completely.

Again inhale through the left nostril and practise moola bandha. The inhalation should be slow, deep and long. Hold the breath in for a count of seven. Maintain the contraction of the perineum. Simultaneously, be aware of the candle flame inside the square. Then open the right nostril and exhale with a slow, deep, long breath. Retain the breath outside for a count of seven. Release the contraction and any muscle pressure in other parts of the body.

This is one round of practice. In this way practise two more rounds. Make sure there is no agitation in the process of breathing. When you finish each round, bring the hand down, but immediately shift the attention from mooladhara to vishuddhi. Do not allow your awareness to linger in the region of mooladhara. As soon as one round of practice is over, immediately come back to vishuddhi chakra. When you begin the second round of practice, go to mooladhara. At the termination of that round come back to vishuddhi. When you move into the third round of practice, the mind should not be allowed to wander uselessly in the area of practice.

Stage 4: Ending the practice

After you have completed three rounds prepare to end the practice. Leave the awareness of mooladhara and vishuddhi. Allow your breathing to return to normal. Become aware of your body, and slowly externalize the mind and the senses. Gently move your body and open your eyes.

Technique 3: The cave of mooladhara
Stage 1: Preparation
Sit in a comfortable meditation posture, body upright and straight. Place the hands on the knees or in the lap, wherever comfortable. Gently close your eyes. For a few moments become aware of your whole body, of the posture in which you are sitting. Awareness of the whole body. Make sure that you are relaxed physically and free from tension. There should be no tightness, you should not feel uncomfortable. Be at ease with yourself.
Mentally observe the posture of your body. Move your attention from one part of the body to the next, from the head to the toes and make sure there is comfort and ease. The feeling of relaxation is all pervading within you. Complete awareness of the whole body. As you go deeper into the experience of the body you will become aware of the stillness and silence that pervades the body. Feel the sensation of stillness and silence in your body. Complete awareness of the body from the top of the head to the toes.
Stage 2: Breath awareness
Mentally observe the flow of the natural breath. As you breathe in feel a gentle cool sensation within the nostrils, and as you breathe out feel a gentle warm sensation. Observe the breath, the natural incoming and outgoing breath, by mentally becoming aware of the temperature of the breath within the nostrils. Intensify the awareness of breath and begin to experience the flow in the spinal passage.
At the time of inhalation feel the breath rise from the base of the spine to the crown of the head. At the time of exhalation feel the breath move from the crown of the head to the base of the spine. Move your awareness with the natural incoming and outgoing breath up and down along the back, from the base of the spine to the crown of the head with inhalation and then down from the crown of the head to the base of the spine with exhalation. Observe and experience this movement of the breath.

Stage 3: Awareness of sushumna
As the consciousness moves up and down with the breath, begin to observe a luminous thread in the spinal passage along which the awareness moves, a bright luminous thread from the base of the spine to the crown of the head. The awareness moves up and then down along this luminous thread with the breath. Gradually you will have to develop the power of visualization. You will have to intensify the will. With the force of the will and visualization begin to experience the movement of consciousness along the luminous thread from mooladhara to sahasrara.

Continue with this practice for a few moments, each time developing more sensitivity, more awareness and identification with the movement of the breath, the ascending and descending of consciousness and the luminous thread. Do not allow yourself to be disturbed by the experiences of the physical body. Experiences of discomfort or aches and pains should not disturb your awareness and your practice of inner visualization. Just focus on the two points of mooladhara and sahasrara: mooladhara at the base of the spine, and sahasrara, the crown chakra. These two centres are connected by a luminous thread running along the spinal passage. The awareness ascends and descends through this luminous path along with inhalation and exhalation.

Stage 4: The cave of mooladhara
Now focus yourself in the region of mooladhara chakra. At the base of the spinal passage visualize mooladhara chakra. Mooladhara is to be visualized in the form of a cave, a deep dark cave. In the centre of that cave is a red, luminous point of light, a deep, dark red point of light. Visualize the cave of mooladhara by taking the awareness down to mooladhara. The visualization has to take place at the location of the chakra, not in chidakasha, not in the head space, but in the space of the chakra. Visualize the cave of mooladhara. Your whole awareness has to be centred in the mooladhara cave. The mooladhara region

feels like the seat of an immense power. There is throbbing, there is energy, there is continuous vibration in this deep dark cave emanating from a point of light on the floor in the centre of the cave.

Stage 5: The shivalingam

As you adjust your mental awareness to the vision, to the experience of the cave, you will notice that the point from which this deep dark red light is emanating is a stone, a rock in the form of a shivalingam. The shivalingam is glowing internally. The colour of the glow is deep dark red and it is that red luminosity emanating from the shivalingam which is also illuminating the cave. Focus your awareness on the symbol of the shivalingam. Visualize this red shivalingam. Do not allow your awareness to be distracted by external surroundings and sounds. Let them be there, keep yourself focused on the image, the symbol of the shivalingam in the cave of mooladhara chakra.

As you intensely observe the symbol of the shivalingam, you will notice that around the base of the shivalingam there is a form, that of a snake, which is coiled around the base of the shivalingam. There is no fear. Just be aware of the mooladhara symbol, the self-luminous shivalingam with a snake coiled around the base. Feel the vibration, feel the *spandan*, the continuous vibration of energy, divine shakti. What is coiled around the shivalingam is kundalini, *Adi Shakti*, the primordial energy, the source of all creation. Experience the light and intensity of energy which is radiating from this shivalingam up into the space of your physical body.

Do not allow your mind to fluctuate. Sensitize the mind. Just as you are visualizing the symbol of the shivalingam and the snake in the cave of mooladhara, just as you are experiencing the reddish glow of the shivalingam filling the whole space of mooladhara, in the same way now you will have to experience the power, the force of that energy which is in mooladhara chakra. Focus your whole awareness in the experience of mooladhara.

Stage 6: Om chanting

Now chant *Om* in the following way. In one breath chant short *Oms* as many times as you can comfortably without becoming breathless. While chanting the mantra *Om* keep your awareness fixed on the symbol of the shivalingam. Visualize the cave illuminated by the reddish glow emanating from the shivalingam. As the sound waves travel in the space of the body, waves of energy from mooladhara also travel upwards. Although the chanting of the mantra *Om* will be done by the body, through the mouth, the vibration of the mantra has to be felt in the cave of mooladhara.

Breathe in deeply and chant *Om* as you exhale. *Om Om Om Om Om Om*. Continue repeating the short *Om* mantras with every breath and keep on visualizing the symbol of the shivalingam. Have the vision of the luminous shivalingam and the cave, and feel the vibrations of *Om* coming up from mooladhara chakra into the body space, up to sahasrara. Pervade the whole body with the vibration, with the force and with the shakti of the mantra Om. *Om Om Om Om Om...*

Stage 7: Ending the practice

Stop the chanting of the mantra *Om*. Remain silent and still for a few moments. Now slowly externalize the senses. Become aware of the sounds around you. become aware of the environment. Let go of the awareness of mooladhara. Let go of the awareness of the symbol, the vibration. Externalize the senses and the mind. Breathe in deeply and chant *Om* three times. Rub the palms of the hands together and place them on top of the closed eyes. Gently open your eyes and move your body.

Technique 4: Mooladhara and vishuddhi dharana
Stage 1: Preparation

Sit quietly in a meditation asana. Focus your awareness within yourself. Complete awareness of the body. Observe your body internally, from the top of the head to the toes. Become aware of the natural breath. Observe the process of breathing and breathing out. Focus the attention on the flow of breath in the nostrils. Observe the natural flow of breath in the nostrils by becoming aware of the slight temperature variation.

Stage 2: Observation of breath in the spinal passage

Observe the breath, and then begin to experience the breath in the spinal passage. At the time of inhalation the breath comes up along the spine, from the base to the back of the neck, and at the time of exhalation the breath moves down along the spinal passage. Experience the flow of breath in the spinal passage between mooladhara to vishuddhi and back down again from vishuddhi to mooladhara.

As you observe the movement of breath in the spinal passage between mooladhara and vishuddhi, you will notice that gradually the process of breathing becomes deeper and longer. The breath gradually becomes deep and long. The consciousness has to rise with the breath from mooladhara to vishuddhi and go down with the breath from vishuddhi to mooladhara.

Stage 3: Repetition of beeja mantras

Now when you descend to mooladhara, stop and retain the breath there for a few seconds and mentally repeat the beeja mantra of mooladhara – *lam, lam, lam, lam, lam,* five times and then when you come up to vishudhhi hold the breath for a few seconds. Then as you breathe in mentally repeat the beeja mantra of vishuddhi – *ham, ham, ham, ham, ham,* five times. In this way continue with breath awareness in the spinal passage between mooladhara and vishuddhi combined with the beeja mantras of the chakras.

As you become fixed and one-pointed in the practice, the body awareness will slowly drop away and you will only be aware of the flow of breath in the psychic passage between mooladhara and vishuddhi, the movement of breath with consciousness, and the repetition, the vibration of the beeja mantras of mooladhara and vishuddhi, *lam* and *ham*. Intensify your consciousness, merge yourself with the process of the ascending and descending consciousness with mantra.

With the repetition of the mantra in mooladhara, feel the waves of vibration moving from mooladhara up into the upper space of the body. At the time of repeating the mantra in vishuddhi, feel the vibrations of the mantra moving down into the lower space. Complete awareness of the mantras *lam* and *ham* in mooladhara and vishudhhi.

Stage 4: Experience of black space and white space
Now you will have to develop the ability to experience the mooladhara region in the form of a totally dark, black, deep space and vishuddhi chakra in the form of a brilliant, luminous, white space. With the breath move the consciousness from the deep, dark, black space to the luminous, bright, light space.

Be aware of the breath flowing in the psychic passage, the spinal passage. Be aware of the mantra in mooladhara and vishuddhi. Be aware of the space in mooladhara and vishuddhi, the black and the white. Nothing else exists except awareness of the deep, dark space in mooladhara and the vibration of the mantra *lam*; pure white luminous space in vishuddhi and the vibration of the mantra *ham*. Go deeper into yourself, without any reservations or fears, go deep.

Sensitize the mind, sensitize the awareness to experience mooladhara and vishuddhi, the vibration, the space, the movement of consciousness along the spinal passage. Have full control over the consciousness, maintain inner alertness, do not become withdrawn and introvert. Remain in command of your mental faculties.

Stage 5: Om chanting in psychic passage

Now stop repeating the beeja mantras of the chakras. Mentally start to repeat *Om* with the ascending consciousness along the spinal passage from mooladhara to vishuddhi and *Om* with the descending consciousness from vishuddhi to mooladhara. Be aware of the deep, dark space in mooladhara and the luminous, bright space in vishuddhi. As you move down towards mooladhara feel that you are being pulled by a force into the depths of mooladhara space, an incredible suction. It is that same suction which propels the consciousness with the mantra *Om* to re-emerge in vishuddhi. Initially this is a mental process, but in the course of time, as the concentration deepens, energy and consciousness will feel the pull of mooladhara and the force of vishuddhi.

Stage 6: Mooladhara and jalandhara bandhas

Now stop this practice. Keep the consciousness tuned to the inner experience of the body and practise moola and jalandhara bandhas. At the time of inhalation breathe in deeply up along the spinal passage, holding the awareness in the vishuddhi region, in the experience of space. Then, while holding the breath in, practise moola bandha, contracting the sphincter muscles until you are able to feel a gentle tingling sensation near the coccyx and sacral region. Along with the practice of moola bandha perform the practice of jalandhara bandha by lowering the chin and placing the chin over the base of the throat, creating a gentle pressure in the neck. Hold this posture for as long as possible, comfortably, while retaining the breath in.

When you feel that you cannot retain the posture any longer, then gradually release jalandhara bandha first, then moola bandha. For ten breaths continue with the practice of moving your consciousness with the normal breath from mooladhara to vishudhhi with the mantra *Om*. The eleventh breath will be combined with the practices of moola bandha and jalandhara, holding them for as long as possible, comfortably, without strain.

Then release the bandhas and continue with the ascending and descending consciousness between mooladhara and vishuddhi with the mantra *Om* for ten breaths. With the eleventh breath again practise the two bandhas. Bandhas are only practised with inhalation, not with exhalation. A total of three rounds of the practice should be performed at your own speed.

Stage 7: Intensifying the practice

In between the practice of the bandhas, whenever you are moving your consciousness between mooladhara and vishuddhi go deep into the experience of space, the suction and the re-emergence of consciousness from vishuddhi. The practices of bandhas are used to sensitize the awareness to the points of pressure and the location of mooladhara and vishuddhi chakras. Remain alert, do not become too introverted and do not lose control of yourself, of your faculties. Intensify the consciousness every passing moment. With absolute faith and conviction of your strength go deep into the practice. Feel the force of suction when the consciousness goes down to mooladhara, and feel the force of expulsion when the consciousness comes up to vishuddhi. Experience mooladhara as the binding force, and experience vishuddhi as the liberating force.

Stage 8: Ending the practice

Now stop the practice. Gradually externalize the consciousness by becoming aware of the body. Externalize the senses by becoming aware of the external environment. Breathe in deeply and chant *Om* three times.

Hari Om Tat Sat

Laya Dharana Two

LOKA DRISHTI

Ritam and satyam: eternal and transient realities

Yogis have described two forms of reality. One is the changing, transforming, evolving reality known as *ritam* and one is the fixed all-pervasive, permanent, eternal reality known as *satyam*. The movement of energy is from ritam to satyam and this is the life force which propels us from one level or state of experience to another level or state of experience. The movement of consciousness is also from ritam to satyam. An example can be given of a crawling caterpillar becoming a butterfly flying in space. Similarly, as human beings we are caterpillars crawling on our leaf, on our branch, in our tree.

In the manifest world we go through the ritam aspect of life. From the time of our birth until death our body goes through a process of continuous transformation. Our perceptions and our faculties also go through a continuous process of change, which is seen in the experience of the chakras. With the dissolution, sublimation or transformation of consciousness, there is the possibility of a human being becoming different, becoming a super-being, changing from ritam and becoming established in satyam.

Mooladhara, at the lowest level, combines both experiences of ritam and satyam: the fixed and the temporal experience. Other chakras do not have this capacity. Other chakras represent transformations and the progressive nature of energy whereas in mooladhara the resting point of the energy represents the fixed reality. Energy has come to rest in the form of solidity, in the form of matter, while the manifest experiences of matter go through change. The potential for evolution is also in vishuddhi chakra, which represents the doorway between the manifest and the cosmic in the form of akasha tattwa. The centres above vishuddhi, including ajna, also represent other doorways which can propel one into different dimensions of experience.

Awareness of the lokas

Just as in the material, physical dimension, we experience transformation and different levels of consciousness through the chakras, in a similar way, once we become established in satyam, we become aware of other dimensions of existence which are beyond the dimension of manifest elements. These are known as the *lokas*.

The planes of the lokas represent further steps of evolution or higher states of consciousness. At the level of the chakras, energy is active and consciousness is the passive support for understanding the energy experience. In the lokas, knowledge and experience of consciousness is predominant or active and energy is a passive supportive factor for that experience. So the roles change from chakras to lokas. It is the knowledge, understanding and experience of the lokas and the different states of perfection and different manifestations of creativity in our life, which is experienced and seen during the process of laya.

Dimensions of consciousness

There are twenty-eight dimensions of consciousness. Humans begin at the fifteenth level of consciousness. Below this there are fourteen other levels known as patalas, from the eighth to the fourteenth, and narakas from first to seventh. The patala level manifests in animal life where every action and every response to a situation is governed by instinct. The narakas can be related with vegetable life for the purpose of our understanding. At these levels even the instincts are not fully active, there is only a dormant conscious state.

The fifteenth to the eighteenth levels: mooladhara, swadhisthana, manipura and anahata, represent the instinctive consciousness. The nineteenth to the twenty-first: vishuddhi, ajna and sahasrara, represent the gunas: tamas, rajas and sattwa.

The seven lokas

Then come the seven lokas: bhuh, bhuvah, swah, mahah, janah, tapah and satya. Bhuh loka, the physical, earthly plane, is related to mooladhara chakra, the refined state of consciousness in mooladhara after the instincts have been cleared and overcome. Bhuvah loka represents the astral plane and is related to swadhisthana chakra. Swah loka, which represents the celestial or divine plane, is related to manipura chakra. Maha loka, related to anahata chakra, represents the plane of balance, also known as the plane of saints and siddhas. Janah loka, known as the human plane or the plane of rishis and munis, is related to vishuddhi chakra. Tapah loka, the plane of austerity or penance, relates to ajna chakra. Satya loka is related to sahasrara and represents the plane or dimension where reality in its true form is experienced, the final, permanent state of consciousness. This is the concept of lokas in laya yoga.

Technique: Loka Dhyana
Stage 1: Preparation

Adjust yourself physically so that you can be comfortable and relaxed in your meditation posture for at least twenty minutes. Make sure that there are no tensions, make sure you are comfortable and at ease with yourself and with your body. There should be no tightness. Observe yourself internally. Become aware of your body internally from the head to the toes. Centre yourself in your body. Be aware of the state of comfort and relaxation.

Stage 2: Space awareness

Become aware of the space within the body, the all-pervasive space. Feel the body to be an empty shell. Within the empty shell, develop the experience of space, space which extends from the top of the head right down to the toes. Observe yourself with total awareness. Observe the space within the body. As you go deeper into the experience of space, gradually drop the external identification, the external awareness of the environment, the world around you and even drop the awareness of the physical body. Remain aware of all-pervasive space.

As you identify more with space and less with the physical body, you will have a sensation of floating – floating in air. With the sensation of floating there will be the experience of inner silence and stillness. During the practice, if at any time you feel the need to move the body you may do so, but the physical movement should be slow and with awareness, and keep your attention fixed on the practice. Do not let the sounds distract you. Do not let the physical experiences distract your attention. Maintain constant and continuous awareness. With each passing moment go deeper within yourself, within the space of the body.

Be aware of the sensation of floating. Gradually disassociate yourself from the physical experiences of comfort and discomfort, aches and pains, states of relaxation and ease. Be aware only of floating in inner space, feeling the motionlessness of the space within, the silence of the space within. The body is just an empty shell with a covering of skin. Beneath the covering of the body exists eternal space, akasha.

Stage 3: Observing the consciousness

The space which is being experienced is consciousness. Be aware of the field of consciousness. Do not identify with the mind. Do not identify with the mental experiences. Do not identify with the thoughts, with the intellect, with the feelings. Just be aware. Observe the field of consciousness, which is infinite at the microcosmic level and also infinite at the macrocosmic level. Only awareness in the form of an observer, the drashta, the sakshi, the seer, remains. Awareness which is part of individuality, the drashta or the seer, the observer which represents individual perception. Observe, witness the field of consciousness extending in all directions of the known manifest universe and the unknown unmanifest universe.

Stage 4: Om chanting

We are going to begin the practice of meditation by chanting the mantra *Om*; continuous short *Oms* are to be chanted with each exhalation. As we chant the short mantras, feel the vibrations of the mantra pervading the entire space of consciousness physically and also in the subtle dimension. The whole being vibrates, the whole being resonates with the chanting of *Om*.

Experience the vibration of *Om* resonating in each and every part of the inner space – the microcosmic space of consciousness. The drashta, the seer, is experiencing waves of vibration extending in all directions in the field of consciousness. We begin. *Om Om Om Om Om...* Experience, observe whatever sensations there may be in the space of consciousness pervading the whole body. Remain silent and observe the play of energy, of harmony or even disarray, experience whatever the sensation may be within the field of consciousness.

Stage 5: Awareness of bhuh loka and janah loka

Now, within the space which is being observed you are going to visualize two centres of energy. One in the region of mooladhara and another in the region of vishuddhi. At the base of the spine is one luminous centre and in the region of the throat is another luminous centre. Develop awareness of the energy centres in the inner space by becoming aware of them one by one. Focus your mind in the region of mooladhara and observe the centre of energy glowing, radiant, in the region of mooladhara.

Intensify your awareness of the mooladhara centre, mooladhara chakra, which, in the dimension of consciousness, is represented by bhuh loka. The other centre is the region of vishuddhi – bright, brilliant, luminous, radiating light. In the field of consciousness this centre is known as janah loka. These are the two centres in the space of consciousness, the bhuh loka and the janah loka, which you should now observe. The bhuh loka in the mooladhara region is not a chakra, rather it represents the dimension of consciousness within the chakra. The janah loka in the region of vishuddhi is not vishuddhi chakra, but the space of consciousness within vishuddhi chakra.

Stage 6: Arohan and awarohan

These two lokas are connected to each other by two passages. One passage extends from the mooladhara area, the bhuh loka, to the vishuddhi area, the janah loka, along the front. The other passage extends down from janah loka to bhuh loka along the spinal cord. Between these two centres the awareness is going to ascend and descend with the help of inhalation and exhalation. At the time of inhalation the consciousness ascends from bhuh loka to janah loka along the frontal passage. At the time of exhalation the consciousness descends from janah loka to bhuh loka along the spinal passage.

Be aware of this movement of consciousness between bhuh loka and janah loka, from the regions of mooladhara to the regions of vishuddhi, and then down. The ascending consciousness is known as *arohan*, along the frontal passage, and the descending consciousness is known as *awarohan* along the spinal passage. Intensify the awareness of movement from bhuh to janah loka and from janah to bhuh loka.

There is no movement of energy, there is no experience of energy moving, only the movement of consciousness, of awareness, the drashta, moving from one loka to the other with the help of inhalation and exhalation. Remain observant of the process and try to merge your awareness more and more into the experience of movement in the field of consciousness. Bhuh loka represents the dimension of consciousness in the world of matter, and janah loka represents the dimension of consciousness in the world of space.

Stage 7: Ending the practice

We are going to stop the practice at this level. Let go of the witness awareness, the drashta awareness of the lokas and the passages connecting the two lokas. Become aware of the state of being. Slowly become aware of your body, the solidity of your physical body. Become aware of the different parts of the body and gradually begin to externalize your awareness into the physical body and into the external environment. Breathe in deeply and chant *Om* three times. Gently rub the hands together and place the palms over the eyes, and then slowly open your eyes.

Hari Om Tat Sat

19

Vyoma Panchaka Dharana

Vyoma, the sky, space or firmament is described in the vedic shastras as the seat of the gods. From the psychic point of view, vyoma represents the highest state of consciousness, described as anibaadha, ourooloka and brihat. *Anibaadha* means 'without any obstacles obstructing the expansion of consciousness', which is the goal of life. With the expansion of consciousness, universal awareness dawns upon the spiritual seeker, so it is known as *ourooloka*. Vyoma is further described as *brihat* by which its vastness and rhythmical identity are conveyed. The boundless and illuminating firmament, shining with the bright rays of the sun by day and with the mellow light of the moon and stars by night, is symbolic of the infinite, so sky or space was chosen as the object for higher meditation. Clouds may veil, storms may break and the sun may disappear, but the sky is always there.

After chidakasha, hridayakasha and daharakasha, the three gross spaces, we come to vyoma panchaka, the five subtle spaces of the intermediate stage of dharana. In this stage, the mind is still functioning in a state of alertness, but the observation faculty is gradually made subtle. The experience of these subtle spaces is in the realm of the unconscious and beyond. Daharakasha, hridayakasha and chidakasha are experienced in the conscious and subconscious. These five spaces are guna rahita akasha, paramakasha, mahakasha, tattwakasha and suryakasha.

Vyoma Panchaka One

GUNA RAHITA AKASHA

Guna rahita akasha is the attributeless space. The word *guna* means 'attribute' or 'quality' and *rahita* means 'without'. According to Samkhya philosophy, at the time of creation there were just two beings existing within the unmanifest dimension. The first being or cause was Purusha, the cosmic soul, who was attributeless by nature. The second was Prakriti, the cosmic nature or energy, who was with attributes. The three gunas are the attributes or qualities of Prakriti whereby the manifest dimension of time, space and object came into existence.

The creation of the world is a result of the interaction of the three gunas. They are the fundamental principle of existence in the individual as well as in the cosmos. By combining in various proportions, the three gunas give rise to all the objects of the world, gross as well as subtle. They not only produce and control matter, but make each object different from another. It is by the three gunas that the imperishable atma is tied down to the body and also to the world itself.

These three gunas undergo transformation from the unmanifest to the manifest. They produce the organic, inorganic, physical, mental, and psychic fields of the universe. The cosmos, society and the entire human nature are operated by the interplay of the gunas. Even the astral planes and subtle lokas are inhabited by the gunas. Only when an individual becomes established in his own essential nature does he become free from the influence of the gunas.

In scientific terms the three gunas are described as vibration, motion and inertia. We must understand the three gunas if we want to know the properties of universal nature. Vibration is *prakasha* or luminosity, which is a kind of rhythm. This vibration is sattwa, motion is rajas and inertia is tamas. When there is harmony between rajas and tamas, they develop sattwa. Therefore, sattwa is not something independent, but an effect of harmonizing these two principles of motion and inertia in their own nature. Thus a harmony of tamas and rajas gives rise to sattwa.

Nature of sattwa

Illumination, equanimity and purity are the qualities of sattwa guna. Sattwa is immaculate, without dirt or taint, and has nothing to do with the physical body directly. It binds the soul to the body and to the world through attachment to happiness and wisdom. This is the inherent nature of sattwa. When sattwa becomes powerful and predominant, it develops an irresistible urge for knowledge or wisdom, and an interest in pleasant experiences. When sattwa predominates, one avoids unpleasant experiences, ignorance and inertia. Sattwa guna is favourable for the pursuit of moksha, liberation, and truth. A sattwic mind is always steady and finds delight internally. It can stick to one place, one work or one pursuit indefinitely. It maintains friendships for a long time. It can study scriptural texts for hours. It can live on a simple, bland diet without difficulty.

Nature of rajas

Just as sattwa guna makes the mind steady and still, rajo guna makes the mind active and restless. It will not allow a person to sit still; it will force them to work. Rajo guna has the nature of *raga* (attraction) and *dwesha* (repulsion). It is born of *trishna* (craving and attachment). While sattwa binds the soul to happiness and wisdom, rajas creates attachment to craving and passion. As a result, there is more karma or action when rajas is predominant. A sattwic person will always seek happiness and knowledge, while a rajasic person will seek satisfaction and enjoyment. When an individual is full of sattwa, he never cares for enjoyment; he cares only for knowledge. When sattwa is predominating, rajas will also be there, but it will be weak. Whenever thoughts of passion and craving come, one will not be happy about it. This indicates the development of sattwa guna.

The sattwic mind unifies and unites, while the rajasic mind divides, separates and diversifies. The rajasic mind always seeks new sensations and variety. It likes certain persons, objects and places for some time, and then it becomes bored with them and wants new people for company, new food to eat, new books to read, new gadgets to use, new places to see.

The mind of a rajo guni always seeks company and talk. It has a tendency to criticize the weaknesses and defects of others. It always remembers the misdeeds done by another and forgets their good acts and virtues. Therefore, it is prone to anger and hatred, and is easily disturbed. The rajo guni is neither compassionate nor considerate of another's happiness unless it somehow concerns his own. He is interested in himself and in his own achievement. Because he is constantly seeking external goals he has no internal satisfaction or contentment.

Nature of tamas

Tamo guna is born of ignorance. It is the negative state of the soul. When an individual is overpowered by the influence of tamo guna, he submits to procrastination, laziness and sleep. When tamas predominates, suppressing the other two gunas, there is nothing in the world that can keep one active, spiritual or blissful. Such is the effect of tamas over the personality. When tamas predominates, the mind enters into an inactive state. As a result there is a process of slow thinking, and at times the thinking ceases altogether. When this state deepens, the mental inactivity becomes acute, manifesting in a state of deep neurosis. This is the dull state of mind.

Predominance of the gunas

Normally, in every individual the three gunas are constantly changing from moment to moment. At every level of our being, body, brain, mind, emotions, astral, psychic and spiritual levels, the gunas are operating. These currents can be seen by persons who are highly psychic. The aura of a person is indicative of the guna predominating in him and, therefore, the aura of each individual is constantly changing. When rajas is predominant the aura becomes scattered, dissipated, broken, indicating a split in the personality. When tamas predominates the aura becomes dull and withdrawn, indicating inertia. When sattwa is predominating the aura becomes very bright, regular and extended.

The three gunas are continuously interacting in the individual as well as in society. When rajo guna becomes predominant and the other two gunas are subservient in an individual or in a society, there is dynamism, action, prosperity and material progress. When sattwa is predominant in an individual and in a society there is elevation of the arts, philosophy and spiritual culture. Knowledge is sought rather than material progress and ways are discovered to go beyond the physical boundaries. However, when tamo guna becomes predominant and the other two gunas are subservient, then there is laziness, backwardness and exploitation. Such a society soon decays and such a person neither prospers nor evolves.

The gunas in meditation

When tamas is predominating it is not possible to practise meditation without falling asleep. The mind is in a dull state, which is known as *moodha*, wherein the awareness is not functioning. When rajas is predominating the mind is dissipated and fragmented, which leads to restlessness and uneasiness. Here one cannot concentrate or even sit still.

This is the *kshipta* state of mind. When rajas moves towards sattwa, the state of *vikshipta* results. This is an oscillating state in which the individual consciousness operates between steadiness and distraction. Vikshipta is the usual mental state of the practitioner when he sits for concentration. Due to the interplay of the gunas, the mind is subject to temporary unsteadiness and distraction. When the flow of concentration, born of sattwa is interupted by unsteadiness, born of rajas, one is said to be in the vikshipta state of consciousness. In this state, inner visions arise and one is very sensitive to moods.

When sattwa has free expression, one-pointedness dawns. When rajas is overpowering, the mind becomes dissipated. When tamas comes into play there is neither one-pointedness nor dissipation, there is only dullness and inertia. In meditation, it is necessary to analyze the predominance of the gunas and to be aware of which guna is in power from moment to moment. It is a rare moment when the three gunas hold equal sway over a person. Usually one guna predominates over the others, even though the other gunas have an equal chance of operation. For example, when rajas is in power there is always a counter movement of the other gunas, resulting in a state of concentration and dissipation following each other.

Therefore, one has to realize which particular guna is in absolute power at the moment and how counter movements are taking place. If there is more dissipation and less concentration, then rajas is in the ascendant. If there is less concentration and less dissipation but more sleepiness, then tamas is predominating. After analyzing the influence of the three gunas over the consciousness, one should eliminate the negative influence of a particular guna and develop the positive influence. For instance, tamo guna is reduced by hatha yoga and karma yoga, and rajo guna is reduced by bhakti yoga and japa yoga. When you find sattwa guna is powerful, although the other gunas are also operating one after the other, then you will have to strengthen sattwa because it is desirable. Tamo guna and rajo guna are undesirable at the time of meditation, so they should be reduced. Tamas is reduced by strengthening rajas, and rajas is reduced by strengthening sattwa. Sattwa guna is increased by the practice of dharana, and by *satsang* (spiritual associations), *swadhyaya* (self-study), simple diet, and peaceful surroundings.

If you find that the mind is concentrated at times but in between there is wavering and oscillation, then it is the vikshipta state. During the meditation practice you must observe which guna is predominant. If tamo guna is more powerful, then you must select preliminary practices which are activating and stimulating. However, if rajas is predominant, you need practices which allow the mind to relax and unwind. Never start concentration directly unless the mind is in the sattwic state, or oscillating between rajas and sattwa. When sattwa guna is predominant, your mind will become concentrated without effort and you will be able to go straight into meditation without forcing the mind.

Transcending the gunas
It is said that yoga begins when the vikshipta state of mind intervenes. Kshipta and moodha are unyogic. In the state of *ekagrata*, one-pointedness, rajo guna and tamo guna are absent and only sattwa guna prevails. When one-pointedness is achieved, then one must aim toward *nirodha*, complete cessation of the patterns of consciousness. This is how the gunas are transcended. In the state of nirodha, neither sattwa, rajas nor tamas function. That is the state of mind known as *trigunatita*, beyond the three gunas, where the consciousness is rendered absolutely free of the three gunas. When your consciousness can remain alone, without any association or reliance upon the three gunas, that state of consciousness is said to be beyond the gunas or free of attributes.

The entire process of the gunas has two purposes: to create experiences for the Purusha and ultimately to bring about liberation. When both of these purposes are fulfilled, the gunas revert to their original state. In nature there is a twofold process which can take place – evolution and involution. In the process of evolution, the objects of experience manifest through various states of *asmita* (memory), *tanmatra* (senses), *bhoota* (elements) and so on, for the enjoyment of the Purusha. The process of involution is opposite to this. The objects merge progressively so that ultimately the gunas remain in an undisturbed condition. This happens when the purpose of the gunas, namely enjoyment and liberation of Purusha, is achieved.

In yoga, Purusha is looked upon as the highest manifestation of consciousness, which is free of the vrittis, the gunas and any entanglement with Prakriti. Usually our consciousness functions through the senses, mind and buddhi, which have evolved out of Prakriti and are under the direct influence of the gunas. In meditation, consciousness functions at a deeper level, but there is still *pratyaya* or content of mind which are under the influence of the gunas. There is also the entanglement of the ego or notion of 'I am'. Ultimately, beyond meditation the pratyaya are discarded and the ego or 'I' feeling also vanishes. What remains then is only pure consciousness or Purusha. This supreme awareness or Purusha, which is not entangled with Prakriti, gives rise to freedom from the three gunas.

Stages of practice

In the first stage, preparatory body stillness is achieved. Next the three gunas are experienced physically, mentally and emotionally. This is done at a very basic level in order for you to familiarize yourself with the experience of the gunas at the different levels.

Then the relationship between the guna and the swara is developed by carefully monitoring the breath flow in the alternate nostrils. Here swara refers to the breath flow in the nostrils. The left swara or breath flow corresponds to ida nadi, the right to pingala nadi, and when both swaras flow together it corresponds to sushumna nadi. Therefore, predominance of the left swara is responsible for introversion or tamas. Predominance of the right swara is responsible for extroversion or rajas, and predominance of both swaras together is responsible for equilibrium or sattwa. In this way, analysis of the breath allows you to observe the influence and interplay of the gunas objectively without identifying with the various qualities and states.

Next the relationship between the guna and the tattwa is discovered. Here the focal point is the different colours which appear spontaneously within the akasha and which indicate the active tattwa. The earth and water elements correspond to tamas; the fire element corresponds to rajas, and the air and ether element correspond to sattwa. As the colours are seen to mix and diffuse, the interplay of the gunas becomes more obvious at an objective level. Observation and analysis of the guna through the swara and the tattwa are excellent methods of gaining mastery over the gunas and gradually eliminating their influence.

In the next stage, the *drashta*, or witnessing consciousness, is projected in order to observe the interplay of the gunas with a view to understanding, mastering and transcending them. The drashta is observing the guna of the components of the antah karana without any objective basis such as swara or tattwa, to filter or separate them. It is very easy to identify with the content of mind at this point unless an attitude of total detachment and dispassion is maintained as the different thoughts and emotions arise. It is by continual dissociation of the interplay of the gunas from the self that the drashta is ultimately able to go beyond their influence on the mental dimension. After observing the interplay of the gunas at the physical and mental levels, we come to the stage of saguna dhyana.

Saguna means 'with quality'. It represents another level where the pure qualities of life, which are beyond the body and mind, are perceived. Saguna dhyana is developing the awareness of the pure qualities. The qualities which we experience in our life are the impure qualities. Meditation on these adulterated qualities takes place in the earlier stages, where we become aware of the tamasic, rajasic and sattwic nature, and their effect on our personal life, behaviour, expression, interaction and so on. The effort to change our life by observing and modifying the patterns of the gunas is made in these stages. However, the pure qualities which exist in the unmanifest dimension are observed in saguna dhyana. The stage of saguna dhyana culminates in the realization of nirguna dhyana.

Nirguna means 'without qualities'. Here the awareness or knowledge of the three gunas merges into one light. This is seen as a complete ring of sunlight or flame of fire, representing the luminous body. This ring of light is beyond the known attributes of the manifest gunas. Developing this vision is the experience of guna rahita akasha.

Technique
Stage 1: Preparation
Sit in a comfortable meditation posture with your spine erect and head slightly back. Place the hands on the knees in chin or jnana mudra. Close your eyes and relax the whole body. Internalize your awareness. Feel your meditation posture becoming steady and still. Concentrate on the steadiness of the body. As the body becomes more steady and immobile, focus your awareness on the inner stillness. Be aware of the body and of stillness.
Stage 2: Awareness of guna
Within the stillness of the body and mind become aware of the play of gunas. Observe your physical condition. Is the body feeling heavy or light, hot or cold, relaxed or tense, uneasy or comfortable? Analyze the physical condition and discern the prevailing guna. Be aware of the interaction and changing of the gunas from moment to moment.
Now observe the mental state. Watch the mind carefully without altering the content or mood in any way. Simply observe whether the mind is active or inactive, dull or alert, dissipated or concentrated, irritated or calm. Observe the emotions also. Do you feel happy or sad, secure or insecure, worried or confident?

Be aware of the different types of thoughts arising in the mind from moment to moment. Do they concern the past, present or future? Are they painful or pleasant? Are they centred around yourself only or around others? Are you able to observe the thoughts and feelings or are they going on without your awareness in a kind of semi-dream state? Go on observing and analyzing the physical and mental state. Try to witness the prevailing or interacting gunas. Be aware when the gunas change over during the practice, as you begin to observe and direct the mental forces.

Stage 3: Swara and guna

Now gradually shift your attention from the body to the breath. Be aware of the natural breath flow as you breathe in and out. Watch each breath carefully. Concentrate at the nosetip and watch the breath flowing up and down the nostrils. When you connect the breathing pattern through the right and left nostrils with the ida and pingala nadis, the breath flow is known as swara. The right breath flow corresponds to pingala nadi, the left to ida nadi, and when both flow together they correspond to sushumna nadi.

Become aware of the left swara. Feel the breath flowing in the left nostril. Mentally direct the breath up and down the left nostril. Then become aware of the right swara. Feel the breath flowing in the right nostril. Mentally direct the breath up and down the right nostril. Develop the awareness of the left and right swara for some time. Then experience the breath moving through both swaras at the same time. Feel the breath moving up and down both nostrils together in a smooth, even flow.

Try to discern which swara is flowing predominantly, whether ida, pingala or sushumna. If the right nostril is blocked and the left nostril is flowing freely, it indicates that ida is predominant and tamo guna is operating. If the left nostril is blocked and the right nostril is flowing freely, it indicates that pingala is predominant and rajo guna is operating.

If both nostrils are open and flowing evenly for one or two minutes, this indicates a time of changeover from ida to pingala or pingala to ida, and hence a changeover in the guna, from rajas to tamas or from tamas to rajas. However, if both nostrils remain open for several minutes or longer, it indicates that sushumna is flowing, and hence sattwa is active.

As you observe the swara, be aware of the concurring mental and physical state which relates with the predominant nadi and guna. If the left swara is flowing, be aware of dullness, sleepiness and dreaminess, which indicates that tamo guna is operating through ida. If the right swara is flowing, you will feel restlessness and mental dissipation because rajo guna is operating through pingala. When both nostrils are flowing, but one is slightly blocked and the other is flowing more freely, there will be interaction of the swaras and the gunas. Depending on which swara is flowing more freely, there will be interaction of rajas with tamas or tamas with rajas. In this case, the awareness will be oscillating between dullness and dissipation or dissipation and concentration. The mind will not be steady.

It is only when both the swaras are open and flowing freely that all traces of dullness and dissipation disappear. At the time when sushumna flows, meditation seems to take place spontaneously. The mental and physical conditions are very favourable for meditation. The mind becomes absolutely steady and one-pointed without any effort and there is no awareness of the body or the external environment.

By observing the swara you can gradually gain control over the guna. After analyzing the breath and determining the active swara and guna, you can decide which guna you require to be active at any given time and change over to it by manipulating the breath and the swara. Concentrate on the influence of the swara on the guna and try to experience the relationship directly.

Stage 4: Tattwa and guna

Now leave the awareness of the breath and become aware of the inner space that pervades the entire body from head to toe. Develop total awareness of the space within the body. Within the space try to perceive the tattwas, the five basic elements, by discovering the colour of your own personality. On account of the three gunas, the five tattwas are continually flowing and changing in the body. These five tattwas are controlled by the three gunas. When a particular guna is operating in the physical system, the corresponding tattwa will manifest and its colour will appear. For example, when rajo guna is operating, the colour red appears and the fire element becomes active.

Observe the inner space. Be aware of colour, any manifestation of colour within the space of the body. Watch the colour which appears spontaneously for as long as you are able to see it. The influence of the gunas is constantly changing, therefore, the colours are also changing. Yellow and white represent the earth and water elements and indicate varying degrees of tamo guna. Red represents the fire element and indicates rajo guna. Varying shades of blue, grey or black represent air and ether and are indicative of sattwa. When these colours combine to make shades of orange, pink, purple, green, brown and so on, this means there is an interaction of two gunas operating.

When you begin this practice, the colour does not always manifest clearly and sometimes you will not see any colour at all. The colours may appear in a particular shape, such as a circle or a triangle, or there may be no particular shape, just bands of colour. When the tattwas are changing, there is a period of transition when you may see a blending or combination of many colours at one time. Go on for some time observing the manifesting tattwa and its corresponding guna within the inner space. Continue observing the changing colours and experience the corresponding guna or gunas manifesting through the psyche. When you understand the relationship between the tattwa and the guna, you will be able to control the guna simply by manipulating the tattwa. If you want to change the guna from tamas to rajas, for example, visualize the colour changing from yellow to fiery red, and hold the visualization of the colour red. If you want to change from rajas to sattwa, visualize the different colours in the spectrum from blue to black and hold them in your vision. The corresponding guna will come into operation. When you are able to apply this knowledge, you will no longer be influenced by the constant rotation of the tattwas and gunas.

Stage 5: Drashta and guna

Now leave the awareness of the five tattwas and become aware of the *antah karana*, the inner instrument or mind field, where the mental elements constantly interact in relation with the changing guna. Experience the antah karana which has evolved from mahat, the greater mind. The antah karana is comprised of four elements or compartments: manas (reasoning), chitta (awareness), buddhi (intellect) and ahamkara (personal identity, ego). Awaken the inner drashta or seer, who is always aware of the changing influence of the gunas. This faculty of awareness is a separate witnessing consciousness apart from the manifestations of the gunas. When this drashta is veiled by the consciousness identifying itself with the gunas, then you are the slave. When the drashta is unveiled and there is detachment from the gunas, it simply remains aware; then you become the master.

Train the seeing consciousness within you to observe the mental process with detachment, to observe the interplay of the three gunas which are operating freely within the mental field. Identify with the detached seer of the mental process and then observe the interaction of manas with buddhi and ahamkara. When rajo guna is predominant, manas operates with ahamkara and so the pain and suffering are intense. When sattwa guna prevails, the suffering is still there, but it is analyzed and understood properly. Hence its effects are neutralized by the application of intellect or right knowledge. When tamo guna is operating, the pain is there but the mind is inactive, so you are not aware of it.

Go on observing the mind. Develop the spectator awareness and separate it from the mental process. See the mind like a TV screen, which displays everything to you. Within the mental play of thoughts and emotions see the interaction of the gunas, which hold sway over the body, mind and senses.

It is a wonderful experience if you are able to develop this phase of consciousness within yourself. Through this process you can learn to see yourself without the help of any drug. When this awareness becomes constant, unfluctuating and spontaneous, it is easy to transcend the effects of the gunas. Learn to see yourself, see what you are doing, see what you are thinking, see what you are feeling, from moment to moment.

Stage 6: Saguna dhyana

Saguna dhyana is meditation with qualities, but these are not the same qualities which were experienced in the previous stages. At this stage you develop awareness of the pure qualities, which is a more subjective experience. The gunas which we refer to as sattwic, rajasic and tamasic are adulterated and modified qualities. Here the pure qualities which exist in the unmanifest dimension are observed.

The original form of the gunas is experienced as light, motion and stability. Be aware of the self effulgent nature of the three gunas. All three represent light and all three are self-effulgent. All the gunas have the qualities to manifest according to the attraction of Prakriti, and at the same time they also have the quality of being able to remain stable and not undergoing the process of change or transformation.

Be aware of the three gunas independently as a force which is pure self-effulgent light. Experience the gunas as a force which has the potential to transform everything and the potential to again become static, motionless and still. Here the vision or perception to be developed is not mental or objective. It is a process of self-expression which is combined with knowledge or awareness.

Stage 7: Nirguna dhyana

Nirguna dhyana is meditation without gunas or qualities. In saguna dhyana there was still awareness or knowledge of the three gunas existing as independent, effulgent entities, but in nirguna dhyana the gunas merge and fuse into one light, the eternal flame of spirit, which is known as *chaitanya jyoti*.

Be aware of total stillness. Experience the whole of creation inside. This experience is unknown and beyond intellectual conception or comprehension. Feel that your entire being is full of divine light, which is pure, infinite, steady, eternal, beyond the sky, beyond measure, colour, form and taste.

Experience this transcendent state, which is blissful and undying, which is the cause of all causes, the support of all, which has the world as its form, which is invisible and omnipresent. Merge your awareness within this principle which is beyond the gunas, beyond time, space and object, and beyond the experience of duality.

Visualize yourself sitting inside a complete ring of sunlight or fire flame. Develop this vision until the light becomes intense. See your body merging into the ring of light, which represents chaitanya jyoti, the eternal flame of the spirit. This ring of fire or sunlight is beyond the known attributes of the manifest dimensions. It is beyond the realm of the physical and mental gunas.

Maintain this vision of the ring of light and nothing else. Here there is no witness or observer, just the pure awareness of the light, the ring of light. Just as you can imagine a rose or any other object if you wish, in the same way, this ring of light also becomes a voluntary vision. Maintaining this vision or visual experience for an extended period of time is the experience of guna rahita akasha, attributeless space.

Stage 8: Ending the practice

Now leave your awareness of the ring of light and get ready to end the practice. Gradually withdraw your awareness from the formless dimension and become aware of the world of forms and objects. Be aware of your physical body which is sitting in a meditation posture. Feel your whole body from head to toe. Be aware of the room in which you are sitting. See your body sitting in the room. Listen to the different external sounds. Take a deep breath in and chant *Om* three times.

Hari Om Tat Sat

Vyoma Panchaka Two

PARAMAKASHA

Paramakasha is described as 'deep, dark space with a twinkling star-like light'. There is a state of perception which is known as *shoonya*, or nothingness. Here total absence of light, cognition and knowledge is experienced with just the awareness remaining in the form of a tiny star or point of light. It is self- contained awareness, not dissipated or expanded awareness, but a fixed, luminous point of awareness. From this, a meditation process has been developed which is known as shoonya meditation. There comes a point after this where there is total absence of external and internal awareness and only undifferentiated awareness is active. That state is the experience of paramakasha. *Param* means 'supreme', therefore paramakasha is the supreme space.

Shoonya dharana
Shoonya meditation is the practice which leads from the state of dharana into the state of dhyana. In the process of dharana there comes a time when, before entering into the state of dhyana, we go through an experience of total dissociation of body with mind, of mind with intellect, of intellect with emotions, of emotions with the experiences of the external object, space and time. This particular stage of experience is the state of shoonya, which is the first step into the actual meditative mind.

The gross mind is transformed into the subtle mind. Saint Kabir eloquently described this state when he wrote:

> *Jal me kumbh, kumbh me jal hai*
> *Baahar bheetar pani*
> *Phootahi kumbh jal jal hi samaanaa*
> *Baat kahe ye jnani.*

"A water pot is inside a body of water, and within the water pot there is water. There is water inside the pot and there is water around the pot. It is simply a matter of breaking the pot in order to mix and merge the water contained inside with the water around the pot."

This is the concept of energy and consciousness contained within the body which fuse at the end of yogic practice with the consciousness and energy of the universe. This is the objective of shoonya dharana. At that time of total shoonya, void, freefall, everything changes. The body changes, the perception changes, the experience changes, the world changes, the universe changes. That connection of the final points of daharakasha and the final point of hridayakasha is a very intimate and close connection. Previously the talented rishis and munis, the determined sadhakas, used to try this method, jumping over the cliff into the void.

Technique
Stage 1: Preparation

Sit down comfortably. Choose a meditation posture in which the body can be maintained upright and straight. Padmasana or siddhasana are the postures recommended for this practice. Place the hands on the knees in jnana mudra or chin mudra. Make sure the spine is erect and upright, the head is straight, the eyes and mouth are gently closed. Make yourself comfortable in this sitting posture and make absolutely certain that there is no tension or tightness in any part of the body. Once the practice begins there should be no movement of the physical body. Therefore, choose the posture carefully and adjust yourself in the posture.

With the eyes closed, mentally become aware of the whole body. Try to experience the body internally. There should be acceptance of the posture and the condition of the body. There should not be negation of pain or discomfort or of the posture. Quickly move your mind throughout the body, being aware of each and every part, making sure that you are comfortable.

Stage 2: Mental mirror

Mentally imagine that in front of you there is a full length mirror. In that mirror try to see a reflection of your whole body. The whole body is reflected in the mental mirror. See the reflection of the body mentally. When you observe the reflection of the body, see the position of the legs, the position of the arms, the position of the back and the head. Develop total awareness of the body internally. The mind is not permitted to move out of the body. Forget about the mind, forget about the thoughts, forget about the experience of pain or pleasure. Simply be aware of the physical body from the tips of the toes to the fingertips, to the top of the head. Awareness of the whole body right from the tip of the toes to the tip of the fingers and to the top of the head. Develop the internal experience of the whole body.

Stage 3: Empty shell

Be fully aware of the physical experiences and make yourself totally motionless and still. After becoming totally motionless and still become aware of the internal physiological state, the experience of silence, stillness, motionlessness that can be experienced when the body is perfectly at ease, comfortable, relaxed and still. Develop experience of total silence internally. Observe the body. Experience the body in the form of an empty shell which is hollow on the inside. There is nothing inside. The body is totally empty on the inside. There is just the soft shell of the skin.

Try to develop, try to intensify this awareness. Let go of the awareness of muscles and bones, of nerves and internal organs. Experience the body in the form of a balloon, in the form of an empty shell. The outer covering of the body is the skin only, and skin is the experience you have to develop, nothing but skin. The body is totally hollow, empty inside.

Within the experience, develop the awareness of akasha, the space that is contained within the body. Do not localize the awareness to any specific area or part of the body but experience the body as a whole. Experience the space, the akasha within the body and experience the akasha surrounding the body, the soft shell of the body.

Stage 4: Who am I?

Ask yourself the question "Who am I? Am I the physical body? No, I cannot be, for the physical body is in a state of continual change. Last year my body was different to what it is now. When I was a child my body was different to what it is now. My body is in a continual state of flux, of change. It cannot be my real nature. Am I the mind? No. My inner nature cannot be the mind, for that too is in a continual state of change. One moment it is happy. Another moment it is unhappy. It is continually fluctuating in mood. How can the mind be my true nature? Am I a Hindu, a Christian, a Jain, a Buddhist, an Englishman, an Indian? No. These are only minor forms of identity. They do not represent my inner nature."

Continue asking yourself this type of question, then ask, "Who am I?" Remember you are the witness behind the phenomena of the universe. You are existence, unchangeable existence. You are consciousness, pure consciousness. You are an indestructible being. Your nature is 'is-ness'. You are what you are, "I am". Within the experience of silence and stillness, develop this understanding of yourself.

Stage 5: Energy and consciousness

Within the awareness of the akasha tattwa develop the experience of silence and stillness within yourself. Develop a total experience of the body, containing nothing, just an external shell of skin. Within the shell of skin there exists energy, there exists consciousness. Become aware of the energy and consciousness within the body. Do not move the body. Do not identify yourself with the body in the form of matter. You are akasha tattwa, space. Contained within that space is consciousness and energy. This is what you have to remember.

You have to get in touch with that experience. Do not move, absolutely no movement. Just be aware of akasha tattwa. Be aware of consciousness and energy contained within the shell of the body. There is just the experience of consciousness and energy pervading the space around the body and nothing else. There is no mind, no thought, no feeling, no emotion, no desire. Just the experience of consciousness and energy within you and around you. Experience everything as divine energy and pure consciousness – infinite, shimmering, vibrant and flowing.

Stage 6: Shoonyata

The whole body is vibrating internally in harmony with the universe. The whole universe is vibrating in tune with the body. Bathe in this sea of infinite energy and consciousness. Float in silence. Float in peace. Float in timelessness. All is energy. Experience the shoonya. The akasha tattwa within the body is in harmony with the akasha tattwa surrounding the body. The silence, the stillness, the motionlessness of the body is in harmony with the silence, stillness and motionlessness around the body.

The emptiness which is experienced within the shell of the body is the experience of timelessness. There is no concept of time and object. Just the concept of space and within this space, the awareness of energy – vibrant, flowing, shimmering. The same experience is taking place around the shell of the body externally. You just have to be the experience. You are nothing but the experience of total shoonyata – voidness, nothingness, emptiness. The experience of shoonyata is not confined to the inner body, but is also projected outward.

Let every type of binding of the ego simply fall away. Every type of bondage has no meaning, no relevance for you at present. Just try to establish the experience of the void, timelessness, emptiness. You are the observer. You are the witness. You are the experiencer of pure consciousness. This is what you have to feel.

Stage 7: Super space

You are nothing but the experience of total shoonyata, voidness, nothingness, emptiness. Establish the experience of the void, stretching beyond time into eternity. Allow your awareness to penetrate deep into the dark space. Experience the deep, dark space of the void which is lit up with a twinkling, star-like light. You are floating in the timeless space, enveloped by the dark night sky lit up by stars.

Now fix your attention on the symbol of a star. Dark space, the space representing consciousness and a point of light, a twinkling starlight, representing the luminous nature of consciousness. No matter how much discomfort or pain you may feel, do not identify with the body. Remind yourself again and again, "I am not this body nor am I the experiences related with the body and I am not affected by the physical experiences of pain and pleasure, comfort and discomfort." Maintain your awareness fixed on the symbol of a tiny star, twinkling star in paramakasha.

Be aware of space, expanding awareness merging with space. Be aware of the luminosity of a twinkling star in the distance and take that image, the symbol of the star, down into your body to the level of swadhisthana and fix it there. Keeping the attention fixed on the symbol of the star begin to chant short *Oms*. With each *Om* feel the vibrations beginning from the star symbol in swadhisthana and gradually expanding outwards, pervading the whole paramakasha. *Om, Om, Om, Om, Om...* Experience the paramakasha within you and outside you. This experience is not confined to your inner being. It is projected outward, beyond the dimensions of perception, of time and space, into infinity. This is what you have to realize. This is what you have to experience in all its splendour.

Stage 8: Ending the practice

Continue with this awareness for a few moments more. Now gradually begin to develop normal body consciousness. Slowly begin to externalize the mind from the experience of shoonyata. Come back into the physical structure of the body. Become aware of the structure of the bones, muscles, internal organs, the solidity of the body. Become aware of the mind and the experiences of the mind. Become aware of the senses and the sensory experiences. Become aware of the environment. Take a deep breath in and chant *Om* three times.

Hari Om Tat Sat

Vyoma Panchaka Three

MAHAKASHA

Mahakasha is described as 'bright like the middle of the sun, which no eyes can see'. You cannot see the brilliance of the sun by going into the middle of it. This shoonya state is evolving. Initially there was total darkness with just a point of light and that represented awareness. The recognition of that point of light is drashta, observing the awareness. But here the merger of drashta with that awareness takes place so that the whole personality is engulfed by total awareness. The whole individual identity has to dissolve in luminosity, nothing but light. It is like being in the centre of the sun, surrounded by brilliance and light. That is known as *maha*, the great.

Technique
Stage I: Akashi mudra
Sit in a steady meditation posture with the hands on the knees. Fold the tongue back in khechari mudra, so that the lower surface presses against the upper palate. Practise ujjayi pranayama and shambhavi mudra. Bend your head backward, but not to the fullest extent. The back of the head should not be leaning on the shoulders. Keep your arms straight by locking the elbows and pressing the knees with the hands. Breathe slowly and deeply in ujjayi. At first you may feel irritation in the throat while breathing in this inclined position, but it will become more

comfortable with practice. While performing this technique, be aware of the inner space. Experience your consciousness in the form of space. Maintain the final position for as long as possible. Then return to the starting position, rest for one or two minutes, and repeat the practice.

Stage 2: Internal space

Sit in a comfortable meditation posture. Close your eyes and internalize your awareness. Feel your physical body becoming steady and still. Concentrate on steadiness and stillness of the body. Within the stillness of the body become aware of the inner space which pervades the entire body from head to toe. Centre your awareness within the space of the body.

Experience the body as being totally hollow, empty inside. Within this experience develop the awareness of akasha, the space that is contained within the body. Do not localize the awareness to any specific area or part of the body, but experience the body as a whole. Experience the space, the akasha within the body, and experience the akasha surrounding the body, the shell of the body.

Stage 3: Luminous space

Within the awareness of akasha develop the experience of silence and stillness within yourself. Develop a total experience of the body, containing nothing but space, just an empty shell. Within the shell of skin, within the space, there exists energy. Become aware of the energy field within the space of the body. Do not move the body. Do not identify yourself with the body in the form of matter. You are akasha, space, and contained within that space is energy, pure energy.

You have to awaken that experience within the stillness of the akasha tattwa. Do not move, absolutely no physical movement. Do not allow the mind to wander or to dream. Just be aware of akasha tattwa. Experience the energy contained within the shell of the body. There is just the experience of energy pervading the body space and nothing else. There is no mind, no thought, no feeling, no emotion, no desire. Just the experience of energy exists within you and around you. Experience everything as divine energy – infinite, luminous, vibrant.

Within this space there is no concept of time and object. The individual identity has dissolved into light. Mahat, the greater mind, has dissolved into light. The illusory world of Shiva and Shakti, of Purusha and Prakriti, has dissolved into light. The attraction of raga and dwesha has dissolved into light. The gross, the subtle and the causal consciousness have dissolved into light. The experience of the existence and the non-existence of the tattwas, the elements, has dissolved into light.

Here all interaction between consciousness and energy has ceased. When the illusory, sensory world is dissolved, only one experience remains, self-luminosity. This luminous space is the base of the omniscient field of consciousness. Having no boundaries, no demarcations or definitions, it is free from the experience of duality. There is no self-identification with body or mind. Just the concept of space exists, and within the space the awareness of energy and light.

Merge your awareness into the infinite expanse of luminosity. See yourself engulfed in surging waves of illumination. Gaze into the vast sea of vibration and luminosity which extends in all directions as far as the eye can see. Visualize infinite waves of light, vibrating, radiating throughout the entire universe. Concentrate on this vision until your consciousness is completely absorbed into the cosmic field of light. Within you and all around you there is nothing but light.

Become one with the infinite expanse of light. Experience the cosmic light field around you and within you. Develop the vision of pure energy, pure light, vibrating and radiating into infinity. You are nothing but the experience of light. Within you is light; outside you is light. All is light wherever you look. Experience the timeless luminous space, which is manifest and unmanifest, which is seen and unseen. Everything is divine light – infinite, radiant, glowing.

Stage 4: The great space

Let every type of ego binding simply fall away. Bondage has no meaning, no relevance for you here. Just be aware of the radiance, the luminosity, the effulgence. Establish your awareness in the vision of luminosity. You are the witness, the observer, the experiencer of pure light. You are nothing but the experience of pure light, extending beyond time into eternity.

Intensify the vision, the awareness, the total experience of light. Like a ray of the sun, gradually draw your awareness back from the periphery to the source. Visualize the intensity of light and energy as you come closer and closer to the blazing orb of the sun. Experience your entire being drawn into the conflagration of heat and light, which comprises the sun. You have to awaken this experience, this vision.

As you enter into the solar sphere, the intensity of light becomes so great that another dimension of vision must open in order to perceive it. This space, which is blazing like the middle of the sun, which no eyes can see, is known as *Maha*, 'the great'. Merge your entire awareness into this space. Experience the brilliance of mahakasha, which is of such an intensity that you cannot perceive its radiance.

Experience the intensity of light within the self-effulgent space of the void. Allow your awareness to merge completely with the luminous space which is like being in the centre of the sun, engulfed by brilliance and light. Your entire awareness is engulfed in the radiant, shining space of mahakasha. This is the vision that you have to experience in all of its luminosity and splendour.

Allow your awareness to dissolve and merge totally into the luminous space of mahakasha. Experience the great space which is indescribably brilliant. Perceive your entire being as one with the shining, effulgent expanse of space which is known as Maha, the great. Experience mahakasha shoonya, the great luminous void in which the total awareness, the total vision, is engulfed by light.

You are floating in the luminous, great space, which is bright like the middle of the sun. Within this space, there is no movement, only stillness and effulgence, blinding effulgence. And within this effulgence is the void, shoonya. Experience the luminous, great space at the centre of which is the void.

Stage 5: Ending the practice

Now gradually withdraw your awareness from the timeless dimension of mahakasha. Again become aware of your physical body which is seated in the meditation posture. Feel your entire body from head to toe. Be aware of the external environment. Listen to the external sounds. Take a deep breath in and chant *Om* three times. Slowly open your eyes.

Hari Om Tat Sat

Vyoma Panchaka Four

TATTWAKASHA

According to modern science, there are three states of matter: solid, liquid and gaseous. In the solid state, the molecules remain dense and compacted. With the application of heat they begin to break apart and their rate of vibration increases. At this stage, solid matter is changed into liquid form. With the application of still more heat, the rate of vibration increases and the volume of substance expands. As a result, even a small quantity of gaseous substance can occupy the space of the vessel containing it.

In this description we find four of the five basic elements: the solidity of earth, the fluidity of water, the heat of fire, and the expansiveness of air. Heat is the fundamental energy of change and transformation. As long as the body and mind are functioning, these four qualities will be active. When the body and mind become empty, the fifth quality of voidness or ether manifests. Our being is comprised of these five elements, and we can feel the change that takes place within us when one or another of them predominates. The predominance of the elements changes all the time, and due to this change the body and mind function, although we may not perceive it as such.

Interaction of the elements

In order to perceive the elemental space or *tattwakasha*, it is necessary to first develop a very clear perception of the tattwas and to understand the subtle role which they play in

Vyoma Panchaka Dharana
Tattwa Akasha

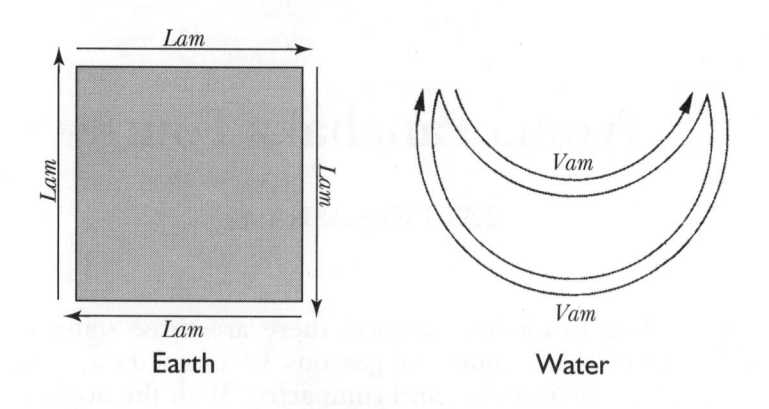

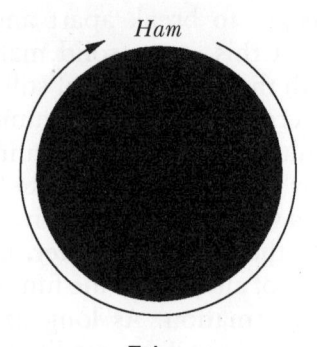

Earth — *Lam*

Water — *Vam*

Ether — *Ham*

Fire — *Ram*

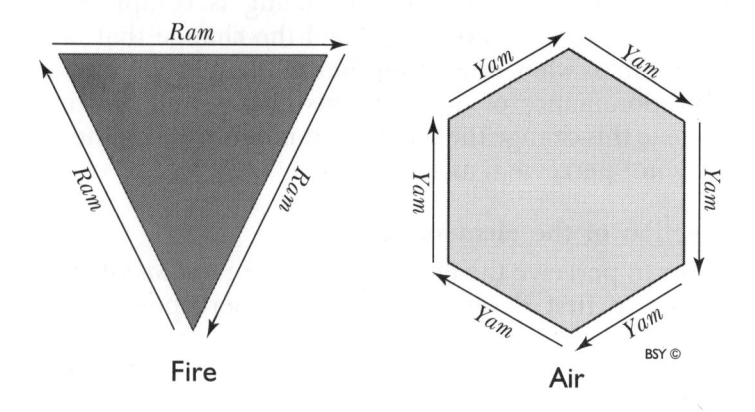

Air — *Yam*

our external and internal life. It is necessary to see how the elements permute and combine according to changing events, situations, moods and thoughts. It is more difficult to observe the elements internally because they do not have a separate independent existence. They are mixed with the different elements predominating at that time.

It is the interconnection of the five elements which constitutes the gross, physical body and the more subtle mental body. We can see the physical role of the tattwas in the respiratory system which is controlled by air but which interacts with fire or heat as it enters the body, with water as it is transported by the blood, and with earth as it is transmitted to and from every cell and part of the body.

Another good example of the interaction of the elements within us is in the digestive process. We consume solid food (earth) and liquid (water). These are both digested by enzymes (fire and water). Also in the digestive process, flatulence, gas or wind (air) is produced. So, in this way, we can observe the different interactions of the tattwas in every physical function.

We can perceive the subtle role of the elements mentally and emotionally as well. For example, some people are known for their dry humour. A rainy day has a dampening effect on our mood. One who becomes angry frequently is hot tempered. A person who does not express feelings or passions is cold or frigid. One who talks too much is a windbag. A person who is not aware of his immediate surroundings is spaced out.

Contemplation on the external elements
Once we have observed and analyzed the various interactions of the elements within, we can extend our study by watching the interaction of the elements in everyday life. This interaction is a continuous one and we can always find an opportunity to observe the elements at work. We may be walking outside, enjoying nature, watching the sunset or a storm gathering. We may be pottering in the garden, paddling

in a stream, climbing a mountain, or hang gliding off a cliff. Outdoors, the basic elements are more obvious and it is not difficult to develop the awareness of the tattwas in everything that we see and do.

Elemental space
When the basic concept of the tattwas has been integrated and understood in our external and internal life, then we will gradually be able to experience tattwakasha, the subtle space which pervades the tattwa. This is elemental space, the seed or essence from which the elements germinate.

This technique is divided into five practices, one for each element, and each practice has four stages. This is to develop the experience of the individual elements further, so that they can gradually be taken back to their source which is tattwakasha, elemental space.

The four stages of each practice follow a similar pattern. The experiences of each stage should be mastered one by one. The first stage involves identification of the consciousness with the physical element. In the second stage a more subtle awareness is induced by concentration on the tattwa symbols and mantras. In the third stage there is total identification with the symbol. Finally, in the fourth stage the symbol is dissolved and the consciousness is merged into the seed or elemental space, which is the source and the end of all manifestation.

This is the technique of tattwakasha dharana. It is an extensive practice which clarifies the elemental substances of our being and transforms the microcosmic body into a macrocosmic body. The mastery of the five elements and elemental space leads to full knowledge and awakening of the higher Self.

Technique 1: Prithvi tattwa
Stage 1: Earth body

Imagine the earth element and all the different kinds of earth: sand, soil, clay, pebbles, rocks, boulders, mountains, valleys, deserts, fields. Merge your awareness into each of these aspects of earth, so that you become one with it. Your identification should be total.

Become aware of the space all around you and within you, like a rock or a mountain. Take your awareness into the depths of the earth, so you are completely surrounded by earth on all sides. Nothing exists but earth. Become the earth.

Feel that your body has become a lump of earth. Your body has solidified and turned to stone. Experience the solidity, the density of matter throughout your being. Say to yourself mentally, "I am the earth; my nature is inert and dense, without movement or fluctuation, like a rock." When this experience manifests in the body consciousness, the finer, subtler qualities of the earth element can be experienced. At a certain point you will lose your awareness of the physical body all together, and feel as if another body has come into existence. This body is made of earth or rock. Centre your entire awareness within this experience. Become the earth. Experience your body in the form of earth, like an anthill or a rock.

Stage 2: Symbol and mantra

Bring your awareness to the mooladhara region of your earth body. Concentrate on this area for a few moments. Be aware of the perineal body, of the entire pelvic floor, of the area between the perineum and the knees. See the shadowy outlines of a large yellow square beginning to form between the perineum and the knees. Visualize the four sides of the square, symbolic of stability. See the yellow earthy colour. As you gaze at the yellow square, the image becomes clearer and clearer.

When you are able to see the form and colour of the square distinctly, without any haziness, then begin to repeat mentally the mantra *Lam, Lam, Lam*. With each repetition of the mantra, move your awareness along the four sides of the square. Continue the repetition for two or three minutes, until your awareness and concentration are absolutely centred on the yellow square in the mooladhara region of your earth body.

Stage 3: Expansion of the symbol

Now leave the repetition of the mantra, but continue gazing at the yellow square. Gradually the square begins to increase in size as you watch it. First see the yellow square filling up the entire region between the perineum and the knees. Then it gradually extends upward, filling the entire pelvic region, abdominal region, chest region, neck and head, until it encompasses the whole body. See the vision clearly.

Be aware of the yellow square which encompasses your whole body and extends outward from the body. Visualize the entire length and breadth of the expansive yellow square, as if you are sitting inside it. Merge your awareness into it. Become the yellow square. Your entire being is merged in the large yellow square. Be aware. Maintain the vision and the experience.

Stage 4: Prithvi akasha

Continue gazing at the expansive yellow square which now encompasses your entire being and extends outward to the limits of your mental and psychic perception. As you gaze steadily at the yellow square, the dense form gradually begins to break up. See the yellow square crumbling and falling away. As the yellow square slowly diminishes and disappears, your entire being also disappears with it, until there is nothing left except empty space and awareness.

Become aware of the empty space in which the earth element had existed in the form of a large yellow square. Concentrate your entire awareness within this space. Experience the space from which the seed or subtle form of the earth element is germinated. Merge your entire awareness in this space. You are the elemental space in which the earth element becomes manifest and again returns to the unmanifest dimension.

Experience this space in which the earth element is existing in a dormant, unmanifest state. There is no activity or movement, no outward expansion within this space. Be aware of perfect stillness, absolute quiet. There is no seed of desire in any form to create action.

Here the concept of duality is completely transcended. All experience relating to name, form and idea has disappeared. There is nothing but pure elemental space. Experience this space which is known as prithvi akasha. Within the space be aware of absolute stillness, shoonya, the void. Merge your awareness in the elemental space. It is the same space which existed at the beginning of time, before creation, and which will exist at the end of time, when all things undergo dissolution. Experience the prithvi akasha where the earth element exists in the dormant, unmanifest state.

Technique 2: Apas tattwa
Stage 1: Water body

Become aware of the water element and all the different kinds of water: in clouds, mist, rains, streams, rivers, lakes, oceans. Immerse your awareness into each of these water forms so that your consciousness becomes one with the bodies of water, to the exclusion of all else. You are the ocean waves, the still lake, the gurgling stream, the flowing river, the clear spring, the deep well.

Submerge your awareness in the water element. Take your awareness into the depths of the ocean. Feel the fluid environment all around you, encompassing your entire being. Develop total awareness of water; become liquid, fluid. Experience the fluidity. Feel that your whole being is immersed in water. You are nothing but water. Experience the flowing, fluid nature of water throughout your being.

However, even in this flowing condition, the earth principle of solidity is maintained. You have the feeling of waves playing on a rock. On the one hand, the body is stable and solid and on the other, it is totally fluid, relaxed, supple and at ease. The feelings of fluidity and firmness are experienced together at the same time. All the qualities of the elements must be kept in perspective as they appear and develop their play.

When this experience of water arises, the quality of suppleness also increases. The body loses all of its rigidity. The mind too seems to melt and flow. As a result you can easily enter into and experience the feelings of others. This is the fluid, flowing condition of the mind.

Stage 2: Symbol and mantra

Now bring your awareness to the swadhisthana region of your water body. Concentrate for a few moments on this area between the pelvic floor and the navel. Gradually you will begin to see the fluid outline of a white crescent moon. Fix your whole attention on the image. See the white colour. As you gaze at the crescent moon, it becomes clearer and clearer. See it filling up your whole pelvic region with cool, white light.

When you are able to see the white crescent moon clearly, then begin to repeat mentally the beeja mantra *Vam, Vam, Vam*. With each repetition of the mantra, move your awareness along the upper curve from left to right and then along the lower curve from right to left. Maintain a clear vision of the white crescent moon as you repeat the beeja mantra. Continue the repetition for two or three minutes, until you feel your awareness is absolutely centred on the white crescent moon in the swadhisthana region of your water body.

Stage 3: Expansion of the symbol

Now leave the repetition of the mantra, but go on gazing at the white crescent moon. As you gaze steadily, the white crescent moon begins to expand. First it fills up the entire abdominal region. Then gradually it spreads outward until it encompasses your whole being within its curve. See the cool, white light all around you.

Visualize yourself sitting in the middle of the white crescent moon with both sides curving up around you. Feel that you are totally enveloped in the cool, white rays of the crescent moon. Be aware of the soft, enchanting crescent moon all around you. Visualize the expanse of the fluid, white crescent moon, as if you were sitting inside it. Merge your awareness into it. Become the white crescent moon. Experience your entire being merged in the fluidity of the white crescent moon. Maintain the vision and experience.

Stage 4: Apas akasha

Continue gazing at the white crescent moon which encompasses your entire being and extends outwards to the limits of your mental and psychic perception. As you gaze steadily at the white crescent moon, the fluid form gradually begins to dissolve and evaporate. See the white crescent moon melting and dissolving into the vast, empty space of the water element. As the white crescent moon slowly diminishes and disappears, your entire being also disappears with it, until there is nothing left but empty space and awareness.

Become aware of the empty space in which the water element had existed in the form of a white crescent moon. Concentrate your entire awareness within this space. Experience this space from which the seed or subtle form of the water element is created. Merge your entire awareness within this space. You are the elemental space in which the water element becomes manifest and again returns to the unmanifest dimension.

In this space experience the existence of the water element in its dormant, unmanifest state. There is no activity, no movement or outward expansion. Within this space, be aware of perfect stillness, absolute quiet. There is no seed of desire in any form to create action. Here the concept of duality has completely vanished. All experiences relating to name, form and idea have disappeared.

There is nothing but space, pure elemental space. Experience this space which is known as apas akasha. Within this space, be aware of absolute stillness, shoonya, the void. Merge your awareness in the timeless, formless elemental space. It is the same space which existed at the beginning of time, before creation, and which will exist at the end of time, when there is total dissolution. Experience the apas akasha, where the water element exists in the dormant, unmanifest state.

Technique 3: Agni tattwa
Stage 1: Fire body

After the water body, the *tejas sharira*, or fire body, will appear. Fire arises out of water. Become aware of the fire element. Imagine fire in all its forms, from the candle flame to the power and fury of the volcano. Immerse your awareness in fire to the exclusion of all other things. Think of fire in its creative and destructive aspects. Be aware of a campfire, a raging forest fire, a bolt of lightning, an electrical fire, a gas fire, an atomic explosion. Become aware of the sun which is the source of all heat, energy and light, a blazing ball of fire.

Merge your awareness into the different aspects of fire so that you become one with them. Your identification should be total. As you identify yourself with the fire element, the body seems to be burning with yogic heat; the mind is also radiant and ablaze. Your entire being burning. Be aware of energy, heat, flames. Experience your body in the form of blazing fire.

Stage 2: Symbol and mantra

Bring your awareness to the manipura region of your fire body. Concentrate on this area for a few moments. See the form of a large red, inverted triangle, emerging between the navel and the heart. Visualize the three sides of the triangle which forms an apex at the navel. See the fiery red colour. As you gaze at the red inverted triangle, the image becomes clear and distinct.

When you are able to see the form and colour of the triangle clearly, without any obstruction or haziness, then begin to mentally repeat the mantra *Ram, Ram, Ram*. With each repetition of the mantra move your awareness along the three sides of the inverted triangle. Continue the repetition for two or three minutes, until your awareness and concentration are absolutely centred on the inverted triangle in the manipura region of your fire body.

Stage 3: Expansion of the symbol

Now leave the repetition of the mantra, but continue gazing at the inverted red triangle. As you gaze at the internal image, it gradually increases in dimension. First it fills up the entire region between the navel and the heart. Then it gradually extends downward and upward, filling up the entire abdomen, chest, neck and head. Ultimately the fiery red inverted triangle encompasses your whole body. Visualize the extended image clearly as if you are sitting inside it.

Be aware of the fiery red inverted triangle, which encompasses your whole body and extends outward from the body. Concentrate on the expanded dimension of the red triangle. Merge your entire awareness in it. Become the fiery red inverted triangle. Be alert. Maintain the vision and the experience. There should be no distraction.

Stage 4: Agni akasha

Continue gazing at the expansive red inverted triangle which encompasses your entire being and extends outward to the limits of your mental and psychic perception. As you gaze steadily at the red inverted triangle, the fiery form gradually begins to disintegrate and to go up in smoke. See the red triangle slowly diminishing and disappearing in a cloud of smoke. As the red triangle dissolves and disappears, your entire being also disappears with it, until there is nothing left but empty space and awareness.

Become aware of the unqualified empty space in which the fire element had existed in the form of a red triangle.

Concentrate your entire awareness within this space. Experience the vast, empty space from which the seed or subtle form of the fire element is germinated. Merge your entire awareness in this space. You are the elemental space in which the fire element becomes manifest and again returns to the unmanifest dimension.

Experience this space in which the fire element exists in a dormant, unmanifest state. There is no activity or movement, no outward expansion within this space. Be aware of perfect stillness, absolute quiet. There is no seed of desire in any form to create action.

Here the concept of duality is completely transcended. All experiences relating to name, form and idea have disappeared. There is nothing but space, pure elemental space. Experience this space which is known as agni akasha. Within this space be aware of complete stillness, shoonya, the void. Merge your awareness in the timeless, formless, elemental space. This is the same space which existed at the beginning of time, before creation, and which will exist at the end of time, when all things undergo dissolution. Experience agni akasha, the space where the fire element exists in the dormant, unmanifest state.

Technique 4: Vayu tattwa
Stage 1: Air body

The domain of the earth, the realm of form extends only up to this point. Beyond it, through the expansion of the fire body, the *vayavya sharira,* or air body, appears. At this point, the fire in the individual becomes universal. It is this aerial body which is the container and carrier of cosmic consciousness. Here form becomes formless, and all that remains is an all pervading sense of energy in constant motion.

Bring your awareness to the element of air. Think of air in all of its forms. Feel the cooling effect of a gentle breeze, or the power and fury of a wind storm. Imagine that you have wings so that you can fly to the heights like an eagle, enjoying the freedom of this new dimension of your existence.

Immerse yourself in the air element. Feel that your body has no density, no restrictions. It is comprised of air only, like a bubble. Experience the lightness and the movement of air throughout your being. Say to yourself mentally, "I am the air; my nature is movement and fluctuation, like the wind." Experience the body of air. Centre your entire awareness within this experience.

Stage 2: Symbol and mantra

Bring your awareness to the anahata region of your air body. Concentrate on this area for a few moments. Be aware of the heart region, of the entire chest from the heart to the throat pit. Gradually you will see the shadowy form of a sky blue hexagon in the chest region of your air body. Visualize the six sides of the geometrical figure. See the sky blue.

As you gaze at the blue hexagon, the image becomes clearer and clearer. Do not make an intense effort to visualize. When you are ready, the image will appear to you. When you are able to see the form and the colour of the hexagon clearly, then begin to mentally repeat the mantra *Yam, Yam, Yam.*

With each repetition of the mantra move your awareness along the six sides of the blue hexagon. Continue the repetition for two or three minutes, until your awareness and concentration are absolutely centred on the sky blue hexagon in the anahata region of your air body.

Stage 3: Expansion of the symbol

Now leave the repetition of the mantra, but continue gazing at the blue hexagon. As you gaze steadily at the six sided figure, it gradually begins to increase in dimension. First it fills up your entire chest region, then it gradually expands, filling up the abdomen, neck and head. Ultimately the figure encompasses your whole body. Visualize the extended blue hexagon clearly, as if you are sitting inside it.

Be aware of the sky blue hexagon which encompasses your whole body and extends outward from the body. Concentrate on the expanded dimension of the blue hexagon. See it all through you and all around you. Merge your entire awareness in it. Become the blue hexagon. Be alert. Maintain the vision and the intensity of concentration. Do not allow the awareness to dissipate.

Stage 4: Vayu akasha

Continue gazing at the sky blue hexagon which encompasses your entire being and extends outward to the limits of your perception. While you gaze steadily at the blue six-sided figure, see the airy form slowly begin to evaporate and disappear. As the blue hexagon dissolves and disappears, your entire being also disappears with it, until there is nothing left but empty space and awareness. Become aware of the empty space in which the air element had existed in the form of a sky blue hexagon. Concentrate your entire awareness on this space. Experience this space from which the subtle form of the air element is created. Merge your entire awareness within this space. You are the elemental space in which the air element becomes manifest and again returns to the unmanifest dimension.

In this space experience the existence of the air element in its dormant, unmanifest state. Here there is no activity, movement or outward expansion. Be aware of perfect stillness. There is no seed of desire to create action. The concept of duality has vanished. All experiences relating to name, form and idea have disappeared.

There is nothing but space, pure elemental space. Experience this space which is known as vayu akasha. Within this space be aware of absolute stillness, shoonya, the void. Merge your awareness in the timeless, formless, elemental space. This is the same space which existed at the beginning of time before creation, and which will exist at the end of time, when all things undergo dissolution. Experience vayu akasha, the space where the air element exists in the dormant, unmanifest state.

Technique 5: Akasha tattwa
Stage 1: Space body

Ether is the most subtle element. It is the underlying aspect of the other four elements. When the air element becomes still and motionless, it is transformed into ether. Ether is pure energy. It is the space between the molecules of gross matter. When the mind is fixed in the ether element there is only consciousness. There is no awareness of the body. You become free of the physical structure.

Bring your awareness to this space and feel the energy which underlies all of creation. This space fills the entire universe. Identify yourself with this space which is full of vibrations, sounds and visions, some of which are beyond the normal range of perception. Through this space you can hear all the sounds around you, and pick up subtle vibrations.

Merge yourself totally with the ether element, the space in which the whole universe is vibrating at incredible speed. Your consciousness is aware of the space behind all matter, pure energy and power of unthinkable magnitude. As you concentrate your mind on the ether element, feel yourself stretching out and expanding into the infinitude of cosmic space.

Feel that you are bodiless. Your being is comprised of consciousness only. Your nature is that of space unsupported and uninhibited by any physical adjunct. Your consciousness moves freely through space, without any obstacles or obstructions. Experience the ether element. Say to yourself mentally, "I am space; my nature is stillness without any fluctuation or movement"

Experience yourself as pure consciousness, free of any gross adjunct. Centre your entire awareness within this experience.

Stage 2: Symbol and mantra

Bring your awareness to the vishuddhi region within your space body. Concentrate on this area for a few moments. Be aware of the throat; be aware of the entire region between the throat and the eyebrow centre. Gradually you will see the shadowy form of a large circle emerging in the throat region. This circle is filled with multicoloured dots which represent space, the ether element.

Visualize the circle and see the multicoloured dots inside it. As you gaze at the circle, the image becomes focused and clear. Look into the circle and experience the empty space, the void, shoonya. When you are able to see the circle of the space element clearly, then begin to repeat mentally the mantra *Ham, Ham, Ham*.

With each repetition of the mantra move your awareness around the outer edge of the circle from right to left. Visualize the circle clearly as you repeat the mantra. Be aware of the space in the centre. Continue the repetition for two or three minutes, until your awareness and concentration are absolutely centred on the circle of ether or the void, in the vishuddhi region.

Stage 3: Expansion of the symbol

Now leave the repetition of the mantra, but continue gazing into the circle of the void. As you gaze steadily at the circular figure, it gradually expands. First it fills up the entire region between the throat and the eyebrow centre. Then it slowly extends downward and outward, covering the chest, the abdomen, and finally the whole body.

Visualize the expanded circle of space encompassing your whole body. See it clearly, as if you are sitting inside it. Be aware of the circular void which pervades your whole body and extends outward from it. Concentrate on the extended dimension of the circle, which is filled with multicoloured dots or pinpoints of light.

Be aware of the circle of space which is all through you and all around you. Merge your entire awareness into the circle. Become one with the space. You are the circular void. Be alert. Maintain the vision and the experience. Do not allow the concentration to slacken. Stillness must be absolute; identification total.

Stage 4: Tattwakasha

Continue gazing at the circle of the void which encompasses your entire being and extends outwards to the very limits of your perception.

While you gaze steadily at the circular figure, see it gradually expanding and expanding, until it takes on universal proportions.

As the circular void expands into infinity, your being also expands, until all sense of individuality is lost. Gradually your entire consciousness is totally absorbed in the timeless, limitless void. There is nothing left but space, endless space, stretching into infinity.

Experience the infinite space in which the akasha or ether element has its existence. Merge your entire awareness into this space. Becoming one with the ether element out of which all the other elements are created. This is the seed or elemental space out of which all of creation becomes manifest and again returns to the manifest dimension.

In this space experience the existence of all the other elements – earth, water, fire and air, in their dormant, unmanifest state. Here there is no activity, movement or outward expansion. Within this space there is perfect stillness, absolute quiet. The concept of duality is non existent here. All experiences relating to name, form and idea have totally vanished.

There is nothing but space, pure elemental space. Experience this space which is the source and the end of all the other elements, which is the beginning and the end of all creation.

Within this space be aware of absolute stillness, emptiness, of shoonya. Merge your awareness into the timeless, formless elemental space. Experience tattwakasha, the space where all the other elements exist in their dormant, unmanifest state.

Stage 5: End of practice
Now get ready to end the practice. Gradually withdraw your awareness from the experience of tattwakasha. Become aware of the mental and physical dimension. Feel your physical body sitting in the meditation posture. Slowly externalize your awareness. Listen to the external sounds. Be aware of the room in which you are sitting. Be aware of your natural breath. Chant *Om* three times mentally and open your eyes.

Hari Om Tat Sat

Vyoma Panchaka Five

SURYAKASHA

The word *surya* means 'sun' or 'he who induces activity'. The sun is the symbol of purification because it burns away all evil and impurities and it can never be made impure. From earliest times people of all continents have worshipped the sun in order to eradicate sin, and to gain protection, prosperity and wealth. Surya is one of the most important vedic deities. In the *Mahabharata*, Yudhisthira, on entering his forest dwelling, prayed to Surya to provide all of his party with food. Surya presented him with the *Akshayapatra*, the 'pot of plenty' which could never be exhausted, to provide them with as much food as they needed.

Surya is depicted as the upholder of the empyreal space, the region of pure fire and light, which is the highest and purest region of heaven. Driving his excellent golden chariot, drawn by seven radiant horses which represent his access to the seven lokas, he rides through the sky, stretching out his golden arms to illuminate the world with his brilliance. Surya is the sun of Dyaus (Zeus in Greek), the most ancient of the gods who rules the firmament.

In the vedic tradition many names have been ascribed to Surya to describe his luminous, universal qualities. Some of his better known names include the following: (i) *Mitra*: friend of all, (ii) *Ravi*: shining one, (iii) *Bhanu*: he who illumines, (iv) *Khaga*: he who moves quickly through the sky, (v) *Pusha*: giver of strength, (vi) *Hiranyagarbha*: golden

Surya Devata

cosmic self, (vii) *Mareecha*: lord of the dawn, (viii) *Aditya*: son of Aditi, (ix) *Savita*: benevolent mother, (x) *Arka*: who is fit to be praised, and (xi) *Bhaskara*: who leads to enlightenment.

Lens of the atma

The existence of the sun is a permanent reality, at least in our lifetime. We are only concerned with the existence of one lifetime, because we are unable to see what exists beyond this life and what existed before this life. It is here that the knowledge of atma is covered by the veil of tamas. To attain the knowledge and the experience of the luminous atma is the purpose of meditation on surya. Once this is known, then it is said that one attains immortality which is spiritual in nature as well as physical.

There is a branch of yoga which is known as Surya Vijnana. There is also a branch of tantra which is called the Surya Tantra. Surya Tantra is the way to realize, to see and to know the vitality and energy hidden in the sun. These two traditions deal with the same concept. They say that the sun is the lens through which part of the radiance of the atma is seen.

When the ancient yogis and tantrics evolved this theory and system of practice for realizing the potential of the sun, they did not consider the external sun as the gateway or the lens through which the radiance of the spirit is seen. They used the sun as an example, as a symbol of the source of light, vitality and energy.

Pure form of the tattwa

According to their concept, the sun, which they describe as the luminous one, is not luminous because of its chemically known components like nitrogen, hydrogen and other gases. It is illuminated by the tattwas, the elements. This ancient yogic philosophy or esoteric system teaches that the atma is the radiant centre of all beings. The sun is the second manifestation of the ever radiant, luminous atma. The third aspect is the tattwa, or elements, which control all the known and unknown experiences of spirit.

There are two basic kinds of tattwas: the first is *deva tattwa*, the divine element, and the second is *mrityu tattwa*, the decayable element. Because of the reaction when these two tattwas meet, a third tattwa comes into being. This is *prana tattwa*, the pranic element. When these tattwas begin to combine and permute with each other, then the different subtle and physical tattwas come into being. These subtle and physical tattwas are thirty-six in number.

The sun represents the pure form of the tattwas at the time of their creation. The tattwas are constantly being created, and according to their density, they take on different life forms. The human life form is one of these, and all the life forms of the original atma and the tattwas can be experienced in this human form. Just as the atma represents the most transcendental aspect of experience, the human life form represents the most dynamic aspect of experience.

These life forms are experienced within the body in the form of chakras and upa chakras, major and minor psychic centres. The surya tradition teaches that apart from these psychic centres, there are thirty-three vertebrae in the spinal cord and each vertebra gives the experience of a set number of life forms. The aspects of energy which control or which manifest in these life forms are known as *devi* or *devata*, the female and the male aspects of luminosity or divinity.

Faculty of sight

Just as the concept of the sun is recognized in the esoteric sense, as the lens through which the luminosity of spirit is seen, in the same way, the eyes are reconized as the lens through which the form and the nature of atma is seen in the human body. The eyes have the ability to see, but they alone cannot decide, act or move. Their main function is just to see, to observe. This observation is understood to increase the awareness of the luminosity of the self.

The surya tradition teaches that by focusing the sight on a flame which is radiating light, it is possible to change the whole visual concept, so that matter is not perceived as matter but as energy. Once matter is perceived as energy, then the sun of the elements is known, and atma, the transcendental form is experienced. To increase the faculty of sight, certain techniques were evolved relating to the third eye.

The third eye is a concept describing a process that happens in the realm of consciousness. In this process the vision which perceived matter, name and form is changed into extrasensorial vision, which sees the energy beyond matter, name and form. In order to reach this stage, it is necessary to control the sensorial faculty of vision or sight. Through the control of this sensorial faculty it is possible to awaken the extrasensorial faculty of vision.

To learn to control this faculty, different practices were evolved. Trataka is one such practice. The surya tradition emphasizes trataka on something luminous, like the sun or a flame. The practice of trataka on a candle flame, the awakening of manipura chakra, and the awakening of the third eye are some of the different techniques used to bring about a change in the sensorial and extrasensorial faculties. The main emphasis is on awareness and control of the mind while the technique is practised. The practice culminates with the vision of surya devata, surya mandala and suryakasha, which depict the three subtler levels of luminosity, before entering into the dimension of pure spirit or atma.

Technique 1: Trataka on a fire flame
Stage 1: Preparation

Light a candle, oil lamp or a small fire if you have some fuel. You can use a metal tray for this purpose if you do not have a fireplace.

Sit in a comfortable meditation posture in front of the flame. Close your eyes for a few minutes and centre your awareness on the body. Be aware of your position. Feel your entire body becoming steady and still. Concentrate on steadiness of the body.

Stage 2: Concentration

Open your eyes and gaze into the fire flame. Look steadily into the base of the flame, just above the wick or the burning wood. Concentrate on the blue part of the flame. Try not to wink or blink. Do not move any part of the body. The burning wood or candle may crackle, but your gaze remains fixed at the base of the flame.

Stage 3: Spinal rotation

Maintaining your gaze steadily on the fire flame, begin to rotate the awareness and the breath up and down the spinal passage, from mooladhara to ajna while inhaling and from ajna to mooladhara while exhaling.

Continue this practice with the eyes open, gazing steadily at the fire flame for three minutes. When you begin to feel a burning sensation in the eyes or tears begin to fall, then close the eyes and relax them. While the eyes are closed, continue with breath rotation and concentrate on the after image of the flame at the eyebrow centre.

At no time during the practice should the awareness wander or drift from the point of concentration. As soon as the after image of the flame fades away, again open your eyes and gaze into the fire flame. The breath rotation should be continuous and effortless throughout. The point of concentration is the fire flame. Continue the practice for ten to fifteen minutes, until the luminous object of concentration permeates your entire field of awareness.

Technique 2: Awakening agni mandala
Stage 1: Awareness of samana

Sit in a steady meditation posture. Close your eyes and relax the whole body. Take your awareness to the manipura region at the navel. Practise slow, deep abdominal breathing. Feel your navel expanding as you inhale and contracting as you exhale. Intensify your awareness of samana, the region between the navel and the diaphragm. Continue the practice for five minutes.

Stage 2: Reversal of apana

Become aware of the lower abdominal region between manipura and mooladhara. This is the region of apana, the downward flowing force. As you inhale, feel the breath and the awareness descending naturally from manipura to mooladhara. As you exhale, the breath and the awareness ascend from mooladhara to manipura.

Next the apana force, which normally flows downward at the time of inhalation, is wilfully reversed and made to flow upward. This reversal is done through the ida channel. First visualize the ida channel emerging from mooladhara, curving upward to the left and crossing swadhisthana, curving to the right and crossing manipura. Now bring your awareness down to mooladhara. Inhale slowly and reverse the flow of apana, directing it upward through ida nadi along with the breath.

Feel the flow of apana reversing and rising up through the passage of ida from mooladhara to manipura. While exhaling, the breath and awareness naturally flow back down from manipura to mooladhara in a straight line. Continue for five minutes.

Stage 3: Reversal of prana

Bring your awareness to the chest, between anahata and vishuddhi. This is the region of prana, the upward flowing force. As you inhale, feel the breath and the awareness ascending spontaneously from anahata to vishuddhi. As you exhale, the breath descends from vishuddhi to anahata. Next the pranic force, which normally flows upward at

Fig. 1: Reversal of Apana

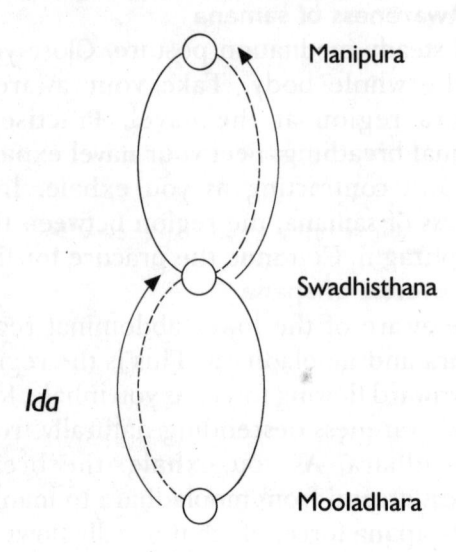

- Manipura
- Swadhisthana
- *Ida*
- Mooladhara

Fig. 2: Reversal of Prana

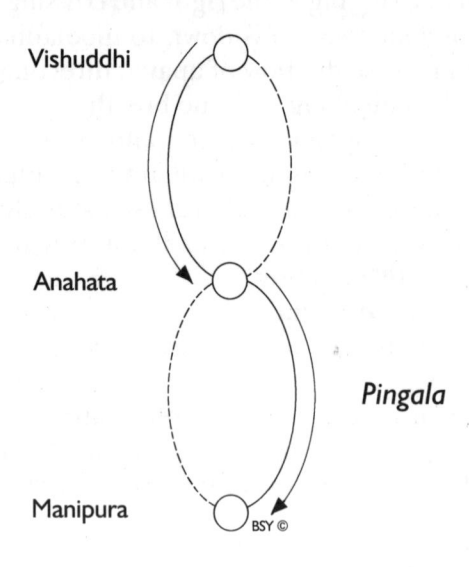

- Vishuddhi
- Anahata
- *Pingala*
- Manipura

the time of inhalation, is wilfully reversed and made to flow downward. This reversal is done through the pingala channel. Now visualize the pingala channel emerging from vishuddhi, curving downward to the left and crossing anahata, then curving to the right and crossing manipura. Now bring your awareness back to vishuddhi. Inhale slowly and reverse the flow of prana, directing it downward through the pingala nadi along with the breath. Feel the flow of prana reversing and descending through the pingala passage from vishuddhi to manipura. While exhaling, the breath and the awareness flow naturally back up from manipura to vishuddhi in a straight line. Continue this practice for five minutes.

Practice note: This technique is very straightforward. However, to reach the level where you can sensitize the awareness to actually feel the upward flow of apana from mooladhara to manipura, and the downward flow of prana from vishuddhi to manipura, may take several months.

Stage 4: Merger of the three pranas

Merging of the three pranas – apana, prana and samana, takes place at manipura. When the forces of prana and apana merge in the region of samana, the vision of manipura in the form of agni mandala, the zone of fire, becomes manifest.

Now, while inhaling, simultaneously direct the flow of apana up the ida channel and prana down the pingala channel. At the end of inhalation practise internal breath retention and feel the two energies colliding with samana at manipura.

The collision of awakens sushumna nadi and the kundalini shakti. Experience the impact of the three energies at manipura, while holding the breath inside. Then exhale and allow the awareness and the breath to separate and return from manipura to vishuddhi and to mooladhara simultaneously. Initially this may be experienced like an electric shock.

Stage 5: Generating energy
Continue the practice with total awareness and concentration. While inhaling, simultaneously reverse the pranic flows. At the end of inhalation hold the breath inside, and experience the explosive merging of the three pranas at manipura. As the energies crash against one another, there is a terrific generation of heat, fire, sparks and light. At this time dharana must be practised on the energy explosion at manipura for as long as the experience lasts. As you concentrate while practising kumbhaka, the three pranas fuse into one, which activates the other two pranas, udana and vyana, and causes the kundalini to arise in sushumna.

A pranic shock is experienced throughout the body as the dormant kundalini begins to wind her way up the timeless passage of sushumna. When kundalini reaches manipura, a tremendous explosion of fire and light takes place which is blinding in intensity. This is the awakening of agni mandala, the zone of fire. With this experience, the awakened kundalini becomes stabilized at manipura, and it no longer gravitates back to its dormant state in mooladhara.

Technique 3: Opening the third eye
Stage 1: Prana shuddhi
Bring your awareness to the trigger point of ajna, in between the two eyebrows. This point is known as *bhrumadhya*. Concentrate at this point for one or two minutes. Try to experience some sensations of heat, light, pressure or pulsation at this point. If you do not feel anything at first, do not be impatient. The experience will come.

Take the awareness down to the tip of the nose. Be aware of the flow of breath moving up and down the ida and pingala nasal passage. The breath flows up from the nose tip, *nasikagra*, to bhrumadhya while inhaling, and down from bhrumadhya to nasikagra while exhaling.

At the end of each inhalation hold your breath and concentrate at bhrumadhya. Try to see a point of light or a tiny, twinkling star. Then exhale slowly and move the awareness back down the nasal passages with the breath. Continue this practice for five minutes.

Stage 2: Anuloma viloma

Begin mental alternate nostril breathing. First inhale slowly through the left nostril. Hold the breath inside for a few seconds at bhrumadhya, then exhale through the right nostril. Next inhale through the right nostril. Hold the breath inside at bhrumadhya for a few seconds, then exhale through the left nostril.

This makes one round. Continue in this way for four rounds, and on the fifth round perform prana shuddhi. In this practice every fifth round, i.e. 10, 15, 20, 25, etc., is prana shuddhi. Each time you retain the breath at bhrumadhya try to experience this psychic centre whether in colours, light, pulsation or any other sensation.

Stage 3: Trikuti dhyana

Now concentrate at the point between the eyebrows, which is also known as *trikuti*, the meeting place of the three psychic passages – ida, pingala and sushumna. Direct the breath in and out through this point. Each time you breathe in feel that you are piercing and opening this centre with the breath. After inhaling, retain the breath inside for a few seconds. Experience the vibration and pulsation emanating from this point as you concentrate upon it.

Continue moving the breath in and out of trikuti. Concentrate intensely on this point to the exclusion of all else. At the time of internal breath retention, visualize this point in the form of a small, closed eye. However, this eye is facing inward, not outward. It is the eye which views the innermost dimensions of consciousness and light that are inaccessible to the outer eyes.

This eye is the mythological third eye, the eye of knowledge or intuition, which is described in all spiritual traditions.

The actual opening of this eye takes place with the awakening of ajna chakra. However, even if it only opens just a crack, we can experience unimaginable inner realms which are beyond the perception of ordinary sight. We gain access to unlimited knowledge which is cognized indirectly, intuitively or spontaneously, without the process of reasoning and analysis.

Concentrate on the small, closed eye as you slowly breathe in and out of trikuti. See the tiny, fleshy protuberance gradually begin to open. As the third eye opens, it illumines the inner worlds which are more vast than the external universe that you know. Infinite worlds of light, form and knowledge unfold before your inner vision. Your perception is unfettered and unlimited by time, space or object. With the opening of the third eye, you are able to enter into the higher domains of luminosity. You become a visionary.

Technique 4: Suryakasha
Stage 1: Invocation of Surya

Sit in a comfortable meditation posture, facing in the direction of the rising sun. Close your eyes and stabilize your position. Take your awareness to bhrumadhya. Visualize the red rising sun as it comes up over the horizon. Concentrate on this image for a few minutes. Feel the glowing, red ball of the sun penetrating and permeating your entire being and filling it with energy, light and life.

Merge your consciousness into the principle of light. The visualization acts as a psychic magnet, drawing the cosmic light fields towards you in greater and greater waves of luminosity. As you gaze into the brilliance, which stretches out in all directions before your inner eye, see the vision of Surya Devata riding on his golden chariot through the luminous firmament.

Visualize the regal and radiant form of Surya, who holds sway over all the dominions of light. See the brilliant form of the sun god, emanating and spreading beams of light in all directions, illuminating the worlds with a gesture of his golden hands. See Surya, seated upon his shining aerial car, drawn by seven effulgent horses, which move faster than the speed of light.

Concentrate on the divine aspect of luminosity in the form of Surya Devata. Gaze upon his brilliant form until your entire awareness is absorbed into it. Become one with Surya, the source of light and energy. Experience yourself as being a part of his cosmic form. Gradually merge your whole being into the radiance of the sun.

Stage 2: Surya mandala

Continue concentrating on the image of Surya until your entire being has merged into it. Your consciousness is totally absorbed into the cosmic field of light. Be aware of the radiance which pervades the inner space of your being. Visualize your whole body in the form of light. This light body is the causal body, or *karana sharira*.

Within you and all around you there is nothing but light. Like a pot which is immersed in water, inside the pot is water and outside the pot is water. Similarly, you are able to experience, without any distraction, the light fields which are within you and outside you. This is the experience of surya mandala, the zone of the sun.

Concentrate on the cosmic light field, the surya mandala. Become one with the limitless expanse of light, vibrating and radiating into infinity. All around you is a sea of infinite vibration, infinite light. Wherever you look, in all directions, there is nothing but light, unending luminosity filling the entire space. Experience surya mandala. Be aware of the zone of the sun.

Stage 3: Suryakasha

Continue gazing into surya mandala, until it gradually merges back into the unmanifest, luminous space from which it arose. Become aware of suryakasha, the space of the sun or the soul, which is pure and untainted. This space of surya or atma is considered to be the source of light which is manifest in every visible and invisible object of creation. It is both seen and unseen.

Suryakasha is a permanent reality. It is undecaying and unalterable. It is unaffected by the manifest dimensions of time, space and object. This space is the source of all the tattwas or elements, hence it is the source of creation and of life itself. It represents the pure form of the tattwas at the time of praylaya, before creation.

Merge your awareness in the pure, unmanifest, luminous space of suryakasha. This space is unqualified and undifferentiated. It is beyond duality. Here no movement, activity or expansion can be experienced. There is only stillness, absolute stillness. Within the stillness, there is luminosity, absolute luminosity. And within the luminosity, there is shoonya, void, absolute emptiness. Experience total stillness, total luminosity, shoonya.

Stage 4: Ending the practice

Now gradually withdraw your consciousness from suryakasha. Come back to the physical dimension where your body is sitting in the meditation posture. Become aware of your physical body. Listen to the external sounds. Visualize the room in which you are sitting. Take a deep breath in and chant *Om* three times. Slowly open your eyes.

Hari Om Tat Sat

20

Nadanusandhana Dharana

The Sanskrit word *nada* means 'sound' or, etymologically, 'flow of consciousness'. Nada is the primal vibration, the divine, ever-present, creative sound. It is the very core of spiritual practice. The word *anusandhana* means 'discovery' or 'search'. The discovery of sound vibration from gross to subtle, from external to internal, from psychic to causal and beyond, forms an entire part of dharana and is known as nadanusandhana, the art of stalking atmic music.

Where there is energy there is movement and vibration, and vibration creates sound. There are sounds which are beyond and beneath the normal range of the ears. The act of moving an arm creates friction in the air and a sound is created. You do not experience the sound as such, but sound does exist as a form of vibration, a form of movement, a pulsation of energy. These vibrations are not confined to the physical body or to the pranic body; they are also in the realm of mind, emotion and intellect.

Even when we think, waves are being generated inside the mind which produce definite vibrations and sounds. When we become introvert, directing our faculties of mind and perception inside, then the sound is experienced and known as nada, the sound of the personality, the sound of being, the sound of the self. This nada is the most subtle sound that we can experience in this dimension. It is not a sound that breaks, it is continuous sound. In yogic

Nadanusandhana
Swara Dharana

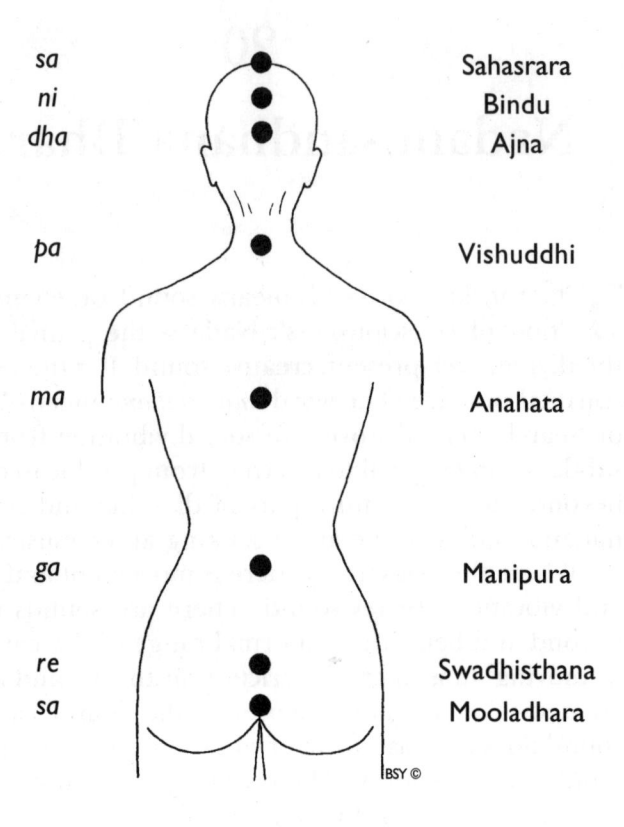

sa	Sahasrara
ni	Bindu
dha	Ajna
pa	Vishuddhi
ma	Anahata
ga	Manipura
re	Swadhisthana
sa	Mooladhara

terminology, these sounds are called *aksharas*, which literally means 'sounds which do not die'. From the birth of humanity until now we have been using sounds to express ourselves. We have been utilizing sound externally. We have experienced the quality, the power, the effect of sound externally. In this practice we experience the quality, the effect and the energy of sound internally.

A well-tuned instrument
Actually being able to hear these internal, subtle sounds, involves a process of becoming more sensitive on the mental or psychic plane and finding the balance between external and internal consciousness. When our mind is externalized we do not hear the internal vibrations and sounds. When our mind is internalized in deep meditation we do not experience the external vibrations or sounds. The aim of nadanusandhana is the discovery, purification and control of these vibrations to the subtlest degree. Eventually we bring our whole being into tune with our true nature. Just like a well-tuned instrument our body and mind begin to play the tune of life in the most harmonious way.

Reference to nada, representing the creative vibration, is to be found in all religious theologies. One should not place any intellectual supposition on it, because if this nada is to be perceived at all it must be done with inner faculties which lie beyond that of surface thought. Nada should be understood as the very life principle from which all aspects of creation derive life and movement. It is in you, in me, in rocks and stones and we have the potential to enter it.

Nadanusandhana can be practised by almost anyone, but it is particularly useful for musicians and all those who are musically or creatively inclined. The masters of nada yoga have provided a systematic progression of techniques which gradually accustom the aspirant to new perceptive sensations which at the same time lead him further on. A person immersed in worldly affairs puts all his nada into external forms which have arisen out of nada itself, whereas one who is established in the vibration of his own Self puts all the worldly forms into the nada of his own being.

Nada, in a confused brain, is like a storm blowing through the head. With the techniques of nada yoga this incoherent force can be focused into a laser beam which shoots inside. By drawing the aspirant inwards, nada forms a link between the individual in his present state of consciousness and his greater inner potential. This provides a gradual process of development and training in sound awareness that is so subtle that one begins to place one's reliance on inner rather than outer perceptions. The mind which usually finds all its pleasure and security in externalized objectivity begins to find peace and happiness in internalized objectivity. Nothing is discarded. The gross aspects of the mind simply fall away like dry leaves from a tree.

Levels of sound
1. *Para nada*, transcendental sound, is the starting point of nada. It is the nada that is heard in the state of superconsciousness. It is way beyond normal levels of perception. It is a sound of such great vibrational frequency that it goes beyond vibration and is of infinite wavelength. The Upanishads call it *Om* and say its nature is *jyoti* or light. Ultimately *Om* is silence. In meditation, light and silence are the same. *Om* is called *anahad*, or unstruck sound, to differentiate it from normal sounds and to show it has an uncaused or spontaneous origin. *Om* is anahada, without any boundaries or quality, indicating non-tone. It is the inner silence, the root sound or possibility of sound. Para is the last stage before samadhi.
2. *Pashyanti*, mental sound, is nearer to the mind than to the ear. This nada can be seen but not heard. It has different specific colours which can be seen by the inner vision. It exists in the deeper layers of the mind beyond the range of audible nada and it can be heard as a sound or a melody that haunts you or as a type of music heard in a dream.

3. *Madhyama*, middle range of sound, is more subtle than *baikhari* or audible sound. The word *madhyama* means 'in the middle', so-called because it is midway between the grossest nada and the more subtle nada. It is at this stage that nada begins to assume form and to crystalize from the formless subtle layers of nada. It can be described as a whispering sound with almost no audible effect. In nadanusandhana the aim is to hear sounds associated with these more subtle levels.
4. *Baikhari*, audible sound, is the grossest form of sound that we hear in the world around us. It is produced by striking two objects together and is the type discussed in physics. This is the place of the spoken word. Audible sound is the starting point of nadanusandhana practice from which one must retread the path through the more subtle realms of nada.

Sound of music

The belief that the universe is a projection of sound vibration alone was formulated from actual experience. In the Indian pantheon the last transcendental sound of para is on the same level as the cosmic source, or Parabrahman. Muslim saints have said the world evolved from sound and form and even the Christian Bible says, "In the beginning was the word (sound) and the word was with God and the word was God."

The development of musical systems in the past was in strict accordance with the logic of nada yoga sadhana. Different waves of nada are attractive to different stages of conscious awareness. Certain vibrations of nada are disagreeable and others are agreeable at a particular time of day or to different people. These nada vibrations in music are known as raga or musical compositions in different scales and rhythms. The morning music of India, with short vibrations, appeals to some but not to all. The ragas appropriate for the evening or midnight music tend to be more popular. This music must be listened to with total attention for the effect to be felt.

In the *Bhagavata*, the story of Krishna and the gopis describes nada yoga. Krishna represents higher consciousness and his flute playing is the nada sadhana. The senses, the gopis, forget the outer reality, their husbands, and withdraw from their sense organs to dance around the divine nada or the flute-like sound. The flute sounds belong to the pashyanti state. In this state actual sounds are not heard, but the frequencies, which are compared with the sounds of flutes and bells, are sensed.

Ten types of nada

Yoga recognizes ten types of nada or internal sounds which are acknowledged as the milestones of kundalini awakening at ajna chakra. These are given in order as follows:
1. *Chini nada* – like the sound of the word 'chini'
2. *Chini-chini nada* – like the sound of the word 'chini chini'.
3. *Ghanta nada* – the sound of bells ringing.
4. *Shankha nada* – the sound of a conch being blown.
5. *Tantri nada* – the sound of a lute (*tantri*) or vina.
6. *Tala nada* – the sound of cymbals.
7. *Bansuri nada* – the sound of a flute.
8. *Bheri nada* – the echoing sound of a drum.
9. *Mridanga nada* – the sound of a double drum.
10. *Megha nada* – the roar of thunder, the ultimate sound.

While hearing the flute music, many people have seen the darkness in chidakasha change to different, bright, flashing colours. There have also been people who could reproduce these vibrant colours into beautiful, three-dimensional art works, or the flute music into celestial and enchanting compositions. These sounds are psychic and are, therefore only an indication of the sounds you may experience. You must perceive the sounds for yourself. The sound that you hear will depend on the depth to which your awareness has penetrated the ocean of your being.

Some describe the ultimate sound as *Om*. Others say it is like the unceasing sound of honey bees. According to nada yoga, it comes from the sphere of anandamaya kosha, or the third dimension of consciousness, which is a body full of bliss. It is the point where the individual realizes his highest consciousness in nada and sees the whole universe in the form of sound.

Nada yoga divides existence into five spheres: the physical, mental, pranic, supramental and ananda or atmic. The nada of each sphere is a symbol enabling the mind to pass into deeper layers of consciousness. The nada of the physical body are the sounds or vibrations of the heart, lungs, brain, blood circulation and the process of metabolism. When the physical plane is transcended the subtle sounds of the movement of pranic consciousness are heard. Nada yogis follow the chain of ever subtler sounds to a point-like centre in their innermost being. For bhaktas this centre is in anahata chakra; for yogis it is in ajna chakra (the third eye); for vedantins it is in sahasrara. Nada yogis find the nada or continuous inaudible and spontaneous sound in bindu.

Stages of practice

The techniques of nadanusandhana are methods of penetrating the deeper layers of mind, utilizing sound as a medium. This science of yoga, as well as various philosophies and religions, regard the manifested universe as having sound as its basis. Science also agrees that everything in the universe is nothing but the continual interplay of vibrational energy. Sound is no more than a particular form of vibration. Yoga believes that even the different layers of mind and body, gross and subtle are nothing but the manifestation of innumerable number of different sound vibrations in a multitude of permutations and combinations.

Nadanusandhana is the means of retracing the path of nada which was the original means for individual growth and being. With extensive practice one's perception becomes more and more refined and sensitive. Eventually one's perception of subtle nada becomes so sensitive that one becomes aware of the bindu. This is the gateway to pure consciousness. This is the essence of nada yoga sadhana.

Beginners should practise at a time when the surroundings are very quiet. This prevents external sounds interfering with the perception of internal sounds. Late at night or very early in the morning are the recommended times. As one becomes able to detect the subtle sounds without difficulty, then nada yoga can be practised at any time, in any place and even without closing the ears. To gain noticeable experiences it is essential to practise every day. Try to devote fifteen minutes or more to this technique in the beginning. After attaining experiences, the time can be extended to suit yourself.

The practices of nadanusandhana guide the practitioner in a systematic way from the gross, external sounds to the deeper and more subtle levels. Although all of the practices can take one to the most subtle level, each one concentrates on one particular level more than the others.

In the first practice of swara sadhana, music is utilized to draw one's awareness inward and to sharpen the inner perception. This practice is in the form of baikhari. As you move up and down the scale, you listen intently to the note you are singing. At the same time you move the awareness through the chakras and feel the vibrations that the music is creating within the psychic centres. Swara sadhana helps to sensitize the awareness of the chakras so that the flows of energy can be felt more intensely. In this way you can more easily perceive psychic sounds as you progress with sadhana.

In the second practice, bhramari pranayama, the ears are closed and a humming sound is produced. The humming sound is soft and less external than the medium of music used in the previous practice. In this practice the awareness is split between concentrating on the external sound, the humming, and then perceiving the effects of this sound within. This humming sound helps to cut off the external sounds and quieten the mind. It creates a quiet space within where one can begin to listen and perceive the internal sounds. When beginning the practice it is usually the internal physical sounds that are heard, such as the heart beat or the metabolic process. These sounds are not ignored or suppressed but are experienced, and you concentrate on them until they fade naturally from you attention. Then you move on to more subtle sounds.

When one's concentration and awareness are more one-pointed then the next practice of shanmukhi mudra should be performed. In the practice of shanmukhi mudra the seven gates of external perception are closed. These are the two eyes, two ears, two nostrils and the mouth. Awareness is concentrated on the internal sounds. The loudest most gross sounds are listened to first, then as the more subtle sounds are perceived, the awareness is transferred to these. In this way the awareness is drawn more deeply inside to perceive the deeper realms of consciousness.

For the practice of nada sanchalana one must be able to remain completely motionless in the meditation posture and to internalize the awareness fully. This is important in order to gain full benefit from the practice. If one is distracted by the discomfort of the body or by outside sounds then it will be difficult to travel into the inner space where the subtlest vibrations are perceived. In this practice the mantra *Om* is moved through the arohan and awarohan psychic passages. The following practice of *Om* chanting is similar to this in that the *Om* mantra is utilized in different ways to create different and deeper effects. The *Om* mantra, which is the original sound, vibrates through the entire being and makes the awareness and perception finer and finer so that it pierces the outer layers of sound and begins to perceive the source of sound itself.

All the preliminary practices lead to and culminate in the actual nadanusandhana practice. This practice seeks to provide experience of the vibration of body, mind, thought waves, desires, emotions and expressions simultaneously, all in one concise shape. In this way the practice moves through the four levels of sound. The practitioner must be open and receptive and allow himself to become one with the vibration and to move on to the stages beyond sound.

Technique 1: Swara sadhana
Stage 1: Preparation
Sit in any comfortable meditation asana with the spine straight. Hold the head erect and the shoulders slightly back. Place the hands on the knees in chin or jnana mudra. Close the eyes and become aware of the whole body. Make any adjustments to ensure that the body is completely relaxed and at ease. If there is any discomfort or pain, then take your awareness to that part of the body and consciously try to relax that part. Feel the body settling into your meditation posture. Become aware of stillness spreading through the whole body. Feel the steadiness and stillness of the physical body.

Stage 2: Breath awareness
Bring the awareness to the natural breath. Do not change the breath in any way, just witness the natural rhythm of the breath. Be aware of each breath entering and leaving the body. As you continue to watch the breath it will become slower and deeper. Bring your awareness down to the abdomen and become aware of the breath in the abdomen. Feel the gentle rise and fall of the abdomen with each inhalation and exhalation. As you inhale feel the abdomen expanding. As you exhale feel the abdomen contracting. Concentrate on the breath in the abdomen. Be aware of every single breath. As the breath becomes slow and steady so the mind will become quiet and calm. With each breath feel the silence becoming deeper and spreading through the whole body and mind.

Stage 3: Awareness of sushumna
Now bring your awareness to mooladhara chakra. As you inhale feel the breath moving from mooladhara chakra up along the sushumna pathway to sahasrara chakra. As you exhale, the breath descends from sahasrara chakra at the crown of the head, along the sushumna pathway to mooladhara chakra at the perineum. Intensify your awareness of this psychic passage. Experience the breath ascending and descending through sushumna. In swara

sadhana, the ascending scale from mooladhara to sahasrara is known as arohan and the descending scale is awarohan.

Stage 4: Singing with chakra awareness

Maintaining awareness of sushumna, begin to sing the ascending and descending scale. As you sing each note of the scale take your awareness to the corresponding chakra point. Feel the vibration of the sound within the chakra. Hold your awareness at the chakra point for the duration of the note. Each note should be intoned for the duration of the exhalation. Then move on to the next note and bring your awareness to the next chakra point. Synchronize your awareness of the chakras with the sound of each note of the scale.

As you ascend the scale, be aware of the note and the chakra in the following order: Sa (mooladhara), Re (swadhisthana), Ga (manipura), Ma (anahata), Pa (vishuddhi), Dha (ajna), Ni (bindu), Sa (sahasrara).

As you descend the scale, be aware each note in the following order: Sa (sahasrara), Ni (bindu), Dha (ajna), Pa (vishuddhi), Ma (anahata), Ga (manipura), Re (swadhisthana), Sa (mooladhara).

This is one round. Then immediately begin the second round with the ascending scale.

In this way move your awareness up and down sushumna, touching each individual chakra point. Experience each note opening and purifying the chakra. Intensify your awareness of the vibration within each chakra point.

Stage 5: Singing with the mantra *Om*

When you have mastered this practice with the scale, the mantra *Om* can be substituted for the individual notes. This is done by singing the mantra *Om* instead of each note. In this way move your awareness up through the arohan and down through the awarohan scale, maintaining careful awareness of the chakra points as before. Be aware of the vibration of *Om* in each chakra. There should be complete awareness of the scale and the vibration of the *Om* mantra at each chakra point. Continue the practice for five to ten minutes. Do not strain the throat.

Stage 6: Ending the practice

Now get ready to end the practice. Complete the scale which you are singing. Then sit quietly for a few moments and experience the vibration of *Om* pervading your entire being. Bring your awareness back to the physical body. Feel the contact between the body and the floor. Feel the weight of the body against the floor. Listen to the sounds in the external environment. Breathe in deeply and slowly open the eyes.

Technique 2: Bhramari pranayama (humming bee breath)
Stage 1: Preparation

Sit in a comfortable meditation asana. The spinal cord should be erect, the head straight and the hands resting on the knees in chin or jnana mudra. The ideal posture is padmasana or siddhasana/siddha yoni asana.

Close the eyes and relax the whole body for a short time. Keep the mouth closed throughout the practice. The upper and lower lips should be touching, but the teeth are slightly apart.

Raise the arms sideways and bend the elbows, bringing the hands to the ears. Use the index or middle finger to plug the ears. The flaps of the ears may be pressed without inserting the fingers.

Stage 2: Awareness of breath and humming sound

Take your awareness to the base of the spine. Then inhale and feel the breath moving upward inside the spinal passage, from mooladhara to ajna chakra. The inhalation should end as you reach ajna chakra. Retain the breath inside for about five seconds. Then begin to exhale slowly and deeply, producing a long continuous humming sound, like that of a bee. Concentrate on the long m-m-m-m... sound and feel it moving down the spine, from ajna to mooladhara. The humming sound should continue for the full length of the exhalation. When you complete the round, again inhale slowly. Feel the breath moving from mooladhara up through the spinal passage to ajna. Retain the breath for a few seconds with concentration at ajna. Then exhale slowly and deeply with the humming sound. Be aware of the sound vibrations moving down the spine from ajna to mooladhara.

The humming sound does not have to be too loud. Your concentration is on the internal sound rather than the external sound.

Stage 3: Awareness of vibrations

Now experience the humming sound vibrating throughout the whole body. While inhaling move the breath and the awareness up through the spinal passage, from mooladhara to ajna. Then while exhaling produce the humming sound and feel the sound vibrations throughout the entire body. Be aware of the inhalation flowing through the sushumna passage, and while exhaling concentrate on the sound vibrations. Continue the practice for five to ten minutes.

Stage 4: Internal sounds

Now stop the humming. Keep the ears closed and listen to any internal sounds. When you become aware of one sound then concentrate your awareness on this one sound. Exclude all other sounds but one and hold your attention on this sound. It may not be very clear at first but as you continue to listen it will become louder and more distinct. Be totally aware of this sound. This is the vehicle for your awareness. Leaving all other sounds and thoughts, let your awareness flow towards this sound.

As sensitivity to the inner sound increases, you will begin to perceive another subtle sound in the background. This sound will be fainter than the first sound. Now transfer your attention to this second sound. Leave the first sound and concentrate fully on the second sound. Again as your sensitivity to the sound increases, the sound will become louder and clearer. Then again try to perceive another sound, a more subtle sound and transfer your awareness to this sound for a few moments.

Continue in this way for a few minutes. Let your awareness become deeper and deeper and try to perceive the more subtle sounds behind the main sounds. The more subtle the sound you perceive, the deeper you will delve into the depths of the mind. Do not become distracted by any one sound. As a particular sound becomes clear and distinct, then move deeper and listen to the next more subtle sound. Feel that you are delving into the depths of your being, going deeper with each new sound. Keep your awareness steady and continuous.

Stage 5: Ending the practice

Now let go of the awareness of the internal sounds. Unplug the ears. Sit quietly for a few moments and just be aware of what you are experiencing at this moment on all levels. Bring the awareness back to the breath. Be aware of the natural breathing process. Become aware of your meditation posture. Slowly begin to externalize the mind. Listen to any sounds in the room and outside the room. Then slowly move the body and open the eyes.

Technique 3: Shanmukhi mudra (closing the seven gates)
Stage 1: Preparation
Sit down comfortably with the spine erect and straight. Place the hands either on the knees or in the lap, wherever is comfortable. Close the eyes. Relax the whole body. Practise kaya sthairyam for a few minutes. Feel the body becoming steady and still, and the breath becoming slow and rhythmic. Be aware of complete stillness.

Stage 2: Performing the mudra
Now raise the hands in front of the face with the elbows pointing sideways. Close the two ears with the thumbs, the two eyes with the index fingers, the two nostrils with the middle fingers and the mouth by placing the ring and little fingers just above and below the lips, respectively. The fingers should gently but firmly close the seven gates. Throughout the practice the middle fingers are used to open and close the nostrils.

Stage 3: Awareness of inner sounds
Inhale deeply and slowly. At the end of the inhalation close the nostrils with the middle fingers and retain the breath inside for a few seconds. While retaining the breath listen to the inner sounds which manifest in the region of

bindu chakra at the top back of the head, in the middle of the head or in the right ear. At first you may hear a lot of sounds or no sound at all. This does not matter, just be aware of whatever manifests.

Retain your breath for as long as is comfortable. Then release the pressure of the middle fingers and breathe out slowly. This is one round. Immediately begin the second round by inhaling slowly and deeply. Close the nostrils and retain the breath inside. Again listen to the inner sounds. After some time release the nostrils and exhale slowly.

Stage 4: Witnessing the subtle sounds

As with the previous practice concentrate on the more subtle sounds within. This should be done in a relaxed manner which will allow the awareness to go deeper. Do not judge any of the sounds or become distracted by any one sound. Just witness them as you move steadily into the more subtle areas of your consciousness. Continue with the practice for five to ten minutes.

Now get ready to end the practice. Place the hands on the knees. Continue with internal awareness for a few more minutes. Now begin to externalize the mind. Become aware of the whole body and the sensations of the body. Become aware of sounds in the environment. When you are ready slowly move the body and open the eyes.

Note: Shanmukhi mudra *means the attitude of the seven gates. It is so called because the two eyes, two ears, two nostrils and the mouth are closed during the practice. These are the seven doors of outer perception. It is through these doors that we receive data from the outside world. These doors are closed to allow the awareness to be directed inwards, towards the source of nada.*

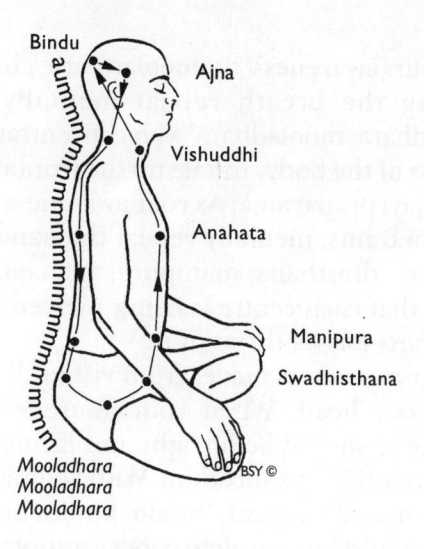

Technique 4: Nada Sanchalana (conducting the sound consciousness)
Stage 1: Preparation
Sit in padmasana, siddhasana or siddha yoni asana. Place the hands on the knees in jnana or chin mudra. Close the eyes. Become aware of the whole physical body. Consciously relax each part of the body. Feel the body slowly becoming quiet and still. Intensify this awareness of stillness. Experience motionlessness throughout the entire body. The body is completely still and steady.

Stage 2: Breath awareness
Now bring the awareness to the breath. Be aware of the slow, steady rhythm of the breath. Begin to practise ujjayi pranayama and be aware of the soft, subtle sound of each inhalation and exhalation.

Stage 3: Performing the practice
Now open the eyes. Though the eyes are open your attention should remain within. Exhale deeply and bend your head forward. Do not press the chin against the chest or make the neck stiff. The position of the head should be such that it is slumped forward as though you are sleeping in a sitting position.

Fix your awareness at mooladhara chakra, and while holding the breath repeat mentally, 'mooladhara, mooladhara, mooladhara' with concentration and absolute stillness of the body. Inhale up the frontal arohan passage with ujjayi pranayama. As your awareness ascends through the kshetrams, mentally repeat the name of each chakra once: 'swadhisthana, manipura, anahata, vishuddhi'. Try to feel that each centre is being pierced by prana as your awareness passes through it.

As your awareness moves from vishuddhi to bindu slowly raise your head. When your awareness reaches bindu your head should be upright and facing forward. Retain your breath for a short time. With your awareness fixed at bindu mentally repeat, 'bindu, bindu, bindu'. Remember there should be complete concentration, stillness of body and no movement of the head while repeating 'bindu'.

Stage 4: Explosion of Om sound

Feel a terrific build up of pressure at bindu, then exhale with an explosive *Om* sound. It is as if the pressure in bindu explodes into *Om*. Move your awareness and the *Om* mantra down through the awarohan passage in the spine from bindu to mooladhara. The *O* sound of *Om* should suddenly explode as your awareness passes from bindu to ajna. The *m-m-m-m* sound should travel from ajna to mooladhara, becoming progressively more subtle so that by the time your awareness reaches mooladhara it is a slight buzzing sound. Repeat the name of each chakra in turn as your awareness passes through them: 'ajna, vishuddhi, anahata, manipura, swadhisthana'. As your awareness descends through the chakras, let the eyes slowly close. As your awareness reaches mooladhara gently lean your head forward. The eyes should be lightly closed. This is the end of one round.

Immediately begin the second round. Open the eyes and with the awareness still at mooladhara repeat: 'mooladhara, mooladhara, mooladhara'. With ujjayi pranayama move your awareness up through the arohan passage, repeating the name of each chakra point. Raise the head as your awareness moves from vishuddhi to bindu. Repeat 'bindu' three times. Feel the pressure building up at this point and exploding into the mantra *Om* as you exhale. The *Om* sound is short and explosive and moves from bindu to ajna. The *m-m-m-m* sound travels with your awareness from ajna down through the awarohan passage to mooladhara. Mentally repeat the name of each chakra as your awareness moves downward. The eyes slowly close as your awareness descends. Let the head move gently forward when the awareness is at mooladhara. Continue in this way.

The sound of *Om* should be strong and penetrating. In this way it has the greatest power to sensitize the chakras. Try to feel the sound of the mantra piercing each chakra in turn, awakening and releasing the prana stored within them. Intensify your awareness of the vibration of the *Om* mantra. Feel it begin to spread out from the psychic passages and penetrate and vibrate through your entire being. With each additional round feel yourself becoming absorbed in the vibration of the mantra. Allow your awareness to flow with *Om* as it explodes from bindu chakra. There must be constant, unbroken awareness.

Stage 5: Ending the practice

Now get ready to end the practice. Stop the *Om* chanting and ujjayi pranayama. Sit completely still and quiet and just be aware of the continuing vibrations within. Experience whatever is manifesting, sounds, colours, whatever. Observe and experience with the same one-pointedness as during the practice.

Now leave this awareness and bring your awareness to the physical body. Feel the meditation posture in which you are sitting. Be aware of the sensations of the body. Become aware of the room in which you are sitting and any sounds in the environment. Externalize yourself completely. Breathe in deeply and chant *Om* three times. Then slowly move the body and open the eyes.

Technique 5: Variations of Om chanting

Sit in a meditation asana with the spine straight. Place the hands on the knees and close the eyes. Become aware of the physical body. Let go of all tensions from the body. Feel the body becoming still and quiet. Be aware of the whole body internally. Centre your awareness on the feeling of space within. Become aware of the vastness of space within. In this vastness of the still inner space become aware of a deep sense of silence.

Visualize or imagine a pillar of air within this vast space. This pillar of air extends as far up and as far down as your perception goes. Observe the pillar of air extending in space. Try to feel that the breathing is taking place in this pillar of air. As you inhale the breath ascends to the top of the pillar of air. As you exhale the breath descends through the pillar of air. Observe this for a few moments with complete awareness. Observe the breathing process taking place within the pillar of air.

Stage 1: Explosive mantra repetition

Now leave awareness of the breath and within the vast silent space become aware of a point of bright light in the region of the heart. Visualize this point of light in the region of the heart. See it as a silvery light which brightens and fades to a glow and again brightens and fades to a glow. Become aware of the pulsation of light. With each pulsation, the whole space momentarily fills up with light, with luminosity, and again the light recedes. Be completely aware of the point of light which explodes and implodes and fills the entire being with luminosity.

Now add the mantra *Om* to the awareness. This chanting of *Om* should be done in rhythm with the expansion and contraction, explosion and implosion of light. The mantra is chanted rapidly in a sharp, explosive manner, but not in such a way that it begins to hurt the throat. As you chant *Om* be aware of the sharp vibrations which it produces in rhythm with the explosion of light in the body space. Continue in this way for five minutes.

Stage 2: Rapid Om chanting

Stop the explosive *Om* chanting but continue to be aware of the internal sound vibrations. Again you will begin to chant the mantra with exhalation. Inhale slowly and deeply and as you exhale begin to repeat the mantra *Om* verbally, repeating it rapidly as many times as is comfortable. You should not become breathless. The sound of the mantra need not be too loud but each repetition should be of equal volume, not becoming fainter as you end the exhalation. Continue chanting in this way for five minutes. Experience the vibration of the mantra. Try to be aware of the different effect created by this rapid chanting. Feel the mantra pulsating within. With the rapid repetition feel as if ripples are being created and are extending outward in ever increasing circles, increasing the sound and intensifying the vibration of the mantra. There is nothing but the mantra.

Stage 3: Medium speed Om chanting

Now stop the rapid chanting of *Om*. Keep the awareness inside and experience the vibrations which are pulsating through your entire being. This time the *Om* chanting is done at a medium speed. The mantra is repeated with exhalation. Inhalation and exhalation should be approximately the same length, creating a steady flowing rhythm with the mantra. As you exhale feel the *Om* sound coming naturally, spontaneously. You should not feel breathless. Again allow the awareness to become absorbed in the vibrations of the mantra. Do not become distracted by any other sounds or by colours or images that may arise at this time, just let them come and go. Try to keep your awareness only on the sound, the vibration created by *Om*. As you are moving from stage to stage, experience the increasing intensity of these vibrations. Continue for five minutes.

Stage 4: Long Om chanting

a) Stop chanting *Om* now. Remain absolutely still and completely aware. The repetition of the mantra will now be long and slow. Allow the breath to become deep and long. Be aware of the slow and rhythmical flow of the breathing. With your next exhalation begin to repeat *Om*, making a long *O* sound which fades into the *m* sound towards the end of the exhalation. Then inhale slowly and deeply and again repeat the mantra with long *O* sound which naturally flows into the *m* sound. Experience the effect of the long *O* sound. There should be constant, steady awareness throughout. Intensify your experience of the vibrations. Continue for five minutes.

b) Again stop chanting. Your awareness is continuous even though you are moving through different methods of chanting. In this stage the *O* sound of the *Om* mantra becomes short and the *m* sound long and drawn out. Inhale deeply and slowly. With exhalation begin to chant *Om* with the *O* sound lasting for just a few moments and then becoming a long, slow *m* sound. The sound of the mantra is not loud but soft and deep. Experience the internalizing effect of the *m* sound. Feel yourself being drawn into deeper and deeper layers of consciousness. Experience the finer and very subtle vibrations here. Continue for five minutes.

c) Stop the chanting now. Feel the vibrations continuing and flowing through your whole being and also all around you. With the next chanting of *Om*, the *O* and *m* sounds are equal in length and volume. So, with your next exhalation repeat the *O* sound for half the length of the breath and the *m* sound for the remaining half. Be aware of the balancing effect between the more externalizing *O* sound and the internalizing *m* sound. It is as if the external and internal dimensions were being drawn together and are becoming one. Continue with full awareness for five minutes.

Stage 5: Mental Om chanting

Again stop chanting. Remain motionless and aware. The repetition of *Om* in this final stage is done mentally. Bring your awareness to the breath. Begin to practise ujjayi pranayama with exhalation only. Inhale normally and exhale slowly and deeply with ujjayi breath. Hear the subtle hissing sound of ujjayi. The ujjayi breath should be controlled, soft and comfortable. With each exhalation mentally repeat the mantra *Om*. Continue mental repetition of *Om*. Simultaneously visualize the pillar of air which is extending in the space of your body.

Feel that the breathing is taking place within the pillar of air. With ujjayi the breath moves down from the top of the pillar towards the bottom of the pillar. With inhalation the normal consciousness comes back towards the top of the pillar. Again with ujjayi exhalation mentally repeat the mantra *Om*, moving down towards the base of the pillar. Intensify your awareness of the pillar of air and the movement of the mantra. Experience the vibrations of mantra within every atom of your being. Become one with the mantra as it moves with exhalation.

Stop the repetition of the mantra and ujjayi pranayama. Remain still and quiet. Become aware of everything you are experiencing right now. Be aware of sounds, colours, images or whatever comes. Let everything come and just observe them. Do not get carried away by any one sound or colour but witness everything. Try to be aware of all the different levels of your being. Continue like this for a few minutes, with steady, receptive awareness.

Now bring your awareness to the breath. Become aware of the sound and flow of the breath. Become aware of the physical body and the feelings of heat or coolness, comfort or discomfort. Begin to externalize your mind slowly and listen to the sounds around you. Become aware of the external environment. Breathe in deeply and chant *Om* three times. Now move the body and open the eyes.

Hari Om Tat Sat

Technique 6: Nadanusandhana (discovering the psychic sound)
Stage 1: Preparation

Nadanusandhana asana is used in this practice in order to facilitate the process of internal listening. Sit on a rolled up blanket or cushion with the knees raised. Place one foot on either side of the blanket or cushion. The feet should be flat on the floor. Adjust the height of the blanket or cushion so that the sitting position is comfortable. The back and head must be straight. The blanket or cushion should be firm and round so that it presses the area of the perineum. Rest the elbows on the knees and place the palms of the hands on each side of the head so that the fingers rest on the side and top of the head. Press the thumbs gently but firmly against the outer flap of the ears. The posture should be comfortable. Make any necessary adjustments to the height of the blanket or cushion, so that you can remain still and steady throughout the practice.

Become aware of the whole physical body. Let go of all tension and tightness from the body. Move your awareness through the different parts of the body and consciously relax each part. Feel your body becoming comfortable and relaxed in the meditation posture. Experience stillness throughout the entire body. Let the body become completely motionless.

Bring the awareness to the breath. Do not change the breathing but begin to watch the natural, spontaneous rhythm of the breath. Feel the breath becoming slow and deep. Follow the breath in and out of the body with each inhalation and exhalation. With the stillness of the body and the slow, steady rhythm of the breath, the mind also becomes quiet and calm. The mental activity ceases.

Stage 2: Physical sound

Now become aware of any internal sounds. Try to distinguish the physical sounds. Each organ of the body has its own rhythm and sound. Although the rhythms may be different, they work in harmony with each other which allows the whole body to function correctly. Move your awareness through the different parts of the body and try to perceive the sound and rhythm of that organ or part. Bring your awareness closer to that sound so that you can hear it clearly. When you perceive the sound, be aware of it for a few moments. Then move on to the next sound.

Become aware of the heart beat. Listen to the slow, steady pulsation of the heart. Try to perceive the sound that this pulsation is creating. Imagine you are inside your heart, listening to this sound and feeling the rhythm. Let go of all the other sounds and just be aware of the heart beat. Move your awareness closer to this sound. Then let go of the sound.

Bring your awareness inside the airway passages and the lungs. Listen to the sound of the breathing there. Try to hear the sound of each inhalation and exhalation, not in the way you hear with the ears but from inside. Be aware of this for a few moments. Then again let go of the sound.

In this way move your awareness through the different physical sounds. Be aware of the gross, physical sounds like gas, wind, gurgling, belching, hiccuping, breathing. Experience each one for a few moments and then move on to the more subtle physical sounds. Continue in this way until your awareness of sound within the physical body becomes penetrating and deep. You should penetrate even into the sound within the cellular structure of the muscles, organs, blood and bones. Be aware of the subtler and subtler sound vibrations manifesting behind the different physical sounds. Then focus on those, one by one. After mastering this stage go on to the mental level.

Stage 3: Mental sound

Let all the physical sounds fade away now. Bring your awareness to the mental level. Try to perceive the sounds that are going on continuously in your mind. These sounds go on without your conscious awareness most of the time. Now you must try to focus on the mental sounds and hear them clearly, not just as a confused buzzing.

Become aware of the mental dialogue that is going on inside your head at this very moment. One aspect of yourself is conversing with another aspect. Focus your awareness on the sound of mental chatter which is going on in the mind. Hear the subtle thought forms that are being expressed within. Thought produces vibration and vibration is subtle sound. Each thought is a form of sound. Listen to each thought as a form of sound.

Sometimes you may also hear the sound of music within the mind. There may be one particular song or melody or perhaps there are several melodies going on at the same time. You can create this music or just become aware if it is happening already. Hear the sound of music clearly and distinctly for a few moments. Then let it go.

On the mental level, sound can also manifest in the form of colours. So, now become aware of any colours which you can see within the mind. Choose the strongest colour first and be aware of it. See it clearly. Concentrate on it until another colour appears behind it.

In this way try to perceive the different sound vibrations at the mental level. Become aware of the subtler sound vibrations manifesting behind the different mental sounds, then focus on those, one by one. Continue with this stage until you feel that you have mastered it. Then go on to the pranic level.

Stage 4: Pranic sound

Allow the mental vibrations to fade. Be aware of complete stillness for a few moments. This stage of the practice requires finer and more concentrated awareness, as you begin to perceive the sound vibrations on the pranic level. The sounds heard on this level are more subtle than in the previous stages. They relate with the purifying, opening and awakening of the nadis and chakras.

You may hear the sound of crickets chirping, or the wind blowing through the leaves and branches of a tree. You may hear the roaring sound of the ocean, the sound of light rainfall or of a heavy downpour. There may be the sound of a frog croaking or other animal sounds.

Go into the quiet space of the pranic level and try to perceive the subtle sounds there. Do not make intense effort. Just listen within to any sounds that come. The sounds are already there and you must simply become aware of them. Let your awareness penetrate deeply into the pranic dimension. Try to experience the sounds within this space. Let each sound come up and be aware of it for a few moments. When another subtler sound arises, transfer your awareness to that sound. Continue practising at this level until you have mastered it. Then proceed to the next stage.

Stage 5: Higher mental sound

Allow the pranic sounds to fade. Bring the awareness even deeper to the higher mental level. On this level the sounds are even more subtle and difficult to perceive. This is where the voice of intuition and revelation is heard or experienced by saints, mystics and prophets, in the form of vision or divine inspiration. Here the awareness must be absolutely one-pointed and continuous.

As your awareness becomes deeper and finer, the subtle sounds of this dimension will begin to manifest. When you are attuned to this level, you may hear the sound of stringed instruments, flute music, bells or cymbals. These sounds are so sweet and melodious that they lead you away from the external senses and draw you ever deeper and closer to your inner self.

Within the supramental dimension, the subtlest sphere where there is still mental perception, become aware of any sound which manifests. Become completely absorbed in this sound. Experience the vibration of the sound fully. Focus your awareness on these sounds for as long as possible. When another sound arises behind the first sound become aware of the new sound and again allow your awareness to become absorbed in it. Continue practising on this dimension until you have mastery over it. Then proceed to the final stage.

Stage 6: Transcendental sound

Allow your awareness to penetrate even deeper still. Be aware of absolute stillness. Experience the whole of creation inside which is beyond intellectual perception. Feel that your whole being is filled with divine vibrations, cosmic sound. Listen to the music of the transcendental spheres. This music is without beginning and without end. It has no cause. It is the unstruck sound which is also known as the anahad nada.

Be aware of the sound or nada at the cosmic level of consciousness. Try to perceive the sounds at this level. You may hear the sound of double drums, tabla, mridanga or the roar of thunder. These sounds will manifest as your awareness transcends the boundary of individual ego and is able to perceive the cosmic vibrations. Your awareness must be absolutely steady and unbroken. Become totally aware of the still, vast space within you. Listen to whatever sound manifests within this vast space. When you hear the sound of drums or thunder, it is then that you will be able to go beyond that sound and hear the ultimate sound which is the unstruck sound, the anahad nada.

Stage 6: Ending the practice
Now get ready to end the practice. Bring your awareness back to the physical dimension. Become aware of the slow, steady flow of the breath. Become aware of the sensation of the physical body. Be aware of heat or coolness, comfort or discomfort, and all the other experiences of the body. Slowly begin to externalize your mind. Listen to the sounds in the external environment. Become aware of your surroundings. Now breathe in deeply and chant *Om* three times. Slowly begin to move the body and open the eyes.

Hari Om Tat Sat.

Glosssary

Abhey mudra – gesture of fearlessness
Acharya – preceptor
Agni tattwa – fire element
Ahamkara – ego
Ajapa japa – continuous, spontaneous repetition of mantra
Ajna chakra – 'third eye'; command centre
Akasha – space
Akasha tattwa – ether element
Akashi mudra – practice of the external stage of dharana; awareness of the inner space
Akshara – sounds which do not die
Akshayapatra – 'pot of plenty'
Anahad nada – unheard, unstruck sound
Anahata chakra – psychic centre located at the heart; centre of emotions
Anandamaya kosha – sheath or body of bliss; beatitude
Anibaadha – without obstacles
Annamaya kosha – sheath or body of matter
Antar – inner
Antar akasha – inner space which forms the substratum for our own individual creation
Anu – to govern over; to control; subtle
Anusandhana – discovery; search
Anusthana – a resolve to perform mantra sadhana with absolute discipline for a requisite period of time

Apas tattwa – water element
Apana – sub-prana which is located in the lower abdominal region; responsible for elimination and reproduction
Arohan – ascending
Asana – physical posture in which one is at ease and in harmony with oneself
Asmita – memory
Atma – individual soul; spirit
Aum – primordial sound; mantra
Awarohan – descending
Bahira – external
Bahira angas – external stages
Bahya – external
Baikhari – audible sound
Bansuri – flute
Beeja – seed
Bhakta – devotee
Bhakti – devotion
Bhoochari mudra – practice of the external stage of dharana; gazing into space
Bhoota – element
Bhrumadhya – eyebrow centre
Bhuh Devi – earth goddess
Bhuh loka – earthly plane
Bhuvah loka – astral plane
Bindu – point; psychic centre at the top back of the head
Brahma – lord of creation; manifest force of life and creation; potentiality of mooladhara chakra
Brahma granthi – perineal knot or psychic block
Brahma nadi – subtle pranic flow within sushumna nadi through which kundalini ascends
Brahman – ever expanding consciousness
Buddhi – discerning, discriminating aspect of mind; from the root '*bodh*' meaning to be aware of, to know; intellect
Chakra – major psychic centre
Chakra shuddhi – purification of the psychic centres
Chaitanya – supreme consciousness

Chandra – moon; representing mental energy
Chandra nadi – name for ida nadi
Chetana – consciousness
Chidakasha – space of consciousness experienced in the head region
Chidakasha dharana – technique of meditation involving awareness of chidakasha
Chin mudra – hand mudra; attitude of chitta or consciousness
Chitta – individual consciousness, including the subconscious and unconscious layers of mind (memory, thinking, concentration, attention, enquiry)
Chitta shakti – mental force governing the subtle dimensions
Daharakasha – lower or deep space, encompassing mooladhara, swadhisthana and manipura chakras
Daharakasha dharana – concentration on the symbols of chakras and tattwas within the lower space
Damaru – an hour-glass shaped hand drum; one of the accoutrements of Lord Shiva
Darshan – to see; to glimpse; to have a vision *Devata* – deity
Dharana – holding or binding of the mind to one point; concentration
Dhri – foundation; base
Dhyana – meditation; seventh step of raja yoga
Drashta – seer; observer
Dwesha – repulsion; dislike
Ekagrata – one-pointedness
Gandha – smell
Gayatri – vedic mantra of twenty four syllables; epithet of the sun
Ghanta – bell
Ghee – clarified butter
Granthi – psychic knot
Guna rahita akasha – first intermediate space of vyoma panchaka; 'attributeless space'
Guru – one who dispels the darkness caused by avidya or ignorance; teacher; preceptor
Hiranyagarbha – golden womb

Hridaya – heart
Hridayakasha – space of the heart experienced between manipura and vishuddhi chakras
Hridayakasha dharana – vedic meditation process involving concentration on the heart space
Ichcha shakti – that desire which is the first manifestation of the greater mind
Ida nadi – major pranic channel in the body; passive aspect of prana manifesting as mental force, chit shakti; lunar force governing the manifest subtle dimension
Indriyas – sensory organs
Ishwara pranidhana – cultivation of faith in the supreme or indestructible reality
Janah loka – plane of rishis and munis
Janma chakra – wheel of life
Japa – continuous repetition of mantra
Jiva – individual identity
Jnana – intuitive knowledge; wisdom
Jnana mudra – hand mudra; gesture of intuitive knowledge
Jnanendriyas – the five sensory organs
Jyoti – light
Karana sharira – causal body
Karma – action
Karmashaya – repository of karma
Karmendriyas – the five physical organs of action (feet, hands, speech, excretory and reproductive organs)
Kaya – body
Khechari mudra – tongue lock
Kheer – sweet rice dish
Kosha – sheath or body
Kriya – action
Kshetram – place; chakra trigger points located in the frontal psychic passage
Kumbhaka – internal or external retention of breath
Kundalini – spiritual energy
Kundalini yoga – path of yoga which awakens the dormant spiritual force

Lakshmi – goddess of prosperity; consort of Vishnu
Lakshya – aim
Laya – dissolution
Loka – higher dimension
Madhya – intermediate,'in the middle'
Madhyama nada – intermediate sound; *Maha* – great
Mahah loka – plane of saints and siddhas
Mahabharata – epic of ancient India, involving the great battle between the Kaurava and Pandava princes
Mahakasha – third intermediate space of vyoma panchaka; 'the great space'
Mahat – total mind, including manas, buddhi, chitta and ahamkara
Manas – rational mind
Mandala – 'area'; 'zone'; pictorial representation
Manipura chakra – psychic centre behind the navel, associated with vitality and energy; 'city of jewels'
Manomaya kosha – mental sheath or body
Mantra – vibration of sound
Mantra yoga – path which liberates the mind through sound vibration
Modaka – rice ball
Moksha – liberation
Moodha – dull state of mind; attribute of tamas
Moola prakriti – mind in its original state
Mooladhara chakra – psychic centre located at the perineum
Mridanga – two-sided drum
Muni – one who contemplates or who has conquered the mind; one who maintains silence
Nada – psychic or internal sound
Nada yoga – yoga of internal sound
Nadi – pranic flow or channel
Nasikagra drishti – nose tip gazing
Nilkant – blue-throated; refers to the blue colour of Lord Shiva's throat, which resulted from drinking the poison churned from the ocean of milk by the devas who were seeking amrit or the nectar of immortality

Nirakara – without form; unmanifest
Nirguna – without quality or attribute
Nirodha – complete cessation of the patterns of consciousness
Niyama – five observances or rules of personal discipline to render the mind tranquil in preparation for meditation; second step of raja yoga
Ourooloka – universal awareness
Padmasana – lotus pose
Pancha, panchaka – five
Panchatattwa – five elements (earth, water, fire, air and ether)
Panchatattwa dharana – concentration on the different qualities and symbols of the tattwas; part of daharakasha dharana
Para nada – transcendental sound
Param – supreme
Paramakasha – second intermediate space of vyoma panchaka; 'supreme space'
Pashyanti nada – mental sound
Patanjali – ancient rishi who codified the meditation stages and states into the system of raja yoga
Pingala nadi – major pranic channel in the body which conducts the dynamic pranic force manifesting as prana shakti
Prajna – knowledge with awareness; the seer who observes the state of nidra; all-knowing, what is known; awareness of the one without a second
Prakriti – manifest and unmanifest nature; cosmic energy
Prana – vital energy; inherent vital force pervading every dimension of matter
Prana shakti – dynamic, solar force governing the dimension of matter
Pranamaya kosha – energy sheath or body
Pranayama – expansion of the range of vital energy
Pratham spandan – first remedial vibration
Pratyahara – withdrawal of the mind from the senses; fifth step of raja yoga

Pratyaya – seeds or impressions in the field of consciousness which do not disappear even in samadhi
Prithvi tattwa – earth element
Purusha – totality of consciousness
Raga – attraction, like
Rahita – without
Rajas – one of the three gunas; state of activity, dynamism and creativity *Rasa* – taste
Rasagulla – Indian sweet
Rishi – seer; realized sage; one who contemplates or meditates on the Self
Ritam – changing, evolving reality
Roopa – form
Rud – 'to cry'
Rudra granthi – psychic knot or block between ajna and sahasrara chakras
Sadhaka – spiritual aspirant
Sadhana – spiritual practice
Sadhu – holy man
Saguna – with qualities
Sakara – with form; manifest
Samadhi – culmination of meditation; state of unity with the object of meditation and universal consciousness; final step of raja yoga
Samkhya – one of the six darshana or systems of vedic philosophy; based on the division of existence into purusha, prakriti and a number of elements *Sampradaya* – tradition
Samskara – unconscious memories; impressions that do not fit into the known categories of our present personality
Samyama – perfection of concentration; harmonious control; culmination of pratyahara, dharana and samadhi
Sankalpa – resolve
Satsang – spiritual association; gathering for discussion pertaining to truth
Sattwa – one of the three gunas; pure, unadulterated quality; state of luminosity and harmony

Satya – absolute truth, reality
Sayujya – fusion with object of concentration
Shabda – sound
Shakti – primal energy; manifest consciousness
Shaligram – black oval shaped stone; symbol of Vishnu
Shambhavi mudra – eyebrow centre gazing
Shankha – conch
Shastra – textbook
Sheshnag – multihooded serpent on which Vishnu reclines; support of the universe
Shiva – auspicious; first yogi; supreme deity of Hindu pantheon; represents cosmic consciousness
Shivalingam – black oval shaped stone; symbol of Shiva
Shoonya – nothingness; void
Shuddhi – purification
Siddha – perfected being
Siddhasana – accomplished pose (for males)
Siddha yoni asana – accomplished pose (meditation asana for females)
Siddhi – psychic abilities
Soma – amrit; potent juice of a plant drunk at religious ceremonies which induces divine intoxication
Spandan – vibration
Sparsha – touch
Sthairyam – steadiness
Sthoolakasha – space pervading the physical body
Surya – sun; representing pranic energy
Surya nadi – name for pingala nadi
Suryakasha – fifth intermediate space of vyoma panchaka; 'space of the sun'
Sushumna – central nadi in the spine which conducts the kundalini or spiritual force from mooladhara to sahasrara
Sutra – 'thread';set of aphorisms in Sanskrit literature
Swadhisthana chakra – psychic centre located at the sacral plexus; 'one s own abode'
Swadhyaya – self-study; continuous, conscious awareness of what one is doing

Swah loka – divine plane
Swara – breathing cycle
Swara sadhana – concentration on the seven notes of the musical scale
Swara yoga – science of the breathing cycle
Tabla – two-piece drum
Tala – cymbals; rhythm
Tamas – one of the three gunas; state of inertia or ignorance
Tanmatra – subtle nature, quality or essence of the elements; five senses (smell, taste, sight, touch and sound)
Tantra – ancient universal science and culture which deals with the development of human nature from the present level of evolution and understanding to the transcendental level of knowledge, experience and awareness
Tantri – lute or vina
Tapah loka – plane of austerity and penance
Tapasya – austerity
Tattwa – element
Tattwa dharana – technique of meditation involving awareness and experience of the tattwas (elements)
Tattwakasha – fourth intermediate state of vyoma panchaka; elemental space
Tejas – luminosity; golden light or flame; the seer who observes the state of swapna
Trataka – to gaze steadily; dharana practice of gazing steadily at one point to focus the mind
Trayate – freed; liberated
Trigunatita – beyond the three gunas
Trikuti – eyebrow centre; meeting place of the three psychic channels of ida, pingala and sushumna
Trimurti – Brahma, Vishnu and Shiva, representing the trinity concept of creation, preservation and destruction
Trishna – craving and attachment
Twacha – skin
Ujjayi pranayama – psychic breathing performed by contracting the epiglottis, producing a light, sonorous sound

Upanishads – vedantic texts conveyed by ancient sages and seers containing their experiences and teachings on the ultimate reality
Vairagya – non-attachment
Vaishwanara – the seer who observes the manifest universe or the external, waking consciousness
Vayu tattwa – air element
Vedanta – one of the six darshana or systems of vedic philosophy; 'end of perceivable knowledge'; the mind experiencing its own limits and going beyond them; gaining realization and understanding of that exploration
Vedas – ancient spiritual texts of Sanatan Dharma written before 5000 BC
Vijnanamaya kosha – higher mental sheath or body
Vikshipta – oscillating state of mind
Vishnu – vedic deity; preserver of the universe; supreme consciousness
Vishnu granthi – psychic knot or block between manipura, anahata and vishuddhi chakras, symbolizing the bondage of personal and emotional attachment
Vishuddhi chakra – psychic centre located at the level of the throat; centre of purification
Vritti – circular movement of consciousness; five mental modifications described in raja yoga
Vyoma – space: sky or firmament
Vyoma panchaka – five intermediate spaces
Vyoma panchaka dharana – techniques of concentration on the five subtle spaces
Yamas – five self restraints or rules of conduct to render the emotions tranquil
Yantra – geometric symbols on which concentration unleashes the hidden potential within the consciousness
Yoga Sutras – ancient authoritative text on raja yoga by Sage Patanjali
Yogi – an adept in yoga

Notes

Notes

Notes